Urban America
Processes
and Problems

John M. Levy
Virginia Polytechnic Institute and State University

D1502188

Prentice Hall, Upper Saddle River, New Jersey 07458

Library of Congress Cataloging-in-Publication Data

Levy, John M.
    Urban America : processes and problems / John M. Levy.
        p.   cm.
    Includes bibliographical references and index.
    ISBN 0-13-287111-4
    1. Cities and towns—United States—History.   2. Metropolitan
areas—United States—History.   3. Urbanization—United States.
I. Title.
HT123.L394   2000
307.76 0973—dc21   99-32735
                                                          CIP

Editorial Director: *Charlyce Jones Owens*
Editor in Chief: *Nancy Roberts*
Senior Acquisitions Editor: *Beth Gillett Mejia*
Editorial Assistant: *Brian Prybella*
Executive Managing Editor: *Ann Marie McCarthy*
Production Liaison: *Fran Russello*
Project Manager: *Marianne Hutchinson (Pine Tree Composition)*
Prepress and Manufacturing Buyer*: Ben Smith*
Cover Director*: Jayne Conte*
Cover Designer*: Kiwi Design*
Marketing Manager*: Christopher DeJohn*

The book was set in 10/12 Stone Serif by Pine Tree Composition
and was printed and bound by Courier Companies, Inc.
The cover was printed by Phoenix Color Corp.

For permission to use copyrighted material, grateful acknowledgment
is made to the copyright holders on page 293.

© 2000 by Prentice-Hall, Inc.
Upper Saddle River, New Jersey 07458

All rights reserved. No part of this book may be
reproduced, in any form or by any means,
without permission in writing from the publisher.

Printed in the United States of America

10   9   8   7   6   5   4

ISBN 0 13 287111 4

Prentice-Hall International (UK) Limited, *London*
Prentice-Hall of Australia Pty, Limited, *Sydney*
Prentice-Hall Canada Inc., *Toronto*
Prentice-Hall Hispanoamericana, S.A., *Mexico*
Prentice-Hall of India Private Limited, *New Delhi*
Prentice-Hall of Japan, Inc., *Tokyo*
Pearson Education Asia Pte. Ltd., *Singapore*
Editora Prentice-Hall do Brasil, Ltda., *Rio de Janeiro*

*To Lucie, Rachel, Bernie,
Kara, and Chris*

Contents

Preface

The focus of this book is the modern American city and metropolitan area. Its subject exists at the intersection of a number of fields—sociology, history, economics, geography, political science, urban planning, and public administration, to name only some. The field of urban studies is huge and not sharply delineated at its edges. Different texts on the subject emphasize different aspects of the subject matter and come at the subject from different analytical perspectives. Many texts on urban studies, perhaps the majority, are written from a sociological perspective. The perspective in this book is somewhat different, with relatively more emphasis on economic, financial, political, and administrative considerations. This approach reflects the author's academic background in economics and public policy, as well as a decade of employment in urban planning and economic development.

Studying urban affairs inevitably takes one into controversy, for urban studies is far from an exact science. In a number of cases this book presents alternate views of questions, whether they be matters of interpreting what has happened or of considering what ought to be done. I believe that it is the role of the author to present facts, hypotheses, mechanisms, and explanations, and to encourage the student to think about the subject—but not to tell the student what to think. Whether I have been successful in this regard is for the reader to judge.

THE PLAN OF THIS BOOK

Part I, the shortest section of the book, presents some general ideas about urbanization and then provides a history of U.S. urbanization in the nineteenth and twentieth centuries. The purpose of these chapters is to provide sufficient background to support the rest of the text. They are not intended as a detailed history of U.S. urbanization.

In Part II we examine the workings of the modern city and metropolitan area. Chapter 4 contains a brief history of the evolution of municipal government followed by a discussion of the workings of contemporary municipal government. Chapter 5 provides a spectrum of views, from pluralists' to political economists' perspectives, on the realities of city government. Chapter 6 presents municipal finance within the framework of the U.S. federal system. It then proceeds to taxation, borrowing, the pattern of expenditures and grants, and municipal budgeting. Chapter 7 explores the economy of the city and the metropolitan region. In addition to some of the standard fare of urban economics, such as the export base model, there is also substantial material on cities in the world economy, as well as on the very fundamental matter of intermunicipal economic competition and the extent to which it shapes and constrains municipal policy. Chapter 8 presents an overview of city planning, in part informed by the author's years as a planner. I have tried to go beyond the forms and legalities of planning into some of the economic, political, and financial realities. Part II concludes with two chapters on housing. The first provides an overview of the U.S. housing situation, a discussion of housing finance, and a section on the mechanics of housing stock change. The second looks at housing policy and housing programs, both past and present.

Part III presents a number of controversies and policy issues. It begins with a chapter on the "melting pot" versus "mosaic" issue. Which way we go on the issue of multiculturalism will have major consequences for many decades to come, and inevitably, much of that controversy will be played out in the cities. There is a chapter on immigration, for in the long term it is hard to identify any issue of public policy that will have more impact upon urban America than what we do regarding immigration policy. The chapter begins with a history of U.S. immigration and then presents a variety of policy positions from an essentially open-door policy to a highly restrictive one. In recent decades poverty has become an increasingly urban problem, and so Part III provides a substantial treatment of that subject. The first of two chapters on poverty lays out the background. The second poverty chapter chronicles U.S. poverty policy from the "War on Poverty" begun in the 1960s to the present era of "welfare reform." Few things effect the tone and quality of urban life more than the matter of crime and public safety. The section contains a chapter on crime and the criminal justice system that presents some background and some history and then examines differing approaches to issues of crime and punishment. Public education is the largest item of expenditure for both local and state governments, employing vastly more people than any other activity of government, and for most people is probably the most important and sustained contact that they have with government. Part III concludes with a chapter on public education and the city. The chapter provides general background on the subject and then turns to pros and cons of three important issues: busing to achieve integration, the question of bilingual education, and, most recently, the movement for vouchers and charter schools.

Parts I and II form a unit, with the first addressing "how we got here" and the second providing a broad picture of the workings of the present-day city and metropolitan area. Part III can be read as a whole, but each of the chapters—or pair of chapters in the case the subject of poverty—will stand on its own once the material in Parts I and II has been presented.

ACKNOWLEDGMENTS

It is not possible to thank everyone who has contributed indirectly to the writing of a book. I have over the years learned a great deal from my colleagues in the Urban Affairs and Planning program at Virginia Tech. In particular, I should note Max Stephenson in regard to urban government, Joe Scarpaci in regard to urban geography, and Diane Zahm in regard to crime and the criminal justice system. The book has benefited considerably from comments by several reviewers for Prentice Hall: Paul E. Teske, SUNY Stony Brook; Laura R. Woliver, University of South Carolina; Phillip A. Beverly, Chicago State University; David M. Littig, University of Wisconsin; N.E. Hart Nibbrig, George Mason University; Edward J. Miller, University of Wisconsin; Michael Johnston, Colgate University; William E. Kelly, Auburn University; and Jan Lin, University of Houston. Finally, I must thank my dear wife, with whom I discussed much of this book, and who was remarkably tolerant when its writing took big bites out of numerous weekends and evenings, as well as several vacations.

John M. Levy

A Note on Data and Definitions

Much of the data on present-day America in this book comes from the Bureau of the Census, and so a few words on the census are appropriate. The Bureau of the Census, a division of the Department of Commerce, does a full enumeration of the population every ten years, and it has done so since 1790. A decennial census is required by Section 2 of Article 1 of the United States Constitution because a count of the population is needed for the allocation of seats in the United States House of Representatives. Over the years the basic task of enumerating the population has grown into a massive data-gathering operation. The censuses conducted by the Bureau of the Census now provide by far the largest source of social and economic data about the United States. If you see a statistic such as the percentage of Americans who have been divorced, how many Americans drive to work as opposed to taking public transportation, the percentage of the population that moves each year, the percentage of Americans who live in households below the federal poverty line, or how many householders own the homes in which they live and how many rent, the chances are that the data originated with the census.

The decennial census, conducted in each year ending in 0, is—so far as is possible—a complete count of the population. The Bureau of the Census obtains as complete mailing lists as it can in order to send a questionnaire to every household in the nation. The majority of the households return the questionnaire without further contact with the Bureau of the Census. For those households that do not return the questionnaire, the Bureau of the Census follows up with a phone call or visit by a census enumerator.

Although the Bureau of the Census attempts to count everyone, the count is inevitably not complete. By law you must respond to the Bureau of the Census request for information. In fact, after every census the Bureau of the Census prosecutes a few people who have made a conspicuous point of refusing to cooperate with the census. However, as a practical matter, most people who do not wish to be counted are not counted. And, of course, many people are missed accidentally.

After the 1990 census, the Bureau of the Census estimated that it had missed about 1.6 percent of the U.S. population. People who do not have a permanent address are hard to count accurately. In the 1990 census the Bureau of the Census attempted to count the homeless by sending workers to homeless shelters, but many of the homeless were undoubtedly missed. People who are in trouble with the law are likely to avoid being counted. People who are in the country illegally are undercounted. The census count in middle-class suburban neighborhoods is more complete than the count in poor inner-city neighborhoods. In short, the Bureau of the Census count of the population is the best measure that we have, but it is far from perfect.

In the decennial census a limited number of questions are asked of the entire population. The demographic items asked of the entire population are age, race, sex, whether or not the person is of Spanish/Hispanic origin, marital status, and relationship to the head of the household. There are also a few housing questions asked of the entire population. These are structure type (mobile home, one-family house detached, one-family house attached, etc.), number of rooms, owner or rental status, and value of the unit or its monthly rent. All other data items in the census reports, such as information on income, education, employment, method of transportation to work, types of appliances in the housing unit, and the like come from more detailed questionnaires that are sent to a sample of the population.

The Bureau of the Census accepts the answers that respondents provide and does not attempt to verify them. To the census you are what you say you are. Some census questions provide better data than other questions. Answers to the age, sex, and marital status questions are likely to provide very good data because they are hard to get wrong. The questions on income elicit less accurate data. The person answering the question may not recall exactly how much income he or she earned from each source in the previous year. He or she may not have read the questionnaire instructions carefully enough to know exactly what items are and are not to be counted as income. If people have not been truthful in filling out their income tax returns, they are unlikely to provide full disclosure on their census questionnaires. Some questions are inherently imprecise. For example, a sample of the population is asked about ancestry. It is from this question that statistics about the national origins of the U.S. population are derived. The instructions for this question in the 1990 census read, in part:

> Ancestry refers to a person's ethnic origin or descent, "roots," or heritage. Ancestry may also refer to the country of birth of the person or the person's parents or ancestors before their arrival in the United States.

The above language provides enough choices so that different people whose ancestry is the same might answer the question differently. In the

1990s it was suggested that the 2000 census add a "mixed race" category, for this represents reality for many people and would prevent people from having to choose which part of their ancestry to acknowledge and which to ignore. That suggestion was ultimately disallowed but the form was redesigned for respondents to check off more than one race. This brings us back to the point that census data, though often the best data that there is on a subject, is neither perfect data nor without ambiguity.

In years other than those ending in 0, the Bureau of the Census conducts a variety of sample surveys in order to provide estimates for years between the decennial censuses. For example, for every year between decennial censuses the Bureau of the Census provides data on family income based upon sample surveys much smaller than the sample used in the decennial census. The Bureau of the Census also makes annual current population estimates for states and municipalities based upon a variety of sources, using the population numbers from the last decennial census as the baseline figure.

Census Geography

In this book you will see terms such as *central city, suburban ring,* and *metropolitan area.* These terms and similar ones refer to Bureau of the Census geographical concepts.

The Bureau of the Census divides the entire nation into metropolitan and nonmetropolitan areas. The basic unit of metropolitan America is the Metropolitan Statistical Area (MSA). For a place to be classified as an MSA it must have a city with a population of at least 50,000. The MSA consists of that city plus any additional counties that are linked to the city by contiguous urbanization or that have strong economic links to the city as measured primarily in numbers of commuters to work. This picture of a central city surrounded by a ring of suburban counties is the basic metropolitan area picture. If the metropolitan area has a population of 1 million or more and if it contains more than one area that, on its own, would meet the requirements of being an MSA, then the entire area may be designated as a Consolidated Metropolitan Statistical Area (CMSA). Each area within it that could meet MSA requirements on its own is designated as a Primary Metropolitan Statistical Area (PMSA). The entire CMSA is composed of two or more PMSAs.

The above acronyms and relationships can be confusing. To summarize, any point of land in the United States is either in a metropolitan area or in nonmetropolitan America. The relationships within the metropolitan parts of the nation are shown below.

Nonmetropolitan Area   Metropolitan Area
                    In MSA or in CMSA
                      Any point within a CMSA is also in a PMSA

As of 1995 there were 253 MSAs in the United States. There were also 18 CMSAs composed of a total of 73 PMSAs. These numbers grow as additional cities pass the 50,000 mark and become eligible to be classified as central cities.

The term *suburban ring* or, sometimes, *part outside* refers to the part of the MSA or CMSA that is not contained in the central city or cities. Statistics that show the growth of metropolitan area populations and the changing relationship between central city and suburban ring populations should be taken only as general indications of trends because of the previously noted designation of new MSAs and CMSAs.

One last point of Bureau of the Census terminology should be noted: the use of the terms *urban* and *rural.* Any incorporated place such as a city, town, or village with a population of 2,500 or more is defined as urban. The rest of the nation is defined as rural. Thus the Bureau of the Census use of the word *urban* is not synonymous with its use of the word *metropolitan.* Hundreds of small towns and cities in nonmetropolitan America are considered urban places because they meet the 2,500-person requirement.

For a more detailed discussion of the Bureau of the Census geographical concepts and for a list of all of the MSAs, CMSAs, and PMSAs, the reader is referred to the Appendix of the *Statistical Abstract of the United States,* a publication of the Bureau of the Census since 1880. For the reader seeking demographic, social, or economic data, the same book is often the best place to start. It contains a wealth of data from the census, from other government sources, and from a variety of private sources, such as industry trade associations. If you cannot find the item in the book itself, very often its footnotes and guides to sources will tell you where it can be found. Virtually any library will have a copy of the *Statistical Abstract of the United States.* It can also be accessed on-line at **www.gov/statab/www/.**

Chapter

1 | The Origins of the City

Although this book is about the city in modern America, a few generalizations about urbanization will be useful before we turn to the American case. Cities endure for a very long time. They are much more permanent than nations. London was a city on the Thames when Britain was a province in the Roman Empire, more than a millennium before the English language came into being. Paris was a settlement on the Isle de La Cité (the present site of Notre Dame cathedral) before Charlemagne ruled. The city bears the imprint of technologies, ideas, and political regimes long gone, and one cannot understand its present state without some sense of how it came to be. Below are a few generalizations about the process of urbanization. In the following chapter we turn to the American case in particular.

In the standard view urbanization was a consequence of the development of agriculture. When the human race lived by food gathering and hunting, population densities were limited to a few persons per square mile and large permanent settlements were not possible. The development of agriculture greatly increased the number of people who could be sustained by a given land area. It also permitted the part of the population that farmed to produce some surplus so that at least a small fraction of the population would be able to live a nonagricultural life. The transition from food gathering and hunting to settled agriculture and the first appearance of permanent human settlement both make their appearance in human history in the Middle East several millennia before the birth of Christ.

Cities have served various functions in ancient and modern times. They have often served as centers of trade and production. Cities have long served a defensive and military function, as exemplified by the walled cities of medieval Europe. Cities have served an administrative function, whether it be for a small area or a worldwide empire. Many cities have served a sacred function as shrines and destinations for pilgrims.

The growth of urban places and the specialization of labor have gone together. Bringing large numbers of people together both makes possible greater specialization of labor and creates the demand that supports many separate trades and activities. Because cities brought many minds together and freed some people from the routine of manual labor, the city has been the locus of much of humanity's intellectual and artistic progress. The archeological record indicates that writing appeared at about the same time as did large, permanent settlements, suggesting that it may have been used originally for commercial and administrative record keeping. Science, technology, art, and architecture have their roots largely in cities. Formalized government and social stratification also seem to have their roots in cities, in part because cities contained sufficient population to permit such developments.[1]

Where Cities Developed

We know that generally cities developed at certain types of sites and that some sites have been occupied for thousands of years. The possibilities of trade make certain sites favorable. Samarkand in Central Asia developed along overland trade routes. A very large number of the world's great cities, like New York and San Francisco, developed at natural harbors. Numerous others, like St. Louis, are located along navigable waterways or, like New Orleans, where rivers empty into the ocean. Before the development of modern land transportation, water transportation was generally the fastest mode. It was, and remains today, the least expensive mode per ton mile. The city with a natural harbor, or the city located on a waterway that gave it easy access to the ocean, like London on the Thames, enjoyed a great commercial advantage. In some cases, its access to the sea gave it the long reach that provided military and administrative advantages as well.

The location on water, whether a river or the ocean, makes the city a "breakpoint" in transportation.[2] Where the mode of transportation must change, as from water to land, employment is created in freight handling and such related activities as warehousing. In modern times, ancillary activities such as insurance and finance related to trade are likely to spring up there. If further processing of goods or raw materials needs to be done somewhere along the route to the final destination, it makes sense to do it where goods have to be unloaded anyway rather than where separate loading and unloading operations would be needed solely for that purpose. Thus breakpoints in transportation are natural locations for the development of manufacturing and refining or processing operations.

Canada's largest city, Montreal, is located at the point on the St. Lawrence River where rapids made further passage up the river by sailing vessel impossible. There, cargoes had to be unloaded, moved around the rapids, and reloaded before they could move farther into the interior of the continent. The city developed around that breakpoint. Buffalo, New York, near the eastern end of Lake Erie, grew largely because it was at a breakpoint for grain transportation. Grain from the Midwest could come that far east by ship but then had to be transferred to another mode (wagon, canal boat, or railroad, depending upon the era) before it could go farther east. The transfer activities themselves were a source of employment. Then, too, as a break-point the city was a natural location for the development of storage facilities and milling of grain into flour.

Many cities are located at choke points, sites that offer control of a pas-sageway. Istanbul, at the Dardanelles, the passage between the Mediterranean and the Black Sea, is one example. Geneva, Switzerland, is located at the point where Lac LeMan (Lake Geneva) necks down to form the Rhone River, which ultimately empties into the Mediterranean. Readily defensible sites have often been choice locations for cities. In many cases the same properties that make the site defensible have also given it control of an important passageway. Quebec was built on a steep, defensible promontory that juts out into the St. Lawrence River, giving it control of the waterway and thus control of access to much of the northern half of North America. When, in 1763, after a number of attempts stretching back almost a century, the English took Quebec from the French, Canada almost immediately changed hands.

Because cities exist partly for trading purposes, and because no city can be self-sufficient, the size of a city depends in considerable measure on how big its trading area is—on how long a commercial reach it has. If the area in which a city can trade advantageously is small, then that trade will support only a small city population. If the reach is great, then a large population is possible. Changes in the costs of transportation and communication change the economic reach of cities and thus the relative fortunes of competing cities. In the nineteenth and twentieth centuries, great decreases in the cost of transporting people and goods and even greater decreases in the costs of communications have given many places and the producers therein a liter-ally global reach. Some smaller places whose less efficient producers had been sheltered by high costs of transportation and communication were eclipsed by larger and more efficient competitors many thousands of miles away.

THE INDUSTRIAL REVOLUTION AND URBAN GROWTH

For almost all of human history the overwhelming majority of people lived an essentially rural life. Agriculture simply did not produce enough of a sur-plus to sustain more than a tiny percentage of the human race in an urban existence. The population of the world, as best it can be estimated, grew very slowly, for population growth was limited by the slow growth of the food supply.[3] The situation changed drastically with the coming of the Industrial Revolution. Assigning a precise date to the beginning of the Industrial

Revolution is necessarily an arbitrary matter, but perhaps the year 1712 would be as good a choice as any. That was the year the steam engine, invented by Simon Newcomen to pump water out of coal mines, made its appearance in Great Britain.

With the coming of the Industrial Revolution the human race experienced something it had never before known, a continuing increase in productivity (output per worker) year after year and decade after decade. One result was enormous population growth, made possible in large measure because the application of machinery and scientific knowledge to agriculture produced rapid increases in the food supply. The second effect was a massive growth of urban populations, for increasing productivity in agriculture freed a steadily increasing percentage of the population from working on the land. We turn to the matter of overall population growth first.

In the time from the first appearance of the human species to the year 1800, the human population of the planet grew to about 1 billion. By 1900 the population of the world had reached about 1.6 billion. By 1950 it had reached about 2.5 billion. In 1996 world population was estimated to be 5.8 billion, and it was projected to reach 6 billion by 1998. In the 11 years ending in 1996 the world population increased by about as many people as it had from the evolution of our species to the year 1800.[4] At this writing world population is growing at about 80 million people per year and is projected by UN demographers to approach 9 billion by the middle of the twenty-first century.

The Demographic Transition

The coming of the Industrial Revolution and the subsequent growth in productivity and wealth has, time and again, produced a somewhat similar sequence of events generally referred to as the Demographic Transition. A very simplified and generalized account of the three stages of the Demographic Transition follows.

Stage 1. Before industrialization begins, the population of the society is relatively stable. Its limit is established by the size of the food supply. Both birth rates and death rates are high.

Stage 2. As industrialization proceeds it raises productivity (output per worker) and thereby raises living standards.[4] The biggest single cause of population increase is usually the increased and more dependable food supply resulting from agricultural mechanization and improved transportation. Well-fed people, even in the absence of any improvement in medical care, resist disease better. Adequate housing and improvements in public health such as safe drinking water, sewage treatment, childhood vaccinations, and the like also lower the death rate. Though death rates fall, birth rates remain high. In fact, they may increase because better-fed and healthier people are likely to be more fertile. The result is rapid population growth.[5]

Stage 3. With continued prosperity birth rates fall, and after a time the society reaches a condition in which both birth rates and death rates are low. Population growth slows or perhaps even stops. But, of course, by this time several generations in stage 2 have produced a much greater than original population.

Whether all nations will go through the Demographic Transition is still an open question. Then, too, we as yet do not know whether or not there is another stage—or other stages—beyond the three that we have so far witnessed.

For a modern society to maintain a constant population decade after decade, the average woman would have to have about 2.1 children, a number sometimes referred to as the "replacement rate."[6] Recent figures from various nations are shown in Table 1–1. A number of nations that are clearly in stage 3 are listed first, followed by a number of nations that are somewhere in stage 2. At this time in history it is hard to name a country that is in stage 1, for, as we soon discover, the effects of the Industrial Revolution cross borders and make themselves felt across the globe.

Clearly, Western Europe has gone through the transition, as has the United States and Canada and some of the more prosperous Asian nations, notably Japan. Judging by fertility rates it appears that much of the former Soviet Union and Eastern Europe has also gone through the transition. Whether that is really the case or whether the low fertility there is a temporary phenomenon related to economic and political uncertainty remains to be seen. A quick look at the selected nations in Table 1–1 or a more detailed look at the larger set of nations from which it is drawn will suggest that the state of economic development appears to be a much more powerful predictor of whether a nation will be above or below the replacement fertility level than are cultural or religious factors. That is not to say that those factors do not have some influence.

Why does the coming of prosperity reduce the birth rate? In Denmark, where childbearing is relatively safe and the apparatus of the welfare state stands ready to help, the average woman has 1.67 children. In Nepal, where childbearing is much more risky and there is no welfare state, the average woman has more than three times as many children. Numerous explanations, some of them overlapping, have been offered.[7]

1. In countries where mortality is high, a couple that wants to have, say, two or three grown children must give birth to more to have a good chance of achieving that goal. In societies where male children are more highly valued than female children, couples may keep trying until they have male children.

2. In countries without social security and pension systems, the only economic security for many people in their old age is having children who will support them.

3. In poor and largely agrarian societies, children become an economic asset at a very early age. In more prosperous societies, the labor that a child

TABLE 1–1 Selected Fertility Rates, 1994

Belgium	1.69	Taiwan	1.76
Canada	1.80	Ukraine	1.87
Czech Republic	1.38	United States	2.06
Denmark	1.67	Afghanistan	6.14
France	1.49	Bangladesh	3.57
Germany	1.30	Ghana	4.59
Great Britain	1.82	Kenya	4.45
Italy	1.27	India	3.20
Japan	1.46	Mexico	3.35
Netherlands	1.51	Nepal	5.06
Russia	1.42	Rwanda	5.99
Poland	1.93	Yemen	7.29
Sweden	1.72		

Source: Statistical Abstract of the United States, 116th edition Washington, D.C.: Department of Commerce, Bureau of the Census, 1996, Table 1327.

can perform is of no market value, and the child, instead of being an economic asset, is a source of expense.

4. In societies where women's wages are high, the opportunity cost (the wages a woman gives up when she has a child) of motherhood is high and thus discourages childbearing.

5. Where male domination of women is very great (more likely to be the case in economically less developed countries), women may have more children than they want because the decision is not under their control.

Some or all of the above may be correct, and there may be other reasons as well. In any case, the overwhelming experience of many countries is that over a long period prosperity has proven to be a very powerful contraceptive.

Today, the population explosion occurs primarily in the Third World, where many nations are in stage 2 of the Demographic Transition. In the nineteenth century the world population explosion was largely a European and North American phenomenon. Industrialization and the accompanying rise in living standards had pushed Europe into stage 2 of the Demographic Transition while most of the rest of the world was still in stage 1.

In the twentieth century, particularly in the last few decades, it has become overwhelmingly apparent that industrialization and the related scientific and technical progress in one nation can push other nations into the second stage of the Demographic Transition. Food imported from industrialized nations with agricultural surpluses, such as the United States, Canada, or Australia can stave off famine. New varieties of such staple crops as rice, developed primarily by researchers in developed countries, have produced the "green revolution," greatly increasing yields per acre in many Third World nations. So, too, can imported pesticides and fertilizers increase the food supply and expand the population. Imported medicines, vaccines, water purification systems, and the like push down death rates. DDT, though banned in the United States, has pushed down death rates in some Third World countries by eradicating mosquitoes and thus controlling malaria. The demographic consequences of the Industrial Revolution cross national boundaries very easily. Much of the spectacular increase in population that we have seen in Third World countries has its root cause in the industrialized First World.

The Industrial Revolution and Rural-to-Urban Migration

Another effect of the Industrial Revolution in Europe and North America has been to shift population from the countryside to the city, partly because it promotes huge increases in agricultural productivity. In the United States in 1800 farmers and other rural workers constituted over 90 percent of the nation's work force. By 1880 farmers constituted about half of the work force. At the present time farm workers constitute only 2 percent of the work force. But that 2 percent is able to produce enough food to feed the entire population and to produce a surplus for export. In fact, it is so productive that the main thrust of federal agricultural policy since the Great Depression has been to restrain production so as to keep agricultural prices from falling too low.

Industrialization has also fostered urban growth in other ways. The development of factory production and its replacement of cottage industry fostered urban growth simply by creating concentrations of employment that, in turn, created nearby concentrations of residence. The development of rail and then truck transportation gave major cities a huge reach, both for customers and suppliers, thus making possible the growth of huge metropolitan areas such as New York, Chicago, and London.

In much of the western world there appears to be little prospect for rapid urban growth now that total population growth is slow and the percentage of the population that is now urbanized is very high. Most of the world's urban population growth in the decades to come will necessarily be in the Third World, where total population growth is still rapid and where the percentage of the population now living in urban areas is generally much smaller than in the West.

SUMMARY

The first urban places appeared when the human race made the transition from hunting and gathering to agriculture, for it was only then that large and permanent populations were possible. We note that cities are much more permanent than nations and that cities tend to develop at certain types of sites, particularly those that are defensible, have some strategic value, and that are breakpoints in transportation. Until the coming of the Industrial

Revolution, world population changed only slowly and the urban population of the world remained a very small fraction of total population. Then, rapid increases in agricultural efficiency and improved living standards promoted huge increases in population. At the same time enormous numbers of people were freed from agricultural labor and moved to cities to take industrial and commercial employment. Most Western nations and some non-Western nations are well into the third stage of the Demographic Transition and are approaching population stability, but much of the rest of the world is still in the second stage and experiencing the rapid population growth that characterized Europe and North America a century earlier.

NOTES

1. For a exposition of the standard view, see V. Gordon Childe, *What Happened in History* (New York: Penguin Books, 1964). For an unconventional view that sees agriculture as beginning after the first small permanent settlements, see Jane Jacobs, *Cities and the Wealth of Nations* (New York: Random House, 1984).
2. The transportation breakpoint is basic principle in location theory and economic geography and can be found in many textbooks on urban economics and urban geography. A good discussion can also be found in William Alonso, "Location Theory," in *Regional Analysis*, L. Needleman, ed. Penguin Books, Ltd., Harmondsworth, U.K, 1968.
3. In the early nineteenth century Thomas Malthus wrote that food supply could grow only arithmetically at best, whereas population tended to grow geometrically. He therefore concluded that humanity would always be bumping up against the limit of its food supply and was fated to have its numbers limited by famine or pestilence. That seemed to describe much of the history of mankind. But at least for a time, the Industrial Revolution and the great increase in food production that it made possible have falsified Malthus's claim. Whether that will continue to be the case remains to be seen. Those, such as the environmentalist Paul Ehrlich, who foresee looming resource crises and who argue that present rates of population growth are unsustainable are sometimes referred to as "neomalthusians."
4. For the earlier estimates see Donald J. Bogue, *Principles of Demography* (New York: John Wiley & Sons, 1969) p. 5. For recent statistics, see Thomas M. McDevitt, *World Population Profile: 1996* (Washington, D.C.: Bureau of the Census Report WP/96, 1996), pp. 8–9. World population statistics can also be found in the United Nations *Demographic Yearbook* New York, United Nations, annual.
5. The transition seems to be a universal phenomenon, but it does not occur in exactly the same manner in all societies, nor are all of its causes fully understood. For a traditional account of the Demographic Transition, see Donald J. Bogue, op. cit. Chapter 3. For a summary of current views and references to the literature see Dudley Kirk, "Demographic Transition Theory," *Population Studies*, 50 (November 1996), pp. 361–87. For a long perspective on human population change, see Robert W. Kates, "Population, Technology, and the Human Environment: A Thread through Time," *Daedalus* (summer 1996), pp. 43–69.
6. That figure accounts for the slight excess of male births over female births and mortality in the years up to childbearing age. In a poor society, where perinatal and childhood mortality is higher, the replacement rate would be higher.
7. See Kirk and Kates, in note 5.

REFERENCES

Bogue, Donald J. *Principles of Demography.* New York: John Wiley & Sons, 1969.
Childe, V. Gordon. *What Happened in History.* New York: Penguin Books, 1964.
Mumford, Lewis. *The City in History.* New York: Harcourt, Brace and World, 1961.

Chapter

2 | The American City in the Nineteenth Century

The general comments about urbanization in the previous chapter, largely drawn from European experience, also apply to the American case. However, there are some aspects of the American case that are special and should be noted.

In Europe the great wave of urbanization that began with the Industrial Revolution occurred in an area that had been settled for many hundreds of years. Migration from an already thickly settled countryside swelled the populations of existing cities. In the United States the processes of settling the countryside and founding cities often took place more or less simultaneously. At other times towns and cities were founded in areas that were not settled at all, other than by a Native American population that was sooner or later displaced, and settlement of the surrounding countryside followed. Thus the European sequence was reversed. Some U.S. cities and towns were founded as a strategic act by government to open up or gain control of a particular region. Pittsburgh, at the confluence of the Allegheny and Susquehanna rivers, is one example. Many more were founded as speculative ventures. Land was acquired, subdivided, and sold as a commercial venture. This, too, was very different from the growth-by-accretion process that had characterized most European cities and probably most cities anywhere in the world.

Still another difference, and an important one, was the speed of the process. Though European populations grew rapidly in the nineteenth century, U.S. population growth in that century was, in percentage terms, much more rapid. First, of course, the United States received immigrants from Europe, thus relieving growth pressures in Europe and accelerating its own growth. A trickle of a few thousand per year at the beginning of the nineteenth century became a flow of hundreds of thousands in the last decades of the century.[1] Beyond that, the U.S. rate of natural increase in the early nineteenth century was one of the highest that had ever been observed. The birth rates that now characterize the most prolific of Third World countries then characterized the United States. In most of the world no level of births could have produced the rate of natural increase seen in the United States because limitations on food supply would not have permitted it. But in the United States the availability of virgin land freed the population from the usual Malthusian limits.[2]

In 1800 the U.S. population was overwhelmingly located east of the Alleghenies and, in New England, east of the Green Mountains. The nation's few cities, which were really the size of small or medium-sized towns by modern standards, were trading and commercial cities, all located on the coast. They served to connect the hinterlands of the United States with the rest of the world, primarily Europe. New York had been founded at the best natural harbor on the east coast. Boston was likewise founded at the best harbor in its region. Baltimore was founded where the Patapsco river empties into the Chesapeake Bay, and Philadelphia near the confluence of the Schuylkill and Delaware rivers before they empty into the Atlantic. The biggest city in the South at that time was Charles Town (subsequently Charleston), South Carolina, located where the Ashley and Cooper rivers join the Atlantic.

In 1800 the population of the United States was about 5 million, and the urbanized population—defined as people living in places with a population of 2,500 or more—was about 5 percent of the total population. New York City had a population of about 60,000, and Philadelphia was second with about 41,000. Baltimore and Boston, the third and fourth largest cities, had populations in the mid 20 thousands. By 1900 the population of the nation had increased by a factor of 15 to about 75 million. Its urban population, however, had increased by a factor of 100 to about 30 million. New York City's population had increased more than fiftyfold to 3.4 million. Philadelphia's population had grown to about 1.3 million. Chicago, which literally did not exist as a settled place in 1800, had a population of about 1.7 million.[3]

THE CHARACTER OF NINETEENTH-CENTURY URBANIZATION

Across the century a variety of forces combined to increase the percentage of Americans who lived in cities, to cause many cities to grow at enormous rates, and to develop in a very compact and extraordinarily dense form.

One force behind urban growth, beyond that of overall population growth, was the increasing efficiency of agriculture. At the beginning of the nineteenth century about 90 percent of the U.S. labor force was in agriculture. The average farm family fed both itself and a small fraction of one nonfarm family. In 1880 the decennial census showed that for the first time in U.S. history as many people were employed off the land as on the land. A large portion of the population was now available to lead an urban life. To the push provided by increasing efficiency in agriculture was added the pull of growing manufacturing and trade.

The growth of manufacturing provided masses of industrial employment in urban centers. Unlike the automated factory of today, the factory of the nineteenth century provided large amounts of employment in machine tending and materials handling that could be done by a relatively uneducated workforce. Industrial employment tended to be concentrated in cities, often in their centers, largely because of the particular properties of nineteenth-century transportation. Overland transportation by horse and wagon was extremely expensive. A team of horses and a man could produce only a few ton/miles per day. The two low-cost modes of transportation at the beginning of the nineteenth century were the oceangoing vessel and the canal boat or riverboat. The first several decades of the century saw a spate of canal building in the United States, generally promoted by local business interests precisely because of the enormous transportation cost advantages that canals provided.[4] The best known of these was the Erie Canal, completed in the 1820s. It was a private venture by a group of New York City businessmen and civic leaders, designed to give the city a commercial reach into the Midwest by linking the Hudson River to Lake Erie. It was in its time enormously successful and is one reason why New York City rapidly outgrew its two main commercial rivals, Boston and Philadelphia.

The coming of railroad technology in the 1830s provided another and superior low-cost mode of transportation, and the canal-building era came to a quick end. Being on a railroad line gave a city a great commercial advantage, and the canal-building story was repeated, this time with rails. Many railroads were built with municipal bonds or with private bonds guaranteed by municipalities. A number of lines were built more on the basis of civic boosterism and competitive spirit rather than rational business calculations. The long-since defunct Oswego Midland Railroad

> zigzagged across the state [New York] in search of municipal bonds, which were its principal source of capital. Midland managed to cross the state for nearly 250 miles from Cornwall on the Hudson to Oswego on Lake Ontario without ever passing through a single major city.[5]

Numerous bankruptcies occurred, along with considerable waste and fraud. But the nation did get off to a fast start in the building of what by the late nineteenth century was a well-developed national rail system. Most of the canals soon lost their traffic to the emerging rail system. Today the Erie canal, now part of the New York State Barge Canal system, serves mainly for recreational boating. The restored towpath of the Chesapeake and Ohio (C&O) canal, which extended from Washington, D.C., to Cumberland,

Maryland, now serves as a pedestrian way in the national parks system. Throughout the Northeast and North Central parts of the nation, there are many hundreds of miles of abandoned canals serving, if anyone, the occasional stroller or hiker.

The transportation technology of the nineteenth century gave a site that could be served by water and by rail an enormous cost advantage. That generally meant an urban site, for that is where the docks and the rail terminals were. The perfect industrial location for a firm that was involved in international trade was a place like lower Manhattan. By the mid nineteenth century, tracks running a few blocks east of the Hudson shoreline linked the area to the Midwest along roughly the same water level route through the Mohawk Valley as did the Erie Canal. Piers on the Hudson side of Manhattan and wrapping around the lower tip of Manhattan to the East River side of the island accommodated ships from all over the world. Goods could move between, say, London and Chicago and make all but a few hundred yards of the trip by low-cost mode. Today the tracks are gone, and the Manhattan waterfront now handles no freight. The most visible remains of this era are the still numerous manufacturing loft buildings in lower Manhattan, now used as residences, as artists' studios, and for a wide variety of commercial purposes.

The Boston Waterfront about 1865. In an age before the automobile and the truck, large amounts of commercial activity clustered around the waterfront.

The pull of factory employment to the cities was abetted by some of the offshoots of manufacturing. Without the great output of factory production the department store could not exist. It was also a source of mass employment at a single point on the map. So too, was the corporate headquarters that came into being because of the existence of the large manufacturing firm. As manufacturing grew, the volume of goods to be transported grew and so, too, did goods handling employment like carting and longshoring.

All these forces pulled large numbers of people into cities. The particular character of nineteenth-century transportation and manufacturing technology also produced great crowding. In Manhattan's Lower East Side, population densities in a few wards (a political district for the election of councilmen) reached as high as 500,000 people per square mile, a figure comparable to the present-day population of the entire city of Cleveland.[6]

In the nineteenth century the preferred structure for a large manufacturing operation was a multistory building. The reason was that power for machinery was generally provided by a steam engine and transmitted through the building by a system of shafts, pulleys, and leather belts. Thus power could not be transmitted very far. The structural shape that put the most amount of manufacturing floor space within a practical distance of the power source was the multistory building. Where waterpower ran machinery, the same situation prevailed—it made sense to mass the operation as close to the source of power as possible. Traces of this latter technology can be seen in old, disused, multistory industrial buildings at the river's edge in New England towns like Lowell, Massachusetts.

Throughout most of the nineteenth century most employees traveled to work on foot. That meant that masses of housing needed to be built near to central employment sites. Beginning in the mid nineteenth century horse-drawn trolley systems were built in some cities, but they were not much faster than walking.

Two nineteenth-century architectural inventions, both made in around 1880, also contributed to very high employment densities. These were the invention of steel frame construction and the invention of the elevator. The steel frame made the skyscraper architecturally possible. The elevator made the skyscraper commercially feasible. As office employment grew, these two inventions made it possible to place huge numbers of jobs in a very small land area.

Concentrated employment meant concentrated housing for working populations. One result was the nineteenth-century tenement.

The residence of the worker in New York City and other large industrial cities in 1850 was frequently the "railroad flat," a walk-up structure that was generally 5 to 7 stories high, 25 feet wide and 75 feet long on a 25 by 100 foot lot. Constructed solidly in rows across entire block faces, these units had four apartments on each floor surrounding a common staircase. The rooms in these apartments were constructed in tandem, with just one room in each apartment provided with a window or two for light and air. No sanitary facilities or water supply were provided for in these structures. A small rear yard contained a multi-seat outhouse and often a well, resulting in deplorable conditions of sanitation and health.[7]

Given the larger family sizes of the era such a structure might contain as many as two hundred people on a 2,500 square foot plot, roughly one-twentieth of an acre. By comparison, a quarter-acre lot (roughly 100×100 feet) is considered a relatively small lot for a single-family house in the modern U.S. suburb. In fact, in many suburbs zoning laws stipulate minimum lot sizes of half an acre, and sometimes one acre or more for a single-family house.

The public health consequences of tenement housing were horrendous. Placing waste disposal and the source of water supply together for a large number of people is a prescription for all sorts of waterborne diseases, such as typhoid fever and cholera. The large number of people in a poorly ventilated space was a recipe for the transmission of airborne disease, most notably tuberculosis, which was a greater scourge in the nineteenth century than any

Hester Street on Manhattan's Lower East Side in 1898. This area contained some of the highest population densities ever recorded in the United States.

disease, including AIDS, is at the present time. This was all, of course, in an age before antibiotics, when doctors could diagnose a disease but could do very little to affect its course. This is how one planning textbook written early in the twentieth century described the urban scene:

> Few municipalities have planned intelligently for this rapid urban growth. Buildings have been crowded upon land and people have been crowded within buildings. Urban living has become in many ways inconvenient, unsafe and unhealthful. . . . Transit facilities fail to develop much in advance of demonstrable need, so the population becomes crowded within a limited area. . . . It becomes used to living a life quite divorced from nature. The responsibilities of home-ownership are felt only by a few. The sense of citizenship and the sense of moral responsibility for evils suffered by neighbors become weak.
>
> In the interest of both hygiene and public morality, the cottage home is much to be preferred to the tenement dwelling. . . . Tuberculosis is responsible for nearly one tenth of all deaths in the United States. . . . The tubercule bacillus can live for weeks outside the human body in a sunless damp room, hall, or cellar. The tenement house may thus at once reduce vitality, through absence of sunlight and fresh air, and may provide abundant opportunity for the transmission of prevalent and dangerous diseases.[8]

Reformers of the nineteenth century focused much energy on the condition of housing for the poor, and some improvements were made. In 1901 New York City's Tenement House Act, considered a milestone in housing reform, limited the lot coverage of tenements to 70 percent and required a bathroom in each apartment. It also required each tenement to have a small courtyard or airshaft space to bring a modicum of light and air to interior rooms. The tenement that met the requirements of the new law, through still substandard and vastly overcrowded by modern standards, was a big improvement for the times.[9]

Many reformers were greatly interested in public transportation, particularly the trolley (also referred to as the electric street railway) and in a few places such as New York and Chicago, the elevated train and the subway. They saw these as instruments to decongest the city and achieve more separation between residential and commercial or manufacturing areas—to let the family of the urban worker enjoy the benefits of the "cottage home" referred to above.

Parks and playgrounds were another preoccupation of urban reformers at the end of the nineteenth century, a reaction to both the high population densities and crowding out of open spaces. So, too, were urban design and public art, for the ninteenth-century city, built at great speed and at great densities was, generally speaking, not an attractive place. Both the Municipal Art movement and the City Beautiful Movement (concerned with improving urban design) that sprang up at the end of the century were a reaction to the crowding and unpleasantness of the nineteenth-century city.[10]

THE GROWTH OF NEW CITIES

Throughout the nineteenth century new towns and cities appeared in the United States with great frequency. As noted, the U.S. pattern sometimes reversed the European pattern. Rather than forming in an agricultural area, the town was started first and the countryside around settled afterwards. Many towns started as speculative ventures. For example, in parts of the Midwest entrepreneurs obtained large blocks of land under the terms of the Northwest Ordinance of 1785, often at less than $1 per acre, laid out towns, subdivided the land, and then made their money selling building lots.

Shortly before the Civil War the federal government began to make grants of land to railroads. Ultimately, approximately 160 million acres, roughly one quarter of a million square miles of land, was given by the federal government either directly or through the states to railroad companies.[11] That made railroads landowners on a spectacular scale. From about 1860 on, railroads made much of their money through land development, by planting towns along the right of way. The building of the railroad boosted land values, and the development of the town provided the railroad with a guaranteed supply of customers.

New cities often grew with unprecedented speed. The most extraordinary case is that of Chicago. The strategic value of the site had long been appreciated, for there the Illinois River almost completed a connection between Lake Michigan and the Mississippi River, thus holding out the promise of a water route from the Great Lakes to New Orleans and the Gulf of Mexico. In 1827 Congress gave the state of Illinois alternate one-mile-square sections of land along the route of a proposed canal between Lake Michigan and the Illinois River. However, until 1830 the only development there was Fort Dearborn. In that year the state set up a Canal Commission, which drew a simple plan for a small area, subdivided land, and began selling lots to raise money for the building of the canal. The development of Chicago then began. The canal was completed in 1848. It apparently had little direct effect upon the growth of the city, other than providing the impetus to plan the city and perhaps lure some people out in the hopes that it would spur commercial development. The city grew slowly at first, reaching a population of less than 5,000 by 1840. But population jumped to about 109,000 by 1860, approximately half a million in 1880 and almost 1.7 million by 1900.

No city in human history had ever grown from nothing to a population of 1.7 million in 70 years. What made Chicago's growth possible? The rapid peopling of the Mississippi Valley provided a hinterland to sustain the economy of the city. Chicago was the biggest link between the agriculture and natural resources of the Midwest and the manufacturing economy of Europe and the eastern United States. In time, the city also became a manufacturing power in its own right. Because the Mississippi Valley had not long been settled, other than by the Native American population, there was not a well-developed network of smaller cities with which it had to compete. Steamboat and railroad technology, both coming along in the first three decades or so of the nineteenth century, gave the city a huge reach that it could not have gained with earlier transportation technologies.

> In a new country the rapid growth of cities is both natural and necessary, for no efficient industrial organization of a new settlement is possible without industrial centers to carry on the necessary work of assembling and distributing goods. A Mississippi Valley empire rising suddenly into being without its Chicago and its smaller centers of distribution is almost inconceivable to the 19th century economist. That America is the "land of mushroom cities" is therefore not at all surprising.[12]

The founding of most of the cities of the western United States took place within the remarkably short time span of the last two thirds of the nineteenth century. Many western cities and towns were founded as commercial ventures, generally by Easterners, and largely settled by migrants from the East. Again, the process of urbanization often preceded or occurred simultaneously with the settlement of rural areas. Writing about the urbanization of the West, the historian John Reps states:

> Most were founded by promoters and settled by migrants from the East who brought with them older urban values, expectations, and institutions. Western towns quickly took on the appearance and character of those in other regions of the nation. The editor of a Portland, Oregon, journal, writing in 1886, suggested that if an Eastern city resident were suddenly "set . . . down in the streets of Portland . . . he would observe little difference between his new surroundings and those he beheld but a moment before in his native city." He would find "the rows of substantial brick blocks . . . , the well paved and graded streets, the lines of street railways, the mass of telephone and telegraph wires, the numerous electric lights and street lamps, the fire-plugs and water hydrants, the beautiful private residences surrounded by lawns and shade trees suggesting years of careful culture, the long lines of wharfs and warehouses on the river front, and the innumerable other features common to every prosperous Eastern City and commercial port."[13]

Perhaps the journalist Reps quotes was given to a bit of civic boosterism, but the larger point that Western urbanization was often similar to the process in the East is important. Reps argues that the process of Western urbanization has gotten less attention from historians than it should have because they have focused so heavily upon rural and frontier settlement. He attributes this overemphasis in large measure to the grip that the frontier hypothesis of the historian Frederick Jackson Turner has exercised upon Americans with regard to the settlement of the West. By focusing on the closing of the frontier as a decisive event in the settling of the continent, and also in the making of the American consciousness, Turner inevitably shifted the focus of attention away from things urban.[14]

THE BEGINNINGS OF DECENTRALIZATION

For most of the nineteenth century the forces of centralization described above were predominant. Cities grew larger and also denser, both in terms of population and of workplaces. But toward the end of the nineteenth century a few dispersing forces began to make themselves known. From about mid-century on, steam railroads made possible the beginnings of what we now call "commuting." For example, there was a trickle of commuting from what is now southern Westchester County into Manhattan by the time of the Civil War. However, the first major instrument of decentralization was the electric trolley. Trolleys are rare now in the United States, though trolley systems, now generally referred to as "light rail," are being built along limited routes in a few U.S. cities.[15] But in their day trolleys were the epitome of high-tech transportation, and they revolutionized urban transportation in the United States.

The trolley required two basic pieces of technology—an adequate electric motor and a dynamo to produce power for distribution through the system's overhead wires. That technology became available in the mid-1880s, and the boom in urban trolley construction began shortly thereafter.

> By 1890 fifty-one cities had installed trolley systems; five years later 850 were in operation with lines totaling 10,000 miles. The suitability of the new system of urban transportation was demonstrated most clearly by the rapidity with which it replaced horse-car lines. In 1890, 69.7 percent of the total trackage in cities was operated by horses; by 1902 this figure had declined to 1.1 percent, while electric power was used on 97 percent of the mileage.[16]

By 1902 trolleys were carrying about 6 billion passengers per year.[17] That compares with a total of about 8.5 billion trips by all types of mass transit in the United States in the early 1990s, despite the more than tripling of the population in the intervening time.

The electric street car marked a new phase in urbanization. The "walking city," whose radius was limited to the distance a person could walk in an hour or so, gave way to a much larger city as streetcar lines were extended into the countryside. Separate towns and villages within many miles of downtown became knitted into a single metropolis as streetcars cut the travel times between them. The almost purely residential subdivision, or "bedroom community," became commonplace as the streetcar made it possible to put some miles between where one lived and where one worked. Not only did the streetcar spread the city, but it enabled developers to leapfrog over the settled areas and plant new streetcar-based communities.

> ... New Orleans interests, through the able use of trolley lines, built a number of profitable suburbs along the Mississippi River and on the north shore of Lake Ponchartrain. Similar communities sprang up around Shreveport.... Another Louisiana real estate firm, the Kent Company of Alexandria, gained control of the

Alexandria Electric Railway Company and used the line to develop a suburban area. The company provided a typical inducement when it promised free streetcar rides for three years to anyone who bought a new lot in its subdivision.[18]

To the extent that the streetcar dispersed the urban population over a larger land area, it was largely those of middle or upper income who were dispersed, in part because it was they who could afford to buy or rent newly built housing in the expanding suburbs.[19] The web of streetcars and interurban trolleys was extensive. Urban historians have claimed that early in the twentieth century it would have actually been possible to travel from the Northeast out to perhaps as far as Wisconsin entirely by street car and interurban trolley.

Electric trolley usage peaked early in this century and then plummeted under competition from the automobile and, to a much lesser extent, the motorbus. It is hard to think of another transportation technology that burst upon the scene so suddenly, became ubiquitous so fast, and then was dis-

The Greely Square elevated steam railway station in Manhattan, 1898. Steam power was replaced by electric power on lines within the city early in the twentieth century. Even with electric power, these lines still devalued adjacent properties. For that reason, and because their supporting columns obstructed traffic flow in the street below, most elevated lines were later torn down and replaced with underground lines.

placed so quickly. However, the electric streetcar left a major, permanent mark upon urban form. In a few of the largest cities, such as New York and Chicago, the dispersing effects of the streetcar was supplemented by elevated railroads, sometimes powered by steam and sometimes by electricity. Because they had separate rights of way, elevated trains had much higher speeds and permitted longer commutes.

At the same time that the electric trolley was dispersing residences, a certain amount of business activity was dispersing as well, for retailers necessarily follow their customers. The beginnings of industrial dispersion were also seen. By the end of the nineteenth century some industry was beginning to move outward from the city center into the suburbs along railroad lines. Cheaper land and the convenience of having the plant's own railroad siding to avoid carting costs were two of the factors, as well as the fact that residential dispersion was providing the labor force for more outlying locations. Radical historians are quick to note that some movement of industry out of the cities was also motivated by the desire of employers to escape from unions. Unions tended to be stronger in cities, in part because many immigrants brought with them from Europe a tradition of union activism.

By the end of the nineteenth century at least one perceptive observer saw the straws in the wind and predicted the transformation of the compact nineteenth-century city into the sprawling metropolitan area of the twentieth century. He was the novelist and futurist H. G. Wells.

> Many of our railway begotten giants are destined to such a process of dissection and diffusion as to amount almost to obliteration. But new forces . . . may finally be equal to the complete reduction of all of our present congestions. . . . What will be the forces acting upon the prosperous household? The passion for nature . . . and that craving for a little private imperium are the chief centrifugal inducements. The city will diffuse itself until it has taken many of the characteristics of what is now country. . . . We may call . . . these coming town provinces "urban regions."[20]

It is hard to find a better prophecy. Wells thought that the chief dispersing agent would be the railroads, but as it turned out the automobile was by far the more powerful force. But in identifying the pull of nature and the desire for personal space as the magnets and improved transportation as the facilitating agent, he was right on target. He was accurate, too, in anticipating that the process of dispersal that came to be called "suburbanization" would occur with greater frequency among the more prosperous. In the following chapter we turn to the process of transformation from city to metropolitan region.

SUMMARY

One way the U.S. pattern of urbanization differed from that of Europe was that in many cases cities were established in advance of agricultural development, sometimes for strategic purposes and sometimes for speculative purposes. Immigration, high rates of natural increase, and a decrease in agricultural employment as a percentage of total employment all contributed to rapid urban growth in the United States during the nineteenth century. Urban population increased from about 300,000 in 1800 to about 30 million in 1900. Nineteenth-century cities often developed at very high densities because the transportation technology of the time favored sites that were served by rail or water. The manufacturing technology, reliant on steam or water power rather than electricity, and the invention of steel frame construction and the elevator (both about 1880) also contributed to the dense concentration of employment. Concentrations of employment, in an age when most people walked to work, necessarily created extremely dense concentrations of housing, such as was seen in Manhattan's Lower East Side, and the deplorable living conditions that went with them. We also note the spectacularly rapid growth of many nineteenth-century cities, most notably Chicago. Toward the end of the nineteenth century we observe the beginnings of dispersal, prompted in large measure by the development of the streetcar (also referred to as the electric street railway).

NOTES

1. The exact amount of immigration in 1800 is not known. The Act of 1819 required masters of ships to provide customs officials with passenger lists, and so good immigration records begin with the year 1820. In that year the United States received somewhat over 8,000 immigrants. In 1830 the number was about 23,000 and in 1840 was about 86,000. Extending that trend backwards would suggest that immigration in 1800 was relatively small. See *Historical Statistics of the United States,* vol. 1 (Washington, D.C.: Department of Commerce, Bureau of the Census, 1975), p. 106 and preceding notes. Decade-by-decade immigration figures for the 1820s though the 1980s are provided in Chapter 12.
2. See the reference to Malthus in the Chapter 1 notes.
3. Accounts of the founding of the city of Chicago can be found in John W. Reps, *Cities of the American West* (Princeton, N.J.: Princeton University Press, 1979), pp. 22–23; and in Charles N. Glaab and A. Theodore Brown, *A History of Urban America* (New York: Macmillan, 1967), pp. 48–50. The Reps book also contains accounts of other cities as well as numerous plans and illustrations. The population figures are from Blake McKelvey, *American Urbanization* (Glencoe, Ill.: Scott, Foresman, 1973), pp. 37 and 73.
4. In the early nineteenth century, overland transportation (horse and wagon) was estimated to be ten times as expensive as transportation by canal boat. See Alan Pred, *City Systems in Advanced Economies* (New York: Wiley, 1977), p. 66.
5. Alfred Eichner, *State Development Agencies and Employment Expansion* (Ann Arbor: University of Michigan Press, 1970), p. 15.
6. Adna Weber, *The Growth of Cities in the Nineteenth Century* (New York: Macmillan, 1899, reprinted by Cornell University Press, Ithaca, N.Y., 1963), p. 460.
7. Frank S. So., et al., eds., *The Practice of Local Government Planning* (Washington, D.C.: International City Managers Association, 1979), p. 27.
8. James D. Ford, "Residential and Industrial Decentralization," in *City Planning,* 2nd ed., edited by John Nolen (New York: D. Appleton, 1929), p. 334. The first edition was printed in 1916, and the article appears to have been written some years before that.
9. For vivid contemporary descriptions of life in the Lower East Side and other poor neighborhoods of New York in the late nineteenth century, see books by Jacob Riis, such as *How the Other Half Lives: Studies Among the Tenements of New York* (New York, Scribner's Sons, 1890).

10. Detailed descriptions of these movements can be found in Mel Scott, *American City Planning Since 1890* (Berkeley: University of California Press, 1971). Short descriptions can be found in John M. Levy, *Contemporary Urban Planning*, 5th ed. (Englewood Cliffs, N.J.: Prentice Hall, 2000), Chapter 2.
11. For a history of land grants to the railroads, see a standard history of the United States, such as Richard Hofstader, William Miller, and Daniel Aaron, *The American Republic* (Englewood Cliffs, N.J.: Prentice Hall, 1970).
12. Adna Weber, op. cit. p. 20.
13. See John Reps, *The Forgotten Frontier: Urban Planning in the American West before 1890* (Columbia, Mo.: University of Missouri Press, 1981), p. 3.
14. Reps, op. cit., p.1.
15. Charles N. Glaab and A. Theodore Brown, *A History of Urban America* (New York: Macmillan, 1976), p. 143–44.
16. Harry Henderson, "Light Rail, Heavy Costs," *Planning* (October 1994), pp. 8–13.
17. Blake McKelvey, *American Urbanization: A Comparative History* (Glenview, Ill.: Scott & Co., 1973), p. 83.
18. Glaab and Brown, op. cit., p. 256.
19. The definitive work on the effects of the streetcar on urbanization in the United States is generally considered to be Sam Bass Warner, *Streetcar Suburbs: A Process of Growth in Boston*, (New York: Atheneum, 1968).
20. H. G. Wells, quoted in *Post-Industrial America: Metropolitan Decline and Inter-Regional Job Shifts*, edited by George Sternlieb and James W. Hughes (New Brunswick, N.J.: Rutgers Center for Urban Policy Research, 1975), p. 176.

REFERENCES

McKelvey, Blake. *American Urbanization: A Comparative History*. Glenview, Ill.: Scott, Foresman, 1973.

Glaab, Charles N., and A. Theodore Brown. *A History of Urban America*. New York: Macmillan, 1976.

Reps, John W. *Cities of the American West*. Princeton, N.J.: Princeton University Press, 1979.

Chapter

3 | The Emergence of Metropolitan America

In the previous chapter we noted the emergence of forces that began to transform the compact "walking city" of the nineteenth century into the metropolitan area. From then until the present time one decentralizing force after another has appeared on the scene. If the streetcar was the first major decentralizing force, the most recent might be a new Internet service or feature that permits you to do from home that for which you previously had to go to a central place. To the effects of technological change were added a number of public policy decisions that also, often unintentionally, had the effect of promoting decentralization.

One fundamental dispersing force, perhaps the most important of all, was simply the growth in personal income that technological change promoted. As people became more prosperous, they could afford to spend more on housing and transportation. Increasing prosperity also led to a decrease in the length of the work week. The nineteenth-century industrial work week of six 10- or 12-hour days evolved in stages to today's 35- or 40-hour week, giving people more time for leisure and more time for travel to work.

The automobile proved to be a tremendous disperser of population. The burst of suburbanization that characterized the 1920s is very closely tied to the beginning of the assembly line production of automobiles in 1915. By 1930, when the "roaring twenties" came to an end and the Great Depression began, there was about one motor vehicle in the United States for every five people. In a little more than a decade the automobile had gone from a luxury item to a standard possession of the middle class and the prosperous working class. Note that by 1990 there was one motor vehicle for every 1.3 Americans—roughly one motor vehicle for every American old enough to drive. As Figure 3–1 shows, since the end of World War II the number (not just the

Lower Washington Street in Boston in the years before World War I. Narrow streets like these were soon to be overwhelmed by the mass production of automobiles.

percentage) of motor vehicles in the United States has been increasing substantially faster than the number of people. Just as the automobile permitted a huge dispersion of residences, the truck did the same for retailing and light industry by freeing them from the need for rail access.

Communications technologies also proved to be decentralizing, for they make it possible to do at a distance what otherwise would have to be done face-to-face. The first big dispersing force in communications technology was the telephone.[1] It was invented in 1876 and became commonplace about the turn of the century as the rotary dial began to replace the switchboard operator. Since then, one new communications technology after another has appeared—teletype, telex, closed circuit TV, computer-to-computer links, fax, e-mail, and the Internet. In the long run the computer chip may be just as powerful a dispersing force as the internal combustion engine.

New entertainment technologies broke the monopoly of downtown on entertainment and thus weakened central places. Motion pictures appeared around the turn of the century, and commercial radio in the early 1920s. The first commercial television transmissions were made very shortly before the

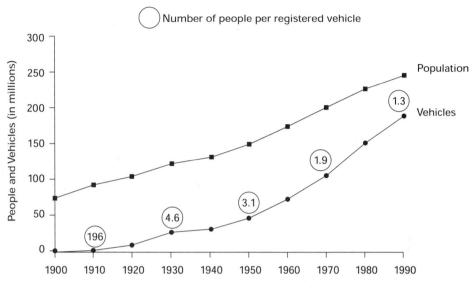

FIGURE 3-1 Motor Vehicles and People, 1900-1990

Sources: Motor vehicle registrations from 1900 through 1970 from table Q, p. 716, Historical Statistics of the United States, Colonial Times to 1970, Department of Commerce, Bureau of the Census, 1975. More recent motor vehicle registrations and U.S. population from the *Statistical Abstract of the United States,* 1996.

Note: Figures are for all motor vehicles rather than just automobiles because large numbers of vehicles are not classified as automobiles, especially pickups, vans, and sport utility vehicles, are used for personal transportation.

beginning of World War II. The TV set became a common consumer item in the late 1940s and early 1950s and by 1960 or so had achieved market saturation in the sense that most homes had one. The VCR, cable TV, and the satellite dish are more recent variations on the same theme. They make it possible to receive one of the traditional attractions of city life—professional entertainment—almost anywhere.

Highway engineers contributed a powerfully decentralizing piece of technology in the form of the limited access highway, a road on which traffic flow is divided and to which access is limited to specific points rather than available to anyone who owns adjacent property. It is believed that the first one built in the United States was the Bronx River Parkway, built in Westchester County, New York, in 1926.[2] The combination of one-way traffic and limited access points is not only much safer than the old highway, but it provides much faster travel and thus encourages much longer trips.

The term *parkway* came from the idea that these roads would enable the auto-owning city dweller to have easy access to parks in suburbia and beyond. And roads like the Bronx River Parkway and Long Island's Southern State Parkway did achieve exactly that. But the much larger effect of such roads was to facilitate commuting and thus enable people who worked in the city to live in the suburbs. The next stage, of course, was that many of the jobs began following the labor force and the buying power out to the suburbs.

None of the above technologies forced the decentralization of either population or employment. Rather, they permitted it to happen. If people wanted to move outward because land was cheaper, because they wanted to be closer to the natural world, because they didn't like the smell of city air, because they didn't like their neighbors in the city, or for any other reason, these dispersing technologies made it possible for them to do so. The same can be said of employment. If employers wanted to locate their businesses outside the city because of cheaper land, lower construction costs, lower taxes, because they themselves wanted to live in the suburbs and not have to commute, or for any other reason, quick transportation and electronic communication gave them that option.

Many of the forces just discussed reinforced one another. For example, in the prosperous decades after World War II automobile ownership in the United States climbed very rapidly. That was one of the forces promoting suburbanization. The fact that more people had cars and wanted to be able to use them efficiently promoted a great surge of highway building. Better roads, in turn, made the automobile a more desirable item and suburban life more feasible. As more automobiles and major public investment in new highways spread out residences and jobs, the state of public transportation declined. Transportation engineers refer to the *collection problem* (getting the transit rider from home to the transit stop) and the *distribution problem* (getting the transit rider from the transit stop to job, store, or wherever he or she actually wants to go). The dispersal of activity complicates both problems enormously. As public transportation became less available, it became ever more necessary to own a car. That weakened public transportation still further, and so the cycle fed on itself. The decline of public transportation was a major turnaround. About 1900 electric street railway stocks were hot items on Wall Street, like semiconductor or Internet stocks in the 1990s. The technology was new and exciting, and the market was expanding rapidly. Today, almost all of the capital costs and about half of the operating costs of public transportation are paid by government, primarily the federal government. Without subsidy, public transportation would die.

Table 3–1 shows the shift of population from the central city to the suburban ring during the twentieth century. The Bureau of the Census refers to metropolitan areas as MSAs (Metropolitan Statistical Areas). The MSA is divided into the central city and the surrounding suburban counties. The latter are referred to as the Ring in Table 3–1. Note that in 1900 about two thirds of all persons in metropolitan areas resided in central cities. Sometime in the early 1960s the number of city dwellers and suburbanites became equal. By 1990 those in metropolitan areas but outside of the central city outnumbered those in the city by about three to two.

TABLE 3-1 Population in MSAs, 1900–1990 (in millions)

Year	Total U.S.	Total MSA	Central City	Ring	MSA as Percentage of Total	Central City as Percentage of MSA
1900	76.0	24.1	16.0	8.1	31.7	66.4
1910	92.0	34.5	22.9	11.6	37.5	66.4
1920	105.7	46.1	30.5	15.6	43.6	66.2
1930	122.8	61.0	39.0	22.0	49.7	63.9
1940	131.7	67.1	41.5	25.6	50.9	61.8
1950	151.3	84.9	49.7	35.2	56.1	58.5
1960	179.3	112.9	58.0	54.9	63.0	51.4
1970	203.2	155.4	72.3	83.8	76.5	46.5
1980	226.5	172.7	73.0	99.8	76.3	42.3
1990	248.7	192.7	77.8	114.9	77.5	40.4

Source: Figures from 1940 and earlier are from Donald J. Bogue, *Population Growth in Standard Metropolitan Areas, 1900–1950,* Housing and Home Finance Agency, Washington, D.C., 1953, pp. 11–13. From 1950 through 1980 they are from the Bureau of the Census, *Census of the Population.* The 1990 figures are from communication with the Population Division, Bureau of the Census.

Note: Over time the number of MSAs (formerly called SMSAs for Standard Metropolitan Statistical Areas) grows. Also, additional counties may be added to the MSA from one census to the next. Thus the above data do not refer to a fixed set of places or a fixed land area and should be taken to indicate only the overall trend. In general, the Bureau of the Census requires that to be defined as a central city the place in question must have a population of at least 50,000. The decision about which surrounding counties to include in the MSA is made largely on the basis of commuting data.

A BRIEF HISTORY OF DECENTRALIZATION

World War II provides a good breaking point for the narrative that follows. This section proceeds very quickly up to the war and then more slowly from the war to the present.

The 1920s saw rapid suburbanization of population, facilitated by rapidly growing automobile ownership and a decade of prosperity and economic growth. In many U.S. metropolitan areas what are now referred to as the "inner suburbs" are largely of 1920s origin. There was some decentralization of business activity, but for a great many suburbanites the city was still the place where they earned their money, went for cultural activities, and made many of their more important purchases.

In October 1929 the stock market crashed, and with that event the United States, along with much of the Western world, began sliding into the Great Depression. The affluence of the 20s was over, and the rush to the suburbs slowed substantially. Metropolitan area growth in the 1930s also slowed for demographic reasons. In the early 1920s the United States' historic open immigration policy was replaced with a system of national quotas, and so immigration slowed to a fraction of its pre–World War I pace, not to return to high levels until well after World War II. The U.S. birth rate was relatively low during the Great Depression, and so a second source of population pressure on metropolitan areas was relieved. Finally, the high unemployment rates of the 1930s discouraged rural-to-urban migration.

The Great Depression lasted through the 1930s. The United States came out of it about 1941 with the coming of the war and the expansion of industrial production for the "war effort." However the suburbanizing process could not resume immediately, for during the war gasoline was rationed, civilian automobile production was halted, and the war effort had first call on construction materials and labor.

World War II ended in 1945, and by 1947 or so the decentralizing process was proceeding rapidly and has continued to do so up to the present time. Perhaps the most important background condition was simply that of continuing economic growth and prosperity. During the war there was considerable anxiety that after the "reconversion" (conversion back to a peacetime economy) process something like the Great Depression might return. That did not happen.[3] In the half century since the end of the war we have had periodic recessions, but nothing approaching the Great Depression in either duration or depth. One reflection of postwar prosperity was the rise in automobile ownership, as shown in Figure 3–1. Increasing automobile ownership went hand in hand with the post–World War II suburban housing boom.

Rapid home building was encouraged by public policy. Beginning in the 1930s the federal government launched a series of programs designed to make home mortgages available on very attractive terms—long durations (typically 30 years), low down payments, and low interest rates. Simultaneously, the federal tax code provided through the deductibility of mortgage interest and property taxes a powerful financial incentive to own rather than to rent. These federal policies, discussed in detail in Chapter 9, provided a very powerful push toward homeownership, and that, for a great many Americans, meant a house in the suburbs.

The combination of rapid suburbanization and increasing automobile ownership created a demand for more and better highways. By 1949 the federal government was providing state and local governments with matching funds for expanding their highway networks. The new roads facilitated suburbanization, which encouraged more automobile ownership in a self-perpetuating process.

Demographic Forces behind Metropolitan Growth

Unlike cities in the Depression years, cities and metropolitan areas in the post–World War II period experienced great population pressure from three separate sources: the "baby boom," increased immigration, and the mechanization of agriculture.

The Baby Boom. From the early 1800s to the early 1940s the U.S. birth rate had been trending down, as described early in the discussion of the Demographic Transition. However, early in the 1940s births began climbing. In 1941 there were 2.5 million births in the United States. The baby boom, generally considered to have begun in the late 1940s, peaked in 1957 with births reaching 4.3 million. Births remained above 4 million for several years and then dropped back to the range of 3.1 to 3.2 million by the early 1970s. The baby boom was much too big and lasted too long to be explained by births deferred because of the Great Depression and the war. Exactly why it happened is hard to say, and it is not easily reconciled with the logic of the demographic transition noted earlier.[4]

Regardless of whether or not we can fully explain the causes, the facts are very clear. The surge of births lasted almost two decades and affected every aspect of American life from increasing the demand for diapers in the 1950s and 1960s to crowding college campuses in the 1970s and 1980s to threatening to put enormous pressure on Social Security and Medicare early in the twenty-first century. To the extent that many people thought their children would be happier playing on suburban grass than on city concrete and asphalt, the baby boom was a big force behind the suburbanization of the postwar period.

Increasing Immigration. Immigration is discussed in detail in Chapter 12, so we note it only briefly here. In the years after the war U.S. immigration policy was loosened up in many ways, and the flow of legal immigrants increased greatly. Now, in absolute terms, it is not very different from what prevailed in the peak years around the end of the nineteenth century. Illegal immigration also increased for reasons discussed in Chapter 12. In the early postwar period most of the newcomers were from Europe, often refugees and displaced persons from the war, who headed toward eastern cities. In the last several decades most of the flow has been from this hemisphere and from Asia, and relatively more has been directed to other parts of the country. It has been a major expander and reshaper of urban and metropolitan area populations.

The Postwar City and the Mechanization of Agriculture. The history of agriculture and the history of urbanization have always been entwined. What made the post–World War II period unusual was the great rapidity with which events occurred. During the 1920s and 1930s the mechanization of agriculture proceeded at a moderate pace, with the increase in population and the increase in agricultural productivity (output per worker) roughly balancing each other. As Figure 3–2 shows, farm population changed little from 1920 to 1940. However, starting shortly after the end of World War II agricultural productivity began to increase at a tremendous pace. In fact, for several decades productivity in agriculture grew much faster than it did in

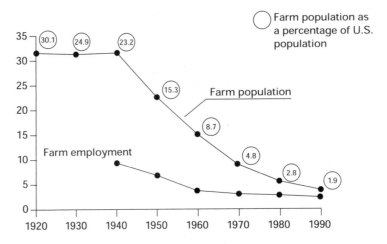

FIGURE 3-2 U.S. Farm Population and Farm Employment, 1920–1990 (in millions)

Source: Statistical Abstract of the United States, sections on employment and agriculture, various years.

Notes: Farm employment as distinct from farm population is not available for 1930 and earlier. In 1974 the definition of farm population was revised so that the 1980 and 1990 figures are not strictly comparable with earlier years.

manufacturing. From 1950 to 1970 farm employment dropped by more than 54 percent, while the U.S. population grew by 35 percent. In 1970 the average farmer was feeding almost three times as many people as he had in 1950. Since then employment in agriculture has continued to decline, albeit at a slower pace, while the total population has grown. The farm population dropped from about 25 million in 1950 to less than 5 million in 1990. The biggest part of that drop, a decline of over 15 million people, occurred during the 1950s and 1960s.

That 15 million drop in farm population gives us some measure of the vast internal migration that occurred in the United States in those twenty years. It was generally the poorer farmers whom mechanization forced out. The prosperous farmer was more likely to be able to make the investment in machinery and to buy or rent more land upon which to use that equipment. For much of the population pushed off the farm, remaining in rural America was not an option, because as farm employment and farm populations shrank, employment in the retailing and service businesses that served the farm population also shrank. Because of this loss of secondary employment, just counting the decline in farm population actually understates the size of the rural-to-urban migration that followed the mechanization of agriculture.

Moving to suburban areas was not an option for most of the displaced rural population for a number of reasons, including the price of suburban housing. That left the cities where there were still the largest concentrations of jobs, where there was a supply of older, lower-cost housing, where it was possible to get around without a car, and where public services such as clinics were generally more developed than in the suburbs.

The great internal migration of a largely poor ex-farm population to the cities from 1950 to 1970 was one of the great events that shaped U.S. cities in the post–World War II period. The effects of this migration are very much in evidence today. Though the process could be seen to be happening, there was no overall national planning to deal with it. Some federal programs were designed to deal with poverty, unemployment, and housing, but by and large, cities were left to deal with the problems this migration imposed as best they could, often in an ad hoc, one-crisis-at-a-time way.

Massive rural-to-urban migration is not an easy problem, and few societies have dealt with it well. In the U.S. case a rural population, often with limited education, found itself in the city, where its job skills were essentially useless. In some ways the situation resembled the one that masses of European immigrants had faced a couple of generations earlier, for the majority of them were people with rural roots, often without much formal education, and who, in addition, faced the challenge of learning a new language. In one way, the situation was somewhat better in the post-World War II case because the United States, largely as a result of the Great Depression and New Deal, had evolved a more substantial system of social services than had existed at the turn of the century. But in another and more important way the new situation was much worse. Technological progress was reducing the need for unskilled labor across the entire U.S. economy. Beyond that, the job mix in many cities was moving rapidly in a white-collar direction. During the 1970s, for example, New York City was losing manufacturing jobs at a rate of several tens of thousands per year, but at the same time it was adding jobs in fields like banking, stockbrokerage, and advertising. For someone with a strong back and willing hands but only a third-grade education, that was not good news. The market for the worker without much formal education was much better around the turn of the century when manufacturing employment in the city was growing, construction was proceeding at a rapid pace, containerized freight was not yet decimating employment on the docks, and the word "automation" had not yet entered our vocabulary.

The post–World War II migration to the cities also had a racial dimension that one must know about to understand the roots of much of U.S. social history in the last four decades. It affects, for example, the degree to which we will be a de facto segregated or a de facto integrated society and whether or not many of the gaps between White America and Black America will close up or remain wide.

In 1940 the majority of America's Black population was rural, and three fourths of all American Blacks lived in the South. There had been a trickle of Black migration to Northern cities for many decades. It had accelerated when the demand for industrial labor shot up during World War I and continued at a moderate pace during the prosperous 1920s. It then dropped off during the Great Depression as the demand for labor throughout the nation weakened. But in 1940 the majority of America's Black population still lived in the states of the old Confederacy. This situation changed with remarkable speed in the two decades after World War II. The mechanization of agriculture discussed above affected all rural populations in the United States, but the effect was especially pronounced for the Black population, for it was more often than not the Black farmer who was poorest and the first to be pushed off the land by the changing economics of agriculture.

The production of cotton provides the most dramatic example. In the Deep South a very large number of Black farmers, mostly sharecroppers, were involved in the production of cotton.[5] Cultivating and picking it was a labor-intensive activity that had been much less subject to mechanization than, say, wheat farming. But for some years engineers had been working on replacing the human hand with a mechanical cotton picker. Much of the work had been done by the International Harvester Corp. on a large Mississippi plantation owned by the Hops family. In 1944 the new equipment was ready and a public demonstration was held. This is how Nicholas Lemann describes it:[6]

> The pickers, painted bright red, drove down the white rows of cotton. Each one had mounted in front a row of spindles, looking like wide mouth, full of metal teeth, that had been turned vertically. The spindles . . . stripped the cotton from the plants; then a vacuum pulled it down a tube and into a big wire basket. . . . In an hour, a good field hand could pick twenty pounds of cotton; each mechanical picker, in an hour, picked as much as a thousand pounds. . . . The unusually precise system of cost accounting that Hops had developed showed that picking a bale of cotton [500 pounds] by machine cost him $5.26, and picking it by hand cost him $39.41. Each machine did the work of fifty people.

In the early nineteenth century the invention of the cotton gin made the plantation system viable on a large scale and concentrated a massive black population in Mississippi, Alabama, Louisiana, Texas, and other states where the climate favored cotton cultivation. In the mid twentieth century another piece of technology came along and drove the descendants of slaves off the land with amazing speed. To quote Lemann again,

> Between 1910 and 1970 six and a half million black Americans moved from the South to the North; five million of them moved after 1940, during the time of the mechanization of cotton farming. . . . The black migration was one of the largest and most rapid mass internal movements of people in history—perhaps the greatest not caused by immediate threat of execution or starvation. In sheer numbers it outranks the migration of any other ethnic group—Italians or Irish or Jews or Poles—to this country.

THE TRANSFORMATION OF THE SUBURB

By the term *suburban* in this context we mean simply that part of the metropolitan area outside of the central city. It is not all suburban in appearance and character. It may include small cities and other places that have an urban look and feel, just as many of the outlying parts of central cities have a suburban look and feel.

In the early post–World War II period, city and suburb had a very intimate economic relationship that, over the decades, has weakened substantially. For a great many suburbanites the central city was still the place where they earned their living, went for entertainment and cultural purposes, made most of their big purchases, and where they went when they had to go to the hospital or get their teeth filled. The suburb was where they lived, raised their children, and bought their groceries. Now the picture of the "bedroom suburb" tied to a central city that is the economic engine of the metropolitan area is much less realistic than it once was. In fact, at present several times as

Times Square, New York, in the 1940s. Television and post-World War II suburbanization had not yet eroded the central city's position as a major center of entertainment.

Midtown Manhattan in the 1940s, looking east along 42nd St. The building at left with the Art Deco top is the Chrysler Building. In the background is the East River and beyond that the Long Island City section of the Borough of Queens.

many workers "cross commute"—that is, commute from one suburb to another suburb, as commute from the suburbs to the central city.

A Scenario of Suburban Economic Growth

The suburbanization of retailing, driven as noted earlier by the suburbanization of population and buying power, was also accelerated by another invention: the shopping center. The invention of the shopping center is generally credited to the architect and planner Victor Gruen, who designed Northland, outside of Detroit, in 1951 and numerous others afterwards.[7] The shopping center has gone through an evolution from being simply a number of stores in the same building that share a common parking area to a huge, climate-controlled megastructure, such as the Mall of America south of Minneapolis. Both the early versions and the more sophisticated modern version share some common features and effects. Because the shopping center requires a substantial block of land for stores and parking, it is much more easily built in suburban or exurban areas than in the city. To acquire a large enough piece of land in the city, the developer must deal with many property owners and generally must spend large sums of money on land acquisition and the demolition of old buildings. Very often, city land is so expensive that structured parking rather than at-grade parking is required, another major expense. Finally, one key to the success of a shopping center is quick and easy automobile access. Such access is generally more available in the suburbs than in the city. A few successful shopping centers have been built in dense urban areas, often with very substantial public subsidy and often as part of an urban renewal project (see Chapter 10). However, on balance, the invention and refinement of the shopping center has favored suburb over city. Not only has the suburban shopping center drawn the suburban customer away from downtown retailing, but it also draws automobile-owning city residents out to the suburbs to shop.

With the growth of suburban retailing we see a growth of wholesaling, for wholesalers necessarily follow their customers, the retailers, just as the retailers follow their customers. There is also growth in both business services and personal services as these activities, too, follow their customers out to the suburbs.

In a few years we begin to see the movement of corporate headquarters from city center to suburban locations. To a great extent this is simply a matter of corporations following their labor forces to the suburbs. Then, too, the members of the board of directors, the vice president in charge of corporate planning, and other people in the organization who have a say in the matter are likely to favor a suburban location, in part because they live there. The janitors and the file clerks, many of whom now live in older housing in the city, may not like the suburban location, in part because it will be hard to get from their city apartments to the new location. But their voice in the decision is limited. At first, the movement of corporate headquarters to the suburbs is slow because it is hard for the headquarters to leave the web of face-to-face contacts that only the city location can provide. They need to be near their bankers, their legal counsel, their consultants, and their advertising agencies. But as the suburban business community grows, more and more business services locate there. Then, too, with each improvement in communications the need for face-to-face contact weakens a bit. With closed circuit TV, people can meet without having to be in the same room. When designs for ads can be faxed, it is not quite so important for the corporate headquarters to be down the street from its advertising agency. When computer-to-computer data links are available, it is easier to coordinate all sorts of record-keeping activity from a distance. In due time, the entire business establishment that was in the central city is replicated in the suburbs. In fact, the suburban business establishment may be larger and more complete than the one that remains downtown.

The Effects of Highway Policy

During the Great Depression planners in the Federal Highway Administration began to envision a highway system that would link America's cities with a system of high speed, limited access roadways. The system would satisfy private and commercial demand for high speed intercity travel. The new highways would also be good for cities, thought the planners, because the new roads would extend the city's commercial reach into its hinterlands.[8] The planning effort stopped during World War II and then resumed afterwards. For a time the federal government hestitated to begin such a system because building it would add to the national debt. But in 1956 Congress decided that the system could be financed by "user charges," namely a federal tax on motor fuel that would go into the soon to be created Highway Trust Fund. This fund would finance the system without dragging the federal government further into debt.

The National Defense Highway Act of 1956 authorized the building of the interstate highway system. The name of the act stems from one of the selling points of the system, that it would permit rapid military mobilization should the nation ever again have to fight a "two ocean" war like World War

FIGURE 3–3 The Washington, D.C., Metropolitan Area and Beltway

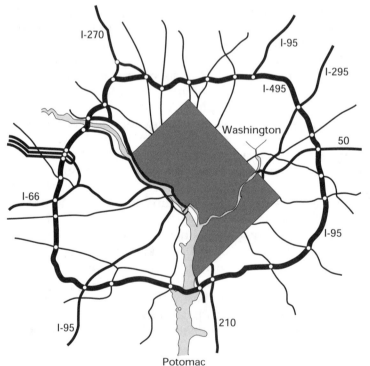

II. This argument may seem archaic now, but it was a serious selling point at the time. Construction of the system started shortly thereafter and was largely complete by the 1980s. The system totals over 40,000 miles of highway and if considered as a single project would be by far the largest construction project in U.S. history.

In the original design, the system was to go from city center to city center. As construction proceeded, that design feature had to be modified. The cost of acquiring city land for rights of way proved to be enormous.[9] In addition, city residents resisted having their neighborhoods sliced up by a block-wide swath of four or six lanes of highway. Citizen resistance proved to be intense and often successful. The solution was to bypass the city by building the now-familiar beltway.

Beltways were not intended to be deurbanizing or decentralizing. They were intended to solve the problem noted above. But their decentralizing effects soon became obvious. The beltway provides a ring of very accessible land outside the central city. It is a magnet for corporate headquarters, business services, shopping centers, and other activities that need easy automobile access. Points where radial highways coming out of the central city intersect the beltway are especially attractive locations.

The mass of jobs along the beltway is a great disperser of population, for those who work near the beltway can live that much farther from the city center. In the larger metropolitan areas, there develops in time a demand for a second beltway, perhaps another ten miles out. At this writing there is much discussion in the Washington, D.C., area about building a second beltway.

THE PHYSICAL FORM OF THE METROPOLITAN AREA

As cities grew in the twentieth century, scholars became interested in formulating models of urban growth. No two cities or metropolitan areas grow in the same way or exhibit exactly the same form, for each metropolitan area is different in history and topography. The form of every metropolitan area will be affected by the decisions of important players such as major landowners, major corporations, and local, state, and national government. The pattern of development in some places can also be affected by catastrophic events such as floods and fires. The question is whether some useful generalizations can be made.

In the 1920s Ernest W. Burgess and other scholars at the University of Chicago formulated what has come to be called the concentric zone model shown in panel A of Figure 3–4.[10] They saw the growth of the city or the metropolitan area as a natural and gradual process. They drew heavily on the idea of competition between groups of people, analogous to the competition between different species of animals and plants within a natural setting, and they used ecological terms such as *invasion* and *succession*.[11] Burgess and

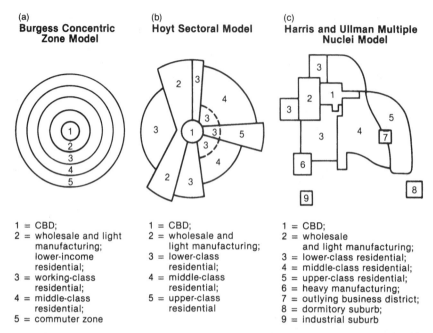

(a)
Burgess Concentric Zone Model

(b)
Hoyt Sectoral Model

(c)
Harris and Ullman Multiple Nuclei Model

1 = CBD;
2 = wholesale and light manufacturing; lower-income residential;
3 = working-class residential;
4 = middle-class residential;
5 = commuter zone

1 = CBD;
2 = wholesale and light manufacturing;
3 = lower-class residential;
4 = middle-class residential;
5 = upper-class residential

1 = CBD;
2 = wholesale and light manufacturing;
3 = lower-class residential;
4 = middle-class residential;
5 = upper-class residential;
6 = heavy manufacturing;
7 = outlying business district;
8 = dormitory suburb;
9 = industrial suburb

FIGURE 3–4 Three Models of Urban Form. Both the Burgess and the Hoyt models assume that growth originates from the center of the metropolitan area. They differ in that the Burgess model sees growth as proceeding in rings whereas the Hoyt model sees different types of activities proceeding peripherally in different sectors. The Harris and Ullman model, more attuned to widespread automobile usage, pictures growth as proceeding from multiple centers.

Source: Chauncy Harris and Edward L. Ullman, *"The Nature of Cities,"* Annals of the American Academy of Political and Social Science, vol. 242, no. 1, 1945, p. 13.) Reprinted by permission of Sage Publications.

others who took this view assumed that all migration into the city would arrive at the center and would spread out from there. They also assumed that economic growth would occur from the center. Note that these assumptions were never entirely true and have been shown to be even less true with the passage of time. As the city or metropolitan area grew, the activities in one ring would expand, forcing the activities in more peripheral rings to move outward, hence the terms *invasion* and *succession.* Burgess identified the second zone as the zone of transition. He believed that residential properties here would be especially prone to decay because of the encroachment of commercial and manufacturing uses. Not only would these nonresidential uses make life there less pleasant, but owners of properties would be less likely to invest further monies in their properties if they expected them soon to be torn down and replaced with nonresidential uses.

The Burgess model has been the object of much criticism on a variety of grounds. Some, like Firey, argued that the ecological model based upon the concept of natural selection was simply not a good description of human be-havior.[12] Another objection was that the scheme takes no account of the role of policy or investment decisions, such as where to locate a highway or a cor-poration's major facility. Finally, the model takes no account of topography. The regular form of the model suggests that it is more likely to be approxi-mated in a relatively flat plain than in an area of uneven topography where the pattern of development is channeled by ridges and valleys, bodies of water, and other barriers. It is perhaps no coincidence that the model was de-veloped in Chicago where the topography is flat.

In the 1930s the land economist Homer Hoyt developed an alternative to the Burgess concentric zone model. He suggested instead a sectoral model, as shown in panel B of Figure 3-4. In his model, based on a federally funded study of sixty-four metropolitan areas, growth radiated out in sectors from the central business district. He recognized both the same push factor from the center as did Burgess but also recognized pull factors from the periphery. He argued that industrial growth was likely to follow the sectoral pattern be-cause it would follow transportation corridors. Sectors of housing might lie close to the industrial sectors, giving workers quick access to their jobs. Rather than seeing the income of households increasing with distance from the center, as did Burgess, he saw income varying from sector to sector.

> The highest rent areas of the city tend to be located in one or more sectors of the city. There is a gradation of rentals downward from these high rental areas in all directions, intermediate rental areas . . . adjoin the high rent area on one or more sides. . . . Low rent areas occupy other entire sections of the city from the center to the periphery.[13]

In the early post-World War II period Chauncy Harris and Edward L. Ullman proposed the multiple nuclei model shown in panel C of Figure 3-4. It differs from both the Burgess and Hoyt models in that it shows develop-ment centered around more than one nucleus. Harris and Ullman did not offer a single explanatory mechanism, as did Burgess. Their model is, in that sense, more empirical and less theoretical than that of Burgess.

All three of the above models capture some piece of reality. If one were to look at a major metropolitan area from a great distance, so that the fine details were lost, one would see some resemblance to the Burgess model. Even though central business districts are of relatively less significance than at the time Burgess wrote, they still exist and in many cases still constitute the largest single mass of commercial activity in the metropolitan area. The Burgess model shows the poorer residents of the region living close to the center and the more affluent residents living farther out. In general, this is still true, as the data for the New York region in Table 3-4 show. Burgess's ob-servations about the zone of transition can easily be verified by observing the areas around downtown in many cities. The Hoyt sectoral model also captures part of the truth, for elements of it can be readily seen in many metropolitan areas. Harris and Ullman's multiple nuclei are present in every metropolitan area, and they provide much of the suburban area's shopping, business and personal services, and employment. We should note that all three models are products of their times. The Burgess and Hoyt models, coming from the periods between the two World Wars, were more adapted to a world in which rail transportation was relatively more important and automobile and truck transportation relatively less important than is the case today. Harris and Ullman, writing two decades after Burgess, had the advantage of seeing how the automobile and the truck were restructuring the pattern of settlement and could incorporate those observations into their model.

In recent years another form of metropolitan area development has become apparent and is beginning to claim the attention of scholars. This is the "edge city," a term invented by the journalist Joel Garreau.

An edge city, such as Tyson's Corner in Fairfax County, Virginia, is a new urban form. As the name implies, it develops at or near the edge of a metropolitan area, though as time passes the metropolitan area may continue to grow around and past the edge city. The edge city develops where there is very good highway access, often provided by one or more interstates. It has most of the economic ingredients of the traditional downtown but a very different physical form. Unlike the traditional downtown, which is intimately connected with the rest of the city through the street grid, the edge city is often more or less disconnected from surrounding residential areas. You can shop there, work there, and do business there. You might have your appendix removed there. But you probably won't live there, nor can you send your child to school there. In fact, you can't even stroll there unless you fancy walking along highway shoulders and through parking lots, for there is no system of sidewalks or even a continuous street pattern. Then, too, as shown in Figure 3–5, the edge city is huge compared to the traditional downtown. It is an absolutely automobile-dependent form of development.

According to Garreau there are more than 200 edge cities in America. This is how Garreau defines the edge city:[14]

1. Has five million square feet or more of leasable office space—the workplace of the information age [to convert that figure into jobs you could use a rule-of-thumb figure of about 200 square feet per worker]. . . .
2. Has 600,000 square feet of leasable retail space. That is the equivalent of a fair sized mall.
3. Has more jobs than bedrooms. When the workday starts, people head towards this place, not away from it. Like all urban places, the population increases at 9 AM.
4. Is perceived by the population as one place. It is a regional end destination for mixed use—not a starting point—that "has it all," from jobs to shopping to entertainment.
5. Was nothing like a "city" as recently as thirty years ago. Then it was just bedrooms, if not cow pastures. This incarnation is brand new.

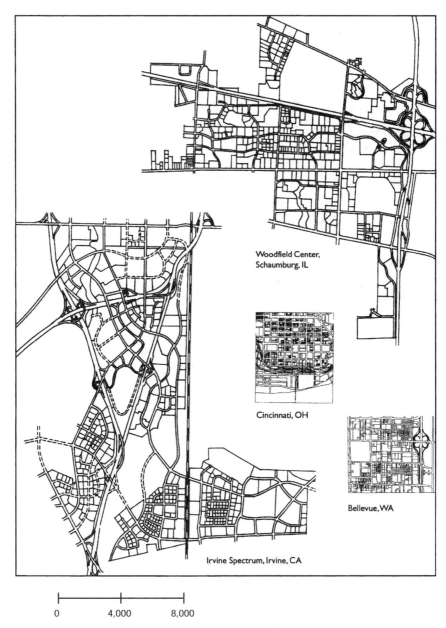

Woodfield Center,
Schaumburg, IL

Cincinnati, OH

Bellevue, WA

Irvine Spectrum, Irvine, CA

0	4,000	8,000

FIGURE 3–5 Edge City Compared with the Traditional Downtown. The maps, all at the same scale, show three edge cities and the downtown of Cincinnati, Ohio. The Bellevue, Washington, edge city is an older edge city that formed from a settled area. Its blocks are about twice the size of those of the Cincinnati downtown.

Source: Reprinted by permission of the *Journal of the American Planning Association,* 64, no. 3, Summer 1998.

Tyson's Corner, in Fairfax County, Virginia. Once on the edge of the DC metropolitan area this "edge city" is now surrounded by extensive suburban development from the growth of the metropolitan area. Though it contains most of the components of the traditional downtown it has a very different physical form and as a practical matter is accessible only by motor vehicle. It is a very "pedestrian unfriendly" design.

Unlike the traditional city, the edge city is usually not a political entity in its own right. Rather, it is a part of another political entity, typically a county. The formation of the edge city requires some basic conditions. As a totally automobile-oriented development, it requires good highway access. Because the typical edge city draws both workers and customers for its retail and service businesses from residential areas outside itself, it can develop only where the surrounding area contains a large supply of labor as well as a large supply of buying power. It also requires large blocks of land in undeveloped or sparsely developed condition. Some edge cities, such as Irvine Spectrum, shown in Figure 3–5, are planned in their entirety at one time. Others, like Woodfield Center in Schaumberg, Illinois, are not.[15] In either case their development requires massive investment. They could not come into being without the existence of large development corporations that have access to hundreds of millions in capital. Unlike the grid pattern of the traditional downtown, the edge city cannot be developed by the smaller builder who has just enough capital to build a single building on a single building lot. The edge city offers its builder(s) the advantages of developing an area where the land assembly problem is simplified because land on the urban fringe is typically owned in large pieces. It reduces or eliminates the need for the builder to absorb the residual value of existing structures (see Chapter 10). It offers economy of scale in development and construction. It also enables the developer to plan a mixture of uses that reinforce each other. For example, retailers may be attracted to the edge city because the large mass of employment constitutes thousands of potential customers. Developers of edge cities pay great attention to that sort of synergy. The edge city, like the private community discussed in Chapter 9, may offer its users greater security than does an urban location. It is, in a general sense, a way to withdraw from many urban problems.

The edge city is an emerging form. One might guess that given its scale (see Figure 3–5 again), it can never be as pedestrian oriented as the typical downtown. Beyond that likely supposition its final form is hard to predict.

THE CENTRAL CITY SINCE WORLD WAR II

Table 3–2 shows population trends from 1950 to 1990 for a number of cities. Most older cities, primarily in the Northeast and North Central regions, have lost substantial amounts of population. The one large, older, Eastern city on the list that has not experienced a major population decline is New York. The most important reason is that the city is a major point of entry for immigrants, typically receiving about one hundred thousand per year in the 1970s and 1980s. They have made up for the outmigration of native-born Americans. The exact path to population loss is somewhat different for each city, but there are some factors that apply to most of them. One is that a city's economic and demographic trends are linked to the region in which it is located, and most of the cities that show major losses are located in relatively slow-growing parts of the nation.

Another factor is population density. In 1950 most of the cities that have since showed big losses were quite densely populated. Chicago had over 15,000 people per square mile. A number of the others, including Detroit, Cleveland, St. Louis, and Pittsburgh, were in the range of 10,000 to 15,000 per square mile. Those population densities inhibited further growth in a number of ways. High population densities and the high employment densities (jobs per square mile) that go with them coexist very badly with the automobile. Traffic flow is congested and parking becomes a major problem. New development becomes very expensive because there are few large pieces of unbuilt land remaining. Thus the developer faces the costs of paying for structures and their demolition costs just to obtain land upon which to build, a point discussed at greater length in Chapter 10 in connection with urban renewal. The high density limits the amount of single-family housing that can be built. And as housing trends in the post–World War II period clearly demonstrated, that is the housing type that a large proportion of the population prefers.

TABLE 3-2 Population of Selected U.S. Cities

City	(× 1,000) Population in 1990	(× 1,000) Population in 1950	Percent change, 1950 to 1990
New York	7,323	7,892	−7.2
Los Angeles	3,485	1,970	76.9
Chicago	2,784	3,620	−23.1
Houston	1,631	596	173.7
Philadelphia	1,586	2,072	−23.5
San Diego	1,110	334	232.3
Detroit	1,028	1,850	−44.4
Dallas	1,007	434	132.0
Phoenix	983	107	818.7
San Antonio	936	63	1385.7
Baltimore	736	950	−22.5
Boston	574	801	−28.3
Cleveland	507	915	−44.6
St. Louis	397	857	−53.7
Pittsburgh	370	677	−45.3
Milwaukee	368	522	−29.5
Miami	359	249	44.2

Source: Population & Housing, CHH-2-1, Table 47, Bureau of the Census and *Statistical Abstract of the United States,* 1955, Table 14.

Most of those cities that have grown rapidly in the period since 1950 have been located in growing regions of the nation, primarily in the "Sunbelt." Regional growth, all other things being equal, expands the city's market area, which tends to expand employment and thus add to the population of the city. In addition, most growing Sunbelt cities still have low population densities. Dallas, after having grown very rapidly for several decades, still had a 1990 population density of under 3,000 per square mile. Phoenix in 1990, after a period of explosive growth, still had a population density under 2,500 people per square mile. Low-density cities are able to coexist well with the automobile, are much more amenable to the building of large amounts of single family housing, and have larger blocks of vacant land available for commercial development. On the list in Table 3-2 the only very large city that showed substantial growth and that had a 1990 population density approaching the numbers for the large older cities was Los Angeles, with about 7,400 people per square mile. This figure is still no more than half the all-time peak densities of many of the older cities, and it should be noted that despite massive freeway building the city's name has become almost synonymous with traffic congestion. A similar phenomenon appears to be occurring in Atlanta. By the late 1990s traffic congestion was causing many corporations to reconsider plans to locate in Atlanta, thus threatening to produce a substantial slowdown in growth.

In the case of a number of older cities part of the decline in population has been caused by a loss of manufacturing jobs, for as employment shrinks population tends to shrink with it. Pittsburgh (steel) and Detroit (automobiles) were major losers of population largely because they lost manufacturing jobs and were not able to replace them with large numbers of jobs in other sectors such as services and trade. Total manufacturing employment in the United States has not changed much in the last several decades, though as total employment has grown it has shrunk as a percentage of all employment. However, the location of manufacturing has changed a great deal. In the decades after World War II much manufacturing employment moved out of cities and into suburban and nonmetropolitan locations. For many products the most efficient plant was the one-story structure. The materials used to produce the product came in one end of the building and moved straight through it, coming out the other end as finished product. The multistory industrial building found in older cities became obsolete, and the land needed to build the new-style industrial building was generally not available in the city. It was available outside the city. The motor truck made nonurban industrial sites accessible for the shipment of goods, and the automobile made the sites accessible to the nonurban labor force. The relocation of manufacturing is discussed in more detail in Chapter 13.

The Suburbanization of Income

Not only have central cities, taken as a group, lost population relative to surrounding areas, but they have also become poorer than surrounding areas. Once we thought of poverty as a largely rural phenomenon.[16] Now we think of it as a largely urban phenomenon. Consider a central city and the ring of communities around it in the post–World War II period. Part of the growth of the suburban areas comes from the migration of central-city residents to the suburbs. In general, it is the prosperous central-city residents who can make the move, for it is they who have the incomes to buy newly constructed suburban housing. When the relatively prosperous central-city resident moves from a central-city apartment into a suburban house, that move raises the average income in the suburbs and lowers it in the city. Migration to the metropolitan area, either from elsewhere in the United States or from overseas, also tends to increase the income gap between central city and the rest of the metropolitan area. Poor people coming to the metropolitan area are likely to head for the central city for reasons noted earlier—a supply of older and cheaper housing, ability to live without a car, and better social services. Wealthier people moving to the metropolitan area for other reasons are more likely to settle outside of the central city. As a general rule personal income in metropolitan areas has increased more rapidly as one gets farther out from the center of the area.

Table 3–3 illustrates this general rule regarding income in the New York metropolitan area. As the largest metropolitan area in the United States, it cannot be entirely typical. However, for illustrative purposes it has the advantage that outside the core area there are three rings of counties. The last column of the table shows the increase in median family income from 1949 to 1989. Note that every county in the outer ring shows a higher rate of increase than any county in the middle ring. Similarly, every county in the middle ring shows a higher rate of increase than any county in the inner

TABLE 3–3 Median Family Income, Counties of the New York Region, 1949 and 1989 (Figures in 1989 dollars)

	1949	1989	1989/1949
Core			
Manhattan	16,010	36,831	2.3
Inner ring			
Bronx	18,818	25,459	1.35
Hudson	18,151	35,250	1.94
Kings (Brooklyn)	17,958	30,033	1.67
Queens	21,470	40,426	1.88
Middle Ring			
Bergen	22,283	57,648	2.58
Essex	19,636	42,150	2.15
Nassau	23,570	60,619	2.57
Passaic	19,146	43,073	2.25
Richmond (Staten Island)	20,032	50,664	2.53
Union	22,465	48,862	2.18
Westchester	22,679	58,862	2.60
Outer Ring			
Fairfield	19,089	57,990	3.04
Middlesex	19,407	51,835	2.67
Monmouth	17,318	53,590	3.09
Morris	19,579	62,749	3.20
Putnam	17,396	58,892	3.39
Rockland	18,516	60,479	3.27
Somerset	17,542	62,255	3.55
Suffolk	17,771	53,247	3.00
United States	16,187	34,213	2.11

Sources: Bureau of the Census, Census of the Population, various years. The original 1949 income figures were multiplied by 5.21 to adjust them for inflation across the 1949–89 period. See Table 745, Statistical Abstract of the United States, 1996.

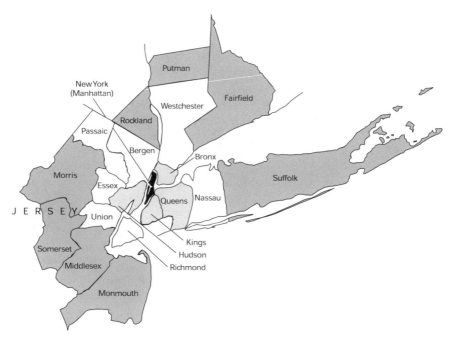

FIGURE 3–6 A map of the counties of the New York region listed in Table 3.3.

ring. Only the core county, Manhattan, appears to be a partial exception to the general pattern described.

Race and Residence

The racial composition of central cities vis-à-vis suburban areas has changed greatly in the last several decades, as shown in Table 3–4. The White population in central cities in 1990 was only slightly higher than it was in 1960, despite the fact that the number of places counted as central cities has increased substantially since then. For the same set of central cities represented by the 1960 data the White population has declined considerably. By contrast, the Black central city population almost doubled from 1960 to 1990. In the suburban ring the White population accounts for almost 90 percent of the total growth in that same time period. It is true that in percentage terms, the Black suburban population is growing faster than the White suburban population, an indication of a growing Black middle class that can afford suburban housing. But note that this high percentage rate is calculated from a very small base in 1960.

The large Black migration to the central cities in the earlier post–World War II decades resulted largely from the mechanization of agriculture discussed before. American Blacks went from being a largely rural and

TABLE 3-4 Race and Residence in Metropolitan Areas, 1960-90 (in millions)

	1960	1990
SMSA population	119.6	192.7
White	105.8	150.9
Black	12.7	25.1
Central-city population	59.9	77.8
White	49.4	51.5
Black	9.9	17.2
Suburban ring	59.6	114.9
White	56.4	99.4
Black	2.9	8.0

Source: U.S. Bureau of the Census, General Characteristics of the Population, 1969 and 1990.

small-town population to a largely urban population in a remarkably short period of time. The net out-migration of White population from central cities can be explained partly in economic terms. A great many people have preferred suburban residence to city residence. For several decades median family incomes of Whites and Blacks have been roughly in the ratio of 10 to 6. That has given Whites a huge financial edge in the competition for suburban housing.

Though the economic factor is important, there are many other explanations for White movement out. One, no doubt, is the choice on the part of some Whites not to live close to Blacks—the "white flight" and "tipping point" phenomena discussed in Chapter 10. Fear of crime, problems in city schools, and simple prejudice have been some of the factors behind these phenomena. Though discrimination in the sale and rental of housing is now banned by federal and state law, it still exists and has acted as a barrier to Black suburbanization. This matter, too, is discussed further in Chapter 10.

REGIONAL TRENDS

Cities exist in a context of regions, and so a few words about regional population change are necessary. Table 3-5 shows regional population changes in the United States since 1960. Growth has been slower in the Northeast and North Central regions of the nation and quite rapid in the North and West. Note that although Southern and Western growth are shown as separate items, a great deal of what is listed as Western growth—Texas, Arizona, Nevada, New Mexico, and southern California—is also Southern growth, at least in a climatological sense.

TABLE 3–5 Population Change by Region, 1960–1995 (figures × 1,000,000)

			Percent change	
	1960	1995	1960–1990	1980–1990
United States	179.3	248.7	38.7	9.8
Northeast	44.7	50.1	12.1	3.7
New England	10.5	13.2	25.7	4.2
Mid-Atlantic	34.2	37.8	10.5	2.7
Midwest	51.6	60.2	16.7	2.3
East North Central	36.2	42.4	17.1	1.8
West North Central	15.4	17.8	15.6	3.6
South	55.0	86.9	58.0	15.4
South Atlantic	26.0	44.4	70.8	20.2
East South Central	12.1	15.3	26.4	4.7
West South Central	17.0	27.1	59.4	14.3
West	28.1	54.0	92.1	25.2
Mountain	6.9	14.0	102.9	23.5
Pacific	21.2	40.0	88.6	25.9

Source: Statistical Abstract of the United States, various tables, chapter on population.

Note: The regions are defined as follows: New England: Maine, New Hampshire, Vermont, Massachusetts, Rhode Island, and Connecticut. Mid-Atlantic: New York, New Jersey, and Pennsylvania. East North Central: Ohio, Indiana, Illinois, Michigan, and Wisconsin. West North Central: Minnesota, Idaho, Missouri, North Dakota, South Dakota, Nebraska, and Kansas. South Atlantic: Delaware, Maryland, District of Columbia, Virginia, West Virginia, North Carolina, South Carolina, Georgia, and Florida. East South Central: Kentucky, Tennessee, Alabama, and Mississippi. West South Central: Arkansas, Louisiana, Oklahoma, and Texas. Mountain: Montana, Idaho, Wyoming, Colorado, New Mexico, Arizona, Utah, and Nevada. Pacific: Washington, Oregon, California, Alaska, and Hawaii.

Table 3–6 shows net migration for the four main regions for one year, March 1993 to March 1994. The pattern of migration from region to region varies from one year to another, based in large measure on U.S. economic trends and also on events abroad. With those caveats, the year shown is reasonably typical.

TABLE 3–6 Net Migration by Region, 1993–94

Region	Net Migration	Net Internal Migration
Northeast	–61,000	–328,000
Midwest	101,000	–31,000
South	827,000	376,000
West	379,000	–17,000

Source: Statistical Abstract of the United States, 1996 (116th edition), Table 32.

As Table 3–6 shows, all but the Northeast shows some net in-migration when immigration is taken into account. Note, however, that when we consider only internal migration the picture changes substantially. The South receives a major influx of migrants, and the Northeast experiences a major net out-migration.

The main reasons for the movement of population to the "Sunbelt" are generally well understood, but knowing how much weight to assign to each reason is a very difficult matter. Some of the main reasons follow.

Historical diffusion. Until well into the post–World War II period the major share of immigration to the United States was into the North and Mid-Atlantic seaboard regions. Thus part of the southward and westward movement of population is simply a natural diffusion process. If, say, the main initial point of settlement had been around the mouth of the Mississippi River, we might now see population diffusing northward and eastward.

Climatic and environmental preferences. The long-term increase in real income (money income adjusted for inflation) has reduced the importance of purely economic motivations and permitted people much more choice about where they will live. A large percentage of the population clearly favors warmer climates. This preference has been reinforced, particularly in the deep south, by the development of airconditioning for homes, vehicles and places of business and entertainment. One has only to visit areas like south Florida in the summer to realize how important a factor this has been. Selected areas of the nation have experienced rapid growth because of particular natural features that make them especially attractive. Parts of Colorado that offer mountain scenery, fine ski slopes, and the like are an example.

Mailbox income. This is really a subcategory of the above reason. An increasing share, currently about one fourth, of all personal income in the United States is portable or "mailbox" income in the form of Social Security, pensions, annuities, dividends on stocks and bonds, rental income of various types, and the like. Much Sunbelt growth has been driven by mailbox income. The retiree who moves from New Jersey to Florida or Arizona or New Mexico brings that mailbox income along, and when he or she spends it locally it builds the local economy. The growing economy, in turn, draws in a working-age population to fill the new jobs.

Improved communications. Better communications both for business purposes and also personal use and entertainment have made the South and West less remote than they once were. Whether it is communication links that made it easier for a Northern firm to open a branch in the South or a satellite dish antenna connected to a TV set, modern electronics has made formerly remote locations much more viable for both business and residential purposes.

The interstate highway system. By linking all the regions of the nation the system made it easier for many businesses, particularly light manufacturing, to move out of the Northeast and North Central regions in search of lower wages, lower taxes, and lower property and construction costs.

A decline in the relative importance of heavy industry. For several decades heavy industry, which generally needs rail transport, has been declining as a percentage of total employment and as a percentage of gross national product. Much of that industry was and still is concentrated in what the urban economist Wilbur Thompson referred to as the "American Ruhr," a belt of states stretching across the Northeast and North Central United States from New York and New Jersey out to Wisconsin. As heavy industry shrank in relative importance, the growth of cities and regions in which it played a major role tended to slow.

The end of "Southern exceptionalism." This is both a cause and a consequence of Southern growth. The phrase refers to a constellation of ways, both political and social, in which the South was different from the rest of the United States. Those differences went back, in large measure, to what before the Civil War was referred to euphemistically as the South's "peculiar institution," namely slavery. Forty or fifty years ago a Northerner could look at the South and see poll taxes, legal segregation, a landscape peppered with "whites only" and "colored only" signs, and feel that the South was really a retrograde and different part of the nation. But today the edifice of Jim Crow is gone from the South and race relations there are no worse, and perhaps somewhat better, than in many other parts of the nation. The Northerner who considers going to the South to attend a university, or teach at one, or take a job, or start a business no longer has to wonder if he or she is perhaps moving to a backward region. There has been a great cultural catch-up in the space of several decades. And for many, that has made the South a more attractive place to live than it once was. One indicator of the end of Southern exceptionalism is that the net migration of Black Americans out of the South has ended and the South now receives net in-migration of Blacks just as it does of Whites. In fact, in the early 1990s, for every Black person who left the South to settle in the Northeast there were about five Black people who left the Northeast to settle in the South.

Business and political climate. Business growth and population growth drive each other. In the last several decades the South has enjoyed some business advantages. Southern wages were generally lower than Northern wages, though as Southern growth has progressed, that gap has narrowed considerably. For reasons of both climate and wages, construction costs are often lower in the South than elsewhere. Relative to many parts of the Northeast and North Central regions, the South has been a low-tax area. The generally more conservative political temper of the South tends to make it rather pro-business, which is often an advantage in competition for firms. Labor unions, in general, are weaker in the South than in the nation as a whole. Many Southern states have "right to work" laws. These forbid making union membership a condition of employment even if the firm is willing to agree to such an arrangement with its union. All of these factors have aided Southern states in the economic competition with Northeastern and North Central states.

One other trend in location deserves a brief note. For several decades an increasing percentage of the U.S. population has lived within 50 miles of a coast—Atlantic, Pacific, or Gulf. One explanation for this shift is simply the loss of population in inland areas because of a decline in agricultural employment. Part is, no doubt, an effect of immigration, particularly in California. Part also is probably amenity based. Coastal climates tend to be more moderate, and many people like to live near water.

SUMMARY

Late in the nineteenth century a process of diffusion began to convert the compact "walking city" into the twentieth century metropolitan area. This process continues to the present time. One major factor was technological change, which gave us better transportation and communication as well as a higher real income and a shorter work week. Public policy also played a role, particularly the federal government's role in housing finance beginning in the 1930s and the post–World War II investment in highways, especially the interstate highway system.

In the post–World War II period the technological forces behind metropolitan area growth were aided by demographic forces as well. These included the "baby boom," the rural-to-urban migration caused by the rapid mechanization of agriculture in the 1950s and 1960s, and the resumption of high rates of immigration after the lull of the Great Depression and war years.

The chapter notes the economic growth of the suburbs and the transformation of many suburbs from "bedroom" communities into suburbs that are in themselves major employment centers. The chapter also notes the growth of suburban subcenters and, more recently, the "edge city" phenomenon.

Metropolitan growth or shrinkage occurs within a regional framework. In connection with the growth of the Sunbelt we note a variety of economic forces, including many of the same ones responsible for the decentralization of metropolitan areas, such as improvements in transportation, communication, and real income. We also note the effect of "mailbox" income in an increasingly prosperous nation.

NOTES

1. The telegraph appeared about four decades before the telephone. It probably facilitated the growth of the modern corporation by permitting quick communication between headquarters and branch operations. It was also essential to the development of a coordinated national rail system. Whether it had any decentralizing effect upon metropolitan areas is not certain.

2. The development of the parkway system in the New York region was to a considerable extent the result of the actions of a single remarkably forceful and politically adept individual, Robert Moses. For a detailed account, see Robert M. Caro, *The Power Broker: Robert Moses and the Fall of New York* (New York: Alfred A. Knopf, 1974).

3. Opinions on why this is so vary. Some argue that the military expenditures necessitated by the cold war provided a macroeconomic stimulus—a sort of giant public works program—that kept aggregate demand sufficiently strong. The economists might argue that greater economic understanding and better management of interest rates and the money supply are a big part of the explanation.

4. It has been asserted that the high rate of childbearing might have been a reaction to the death and destruction of the war. But in Western Europe, where the population experienced much more death and destruction than did the U.S. population, the rise in postwar births was much smaller. Perhaps the baby boom was, in part, a response to the glow of postwar prosperity and a sense of expanded opportunity both for one's self and one's children. But note that such an explanation seems to contradict the proposition advanced when we discussed the demographic transition, namely that in a society-wide sense prosperity seems to be an effective contraceptive. It has been noted that women's labor force participation rates were much lower in the immediate postwar years than later on. Thus the opportunity costs (loss of wages because of having to stay home with children) of children were lower. But one can argue about whether that really explains much or whether it is just the opposite side of the high birth rate coin. Births rose back up to about 4 million in the early 1990s, in large measure a result of the large number of women of childbearing age, the so called "echo" of the baby boom. But the 1957 figure has never been equaled since, despite the fact that the nations' population is now much larger.

5. The term means a farmer who rents the land he cultivates and pays the rent by giving part of his crop to the property owner; hence the term *share*cropper.

6. Nicholas Lemann, *The Promised Land: The Great Black Migration and How It Changed America* (New York: Alfred A. Knopf, 1991), pp. 5–6.

7. The reader interested in the history of the shopping center might see Victor Gruen, *Shopping Towns USA: the Planning of Shopping*, Reinhold Publishing Corp., New York, 1960.

8. A history of the planning and building of the interstate highway system, from an official perspective, can be found in *America's Highways, 1776 to 1976: A History of the Federal Aid Program* (Washington, D.C.: U.S. Department of Transportation, Federal Highway Administration, undated). For an account of the politics of building the interstate highway system, see Mark H. Rose, *Interstate Express Highway Politics*, revised edition (Knoxville: University of Tennessee Press, 1990).

9. Government has the power to take private property for public purposes. But it must pay for it, for the 5th Amendment of the Constitution states ". . . nor shall private property be taken for public use, without just compensation." If agreement between property owner and government cannot be reached by negotiation, then there is a "condemnation" proceeding in court and government must pay the fair market value of the property as established by the court. Government's power to take is generally referred to as the power of "eminent domain." All governments in the United States as well as some quasi governments such as school districts have the power of eminent domain.

10. Ernest W. Burgess, "Growth of the City," in Robert W. Park, Ernest W. Burgess, and Roderick D. McKenzie, *The City*, (University of Chicago Press, 1925), pp. 47–62.

11. Their work was heavily influenced by that of Charles Darwin, whose book, *Origin of Species*, was one of great intellectual events of the second half of the nineteenth century.

12. Walter Firey, "Sentiment and Symbolism as Ecological Variables," *American Sociological Review* 10, no. 2 (1945), pp. 140–48.

13. Homer Hoyt, "The Structure and Growth of Residential Neighborhoods in American Cities" (Federal Housing Administration, 1939), p. 76.

14. Joel Garreau, *Edge City: Life on the New Frontier* (New York: Doubleday, 1991), p. 6.
15. Brenda Case Scheer and Mintcho Perkov, "Edge City Morphology: A Comparison of Commercial Centers," *Journal of the American Planning Association,* 64, no. 3, (summer 1998), pp. 298–310.
16. Many of the New Deal programs were directed specifically at rural America. Among these were rural electrification under the Rural Electrification Administration (REA), The Tennessee Valley Authority (TVA), and the agricultural price support programs. For an account of New Deal programs, see William E. Leuchtenburg, *Franklin Delano Roosevelt and the New Deal* (New York: Harper & Row, 1963).

REFERENCES

Downs, Anthony. *New Visions for Urban America.* The Brookings Institution, 1994.

Garreau, Joel. *Edge City: Life on the New Frontier.* New York: Doubleday, 1991.

Gorham, William. and Nathan Glazer, eds. *The Urban Predicament.* The Urban Institute, 1970.

Lemann, Nicholas. *The Promised Land: The Great Black Migration and How It Changed America.* New York: Alfred A. Knopf, 1991.

Chapter

4 | City Government: Part 1

This chapter begins with a brief summary of the history of city government in the United States. We then turn to discussion of city government at the present time. In the following chapter we examine some alternative views of city government and some policy questions. Though we present the history of city government in terms of eras, the reader should be aware that these are only the roughest of generalizations. Eras overlap, and some survivals of the earliest eras are with us today. Then, too, city government and its history vary from one part of the nation to another. In this chapter we use the term *city* or *city government* generically to refer also to town, county, and other substate units of government.

THE MERCHANT CITY OF THE EARLY NINETEENTH CENTURY

This section refers to the period before the Industrial Revolution was well underway in the United States and before the coming of transatlantic steam service (about 1840) made possible the huge waves of immigration that characterized the latter part of the nineteenth century. Even the largest cities were small by modern standards. In this preindustrial era their economies were devoted much more to trade, either overseas or with their own hinterlands, than to the production of goods. The range of municipal services that cities provided to their residents was small. Property requirements for voting were widespread, and women's suffrage was still decades in the future. The electorate consisted largely of White males who owned at least some property.

In a era of rapid physical and commercial expansion it is not surprising that the focus of many city governments was the promotion of growth and

55

economic competition with other cities.[1] The fact that suffrage was generally limited to those who owned some property contributed to this emphasis. City governments often used their power to issue bonds to finance railroads and canals, for low-cost transportation was often the key to commercial success. Municipal borrowing was not regulated as it is today (see Chapter 6), and so fraud, malfeasance, and unwise investment were common in this age of "urban mercantilism."[2] Unlike the modern city, the city of this era was very much on its own. The present apparatus, discussed later in this book, of financial aid from state and federal government did not exist. Nor did there exist the mass of regulations and mandates from higher levels of government that now forms much of the context in which municipal governments function.

The most common form of city government was a type later designated as the "weak mayor" form. In this system the mayor was *primus inter pares* (first among equals). He had few powers that the other city council members did not. He presided over meetings and had some symbolic and administrative duties. But his vote counted no more than that of other council members. He could not veto legislation, nor set the council's agenda, nor hire or fire employees. It was a weak system for an age in which not very much was expected of municipal government. As cities grew larger and the demands made upon city governments grew greater, the weak-mayor form generally proved inadequate and was supplanted by other forms.

THE AGE OF MACHINE POLITICS

About the middle of the nineteenth century a new form of political organization, the "political machine," began to appear in American cities, and the nation entered into the age of machine politics. The "machine politics" to be described was more characteristic of the Northeast and North Central United States than it was of the South and the West for reasons discussed subsequently. Machine politics probably peaked about the turn of the century but in some cities persisted deep into the twentieth century. The last-full blown example of the political machine in the United States is often considered to be the administration of Richard Daley in Chicago from 1955 to 1976.

The central element in machine politics was the political party and its organization. The party sustained itself by a combination of loyalty, graft, favors, and coercion. How did the machine work? The following describes the Chicago of Mayor Daley, but the basic outlines would fit turn-of-the-century New York or Boston or many other large cities just as well.[3] Chicago was divided into 50 wards, each of which elected an alderman to the city council. Each ward, in turn, was divided into a number of precincts. Within the party there was for each ward a ward boss and a number of precinct workers (a derisive term of the times was "ward heelers"). Their role was to get out the

vote and so maintain the machine in power. In the system of sticks and carrots the biggest carrot was patronage. City government had jobs to give out,
and the number one and absolutely necessary qualification for a city job was
party loyalty. That patronage produced an army of loyal ward and precinct
workers. This is how Mike Royko, a Chicago reporter and columnist and one
of the great chroniclers of day-to-day urban life in America, described the system in Chicago of the 1950s.

> The Hawk got his nickname because in his younger days he was the outside
> lookout man at a bookie joint. Then his eyes got weak, and he had to wear thick
> glasses, so he entered politics as a precinct worker. He was a hustling precinct
> worker so he was rewarded with a patronage job. . . . The Hawk keeps his job by
> getting out the Democratic vote in his precinct, paying monthly dues to the
> ward's coffers, buying and pushing tickets to his ward boss' golf outing and $25-
> a-plate dinners. His reward is a job that isn't difficult, hours that aren't demand-
> ing, and as long as he brings out the vote and the party keeps winning elections,
> he will remain employed.[4]

Patronage jobs spanned a range from low to high. The better ones went
to those who best delivered the vote. But whether the job was a little one or a
big one, the first requirement of the job holder was party loyalty.

> A ward boss who was given a job paying $28,000 a year [equivalent to about
> $150 or $200 thousand in today's dollars] as head of the city's huge sewer sys-
> tem was asked what his experience was. "About twenty years ago I was a house
> drain inspector." "Did you ever work in the sewers?" "No, but many a time I
> lifted a lid to see if they were flowing." "Do you have an engineering back-
> ground?" "Sort of. I took some independent courses at a school I forgot the
> name of, and in 1932 I was a plumber's helper." His background was adequate:
> his ward usually carries by fifteen thousand to three thousand votes.[5]

Royko notes that the law was a powerful instrument of patronage.
About a third of the ward bosses were lawyers, and many judges were former
ward bosses who had gotten their judgeships partly as a reward for years of
loyal and effective service in the wards. Being connected to the machine was
a real business asset for such a boss. Assume, for example, that you were involved in a lawsuit in the Chicago of Mayor Daley. Wouldn't you feel a bit
more secure with your case in the hands of lawyer who was well connected?
As Royko puts it, "This doesn't necessarily mean that cases are always rigged,
but one cannot underestimate the power of sentimentality."[6]

Along with the carrots of patronage there were some sticks too. If you
owned a bar and grill you might want to display some party loyalty, or at
least not display any disloyalty, lest city inspectors become extraordinarily
scrupulous when checking your kitchen facilities or looking to see if there
were any violations that might imperil your liquor license.

Among the poor the precinct worker might have a threatening aspect.
Again, to quote Royko,

Don't vote and you might lose your public housing apartment. Don't vote and you might be cut off welfare. Don't vote and you might have building inspectors poking around the apartment.[7]

In Chicago in the Daley period there were, despite civil service reforms discussed in the next section, about 25,000 patronage jobs at the command of the Daley machine. And, of course, those 25,000 workers had wives, husbands, children, parents, and other relatives. That was a formidable block of voters, even in a city with a population of several million. More important, it was a formidable army of party loyalists and precinct workers.

Another source of machine strength was the city budget. The city had money to spend on paving contracts, insurance, construction, and the like. Firms vied for that money, and one way they did so was by supporting the machine with contributions. They also supported the machine by making a certain number of jobs on their payrolls available to loyalists designated by the party—thereby extending the web of patronage jobs beyond those on the city payroll itself.

Though political machines did place some unqualified people in jobs, in some cases created "no show" jobs to reward loyalists, did not always buy goods and services from the most competent supplier or for the lowest cost, and generally used a certain amount of the public treasury for other than legitimate public purposes, there were positive things to be said about them. Many political machines were effective at getting things done, for getting things done takes power. And power was one thing the political machine had. When a group of experts, including a number of political science professors and many journalists who had covered Chicago politics, were ask to rank Chicago's mayors from Edward Kelley in 1933 to Harold Washington in the late 1980s, Richard Daley came in first by a large margin.[8] The voters of the city of Chicago thought well of Mayor Daley too. At this writing the mayor of Chicago is Richard Daley, Jr. He governs in a much more modern and very different style than did his father. But there is no doubt that the family name has been a big political asset.

Having pictured the typical workings of a big-city machine using a twentieth century example, let us return to the nineteenth century and the origins of the machine. On this matter there is some dispute among scholars. One line of argument is that as cities became larger and began to face increasing responsibilities, such as the need to construct and maintain such major public works as water supply systems, the machine evolved to meet that need.[9] It could mobilize power and make decisions in a way that the weak-mayor form could not. The system of election by ward favored the development of the machine because it favored the development of the patronage system. The ward boss and precinct workers were the patrons. They delivered jobs to the working class, contracts to entrepreneurs, Thanksgiving and Christmas turkeys to the poor, and intervention with the police and the courts for people who got into trouble. And they got loyalty and contributions in return.

There is a large ethnic side to the development of nineteenth-century political machines. America at mid ninteenth century was an overwhelmingly Protestant nation. But in the second half of the century much of the immigration it received was not Protestant. Rather, a great many of the immigrants it received then were Catholic, whether from Ireland, Italy, or Eastern Europe. In the late nineteenth century a substantial number were Jewish, coming primarily from Czarist Russia (which then included much of the present-day Eastern Europe). Non-Protestant immigrants often felt uncomfortable with the WASP establishment and often were on the receiving end of a great deal of prejudice. The Irish, for example, encountered enormous prejudice when they began to arrive in the mid nineteenth century. Want ads that included the phrase "No Irish need apply" were common and perfectly legal. The ethnically oriented machine—an Irish ward boss for an Irish ward, a Polish ward boss for a Polish ward, and so on—furnished an immigrant population with a powerful political counterweight to dominance of the WASP. The patronage system with its precinct worker intermediaries was well adapted to an immigrant population, much of which was not yet literate in English and not fully oriented to or comfortable in its new home.

While the above is the more common view, it is not universal.[10] DiGaetano argues that the machine did not come into being to solve problems so much as it came into being after municipal governments had grown substantially and therefore after there were some major assets to be taken over. His argument is a statistical one. He shows that for a sample of cities machine politics did not become institutionalized until the city had already begun to provide a number of major urban services such as police protection, water supply, sewage disposal, and so on. Each of the preceding arguments probably captures a piece of the truth.

It is argued that the big-city political machine and its ethnic politics performed a very useful function by giving many immigrants a foot up on the economic ladder, primarily through patronage jobs. For example, in New York City and Boston the Irish more than any other ethnic group dominated machine politics, and for many decades thereafter the police and fire departments were dominated by the Irish. The Irish were also prominent throughout the city's workforce. For example, Irish teachers and administrators constituted a very large presence in the cities' public school systems. However, it has also been suggested that while that sort of patronage-driven employment helps some individuals it may also blunt a group's entrepreneurial drive or reduce its push toward higher education; and therefore, on balance, it may not always be a positive force.[11]

The political machine was a predominantly American phenomenon, and a number of political scientists have theorized about why it occurred in America and not in Europe, the place to which the overwhelming majority of nineteenth-century American city dwellers traced their ancestry. One argument is that political regimes in a number of European nations in the nineteenth-century were much more repressive than in the United States. As a result European political parties tended to organize along class lines rather than ethnic lines.

> The American political order in the late nineteenth and early twentieth centuries, in turn, can be characterized as both less exclusionary and less repressive [than many European regimes]. American statemaking eliminated property requirements [for voting] in the preindustrial era, so the urban industrial working classes encountered no official obstruction to political integration. The American regime, in addition, did not ban or uniformly impede working class organization. This less exclusionary, less repressive context for working class formation fostered Democratic and Republican cross-class party coalitions rather than ideologically based, single class ones.[12]

Another argument is that in the U.S. federal system city governments had much responsibility and power. That is likely to make city politics a livelier, higher-stakes game than in a nation where political power is more centralized. It is also more likely to cause political factions to organize on geographic rather than class lines.

THE REFORM MOVEMENT IN AMERICAN CITY GOVERNMENT

In the late nineteenth century a powerful reform movement arose, determined to change the way in which American cities were governed. The cronyism, patronage, and corruption associated with big-city political machines fueled this movement. Not only was the seamy side of machine politics evident to many in their daily lives, but "muckraking" journalists like Jacob Riis and Lincoln Steffans and the political cartoonist Thomas Nast did all they could to publicize it. The reformers believed that city administration could be made into a much more scientific and rational process. Reformers were fond of noting that there are not separate Republican and Democratic ways of paving the streets—a statement that is absolutely true but, as we shall see, is far from the whole truth of the matter. Ethnic, religious, and class prejudice is also thought by many scholars to have played a part in the Reform movement. Much of the support for reform came from the WASP middle and upper classes, and the political regimes that they sought to reform were often dominated by Catholics of working-class origins from Ireland or from Southern and Eastern Europe. The fact that the movement was driven partly by idealism and partly by prejudice should not surprise us. Most of us are mixtures of more and less admirable qualities. There is no reason why feelings of genuine idealism can not exist in the same head that also harbors some ugly prejudices.

The reformers had an extensive agenda for city government. Below are some of its main elements.

The council-manager form of city government. In this scheme, now in very wide use in the United States, the city council would hire a nonpolitical, professional city manager as the city's chief executive. He (at this time in American history *he* was more accurate than *he or she*) would serve in a nonpolitical way so long as the council chose to periodically renew his contract. City management was to a be a profession for which there were formal qualifications. Cities were not to be run by former saloonkeepers whose main qualifications for office were years spent as precinct workers and ward bosses.

At-large election of city council members. The patronage system of the political machine was built on the ward system, with ward bosses and precinct workers bringing out the vote for the party's nominee for councilman of that ward. Reformers favored a system in which each candidate for city council ran at large, meaning that the candidate was elected by the voters of the entire city. Not only would this attack the roots of the patronage system, but, reformers argued, it would improve the quality of municipal government by causing city council members to place relatively more weight on the interests of the city as whole and less on the interests of particular neighborhoods.

The nonpartisan ballot. The heart of the machine was the political party. Reformers favored a ballot that contained only names and no party identification.

The short ballot. Reformers argued that it was unreasonable to expect citizens to cast informed votes for a mass of officials. Rather, they favored selecting only a few officials through the ballot. Other officials, such as judges and department heads, would be selected by the elected officials of the city. For example, in the case of judges it was easy to argue that most citizens do not know enough about the law to make a well-informed choice. Better to let the city council choose, perhaps from a list supplied by or at least approved by the city or state bar association.

The civil service system. Patronage—the giving of public jobs on the basis of party loyalty and favors done—was the lifeblood of machine politics. Reformers wanted to replace the patronage system with civil service. Under this system the overwhelming mass of municipal jobs would be filled by people who passed exams, had clearly defined educational or experiental qualifications, and whose names appeared on a list ordered by their examination grades. Not only would this strike at the roots of the patronage system, but it would produce a more competent and professional cadre of public employees.

The Reform movement reshaped city government. Thousands of cities, towns, and counties now use the council-manager form of government. There is now a city manager profession. There is no one academic path to that profession, but if one were considering a career in city management one might think first of getting a master's degree in public administration (M.P.A.). Cities and towns routinely hire managers who are not local people, who have no local connections, but who make a career of city management.

The civil service system is ubiquitous in American cities, and in most if not all cities the great majority of people on the city payroll are civil service employees. Patronage is not entirely gone from urban government, but it is a shadow of its former self. The short ballot and the nonpartisan ballot are not universal, but they are very commonplace. The at-large electoral system is not universal, but it is widespread.

Though the council-manager system—the favored system of the reformers—is widespread, it is not universal. The biggest cities in the United States, such as New York, Chicago, Philadelphia, Los Angeles, and Detroit, do not use it. Why is this?

We might come back to the statement that there is no Republican or Democratic way to repair a street. Republicans and Democrats do not disagree about how to spread asphalt, but they can disagree about which streets to pave. They can disagree about spending to pave the streets versus spending for social services. They can disagree about what sort of tax system should be used to pay for street paving. They can disagree about whether or not there should be minority set-asides in the awarding of paving contracts. Given a diversity of interests and of political and social philosophies, one cannot reduce political decision making to a purely engineering exercise. One cannot make governance nonpolitical. One may bring great objectivity to deciding how to do a clearly specified task. But when one comes down to the larger issues of what shall be done for whom and who shall pay for it, one is inevitably back in the political realm. The council-manager form is likely to be easiest to institute in a city where there is not a great deal of disagreement about political questions. That need for consensus is probably the biggest reason why the council-manager form is not to be found in the largest cities.

There are also some regional considerations to be noted regarding type of city government. In the eastern United States many cities reached the size at which the weak-mayor form discussed earlier became inadequate during the late nineteenth century. Thus their governments, in effect, came of age during the heyday of machine politics. It is only natural that many of them retain the strong-mayor form. In the southeastern United States the council-manager form may be somewhat more common because a kind of pseudo-agreement on many political issues was reached. In the era before the Civil Rights revolution, a period of some decades prior to the 1960s, the Black populations of southern cities had little political voice. Most southern Blacks were, one way or another, blocked from voting. In fact, many poorer Whites were also disenfranchised in a *de facto* sense by the existence of the poll tax, for the few dollars required to vote was a serious barrier. If the political regime in power represented primarily a White elite, there might not be much effective disagreement on basic issues. In that case, the city-manager form was more feasible than in the Northeast or North Central regions of the nation. Of course, suppression of the voice of some segments of the population is an ironic path to the governmental form favored by reformers.

In western states the council-manager form is more common than in the East, but for a very different reason. Many western cities did not reach the scale at which they needed a more effective city government until late in the nineteenth or early in the twentieth century. Thus their coming of age coincided with coming of the Reform movement, and they were therefore more likely to chose the form favored by that movement.

Though one cannot assign a precise year, the Reform movement in the United States probably reached its peak in the early post–World War II period, perhaps sometime in the 1950s. One of the hallmarks of Reform administration was a relative agreement on goals and a strong focus on the pragmatic and the technical. In the 1960s American urban politics became more contentious and a little less like the rational vision of the turn-of-the-century reformers.[13]

THE POST-REFORM ERA

In the 1960s new voices began to be heard and new programs appeared. One force for change was the Civil Rights revolution of the 1960s. America's Black population became much more politically active and began to vote in much larger numbers. The urban Black population grew rapidly as a result of the rural-to-urban migration set in motion by the post–World War II mechanization of agriculture. Just as immigration from Europe in the late nineteenth century reshaped urban politics then, so too did this new activism and great internal migration reshape urban politics in the 1960s. To these underlying forces were added some changes in policy as well. As discussed in Chapter 14, much federal policy was designed to empower poor people and thus posed a challenge to city governments. For example, Community Development programs, among other federally funded programs, contained requirements that the population served by the program be represented in program design and program operation. Federally funded Community Action Programs (CAPs) provided funds for lawyers who frequently assisted their clients in suing municipal governments.[14] In general, city officials found themselves operating in a more litigious and contentious environment. For example, welfare recipients had long been a very passive group, taking what the welfare system would give them and not complaining. However, in the late 1960s in New York City the National Welfare Rights Organization, headed by George Wiley, staged a "strike," and welfare recipients held sit-ins and took over social service buildings, an event that would have been amazing a decade earlier.

Implicit in the Reform movement was the idea that there is a public interest and that city governments could rationally and efficiently serve that interest. The conflict of the period raised serious questions about whether or not there was a such a single, identifiable public interest or whether there were simply many separate and conflicting group interests.

The conflict described above occurred against a background of fiscal stress in many cities. Many cities, for reasons noted earlier, were losing manufacturing, retailing, and other jobs to the suburbs and were also experiencing a substantial out-migration of their more prosperous residents. Both these trends entailed significant loss of revenues at the same time that the city was experiencing net in-migration of poorer residents who needed more in the way of social services. The crunch between needs on the one hand and financial resources on the other tended to make the fighting over goals and programs more intense. That the urban scene had grown rougher and more confrontational was confirmed by the wave of urban riots that hit forty or so of the nations' big cities from Newark to Los Angeles in the years between 1965 and 1968 (see Chapter 14).

One result of the changed political situation in the "post-Reform" era was a move toward "community control."[15] In a way this looked a bit like a return to the days of the big-city machine and ward politics, for it shifted the focus back from the interests of the city as a whole to the interests of a neighborhood or a particular group.

Community control became common in public education. Many minority parents felt that the public schools were failing to meet the needs of their children. Low scores on tests like the SAT and high dropout rates were often cited as evidence of this failure. So, too, were crimes on school properties and high rates of absenteeism. Community control looked like a way to make the schools more responsive to the community's needs.

There was also a move toward community control in planning. The argument was that city planning departments and the city governments of which they were a part tended to ignore the interests of neighborhoods—particularly poor and minority neighborhoods—in the pursuit of larger goals. For example, urban renewal projects often pitted the interests of developers, property owners, and those who viewed the city primarily as an economic machine against the interests of people who lived in renewal areas—people who lived in the path of "the federal bulldozer." Transferring some planning responsibility to neighborhood planning boards was a way to see that local interests were better represented.

However, community control has its downside. In the realm of education it has the capacity to transfer a great deal of responsibility to people without much professional background in the field. It also opens up many opportunities for corruption. In 1970 New York City decentralized its huge public education system from a single board of education to thirty-two community boards in the five boroughs (counties) that make up the city. That system is still in use, but it has had a turbulent history complete with periodic charges of corruption and election fraud. Whether it is better or worse than the old system is debatable. Certainly it has not proven to be a panacea.[16] In the realm of planning, the downside is that transferring too much power to community boards makes it difficult to plan for the city as a whole. If power is dispersed among many boards, too many people can say "no" and too few people can say "yes." Planning roads and utilities requires that the city or perhaps the metropolitan region must be viewed as a whole. But community control takes city governance in just the opposite direction.

One effect of the Civil Rights movement and the rural-to-urban migration discussed before was the coming to power of Black mayors in many U.S. cities from the 1960s to the present time. Just as demographic change brought White ethnic mayors to power in the late nineteenth and early twentieth century, so too did it bring Black mayors to office in the later part of the twentieth century. One difference, though, was that Black mayors such as David Dinkins in New York, Harold Washington in Chicago, Kurt Schmoke in Baltimore, Thomas Bradley in Los Angeles, Willie Brown in San Francisco, Coleman Young in Detroit, Maynard Jackson in Atlanta, Carl Stokes in Cleveland, and a number of others arrived on the scene well after the great age of machine politics was over. Then, too, many cities were losing population or at least were many decades past their period of peak growth. Consequently, the election of Black mayors generally did not mark the establishment of permanent Black political power in the city, though it did have the effect of permanently opening up city politics and public employment at all levels to Black people. Rather, leadership has swung back and forth between Blacks and Whites. Moreover, in many cities to talk simply of Blacks and Whites greatly simplifies a complicated ethnic politics. In Los Angeles or New York City, both Blacks and non-Hispanic Whites constitute minorities, albeit large ones. Hispanics and Asians also constitute major blocs of voters. As immigration, particularly from Central and South America and from Asia, continues to move America further from being a largely biracial nation to being a multiracial nation, the previous comments will become true of more and more cities.

THE "NEW PROGRESSIVES"?

The Reform (Progressive) era is decades behind us, but many commentators on the urban scene discern echoes of it in some of today's mayors.[17] To understand this consider some of the basic ideas of the Reform movement. Reformers believed it was a good idea to depoliticize (though that word was not in use at the time)—to take as much out of the political realm as possible and decide it instead in rationalistic engineeringlike terms. They also believed that there was an overall, unitary public interest and that the mayor or city manager should give first priority to that interest. For a city that is hard pressed financially and is confronted with fierce economic competition, the drain on resources and energy that go into zero-sum-game fighting between factions may be a loss that the city cannot afford. In such a city, a progressive style of administration that seeks to identify and focus on a citywide public interest may be very attractive. A number of those mayors whom one might identify as new progressives have made a conspicuous point of bypassing "identity politics" (politics based on racial, religious, and ethnic groupings).

> While men like Bradley and Dinkins stressed their sensitivity to distinct inter-ests of various groups, talking at length of their connections to different com-munities, Riordan, Guiliani, and other reformers conspicuously reject the lan-guage of group interest. Underlying the reformers' almost breezy lack of interest in identity politics is a deep confidence that they can bypass deep issues of race and ethnicity by simply making city government more effective: voters of every color want the garbage picked up and the streets made safe. It is their faith that such a thing as the public interest—as opposed to shifting coalitions of group interests—exists in America's big cities that links today's "new progressives" to the Reform movement of a century ago.[18]

The names in the above quote are Tom Bradley and David Dinkins, the former mayors of Los Angeles and New York City, respectively, and Richard Riordan and Rudolph Guiliani, the mayors of Los Angeles and New York City, respectively, at the time the article was written. (Both men were elected to second terms in 1997.) Though both Riordan and Guiliani are Republi-cans, both are liberal on a variety of social issues. Guiliani, for example is pro-choice, pro-immigrant, and pro–gay rights. But he cannot be pigeon-holed politically or ideologically. He is a hard-liner on crime (see Chapter 15). When it comes to behaviors like panhandling, he is willing to abrogate some civil rights in the interest of public order, a stance that has alienated many liberals who agree with him on matters such as abortion and gay rights. He is clearly pro-business, for he concludes that his city needs to re-tain and expand its employment base, and that means taking a pro-business stance to attract investment.

Efficiency and competitiveness are top priorities with the "new progres-sives." They are, in general, big proponents of privatization, as discussed sub-sequently. While none of the "new progressives" have attempted to elimi-nate civil service in their cities, they have, in general, tried to loosen up civil service and eliminate some of its rigidities—in short, to retain the benefits of the "merit" system while rendering it more efficient.

Among the mayors whom Beinart identifies as new progressives, in ad-dition to the two mentioned above, are Michael White of Cleveland, Steven Goldsmith of Indianapolis, Ed Rendell of Philadelphia, John Norquist of Milwaukee, and a name mentioned before in this chapter, Richard Daley, Jr., of Chicago.

A SHIFTING BALANCE OF POWER

Another change in the post–World War pattern of urban politics was the growth in the political strength of suburban governments as compared to central city governments. This is not apparent from considering any single municipal government, but becomes apparent when one considers the situation from a metropolitan or national perspective. As the decentralizing trends discussed in Chapter 3 proceeded, the strength of suburban communities relative to central cities increased, whether measured in terms of population, total and average personal income, or employment. This shift in relative power has many manifestations.

At the national level it means that more members of the House of Representatives come from suburban districts and also that suburban areas will have more political influence in all of the ways that economic strength counts in politics. Thus there will be more political force behind programs and grants that appeal to a suburban rather than an urban constituency. For example, suburban and city residents are likely to have different priorities regarding public transit and highway expenditures.

At the state level there was also a power shift from city to suburb for the same reason. Proportionately more state legislators come from suburban districts as suburban populations grow relative to city populations. The most important ramification here is financial, for as discussed in Chapter 6 a great deal of most cities' revenue comes down from the state government. However, this power shift at the state level may also manifest itself in other ways such as state level decisions about public capital investment and state economic development policy (see Chapter 7). The distribution of political power within the state legislature needs a brief historical note here. Through the 1960s many state legislative districts were drawn so that rural districts had smaller populations than urban or suburban districts and thus rural residents were over represented. In 1963 the Supreme Court's "one man, one vote" decision banned this practice and so when the population totals from the 1970 decennial census became available states that had followed this practice had to redistrict. The result was a shift in legislative representation away from rural areas and to metropolitan areas, both central city and suburb. With the continuing growth of suburban populations relative to central city populations, much of that increase in representation at the metropolitan area translated into increased suburban representation.

Within the metropolitan area itself, the shift in political power may manifest itself in greater suburban influence in Councils of Governments (COGs) and in authorities, both discussed later in this chapter.

CITY GOVERNMENT TODAY

In this section we describe some basic features of most U.S. municipal governments. One common form of city government, especially in the larger cities, is the strong-mayor form noted earlier. The mayor is elected at large and council members by district. The mayor appoints department heads and other top officials, but does so subject to confirmation by the city council. Laws are passed by the city council, subject to mayoral veto as well as to legislative override of that veto. Taxes are levied and funds appropriated by the council, generally working from an initial budget request submitted by the mayor. The strong-mayor system is analogous to that of the federal government.

In many smaller cities the council-manager system is used. Here, the council hires a professional city manager who does the day-to-day work of governing. In general, the city manager is not as powerful a figure as the mayor in a strong-mayor system, for the manager does not have his or her own electoral base. The manager knows that if he or she displeases too many members of the council too often they will vote *no* at contract renewal time. Some cities with council-manager governments also have a mayor. In such cases the mayor is usually not full-time and plays a largely ceremonial role.

Some smaller cities use the commissioner system. Its invention was accidental. In 1900 a hurricane devastated the city of Galveston, Texas. In its wake the state legislature appointed a group of five businessmen to run the city. The system worked well and has been adopted in several other states, notably Pennsylvania, New Jersey, and Illinois. The city is run by an elected commission, generally of five members. Each commissioner serves both as a member of the commission and as a department head. The chairmanship of the commission rotates. Power is much more dispersed than in either the strong-mayor or council-manager system, and therein lies the system's weakness. It is hard to say exactly who is in charge, and thus there is a political accountability problem. Note the resemblance to the weak-mayor form discussed earlier.

Creatures of the State

Cities are said to be "creatures of the state," meaning that the city has only those powers given it by the state government. These powers are spelled out in the state constitution or in enabling legislation passed by the state legislature. This principle, that the city derives its powers from the state rather than possesses them inherently, is referred to as Dillon's Rule, after an opinion by Judge John F. Dillon of the Supreme Court of the State of Iowa in 1868. One might wonder if cities do not have some powers that come from the Constitution of the United States. But the answer to that question is no. The words *city* and *town* do not appear anywhere in the Constitution. There is thus no clear implication in the Constitution that there shall be any subnational units of government other than the states.

Though the powers of city government come from the state, the obligations of the city government can come from other sources as well. Specifically, municipal governments, in addition to obligations laid on them by state governments, also face obligations from the federal government. Congress makes laws that impose obligations on city governments, and the federal courts also impose obligations. For example, the obligation to bus children for purposes of school integration was an obligation imposed upon cities by the federal courts, as discussed in Chapter 16. More recently, the Americans with Disabilities Act (ADA) passed by Congress imposes obligations on all levels of government. Those obligations come from the law itself, from the regulations issued by federal agencies pursuant to that law, and from the manner in which the courts interpret that law. If a parent decides that the city school system is not providing her child with the education that the child is entitled to under the ADA, she can go to court. If she is successful, the decision of the court will be binding upon the city.

Staffing City Government

The top posts in city government—mayor (if there is one) and council members—are filled by election. Posts at the commissioner and deputy commissioner level are generally filled in the same way as cabinet positions in the federal government, by executive nomination subject to legislative confirmation. In some cases there may also be formal requirements for the position. For example, the commissioner of public works might be required to have an engineering degree or a Professional Engineer's license. A few positions close to the mayor or manager—aides, press secretary, and the like—are generally left to be filled at that individual's discretion.

Almost all the remaining city labor force is filled through Civil Service (sometimes also referred to as the merit system). Civil Service is one of the most important legacies of the turn-of-the-century Reform movement, and it deserves a brief description here.

With variations from place to place, it works approximately as follows. The great mass of jobs within the city government have clearly defined educational and experience requirements. For example, the Social Worker I position might require a master's degree in social work or a bachelor's degree and three years of experience. Only the candidate who possesses those qualifications is eligible to take the exam for the position. The exam is given periodically, perhaps once or twice a year. Those who pass are listed in order of their scores on the exam. The agency must then fill positions from the top of the list. A typical requirement might be that the agency must offer the job to one of the three top candidates. If that person declines, the agency may hire one of the remaining two or offering the job to number four.

The newly hired worker then goes through a probationary period, typically a year. If the worker's performance is satisfactory, he or she then receives a permanent appointment. The worker then has a more or less permanent lock on the job. He or she can be discharged only if the position is abolished or for cause. Discharging a civil service employee for cause generally involves a hearing, an appeals procedure, and often a probationary period during which an employee who lost in the hearing can try to improve his or her performance and thus retain the job. It is usually a cumbersome and tedious procedure and one that few supervisors will undertake if they can possibly avoid it.

Within the civil service personnel structure, there is a series of pay grades and steps within each grade. For each year in grade the employee automatically advances another step. Moving to the next grade requires being promoted and, often, passing another exam. The pay for each grade and step is specified and, like all financial data of government, a matter of public record. In recent years, to motivate workers some civil service systems have introduced merit pay increases above and beyond the grades and steps just described.

The system has advantages and disadvantages. The advantages are those that the turn of the century reformers foresaw. It goes far in avoiding the use of the public payroll for political payoffs and nepotism. It also goes far in keeping out grossly unqualified people, therefore professionalizing public service. It has a great element of fairness. The person who grades the exam—or now, the computer that scores your answer sheet—does not worry about whether he or she likes your face or whether you come from a "good family." The system also has some disadvantages. It is rigid. An agency cannot hire someone who obviously can do the job but does not have the formal qualifications. Discharging a nonproductive or disruptive employee is very difficult. For the worker who has a permanent appointment and who has decided that there is no possibility for further promotion, management has few carrots or sticks to motivate him or her. The permanent appointment system is not well adapted to fluctuating workloads.[19]

Purchasing Supplies and Services

Just as reformers saw that patronage was a major source of power for a political machine, they also saw that the ability to favor political friends with contracts for supplies and services was also a major source of power. One heritage of the Reform era is that supplies and services are now procured on the basis of competitive bids. Before any good or service can be purchased, whether it be office supplies or paving the streets, a detailed description of the required item(s) is prepared and companies that wish to supply it bid for the contract.

At a designated time all the bids are opened and the contract is awarded to the lowest qualified bidder. In some cities the system has been modified somewhat to favor minority-owned firms. For example, the bidding rules might specify that if a minority-owned firm comes within, say, 10 percent of the bid of the lowest bidding nonminority-owned firm, then it will get the contract. But although the rules are clearly specified, that fact does not mean that this system is never violated.[20] However, it is much cleaner than municipal purchasing and contracting was in the heyday of machine politics.

MAKING GOVERNMENT MORE EFFICIENT

City governments are under much pressure to become more businesslike, more efficient, more "bottom line" oriented. Some of this pressure comes from the inevitable squeeze caused by citizens who want both good public services and low taxes. Some of the push comes out of the process of politics. Charges of waste and inefficiency are always a stick with which the challenger can beat the incumbent. Then, too, as the United States has moved toward the Right politically in the last several decades, the prestige of the private sector relative to that of government has risen; and with that change has come the idea that government should become more "businesslike." The pressure for efficiency is likely to be particularly great in the central city, which is losing some of its more prosperous residents and some of its industrial and commercial employment base to its suburban or exurban rivals. However, it is felt in all cities to some extent. Before we discuss the matter of efficiency, we need to say a few words on behalf of the municipal government facing this sort of pressure.

Consider the contractor who has just gotten a paving contract with the city. He is expected to be efficient. As long as he obeys the law and lives up to the specifications of his contract, efficiency is all that we expect of him. If he drives a hard bargain with his workers or his suppliers, so much the better. He is being an efficient businessman.

Now consider the city carrying out a project itself. It, too, is expected to be efficient. We don't want the city government to squander funds. But we also expect it to be fair and compassionate. If the city drives too hard a bargain with its workers, we may take it to task for that. And, of course, its workers are also voters, as are their friends and relatives. If the city operates a public facility such as a golf course, we do not expect it to charge a profit-maximizing fee as would a private owner. Rather, we expect it to charge a fair or a reasonable fee, whatever that means. If the city is locating some low- or moderate-income housing, we expect it not only to consider money issues but also neighborhood impacts—perhaps the competing demands of different racial or ethnic groups, the effect on traffic flow, effects on school enrollments—a myriad of considerations that a private developer would not be expected to consider.

The point of the above digression is that it is not reasonable to judge municipal government purely in terms of efficiency, because we expect other things as well from government. And often those other things conflict with the goal of efficiency. Below, we discuss some of the techniques for making municipalities more efficient providers of public services.

Privatization

Privatization means contracting out to the private sector work that otherwise would be done by the municipal work force. In recent years many more functions have been contracted out. Some of these services include trash collection, maintenance of municipal vehicles, operation of 911 services, some types of social services, and even the operation of jails and prisons.[21]

Privatization can lower costs in several ways. It often lowers labor costs. Firms may pay lower wages in some job categories. Even where firms' hourly wages are no lower, they may pay less in pensions and benefits. Where work loads fluctuate, firms can hire and lay off workers rapidly, something that cannot be done in a civil service system with examinations and permanent appointments.

In some cases privatization has saved money because it can achieve economies of scale. For example, for a small community to keep a 911 service manned continuously may mean having several people on the payroll who are idle a good part of the time. If a firm provides this service to several municipalities, it can keep its operators busier and lower the cost per call. (This kind of economy can also be, and often is, achieved by cooperative agreements between municipalities.)

Free market ideology holds that competition breeds efficiency. If that is so, then privatization enables municipal governments to tap those competition-bred efficiencies by shifting work from the public to the private sector. One extension of the privatization theme is that of introducing competition into the operation of government itself. If we believe that competition makes firms more efficient, shouldn't it also make government more efficient? The guru of this movement has been Mayor Steven Goldsmith of Indianapolis.[22] His most important innovation has been to open up many government functions to competitive bidding but then to let government departments bid on an even footing with firms.[23] For example, his administration put the repair of municipal vehicles out for bid but allowed the government workers who had been doing the work to bid in direct competition with outside firms. The government employees were highly motivated because their jobs were on the line. (Recall that a civil service appointment generally does not offer any protection if the job itself is abolished.) As it turned out, the government employees put in the low bid and the work stayed inside of government. But in order to make the low bid they first had to go to their superiors and get permission to abolish work rules that held back productivity. In effect, this policy initiative was Goldsmith's answer to the question of how competition can be introduced into a monopoly situation when there is only one government for the city.

Public-Private Partnerships

Another route to efficiency in accomplishing the goals of government has been the public-private partnership. These partnerships become feasible when the interests of government coincide with those of firms or nonprofit organizations.

The area in which public-private partnerships are most common is economic development. The city government wants to promote economic growth as a response to citizen pressure for lower taxes and stronger local labor markets. The business community wants economic growth because it is good for business. Economic growth increases the value of commercial and residential property. It means more sales for local businesses, more commissions for real estate brokers, more work for the local construction industry, and more bank deposits.

A common arrangement is that the public-private partnership for economic development gets some of its funding from government and some from the business community. The board that runs the organization has some members from the business community, perhaps some from civic or other nonprofit organizations, and some who are high-ranking officials of the municipal government. When officials from a firm that the city is trying to recruit come to town, they see a smoothly functioning partnership. The presence of bankers and businessmen reassures them that the partnership understands business. The presence of municipal officials reassures them that there will not be undue delays in getting the necessary water and sewer hookups and that their problems with zoning or waste discharge permits will receive a sympathetic hearing in city hall. If there is a representative of organized labor on the board, that too is reassuring for it suggests that there will be cooperative rather than confrontational relations with their labor force.

The public-private partnership is not limited to economic development. A city that operates an art museum might share the management with a nonprofit or philanthropic organization with a commitment to the arts. Both city social service agencies and philanthropic or church-based organizations may have similar goals and may service overlapping client populations. Their mutual interests create an opportunity for cooperation and perhaps shared funding of some activities. Because the partnership is not a part of the municipal government, it is likely to have much more flexibility of operation; it can more readily initiate new approaches or drop old approaches that do not work well.

Public-private partnerships are growing in number, and the trend has many supporters.[24] Do they have a downside? It could be argued that in some cases such partnerships may pull government in the direction of a set of particular interests. For example, a public-private partnership for economic development might pull municipal government in a direction that favors corporate interests over other interests. Suppose the issue is how much of a tax break to provide a new firm or whether low-income residential property should be condemned to make room for industrial development. Would the fact that public officials have become involved with real estate and other development interests through the partnership tip the scales in favor of business interests? To generalize, the question is whether the existence of public-private partnerships, whether for economic development or some other purpose, might favor particular interests and give them undue weight in the decision-making process.

QUASI-GOVERNMENTAL ORGANIZATIONS

A good deal of the work of local government is done by organizations that we might call quasi governments—organizations that have some but not all of the responsibilities and powers of general-purpose municipal governments.

The quasi-governmental agency with which most readers of this book have had extended contact with is the school district. About five sixths of all public school students in the United States attend schools run by school districts. The most important governmental power that school districts have is the power to tax, and school districts collect many tens of billions of property taxes to support public education. Many school districts have the power of eminent domain, so that they can condemn property for uses like school construction. In some states, such as Virginia, school board members are chosen by municipal governments, and so the quasi government is really a creature of the general-purpose government. In other states, such as New York, school board members are elected separately and the relationship of the school district to the general-purpose government is a parallel rather than a subsidiary one.

There are many other types of districts. These include water [supply] districts, sewer districts, street lighting districts, conservation districts, and transportation districts. As in the case of school districts, their relationship to municipal government varies from place to place. Districts may work harmoniously with general-purpose governments, or they may work at cross-purposes. In many cases district boundaries do not correspond to municipal boundaries. For example, some school districts may contain several towns and parts of more than one county. Conversely, parts of the same town or county may be in more than one district.[25] Such overlaps can complicate the task of government and intergovernmental coordination.

Authorities

In many places some functions that could be performed by general purpose governments are performed by authorities. There are hundreds of authorities in the United States for airports, seaports, bridges and tunnels, public transportation, housing, dormitories (for universities), and many other purposes.

Typically, these public organizations are created by act of the state legislature and charged with a particular set of responsibilities. The legislation will charge, or "task," the authority with responsibility for a clearly defined set of goals and also assign to it some of the powers of government to aid in pursuing those goals. The idea behind the authority is that an organization that is outside the structure of general-purpose local governments can pursue a single goal or a small set of goals in a more single-minded and effective way than can a general-purpose government. In effect, the authority can bypass some of the normal political processes.

The first authority created in the United States was the Port of New York Authority, subsequently renamed the Port Authority of New York and New Jersey and referred to here simply as the Port Authority.[26] It was created in 1921 by acts of the New York and New Jersey state legislatures and was patterned on the port authority of the city of London. The authority's original charge by the legislatures was to improve the transportation of rail freight in the New York metropolitan area. The area is broken up by various bodies of water, and it lies in two states. The political situation was further complicated by the fact that the part of the New York region on the New Jersey side of the Hudson River is composed of numerous municipalities. It was a situation that clearly called for interstate cooperation and some entity that could pursue the goal in a single-minded way. The authority soon perceived that the automobile and the truck were the transportation of the future and redefined its primary mission as the building of bridges and the operation of tunnels to unify the region. In this it has been extremely successful. Most of the bridges and tunnels that bind the region into a single economic entity were built either by the Port Authority of New York and New Jersey or by another authority, the Triborough Bridge and Tunnel Authority (TBTA), which has subsequently been merged with still another authority, the Metropolitan Transit Authority (MTA).[27]

As time passed, the Port Authority grew and its role gradually expanded. At present it operates bridges, tunnels, the region's major airports, harbor facilities (Port Newark), some of the region's commuter trains, bus lines, and bus terminals, and miscellaneous other facilities. It has almost 8,000 employees, an operating budget of over $2 billion a year, and about $6 billion in outstanding debt. It has been a very effective organization and a very powerful force in shaping the region.

The Port Authority is self-financed. Tolls on bridges, landing fees at airports, fares on buses, and so on pay its costs. One of the powers of government that the agency has is the power to issue tax exempt bonds (see Chapter 6). It is thus able to borrow at the same rate as a municipal government rather than the higher rate that would usually be paid by a corporation or individual. The authority is run by a board of twelve directors, six of whom are appointed by the New York state legislature and six by the New Jersey state legislature.

Though we have focused on this original and very powerful authority, it is a prototype for numerous other authorities. Consider some of its characteristics. In principle it is under the political control of two general-purpose governments, the state governments of New York and New Jersey. But in fact, it operates with a high degree of autonomy. It is one remove further from the voter than is a city government, whose mayor and city council members stand for election and are known to the public. Though created for a specific purpose, which it has long since accomplished, it is in no danger of being abolished, for it has periodically defined new roles for itself. The statistics cited above on its workforce and expenditures are those of a good-sized city government. It is thus a powerful political force in its own right. None of these remarks are criticisms of the Port Authority or a reflection upon how well it has served the interests of the region. They are simply generic comments on the politics of authorities, using this particular authority as a case in point.

Those who like a particular authority may point to its accomplishments that may transcend the capabilities of municipal governments. Those who dislike an authority may complain that it exercises some of the powers of government without having the political accountability of a government. And, they may argue, if the resources that flow to the authority flowed instead to the general-purpose government(s) of the area, they would be used in at least somewhat different ways. Because an authority is not part of government, it lies outside the debt limits imposed upon state and local governments, and no referenda are necessary for an authority to issue bonds (see Chapter 6). This presents both opportunities for doing useful things that could not otherwise be done and opportunities for misuse.[28] At least one scholar has argued that where a great deal of the total responsibility for the provision of public services is in the hands of authorities, the total pattern of public expenditures is pushed somewhat more in the direction of physical investment and away from services to individuals than it would otherwise be.[29] This is not surprising, for, in general, authorities are created to build and operate public infrastructure. It seems natural to expect that they will continue to do what they were created to do and are comfortable doing. Then, too, because the authority is more insulated from political pressures than is a general-purpose government, it can more easily resist pressure to change.

Intergovernmental Cooperation within Regions

In many metropolitan areas, particularly in the eastern United States, political subdivisions are much smaller than what we might term the "real" city as defined by items like commuting and shopping behavior. Therein lies a serious problem for governance. This is clearly true with regard to public finance, as discussed in Chapter 6. But it is also true wherever the scale of the activity does not correspond to the scale of the political jurisdictions. Districts and authorities, as just pointed out, are one way to address this problem. So too are intergovernmental agreements. For example, two or more municipal governments may agree to jointly fund and operate a facility where there are economies of scale to be realized. In principle, it might be possible to bring the political city and the "real city" into a proper relationship by means of governmental consolidation, perhaps by having a single government for an entire metropolitan area. But this is not in the cards politically. The political force to compel the citizens of suburban municipalities to cede their sovereignty to a metropolitan government simply does not exist.[30]

The most recent device for achieving cooperation within metropolitan areas is a Council of Governments (COG). Local governments representing most of the population and most of the land area of the United States belong to COGs. The National Association of Regional Councils estimates that there are 450 COGs in the United States. A COG is very much the creature of its member governments. For the National Association of Regional Councils to count an organization as a COG, at least 51 percent of its governing board must be made up of elected officials from its member governments. In most cases the actual figure is much higher, and many of the nonelected members are there by appointment of the member governments' legislative body.

The growth of COGs has been driven partly by the realization that a vehicle for intergovernmental cooperation is needed. It has also been driven by federal policy. A great many federal grants are conditioned by requirements for intergovernmental cooperation. For example, the 1998 highway bill appropriated $203 billion for highway funding over the next six years. Most of the money is to be spent by state and local governments. For a government in a metropolitan area to apply for grant money, its application must come through a metropolitan planning organization (MPO) and the bill designates councils of governments (COGS) as the MPOs.

COGs serve as a mechanism for intergovernmental cooperation over a range of issues that transcend municipal boundaries. For example, COGs are the venue for area-wide planning efforts regarding transportation, water supply, and environmental protection. COGs also serve as a vehicle for intergovernmental cooperation where there are economies of scale to be gained, as in the provision of social services such as Medicaid.

Because COGs are very much the creation of the political establishments of their constituent municipalities, they are as effective or as ineffective as those municipalities choose to make them. COGs thus can vary from highly effective organizations to organizations that are not much more than pro forma entities whose main purpose is satisfying federal requirements for intermunicipal cooperation as a prerequisite for federal grants. Though many COGs do make a considerable contribution to intermunicipal cooperation, the problem of intergovernmental cooperation at the metropolitan level is still far from solved.

SUMMARY

The chapter begins with a brief history of urban government in the United States. In the first half or so of the nineteenth century, urban governments were generally weak and had a limited range of responsibility. Suffrage was largely restricted to White males and often to those among them who owned property. Much of the attention of many municipal governments was directed to essentially commercial concerns, such as economic competition with other municipalities and the promotion of land subdivision and development. As urban populations grew and the range of necessary urban services expanded, powerful political machines emerged in many cities, especially in the Northeast and North Central regions of the United States. At the core of machine politics was the system of election by ward and the widespread use of public jobs and municipal contracts to retain the loyalty of ward captains and precinct workers. As the turn of the century approached, a powerful municipal reform movement developed and reshaped U.S. urban governance. Among the reformers' goals were the council manager form of government, the use of civil service for filling city jobs, at large elections, and the short ballot. Reform government in U.S. cities probably reached its peak in the years shortly after World War II. The period after that is sometimes referred to as the post-Reform era. Urban politics became much more contentious and, in a very different guise, some of the "identity" politics of the machine era returned, this time often centered around race. At present a number of U.S. cities have administrations that represent a return to some of the ideas of the reform movement and whose mayors have been referred to by some as "the new progressives."

Many small and medium-sized cities employ the council-manager form, but the largest cities still maintain the strong-mayor system. Like all substate governments, cities are "creatures of the state" and have only those powers given to them by state constitutions and state legislatures ("Dillon's Rule"). They are bound not only by rules and obligations imposed by the states but also by rules and mandates from the federal government and often by rulings of the state and federal judiciary as well. We also note the essentially universal use of civil service for filling the majority of city jobs and the use of sealed bid systems for awarding municipal jobs, two heritages of the Reform movement. Privatization is increasingly used as a way of improving the efficiency of city services.

Many urban services are delivered not by general governments, but by a range of quasi governments. These are organizations that have some but not all of the powers of government and a much narrower range of responsibilities than have general-purpose governments. For example, school districts rather than general-purpose governments educate about five sixths of all public school pupils in the United States. We also noted the role of authorities in providing public infrastructure and infrastructure-related services. Councils of Government (COGs) are a widespread device for addressing the difficult problem of intermunicipal competition.

NOTES

1. In the years after the Revolution the nation came to view individualism and entrepreneurship in a much more favorable light than it had in prerevolutionary times and to view status, hierarchy, aristocracy, and authority in a much less favorable light. That change in world view underlies some of the wild and freewheeling character of the early nineteenth-century U.S. city and city governance. For a discussion of this change in outlook, see Gordon S. Wood, *The Radicalism of the American Revolution* (New York: Random House, Vintage Books, 1991).
2. The phrase "urban mercantilism" comes from Alfred Eichner, *State Development Agencies and Employment Expansion*, (Ann Arbor: University of Michigan Press, 1970). The book contains accounts of some of the early municipal financings of rail and canal development.
3. The novel *The Last Hurrah*, by Frank O'Connor (Boston: Little, Brown, 1956) contains a very good picture of machine politics in Boston around the turn of the century. The book's protagonist is modeled on Mayor James Curley.
4. Mike Royko, *Boss: Richard J. Daley of Chicago* (New York: E. P. Dutton, 1971).
5. Royko, op. cit. p. 64
6. Royko, op. cit. p. 64
7. Royko, op. cit.
8. Melvin G. Holli, "Ranking Chicago's Mayors: Mirror, Mirror, on the Wall, Who Is the Greatest of Them All?" in *The Mayors: The Chicago Political Tradition*, edited by Paul M. Green and Melvin G. Holli (Carbondale and Edwardsville: Southern Illinois University Press, 1987).
9. See Robert K. Merton, "The Latent Functions of the Machine," in *The Politics of Urban America*, 2nd ed., edited by Dennis R. Judd and Paul R. Kantor (Boston: Allyn and Bacon, 1998). Note: The article first appeared in 1957 in Merton's *Social Theory and Social Structure* (New York: The Free Press).
10. Alan DiGaetano, "The Rise and Development of Urban Political Machines: An Alternative to Merton's Functional Analysis," in *The Politics of Urban America*, 2nd ed., edited by Dennis R. Judd and Paul R. Kantor (Boston: Allyn and Bacon, 1998).
11. In *Ethnic America* (Basic Books, 1981), Thomas Sowell makes this sort of argument. He notes that a large part of the Irish immigration to America occurred in the mid nineteenth century. By 1950—roughly a century later—the Irish by every statistical measure, such as family income, professional occupations, rate of college graduation, and the like, had completely caught up with the rest of the American, White, native-born population. That catch-up, by his reckoning, took a century. He notes that the Italian immigration to America peaked in the late nineteenth and early twentieth century. By 1950 the Italians had made the same catchup as the Irish, but in half a century. He attributes the greater speed of the Italians partly to the fact that they showed much less interest in politics than the Irish (he notes that Italian wards were often represented by Irish politicians) and instead focused on small business, which, he argues, proved to be a more efficient engine of economic progress. In *Still the Promised City: African Americans and New Immigrants in Post-Industrial New York* (Cambridge: Harvard University Press, 1996), Roger Waldinger provides some reflections on an analogous theme. He notes that in New York City American-born Blacks have obtained a very large share of civil service employment relative to immigrants because they are citizens, are native English speakers, and often have the requisite high school or college degree. However, many immigrant groups are doing as well or better economically. This, like Sowell's example, suggests that government employment may not be the fastest route to economic success, considering the group as a whole. For a case study of one group's rapid economic progress via the small business and education routes and without much reliance on public employment, see Heather MacDonald, "Why Koreans Succeed," *City* 5, no. 2 (Spring 1995), pp. 12–29.
12. Alan DiGaetano, "The Origins of Urban Political Machines," *Urban Affairs Quarterly* 26, no. 3 (March 1991), pp. 324–353.
13. For an elaboration of the idea that one can identify a post-Reform era, see Chapters 8 and 9 in *Urban Policy and Politics in a Bureaucratic Age*, by Clarence N. Stone, Robert K. Whelan, and William J. Murin (Englewood Cliffs, N.J.: Prentice-Hall, 1978).
14. For an insider's account of community action and related programs, see Daniel P. Moynihan, *Maximum Feasible Misunderstanding* [taken from the phrase "maximum feasible participation" in federal regulations referring to participation by the poor in program operation] (New York: Free Press, 1969).

15. For contemporaneous discussion of community power, see Stone, et al., op. cit., the first part of Chapter 9.
16. For the reader interested in a history of school decentralization in New York, the best source is the *New York Times* Index.
17. Peter Beinart, "The Pride of the Cities," *The New Republic* (June 30, 1997), pp. 16–24.
18. Beinart, op. cit. p. 21.
19. For a detailed and very critical presentation of the disadvantages of civil service, see David Osborne and Ted Gaebler, *Reinventing Government: How the Entrepreneurial Spirit Is Transforming Government* (New York: A Plume Book, Penguin Group, 1993), Chapter 4.
20. For example, a city employee on the take might manage to see the bids before their official opening and inform a favored firm about other bids. Where there are only a few qualified firms, these firms might conspire ("bid rigging") to not compete with each other but to decide among themselves which firm will get which contract and then adjust their bids accordingly. In one variation, which this writer witnessed, the request for bids included some specifications that the purchaser did not really care about and that the favored firm knew about. The favored firm was thus enabled to be the low-bidding firm because it knew that the buyer would never check for these items. But firms not in the know would have to build the cost of meeting those specifications into their bids. In the case of minority set-asides, a nonminority firm might masquerade as a minority firm by using a minority individual as a figurehead.
21. The most prominent academic advocate of privatization and one of the earliest to write about it is Emanuel E. Savas. See *Privatization: The Key to Better Government* (Chatham, N.J.: Chatham House Publishers, 1987). See also Osborne and Gaebler, op. cit.
22. Jon Jeter, "A Winning Combination in Indianapolis: Bidding for City Services Creates Public-Private Success," *Washington Post* (September 21, 1977), p. A3.
23. Whether the footing is entirely equal is open to argument. Firms pay taxes that government departments do not. Governments can borrow money in tax-exempt markets, whereas firms, in general, must borrow in taxable markets and thus typically pay perhaps 2 percent or so more interest. Thus the same capital expenditure costs the firm more than it costs government.
24. Osborne and Gaebler, op. cit.
25. See, for example, Ronald C. Fischer, *State and Local Public Finance* (Chicago: Irwin, 1996), p. 4–5, for a map and discussion of such overlaps in Michigan.
26. For an account of the creation of the Port Authority see Jameson C. Doig, "Politics and the Engineering Mind: O. H. Amman and the Hidden Story of the George Washington Bridge," in *Building the Public City*, edited by David C. Perry (Sage Publications, 1995).
27. For an account of the TBTA see Robert Caro, *The Power Broker* [the career of Robert Moses, the creator of the TBTA] (New York: Alfred A. Knopf, 1974).
28. David C. Perry, "Building the City Through the Back Door: The Politics of Debt, Law, and Public Infrastructure," in *Building the Public City*, op. cit. Perry argues that New York State's former governor, Nelson Rockefeller, created numerous authorities as a way of bypassing legislative and public control of expenditures. While the Port Authority provides the types of services that can be supported by user charges, this was not the case for many of the authorities created by Rockefeller.
29. Katherine Foster, *The Political Economy of Special Purpose Government* (Washington, D.C.: Georgetown University Press, 1997).
30. Even limited tax base sharing between municipalities is rare in the United States. The one well-known example is Minneapolis–St. Paul. There are some theoretical objections to municipal consolidation, but they are outside the purview of this book. The interested reader, however, can look them up under the name "Tiebout hypothesis," a subject covered in many books on public finance, including Ronald C. Fisher, *State and Local Public Finance*, 2nd. ed. (Irwin, 1996). The original source of the argument is to be found in Charles Tiebout, "A Pure Theory of Local Expenditures," *Journal of Political Economy* (October 1956), pp. 416–24.

REFERENCES

See the following chapter.

Chapter

5 | City Government: Part 2

I n this chapter we examine five different viewpoints on urban government. The viewpoints to be discussed cast city government in very
different lights and leave one with very different feelings about city government. They are all great simplifications of a complex reality and a few
words need be said about such simplifications.

In the physical sciences very simple (parsimonious) assumptions or generalizations permit the building of powerful and useful structures of
thought.[1] In the social sciences there is always a conflict between the need
for such simple statements and the need to take into account the complex
context of each situation. In effect, context is the enemy of parsimony.[2] The
more the social scientist reaches for a powerful, parsimonious generalization
or assumption on which to build a theory, the more he or she has to ignore
the context of the situation—to simplify or distort reality to make it possible
to theorize.

The various theories discussed in the following section necessarily re-
flect the tradeoff between parsimony and context. They all simplify reality,
and in this writer's view they all capture a piece of the truth. The question is
not which one is right or wrong, but which one captures more of reality and
perhaps also which one raises more useful questions.

The reader should also be aware that different viewpoints and their vo-
cabularies carry different emotional loads. Consider the language of mainstream (neoclassical) economics. Phrases like "adjustment at the margin" or
"if the supply curve shifts to left then, *ceterus paribus*, . . ." have a calm tone
to them. On the other hand, the language of Marxian analysis with terms
like "exploitation, expropriation of surplus value, immiseration, and monopoly capital" tends to stir the blood a bit more. The neoclassical language

conjures up a world of incremental and rational behavior—nothing to get excited about. The Marxian language conjures up a world in which some dominate and exploit others—a world of haves and have nots. The emotional loading behind or implicit in the work of social scientists is important because it affects how we act and the political and social choices that we make. Perhaps, too, some of us are attracted to particular schools of political and social thought in part because we like their tone, because they fit our emotions as well as our intellects.

Below we present five alternative views of city governance, arranged more or less in the order in which they have appeared on the scene. These views are

Pluralism

Elite and Regime theories

The city as "growth machine"

The Peterson view of the limits of municipal governance

The Political Economy perspective

PLURALISM

The seminal book in pluralist theory is Robert Dahl's *Who Governs?*, a detailed study of the government of the city of New Haven, Connecticut, from the immediate postrevolutionary period until the mid twentieth century.[3] He begins with this question:

> In a political system where nearly every adult may vote but where knowledge, wealth, social position, access to officials, and other resources are unequally distributed, who actually governs?[4]

Dahl's answer to the question is what has come to be called *pluralism.* Dahl concluded that political power had been widely dispersed and that no single group achieved permanent dominance. In *Who Governs?* he divides the populace into three groups: a large number of people he terms *constituents,* a smaller number of people he terms *subleaders,* and a still smaller number he terms *leaders.* The last two groups together make up the "political stratum." For the great mass, the constituents, politics is most of the time a minor issue in their lives. For the political stratum it is a major focus of their lives.

A member of the political stratum has far more influence on the actions of government than does a member of the constituency. But the actions of the political stratum are very much limited by the will of the mass of constituents. Even if the constituents are quiescent at the moment, the political stratum is very much attuned to their likes and dislikes and is strongly motivated not to do what will displease them, for after all, politicians must stand for election. Dahl also argues that the political stratum is neither homogeneous nor hard to enter.

> In the United States the political stratum does not constitute a homogeneous class with well defined class interests. In New Haven, in fact, the political stratum is easily penetrated by anyone whose interests and concerns attract him to the distinctive culture of the stratum. It is easily penetrated because (among other reasons) elections and competitive parties give politicians a powerful motive for expanding their coalitions and increasing their electoral followings.
>
> In an open pluralistic system, where movement into the political stratum is easy, the stratum embodies many of the most widely shared values and goals of the society.[5]

Dahl asserts that his detailed study of the city supports such a view. For example, he studied the city's decision in the late 1950s to engage in a major Urban Renewal project. He argues that although the idea came from within the political stratum as well as from some major institutions, it did not come to pass until a mayor who campaigned in support of it was elected by a large majority—that is, until the constituency gave its consent.

Dahl also argues that the political stratum changes composition over time. For example, he lists all the mayors of New Haven from 1784 to 1953. The first group (until about 1840) he terms the "patricians." They were primarily judges, lawyers, and former congressmen, as close to an aristocracy as postcolonial America had. He then identifies the group from roughly 1840 to 1900 as the "entrepreneurs." They are primarily the heads of successful businesses, many in manufacturing. The third group, from the turn of the century to the 1950s, he terms the "ex plebes," basically men who rose from relatively modest origins and who, in many cases, were neither wealthy nor highly placed in society at the time they became mayors. The last three in this group were the business agent for the Cigar Workers union, the secretary-treasurer of a group of funeral homes, and the director of the Yale News Bureau—a group very different from the "patricians" of a century earlier.[6] The point he makes is that to the extent that there is a political elite it is a shifting and permeable one. There is no one group that has the leadership locked up for very long.

The pluralist view is a very reassuring view. There is no ruling group, a diversity of interests are represented, the top of the political stratum at different times represents a variety of people, and its general composition is subject to considerable change. It is a situation very much in keeping with our democratic egalitarian ethos. In that it affirms the basic equity of the system and suggests no need for major change, it is fair to characterize the pluralist view as a conservative position.

REGIMES AND ELITES

Not long after it was enunciated the pluralist view came under heavy criticism. Its critics argued that it presented a naive and overly benign picture of how city governments worked and how decisions really got made. Critics argued that the pluralists ignored the fact that different groups had very different access to the political process, due, for example, to poverty or to racial prejudice. They argued that the pluralists were wrong in saying that people outside the political stratum participated in politics only sporadically. Rather, they contended, there were some groups that participated continuously and effectively to their own advantage and to the detriment of other groups. In short, they argued that beneath the appearance of widely dispersed power and democratic participation, the most important decisions were made by an affluent and well-connected elite.

Some of the difference in outlook may have been the difference in viewpoint between political scientists and sociologists, for the pluralist view was largely the work of political scientists and the emerging *elite* view largely the work of sociologists.[7] The political scientist is likely to focus on political processes, laws, and voting behavior. Sociologists are fond of the distinction between manifest and latent functions. The *manifest* function of a thing is the purpose or role it is supposed to have. The *latent* function is the unstated purpose that it also serves. To elite theorists it seemed as if the pluralists were looking at manifest functions and not perceiving more powerful latent functions—that they were looking at formal processes such as votes by the city council and not giving due weight to influences behind the scene.

In time, writers on urban government began to speak of urban "regimes." The regime, the groups that actually makes and influences the major decisions of city government, is composed not just of elected officials but also of an elite who by virtue of their wealth, as well as their business, institutional, and social connections, are able and motivated to exert a major influence upon public affairs.

Clarence N. Stone in an often cited study of Atlanta noted:

> The exercise of public authority is thus never a simple matter; it is almost always enhanced by extraformal considerations. Because local governmental authority is by law and tradition even more limited than authority at the state and local level, informal arrangements assume special importance in urban politics.[8]

Stone distinguishes between elite theory and regime theory, a distinction not made in this chapter.[9] But an elite view and regime view are clearly linked, for it is the elite who possess wealth, economic power, and connections who make up much of the regime. Among those who might make up the regime are elected officials and perhaps some other important public officials, owners and directors of major businesses, major property owners, owners of newspapers and other media, and directors of major nonprofit institutions. Among most regime theorists special weight has been placed upon the owners and directors of capital— upon business. Stone asserts,

> The mix of participants [in the regime] varies by community, but that mix is itself constrained by the accommodation of two basic institutional principles of

the American political economy: (1) popular control of the formal machinery of government and (2) private ownership of business enterprise. Neither of these principles is pristine. Popular control is modified and compromised in various ways, but nevertheless remains as the basic principle of government. Private ownership is less than universal. . . . Even so, governmental conduct is constrained by the need to promote investment activity in an economic arena dominated by private ownership. This political economy insight is the foundation for a theory of urban regimes.[10]

The last sentence of the quote is the key one. In the minds of many regime theorists the key players in the regime are those who own and control capital and the regime is their vehicle for getting municipal government to serve the interests of capital. This does not mean that they are always successful in doing so or that there are no members of the regime who are not tied to capital. It means simply that regime theorists see those who represent the interests of capital as being the primary players. Regime theorists see city governments more often than not acting in the interest of capital rather than of some other interests. This preference might manifest itself in decisions about such matters as land development, the subsidization of economic development, or about how much of the city budget is to be spent on public capital investment versus how much is to be spent on social services for the poor.

THE CITY AS "GROWTH MACHINE"

The "growth machine" hypothesis is distinct from elite theory or regime theory, but it bears a relationship to them in that it too places great emphasis on the idea that municipal government largely serves the needs of capital. It appeared in a very persuasively written article by Molotch in 1976.[11] This is how Molotch describes his view in the summary statement at the beginning of his article:

> A city and, more generally, a locality is conceived [by Molotch] as an areal expression of the interests of some land-based elite. Such an elite is seen to profit through an increasing intensification of the land use of an area in which its members hold a common interest. An elite competes with other land-based elites in an effort to have growth inducing resources invested within its own area as opposed to that of another.

He argues that the "land-based elite," those who own property and stand to benefit from growth, bends city government to its will and makes the city into a "growth machine," a government whose first priority is growth.

He argues that growth serves a fairly narrow set of interests, primarily those of property owners. Growth, in his view, does little to reduce unemployment, for employment growth promotes in-migration. He but-tresses this position with statistics on a number of metropolitan areas show-ing that there is little or no correlation between growth rate and unemploy-ment rate. He also cites a number of studies that showed or attempted to show that economic growth often costs as much in new services as it con-tributes in new revenues. He does this to refute two of the main arguments behind the promotion of growth, that it will improve labor market condi-tions and that it will reduce tax (particularly property tax) burdens.

The article ends by saying, in effect, that it does not have to be this way, that we would be much better off as a nation if we decided on a very differ-ent basis where capital was to be invested. Clearly Molotch does not like the growth machine and hopes that we can change our ways. His overall view fits very comfortably with a Marxian outlook, for it is consistent with the Marxian view that "the state is the executive committee of the bourgeoisie." In this view, underneath democratic rights like universal suffrage—the "for-mal freedoms," as Marx termed them—government basically serves the inter-ests of capital. But, as will become apparent, others have come to Molotch-like conclusions from many points on the political spectrum. In fact, one can even come to some Molotch-like conclusions about how things work from the apolitical perspective of systems engineering.[12]

CITY LIMITS: HOW MUCH CAN A CITY DO?

One very basic question about city governance is simply that of how much one can reasonably expect a city to do. This question is not only relevant to practical questions of policy, but it is also relevant to broader normative questions.[13] Let us say that we observe that the city is spending a great deal of money to promote economic growth. Some of that money ultimately ends up in the pockets of wealthy individuals as dividends, profits, and capital gains on the sale of land and buildings. At the same time we observe that although there is a substantial amount of poverty in the city, the city does not do much by way of income redistribution. We observe that the city does not attempt to tax the prosperous heavily in order to aid the poor. It has no income tax nor does it levy an excise tax on luxury goods. Is the city gov-ernment to be faulted for such behavior? If one thinks that those who govern had many options and chose of their own free will to favor the interests of the well-to-do over the interests of the poor, one is likely to find them much at fault. On the other hand, if one sees them as having no other realistic op-tions because the city is locked in economic competition with other cities, then one may see them as blameless. One cannot fault the city government for not doing what it cannot do. Cast more generally, the question is just how much freedom of maneuver does a city have.

A very influential book that attempts to answer this question is Paul E. Peterson's *City Limits*, published in 1981. Peterson's argument in brief is that one cannot analyze the political behavior of cities as one can that of nations, because cities operate under so many more constraints.

> They cannot make war or peace; they cannot issue passports or forbid outsiders from entering their territory; they cannot issue currency; they cannot control imports or erect tariff walls. There are other things that cities cannot do, but these are some of the most crucial limits on their powers.[14]

Peterson looks back at the pluralist, elitist, and regime theorists described previously. He argues that they all have some portion of the truth but that they all miss a larger reality. The larger reality is that cities all operate under much greater constraints than do national governments and that their range of choices, regardless of which pluralities, elites, or regimes are in power, is very limited.

> The place of the city within the larger political economy of the nation fundamentally effects policy choices that cities make. In making these decisions, cities select those policies which are in the interest of the city, taken as whole. It is these city interests, not the internal struggles for power within cities, that limit city policies and condition what local governments do.[15]

Note the phrase "interest of the city, taken as a whole." This is very much at variance with those who argue that regimes and elites generally do what is in the interests of their own members but that what they do may be very much to the disadvantage of other parts of the city's populace. The Peterson argument is that the city is faced with so many external constraints that its various factions cannot simply ignore the outside world while they fight with each other. If the ship is cruising along in calm waters with no problems, then the crew can devote most of their energies to fighting with one another about minor matters such as who gets the best cabins. However, if the ship has a hole below the waterline and is in danger of sinking, the crew have to make common cause with one another and deal with the problem no matter how selfish they may be or how much they may dislike each other.

Specifically, the constraints on the city that Peterson considers most important are those alluded to in the first quote—the openness of the city's economy. People are mobile and capital is mobile. If the city adopts policies that discourage capital investment in the city and drive out more prosperous residents, budget deficits will loom, the city will find it more and more difficult to provide public services, and the pain inflicted by a shrinking economy will be felt by very large numbers of city residents. The city will have to deal with the problem by changing its policies. Regardless of what sort of policies those who rule would prefer, they will have to make similar adjustments because they face similar economic necessities.

Peterson argues that cities cannot do income redistribution. Income redistribution necessarily means taxing the prosperous to distribute money to the poor. The city that does this drives out those it would seek to tax, for the city has no control over its borders.[16] Likewise, if the city lays a heavier burden on capital than competing jurisdictions do, then it risks seeing new investment diverted to other jurisdictions, and it may also see parts of its own economic base moving out as well. When that happens, it will have fewer resources to support the functions of city government, including redistribution.

Peterson's argument that cities cannot do significant amounts of income redistribution parallels the conclusions of theorists of public finance. Richard Musgrave in *The Theory of Public Finance*, a standard text whose first edition appeared in 1959, stated that income redistribution in an ideal fiscal system would be entirely the responsibility of the federal government.[17] He argued that if income redistribution were left to city and state governments, disparities in the generosity of different places would lead to migration from place to place simply to obtain assistance. Only if the federal government provides a standard pattern of income redistribution throughout the nation can this wasteful movement be avoided. There is also the clear implication that if one place offered generous redistribution while another place was relatively stingy, the more generous place would be at a clear competitive disadvantage because of the drain upon its treasury by the poor.

Whether Peterson was influenced by Musgrave's work or whether he arrived at the same conclusion about income redistribution by a different path is not clear. Peterson lists Musgrave's book in the bibliography of *City Limits*. On the other hand, he makes no mention of Musgrave in the text of his book.

Note that Peterson and Molotch, described in the previous section, see a great deal of the same reality. Molotch comes at it from a Marxian perspective. Peterson comes at it from a relatively centrist perspective. Molotch deplores what he sees. Peterson simply describes what he sees and urges us to be realistic. Both see, for different reasons, a municipal preoccupation with the issue of economic growth.

THE POLITICAL ECONOMY PERSPECTIVE

In the last two decades or so what has come to be termed the Political Economy perspective has become very prominent in urban studies. The term *political economy* is a very old one. Before economics assumed its modern and highly mathematical form, the subject was often referred to as "political economy." At that time economics and political science were not regarded as separate subjects. Adam Smith, John Stuart Mill, David Ricardo, and other classical economists were "political economists." So, too, was Karl Marx. The present Political Economy school represents a combination of economic and political thinking and in that way harks back to the old political economy tradition. Note that the Political Economy school is not the only contemporary school of thought that harks back to the political economy tradition. The Public Choice school, which comes from much further Right on the political spectrum, also seeks to unify political and economic thinking to analyze events and to propose policies.[18]

Political Economy is partially rooted in Marxism and shows that lineage in many ways, but one does not have to be a Marxist to take its arguments seriously or to view many issues from its perspective. The Political Economy school is large and represents a diverse group of scholars, so no one statement will fit all its adherents. Below are a few general positions held by many members of the school.

1. Most Political Economists assign a central role to capital—to large corporations and major financial institutions—in shaping the urban environment. They see major links between government and capital, and they see government as largely serving the interests of capital. And they do not see the power of capital or the nexus between capital and government as being benign.

2. Members of the Political Economy school place a great deal of emphasis on class conflict and "class struggle" and see the results of such conflict reflected in many aspects of the urban scene.

3. Members of the school believe that much of what happens in cities can be understood by viewing cities as nodes or elements in the world capitalist system (see Chapter 7).

4. Many members of the Political Economy school take a different view of the matter of consumer choice than do mainstream economists. Traditionally, economists have taken consumer preferences as given and then have seen businesses as competing with each other to meet those preferences. This is not to say that they deny that consumers' preferences are modified somewhat by advertising, packaging, merchandising, and the like. Political Economists tend not to see consumer preferences as essentially given. Rather, they see consumer demand as being largely shaped and manipulated by producers. And they hold this view whether the consumer preferences in question are for transportation, for the ordinary run of merchandise, for housing, or almost anything else that people spend money on.

Note that none of the above is unique to the Political Economists. One does not have to be a Political Economist to be concerned about the power of capital, nor is such concern new. The Standard Oil Corporation was broken up by antitrust prosecution in 1911 because of that concern. The antitrust prosecution of Microsoft at this writing is a modern expression of that concern. The present-day push for campaign finance reform is in part an expression of concern about the power of big business to influence the process of government. Similarly, one does not have to be a Political Economist to be aware of the growth of world trade and the flow of international capital and the fact that these can have powerful influences upon urban economies. Political Economists take a baleful view of the actions of multinational corporations. At the other end of the political spectrum so too does the populist conservative Patrick Buchanan.[19] Many who are not Political Economists have viewed with alarm the power of advertising to mold consumer choice.[20] Thus it is often not possible to draw a hard line between the views of the Political Economists and more centrist tendencies. Rather, the distinction is more one of emphasis and degree.

Though the Political Economy school has become extremely prominent in urban studies, it has made very little impression upon mainstream economics. In fact, Political Economists and mainstream economists largely ignore each other. Political Economists are rarely cited in the mainstream economic literature, nor do they cite mainstream economists very often.[21]

To provide some sense of the Political Economy perspective we look at a few issues below.

In general, members of the Political Economy school see the metropolitan land use pattern as shaped in large measure by the owners of capital. Rather than seeing investment decisions as being responses to larger, impersonal economic forces, the Political Economist is more likely to see them as the result of conscious decisions by major players who have considerable freedom of choice. Again, there is not an absolute disagreement between the Political Economy and the ecological or neoclassical economic view. The Political Economist will not deny that the owners of capital do face many constraints in the marketplace. Conversely, the scholar of more mainstream orientation will not deny that a single investment can have a major effect on the pattern of land use. Nor will he or she deny that major property owners or developers can influence the decisions of government about infrastructure investments like water and sewer lines or highway interchanges that shape the pattern of land development. Instead, there is a difference in emphasis. Consider how Michael Smith (who writes from the Political Economy perspective) characterizes the land development process.

> The adage that people can vote with their feet if they are unhappy with their environment tends to distort reality. The single most important determinant of "why people move" has been shown to be "where the jobs are." This means that corporate elite decisions about where work will be available contribute significantly to the pattern of population movement to suburbia, to rural areas, to the South, and to the Sunbelt. Neither random citizen choice nor public planning has determined the pattern of population distribution; rather, employers pursuing criteria of profit, economic efficiency, and internal convenience have set that pattern.

Referring to decisions about where to build shopping center, he asserts:

> These kinds of large scale investments no longer follow population flows but shape the pattern of population movement, so as to yield further profitable mo-

bility. . . . Needless to say, the auto-highway-rubber-oil-asphalt industrial complex remains supportive of suburban sprawl and the speculative investments that contribute to it.[22]

Note the emphasis on the power of choice assigned to capital and also upon the link between capital and government. In this vision it is capital that makes the primary decisions and the rest of society that follows along. A writer of a different school might describe the process of shopping center location as being driven largely by a mass of individual or "atomistic" residential decisions. Those atomistic decisions would determine the distribution of buying power. In this picture the shopping center investor would assiduously study census and other data to decide where the buying power is or will be, where competing retailers were located, and the like, and would then choose the shopping center site largely on those bases. It is not the purpose of this chapter to argue the point, but only to note the difference in perspectives.

As another example of the Political Economy perspective, consider the explosion of the automobile population of the United States and the concurrent decline of public transportation. The reasons offered earlier in this book were essentially a natural-process explanation. We noted rising real incomes, an apparent preference for the car because of flexibility of route and schedule, and an apparent preference on the part of much of the population for a relatively low-density pattern of settlement that favors the automobile and disfavors public transportation. We also noted federal and state investment in major highways, largely in response to the public's demand for a road system suitable to its newly acquired cars and emerging suburban pattern of settlement.

The Political Economist may not deny any of these factors. But he or she will ask us to consider the hand of major corporations in this process as well. Perhaps it was not all quite so natural and inevitable as the explanation in this text suggests. He or she might ask us to consider just how much influence the automobile companies, the oil companies, and the major construction firms have had on decisions about highway construction. In the United States gasoline costs about one third or one fourth as much as it does in most of the nations of Western Europe. The difference in price is almost entirely a difference in taxation. Low fuel costs obviously favor the automobile. The Political Economist might ask us to consider why the United States taxes gasoline so lightly relative to how the Europeans tax it. He or she might suggest that we consider the role of big capital when we conduct this inquiry.

In Chapter 3 the rapid decline of the streetcar was explained in terms of impersonal economic and technological forces such as dispersion of population, widespread automobile ownership, and the interference effects of automobiles and vehicles that run in fixed tracks on the same streets. Again, the Political Economist will not deny these arguments. But he or she will point us to the buying up of streetcar lines in a number of cities by automobile and oil companies and their replacement with bus lines that were ultimately discontinued.[23] The economist or urbanologist of more mainstream tendency may retort that this did indeed happen in a number of cities, but that overwhelming economic and technological forces would have taken us to the same place in any case. And there the matter may be argued back and forth. The point is simply that there is a substantial difference in perspective.

More generally, members of the Political Economy school take a different view of the matter of consumer choice than do mainstream economists. The Political Economist, with that school's emphasis on the pervasive power of capital, sees consumer demand as less autonomous and more manipulated than does the mainstream economist. From a mainstream position, one might explain the great waves of suburbanization after World War II in terms of the public's housing preferences coupled with rising real incomes. The mainstream writer would admit that the favorable tax treatment of housing and the availability of mortgage credit on favorable terms are part of the equation. Thus political decisions, specifically actions of the Congress, play a role here. But he or she might also argue that such legislation was to a great extent a congressional response to the preferences of the electorate. The Political Economist might view it somewhat differently and ask us from whence the consumers' preferences really come?

> While many suburbanites moved out of the cities to escape crime, crowding, noise, and the presence of minorities, the families who made the suburban move exercised less choice about it than is commonly supposed. . . . In their attempt to market the new subdivisions, developers virtually invented the images that came to be thought of as the American Dream, with the suburban house at its center. The suburbs were *created first by decisions of entrepreneurs and only second by the choices of suburbanites themselves.* . . . [italics added][24]

The marketplace pictured above is very different from the mainstream economist's concept of "consumer sovereignty."[25]

SUMMARY

In this chapter we presented five different perspectives on city government.

1. The pluralist perspective. This view is most closely associated with the political scientist Robert Dahl. In this view political power is widely dispersed. The political establishment, which he terms the "political stratum," is very much guided by the will and interests of the mass of the "constituents" even when the constituents are not actively participating in politics. The political stratum is an open group, and the sorts of people of whom it is composed can change substantially from time to time.
2. Elites and regimes. Those, like Clarence Stone, who see city governance in terms of elites and regimes argue that power is much less widely dispersed than the pluralists claim. Elite and regime theorists see city governance as largely reflecting the interests of a relatively narrow range of affluent and well-connected in-

dividuals. In particular, they see city government as being influenced by and serving the interest of those who own or control large amounts of capital.

3. The city as growth machine. In this view, of which Harvey Molotch is the best-known proponent, the city can be regarded as a growth machine whose policies are primarily directed to pursuing economic growth. This behavior primarily serves those who stand to benefit from development because they own property—in Molotch's words, "a land-based elite."

4. How much can a city do? In this section we discussed the argument of Paul Peterson that city governments are very much constrained because their economies are completely open to the rest of the nation. Because cities can exercise no control over the movement of people, goods, or capital, their range of policy choices is very limited. According to Peterson it is largely the necessities of interplace competition rather than the details of city politics that shape municipal policy.

5. The Political Economy perspective. This perspective, which draws heavily on Marxian thought, emphasizes the role of capital in shaping public policy and sees both municipal and higher levels of government as largely serving the interests of capital.

NOTES

1. An example of a parsimonious statement in the physical sciences would be Boyle's law (formulated by Robert Boyle in the seventeenth century). It states that if temperature is held constant, the pressure of a gas in a container is inversely proportional to its volume. It can be expressed very compactly as $PV = K$. There are no further qualifications. It has proven useful and satisfactory for many purposes over more than three centuries.

2. I have adapted this phrase from a more complex formulation by Clarence Stone in "The Study of Politics in Urban Development," in *The Politics of Urban Development*, edited by Clarence N. Stone and Heywood T. Sanders (Lawrence: University of Kansas Press, 1987), p. 18. "In political science, parsimony is always at war with the importance of context and with the capacity of humankind to analyze context and to take some hand in altering social conditions."

3. Robert A. Dahl, *Who Governs?* (New Haven: Yale University Press, 1961). For another presentation of the pluralist view written in the same period, see Edward C. Banfield, *Political Influence* (Glencoe, Ill.: The Free Press, 1961).

4. Ibid., p. 1.

5. Ibid., p. 91.

6. Ibid., pp. 12–14.

7. Peter Bachrach and Morton S. Baratz, "Two Faces of Power," in *Readings in Urban Politics*, 2nd edition, edited by Harlan Hahn and Charles H. Levine (University of Kansas Press, 1984), pp. 149–158.

8. Clarence N. Stone, *Regime Politics: Governing Atlanta from 1946 to 1988* (University of Kansas Press, 1989), p. 1.

9. See the Introduction in Stone, op. cit.

10. Stone, op. cit., p. 6.

11. Harvey Molotch, "The City as a Growth Machine: Toward a Political Economy of Place," *American Journal of Sociology* 82, no. 2, pp. 309–332.

12. Jay Forrester, *Urban Dynamics* (Cambridge: M.I.T. Press, 1969). Forrester uses a systems model of his own devising, System Dynamics, which contains standard ideas in systems analysis such as set points and feedback loops. He then models urban behavior with no political content at all and reaches some conclusions similar to Molotch's as well as to Peterson's.

13. In social science and policy literature one often sees references to "positive questions" and also to "normative" questions. The former type are questions about how things work, and

they have no more element of moral judgment attached than do questions in chemistry. The latter refer to questions that involve moral or value judgments. What will happen if we reduce the funds available to aid poor people? is a positive question. Should we do this or is it right to do this? is a normative question. The two are linked in that before we make the normative judgment we may want to have the positive "what will happen if" question answered. They are also linked in that where we stand on normative issues may determine on which positive questions we choose to focus. Nonetheless, in principle they are two fundamentally different types of questions.

14. Paul E. Peterson, *City Limits* (University of Chicago Press, 1981), p. 4.
15. Ibid.
16. It has been argued by some that New York City's brush with bankruptcy in 1975 was in large measure brought on by the city's attempt to do a great deal of redistribution, such as free tuition at city universities. For a detailed presentation of this position, see Ken Auletta, *The Streets Were Paved with Gold* (New York: Random House, 1979).
17. Richard Musgrave, *The Theory of Public Finance* (New York: McGraw-Hill, 1959). See also subsequent editions with Peggy Musgrave. For many years the book was the standard text in public finance.
18. The Public Choice school argues that economic man, the behavioral model of economics, is also the right model for political science, and it seeks to unify the two disciplines around this model. Though agreed on the need for blending political and economic analysis, the Political Economy school and Public Choice school are quite far apart on many issues. Their origins are different too, for the Political Economy school has many Marxian roots, whereas the Public Choice school is clearly on the right-hand side of the political spectrum. For a brief and very readable introduction to the Public Choice viewpoint, see James Gwartney and Richard Wagner, "The Public Choice Revolution," *The Intercollegiate Review* 23, no. 2 (Spring 1988), pp. 17–26. For more formal and extended exposition, see other writings by these two authors as well as works by James Buchanan and Gordon Tullock.
19. Patrick Buchanan, *The Great Betrayal* (New York: Little Brown, 1998).
20. In *The Affluent Society* (New York: Houghton Mifflin, 1969), John Kenneth Galbraith takes the view that consumer preferences are strongly manipulated by advertising and marketing and that if consumers' choices are really engineered the traditional notion of "consumer sovereignty" is largely a myth.
21. Some years ago, the Nobel Prize–winning macroeconomist Robert Solow was asked why standard economics textbooks offered so little discussion of Marxism. His rather haughty reply was "we neglect it because it is negligible." Right or wrong, the reply does indicate how many mainstream economists view the matter. Marxian and mainstream economics have followed separate paths for many decades. The first big conceptual break was over the labor theory of value, which the Marxists retained and which mainstream economics abandoned at the time of the "marginalist revolution" in economics about 1870.
22. Michael P. Smith, *The City and Social Theory* (New York: St. Martin's Press, 1979), pp. 239–40.
23. See Glenn Yago, *The Decline of Transit: Urban Transportation in German and U.S. Cities, 1900–1970* (Cambridge: Cambridge University Press).
24. Dennis R. Judd and Todd Swanstrom, *City Politics: Private Power and Public Policy* (New York: HarperCollins College Publishers, 1994), p. 192.
25. This chapter sketches only a few aspects of the Political Economy perspective. For the reader interested in pursuing it further there is a huge literature to be explored. Among textbooks, the reader might look up Thomas Shannon, *Urban Problems in a Sociological Perspective* (Random House, 1983); M. Gottdeiner, *The New Urban Sociology* (McGraw-Hill, 1995); Nancy Kleniewsky, *Cities Change and Conflict: A Political Economy of Urban Life* (Boston: Wadsworth, 1997); or the Judd and Swanstrom book quoted previously. There is also a very large literature of journal articles and books other than texts. For academicians who write from the Political Economy position or from nearby terrain, the reader might look into the work of David Harvey, Manual Castells, Michael P. Smith, Joe R. Feagin, Neil Smith, P. L. Knox, Saskia Sassen, Harvey Molotch, Ann Markusen, Pierre Clavel, John Forester, Robert Beauregard, Bennett Harrison, Barry Bluestone, M. Gottdeiner, John H. Mollenkopf, John Freidman, and Susan S. and Norman I. Fainstein.

REFERENCES*

Dahl, Robert A. *Who Governs?* New Haven: Yale University Press, 1961.

Gottdeiner, M. *The Decline of Urban Politics.* Thousand Oaks, CA.: Sage Publications, 1987.

Hahn, Harlan, and Charles H. Levine, eds. *Readings in Urban Politics.* New York: Longman, 1984.

Judd, Dennis R., and Paul P. Cantor, eds. *The Politics of Urban America.* Boston: Allyn and Bacon, 1998.

Osborne, David, and Ted Gaebler. *Reinventing Government.* New York: Plume, The Penguin Group, 1993.

Perry, David C. ed. *Building the Public City.* Thousand Oaks, CA.: Sage Publications, 1995.

Peterson, Paul E. *City Limits.* University of Chicago Press, 1981.

Savas, Emanuel E. *Privatization: The Key to Better Government.* Chatham, N.J.: Chatham House Publishers, 1987.

Stone, Clarence N., Robert K. Wheland, and William J. Murin. *Urban Policy and Politics in a Bureaucratic Age.* Englewood Cliffs, N.J.: Prentice-Hall, 1979.

Stone, Clarence N. *Regime Politics.* University Press of Kansas, 1989.

Stone, Clarence N., and Heywood T. Sanders, eds. *The Politics of Urban Development*, University Press of Kansas, 1987.

*Includes references for previous chapter.

Chapter

6

City Finances: Raising the Money and Paying the Bills

For many mayors, city managers, and county executives the item that causes most concern is the municipality's finances. Almost inevitably department heads will ask for more money than is available in the budget. Hard choices have to be made. The citizens both demand high-quality public services and resist increases in the tax rate. For any municipal administration, raising taxes in the face of an upcoming election is a high-risk proposition, no matter how justified the increase may be. If the city or town or county is mounting an economic development program (see Chapter 7), its leaders will worry that higher tax rates will drive away prospective firms. But of course prospective firms will want both low tax rates and also high-quality municipal services. Not only will the municipal government have to concern itself with how it will finance what it wants to do, but it will also have to concern itself with paying for things that it is required to do by higher levels of government but for which it is not given additional funding. This sort of "unfunded mandate" is a fine raiser of mayoral blood pressure.

The municipal picture is complicated for several reasons. Cities vary greatly in size and in the responsibilities that they must meet. Some cities must provide for public education, but in other locales that function is taken care of by an independent school district or by county government. Some cities must handle public welfare, but in other cities that is a county function. Fiscal capacity—the size of the tax base—relative to need varies greatly from one municipality to another. A growing city in the suburbs that has an affluent population and has been successful in attracting business investment is likely to be in a far better fiscal position than an old central city that has difficulty in attracting new business investment and has been steadily losing its more affluent residents.

Terms like *city* and *town* are legal terms. Though *city* conjures up the image of a large urbanized place and *town* a smaller and less urban picture, the categories overlap greatly. Some towns are larger and more urban than some of the cities in the same state. Sometimes an area can be highly urbanized and have no cities. For example, Nassau county in New York State has a population of almost 1.3 million and is to all intents and purposes as urban as many cities. It contains no cities. It does, however, contain the town of Hempstead with a population of 725 thousand. Were Hempstead to be incorporated as a city, it would be the eleventh largest city in the United States. In the material that follows we use the term *municipality* or *city* generically for any substate unit of government whether it is legally a city, town, or a county.

MUNICIPAL FINANCE IN THE LARGER PICTURE

Municipal governments exist in a national framework of public finance, so we begin with a few words about the overall picture. Figure 6–1 shows an overview of the U.S. system of public finance. The local government block in

FIGURE 6–1 The U.S. Fiscal System. There is a large downward transfer from the federal to the state governments and an even larger transfer from the state governments to local governments. There is also a much smaller transfer from the federal government directly to local governments. In this figure the term *Local Governments* includes numerous quasi governments, such as school districts.

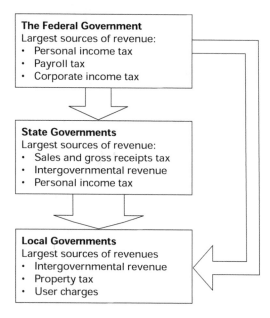

The Federal Government
Largest sources of revenue:
• Personal income tax
• Payroll tax
• Corporate income tax

State Governments
Largest sources of revenue:
• Sales and gross receipts tax
• Intergovernmental revenue
• Personal income tax

Local Governments
Largest sources of revenues
• Intergovernmental revenue
• Property tax
• User charges

the figure includes not only municipal governments but also a variety of districts, most notably school districts.

The federal government is the largest collector of taxes and also transfers a great deal of money downward. The states receive most of these transfers but, in turn, transfer even larger sums to local governments. Except for some very minor flows, intergovernmental transfers go only one way—downward. Note that the three levels of government rely upon a substantially different set of revenue sources. Both the downward transfers and the different revenue sources make considerable sense when viewed in terms of intergovernmental competition.

The largest revenue sources of the federal government are the personal income tax, payroll taxes (social security), and the corporate income tax. Compared to state governments the federal government taxes both individuals and corporations at relatively high rates. One reason that it can do this is because it has no competitors. It is difficult to escape the reach of the Internal Revenue Service (IRS) by moving. No state could tax individuals or corporations at rates approaching those employed by the federal government because it would very quickly find itself quickly losing jobs and more affluent residents to other states.

Most states make use of a sales tax of no more than several percent. Even at these relatively low rates, state governments must be concerned about diverting sales to other states, the so-called "border effect" of sales taxes. The majority of states also levy a personal income tax, but at a small fraction of the federal rate.[1] Those states that levy a corporate income tax also use a rate that is a fraction of the federal rate.

Local governments are even more restrained by competition for businesses and more prosperous residents than are the states. Very few municipal governments make use of either the personal or the corporate income for fear of driving individuals or business across the municipal line. Those that do make use of these taxes do so at very modest rates. Some municipal governments make use of sales taxes, usually as an add-on to the state sales tax. Typically, the municipality that does so will use a low rate, such as 1 or 2 percent, so as not to drive too many sales across the municipal line.

The one tax upon which municipal governments rely heavily is the property tax. In fact, they raise several times as much revenue from this tax as from all other taxes combined. A major reason for favoring the property tax is that property is immobile. One generally cannot put one's house on a trailer and tow it across the town line because the town has just raised property taxes. But even in the case of the property tax municipal governments must pay attention to how their tax rates compare with those of their neighbors. Property tax rates that are higher than those of nearby communities may divert new investment in residences and commercial buildings to other communities. And in some municipalities, high property tax rates may increase the rate of building abandonment or may discourage investment in the maintenance and improvement of existing buildings. In that indirect sense, even buildings are mobile in the face of high property taxation.

As the employment figures in Table 6–1 suggest, it is substate governments that provide the largest share of public services. Note that school districts alone have two million more employees than does the federal government. The reader might wonder how state and local employment can exceed federal employment by such a large ratio when the federal government collects more in taxes than both state and local governments combined. The main reason is that much of the revenue that the federal government collects is not used for the delivery of services but for the making of transfers. There are the transfers to state and local governments shown in Figure 6–1. In addition, even larger sums are transferred to individuals. When federal expenditures are categorized by function, over 60 percent are for human resources, of which the vast majority are payments to individuals. In some cases, such as

TABLE 6–1 Government Employment, Own Source Revenues, and Expenditures by Level, 1994 (Employment in thousands, revenues in billions)

Employment	
Federal (civilian)	2,993
Federal less U.S. Postal Service and Department of Defense	1,243
State	4,673
Local	11,151
Counties	2,270
Municipalities (cities, towns, and boroughs)	2,665
Townships	424
School districts	5,134
Special districts	627
Revenues exclusive of transfers (in billions)	
Federal	1,397
State	637
Local (including districts)	479
Expenditures	
Federal	1,630
State	775
Local	719

Source: Statistical Abstract of the United States, 117th edition, chapters on federal and on state and local finances.

Notes: The revenue figures and the federal employment figures are from 1994. The state and local employment figures are from 1993 and 1992. The revenue figures include taxes, user charges, and intergovernmental transfers. They do not include borrowing. The expenditure figures include some double counting because of intergovernmental grants. (The same dollar that appears as an expenditure for the grantor government will also show up as an expenditure when spent by the grantee government.)

Social Security and Medicare, the transfers are made directly. In other programs, such as Medicaid, the payments go through the states. In either case, it is this "money pump" characteristic of the federal government that accounts for its much higher ratio of expenditures to employees as compared with either state or local government.

Table 6–2 shows how local governments, considered as a whole, spend their funds. As you can see in Table 6–2, by far the biggest item is public education. This is hardly surprising. In the mid-1990s there were about 47 million students in grades K through 12 in public schools at an average cost of approximately $5,000 per pupil. Because of its singular importance in municipal finance, public education is discussed separately later in this chapter.

Public welfare, which includes Aid for Families with Dependent Children and a variety of other programs for poor people, is usually a county function, with the funds being a mixture of federal, state, and county monies.[2] Most cities thus have no expenditures for this category. However, a

TABLE 6–2 Local Government Expenditures, 1993 (figures in billions)

Direct expenditure	685.3
Education	252.2
Elementary and secondary education	238.1
Higher education	14.2
Public welfare	30.0
Hospitals	35.0
Health	15.0
Highways	26.1
Police protection	31.2
Fire protection	15.8
Corrections	10.5
Natural resources	2.6
Sewerage	21.6
Solid waste management	11.4
Housing and community development	16.7
Governmental administration	31.3
Parks and recreation	13.3
Interest on general debt	31.1
Utility and liquor store	75.0
Insurance trust	11.9

Source: Statistical Abstract of the United States, 116th edition, 1996, Table 472.

Notes: The utility and liquor store category consists primarily of utilities. Of these, the most important are water supply and sewerage, electric power, natural gas, and transit. These are all supplied on a user charge basis. In some states the sale of liquor is a state monopoly and hard liquor is sold only in state licensed liquor stores. The insurance trust is primarily contributions for employee pensions.

few, such as New York City where the city is coterminous with five counties (boroughs), have very large expenditures in this category. In the mid-1990s New York City spent about $7 billion in this category for a case load of about one million people.

The other functions listed under general expenditure constitute the great bulk of local government expenditures. How much in any category will be a county function and how much a municipal function will vary greatly from state to state and often within the state as well.

For the taxpayer the important thing about local government taxes is not exactly how those taxes are divided between local governments and districts, but how much is the total load. In many cases the taxpayer may not be aware of exactly how the burden is divided. For example, the biggest tax used at the local level is the property tax, and that may go to a number of different jurisdictions. In many states, cities and towns are contained within counties, and all of these jurisdictions levy property taxes. In many states school districts are separate from general-purpose governments, and they, too, levy taxes.

Revenues and Taxes for Local Governments

For the reasons discussed before—major responsibilities for providing public services and severe limits on how steeply they can tax—local governments are heavily dependent upon intergovernmental transfers. Most of the transfer money they get comes to them from the state government. Another significant source of local revenue is charges. These are fees charged for a variety of services, including transportation, hospitals, water, sewer, and trash pickup, as well as the use of facilities such as parks. By far the biggest tax source for both local governments and school districts is the property tax. Because it is such a mainstay of local public finance, the property tax is worth special attention.

The Property Tax

In late 1990s local governments collected over $200 billion in property taxes, or roughly $800 for every person in the United States. Of that figure about two fifths was collected by school districts.

One reason that local governments rely heavily upon the property tax is the immobility of property. Another reason is simply tradition. The tax has been in use by local governments since before the Revolution. Finally, the tax is simple to administer and, because land and structures cannot be concealed, it is extremely difficult to evade.

The basic mechanics of the property tax are fairly simple. The municipality has an assessor or an assessment department. The role of the assessor is to determine the value of each piece of real property in the city and record that value on the tax rolls of the municipality. By value we mean what the property would sell for in a fair market or "arms length" transaction.[3] There are two main categories in the tax roll, land and improvements, the latter term meaning structures. Generally speaking, property that is privately owned, whether by individuals or businesses, is subject to property tax. Property owned by government and by nonprofit institutions such as philanthropies and churches is not subject to property taxation. The property tax base of the municipality consists of all of the land and improvements subject to tax.

The same rate—so much per $100 or $1,000 of assessed value—is applied to every property in the municipality. The process of collection is quite simple. The municipality's receiver of taxes sends a bill to each property owner. If the bill is not paid by a certain time, the municipality can go to court, take the property, sell it at auction, and recompense itself for unpaid taxes and expenses. The basic equation of the property tax is

$$\text{tax base} \times \text{tax rate} = \text{tax yield}$$

If, for example, the municipality contains $500,000,000 of taxable real property and has a tax rate of $2 per $100 of assessed value, then the tax yield will be

$$\$500,000,000 \times 2/100 = \$10,000,000$$

The municipality has no direct and immediate control over the size of its tax base. However, it can adjust the tax rate on the basis of its revenue needs. In principle, the municipality or district can set the property tax at whatever rate is required to generate the necessary revenue. The reality is very different. High property tax rates will slow the growth of the tax base by making the community less attractive as a business or residential location. A decision to raise the property tax above the rates in competing districts thus reduces the future capacity of the municipality to raise revenues because it reduces the growth of the property tax base. High property tax rates may have adverse effects on the quality of properties. For example, if high property tax rates sharply reduce or eliminate profits on a rental property, the property owner may try to squeeze out some profit in the short term by skimping on repair and maintenance—the disinvestment process discussed in Chapter 9. Over the long term that will cause the quality of the structure to decline. Such decline ultimately reduces the structure's market value, and that, in turn, shrinks the property tax base.

Property taxes are often a major source of political contention. For example, in a reasonably prosperous but not especially affluent suburb the average single-family house might pay several thousand dollars per year in property taxes. Thus an attempt to raise the property tax rate by even a few cents per $100 of assessed value may encounter considerable resistance from the citizens. In a number of states citizen resistance to increases in property taxes has resulted in referendums that limited the rates at which property taxes could be increased and, in some cases, actually rolled property taxes back. The best known of these is referenda California's Proposition 13, passed by the voters in 1978.

In many suburban areas the property tax bill from the school district is as large as that from the municipality. Many school districts have seen great controversy over school budgets because of their property tax implications. In states where school district budgets must be approved by voters in the district, many a budget has been voted down. A pared-down budget is then submitted and the district residents vote again.

The property tax is not directly tied to the taxpayer's ability to pay, as is an income tax, but rather to the amount of taxable real property that the taxpayer has. Thus it can fall with particular weight upon a low income taxpayers. It might, for example, be a particularly onerous burden upon a retired person whose house was purchased when his or her income was subtantially higher than it is now. Many states attempt to deal with this issue of fairness. In some states a portion of the assessed value of a residential property is exempt from the property tax. These "homestead exemptions" may apply to all residential properties or may be limited to lower income taxpayers. They cause the effective property tax rate to be lower on less valuable properties. Another common arrangement is for the state to allow lower income individuals, or, in some cases, all senior citizens regardless of income, to deduct some of their property tax payments from the amount due on their state income tax. Such arrangements are often referred to as "circuit breakers" with the idea that they prevent a tax overload.

Property Taxes and Zoning

The property tax is intimately involved with the matter of zoning discussed in Chapter 8. For the municipality that is seriously concerned with holding down its property tax rate—and that means almost all municipalities—the nexus between land use controls and property tax rates may be of considerable concern. Some land uses will yield more in property taxes than they will cost in additional services. An example of that case might be corporate headquarters. Acquiring such a facility will put downward pressure on property tax rates. The municipality will be able to fund either the same level of public services at a lower rate or a higher level of public services at the same rate. Other land uses, such as low-cost housing, will cost more in public services than they will provide in tax revenues. Using zoning and other land-use controls to encourage a land-use mix that will hold down property tax rates is generally referred to as *fiscal zoning*. Exactly how far a municipality can go in this regard has been the object of considerable litigation.[4]

A land-use pattern that one sees in some affluent suburban areas such as Connecticut's Fairfield county—large areas devoted to large-lot, single-family development with an occasional corporate headquarters—is in large part a result of fiscal zoning. The municipalities will grant rezonings for corporate headquarters largely for fiscal reasons. The headquarters pay substantial property taxes but do not impose many costs upon the municipality for public services. If the large-lot zoning limits the housing supply nearby and causes many of the corporation's employees to live in other jurisdictions, then it is other jurisdictions that will have to bear the cost of educating their children and providing them with other public services such as fire and police protection. The property tax has been subject to considerable criticism because of its presumed effects upon the land-use pattern and also because it is one of the motivations behind exclusionary zoning, a matter discussed in Chapter 8.

BORROWING BY MUNICIPAL GOVERNMENTS

Municipal governments, like state governments and districts such as school districts, borrow money to make capital expenditures. For several reasons capital expenditures are usually paid for through borrowing rather than out of current expenditures. First, capital expenditures tend to be "lumpy." This means that they occur in an irregular pattern so that paying for them out of current revenues would mean that tax rates would have to move irregularly from year to year.

Writers on public finance speak of "user benefit equity," the idea that those who benefit from a capital expenditure should be the ones who pay for it. Thus, one can argue that if a project such as a highway delivers its benefits over a period of decades it seems reasonable that it should be paid for over a long time period rather than all at once. Municipal governments could pay for some capital projects by putting funds away in a sinking fund and then building the project when they had accumulated sufficient funds. However, this would violate the "user benefit equity" principle. As a more practical matter, allocating funds in this manner would be very unattractive politically for it would put the municipal government in the position of raising taxes without delivering any immediate benefits. This technique is rarely used.

The financial instrument through which state and municipal governments borrow is the municipal bond. A bond is basically a promissory note—a commitment to repay funds that are borrowed. For example, assume that a municipal government sells a $10,000 bond with an interest rate of 6 percent and a maturity of 20 years. This means that every year the municipal government will make an interest payment of $600 (.06 × $10,000) and at the end of the 20 years, on the day that the bond "matures," the municipal government will pay back the original $10,000.

Municipal governments borrow money under strict limits. First, the amount of outstanding debt that they may carry at any time is strictly limited by the state, generally to a percentage of the value of taxable real property in the municipality. For example, in the state of Virginia the outstanding debt of a municipal government may not at any time exceed 10 percent of the value of its real property tax base. Thus a municipality whose municipal tax rolls showed $500 million in taxable real property would be forbidden by state law from at any time having an outstanding debt of more than $50 million. This limit is a matter of state law—recall that municipal governments are "creatures of the state"—and cannot be changed by the municipality.

Second, municipal governments can borrow money only to make capital expenditures. They cannot borrow in order to fund current expenditures or to pay off debt.[5] Payments ("debt service") on outstanding debt must come from current revenues.

Finally, in many states neither the state nor local governments can issue general obligation bonds (see below) without placing the matter on the ballot and submitting it to a referendum. Thus there is direct citizen control in a way that is not the case for other tax or expenditure decisions.

There are two main types of municipal bonds: general obligation (G.O.) bonds and revenue bonds.

1. *General obligation bonds.* These are backed (secured) by the "full faith and credit" of the municipal government. In the event that the municipal government fails to make timely payments on interest or principal, the bond holders can go to court and the court may compel the municipality to use any resource at its disposal to repay the bondholders. Because these bonds are an obligation of the municipal government, they are subject to the debt limits noted above.

2. *Revenue bonds.* These are not backed by the full faith and credit of the municipality. They are, instead, backed by the stream of revenues produced by the project that they are used to construct. Such facilities as toll roads, airports, parking structures, and water and sewer systems that are expected to produce a predictable stream of revenues can be built with revenue bonds. On the other hand, a structure such as a new city hall could not be built with revenue bonds because it does not produce a stream of revenues. Revenue bonds are not an obligation against the full faith and credit of the municipal government but are only an obligation against the project that they were used to finance. For that reason, they are not subject to debt limits. Because revenue bonds do not fall under the municipal debt limits and do not constitute an obligation of municipal government, municipal governments will use them in preference to general obligation bonds when it is feasible. The revenue bond debt of all subnational governments in the United States was more than twice that of general obligation bonds. Most revenue bonds are issued to finance public capital investment. However, some revenue bonds are issued to support private investment. These bonds are generally referred to as industrial development bonds (IDBs) or industrial revenue bonds (IRB)s.

The balanced budget requirement and the limitation on debt often frustrate municipal officials because they may block expenditures or projects that the officials find useful. But the rules are there for a good purpose.[6] They prevent municipal governments from incurring financial obligations beyond their ability to handle them. Many of the restrictions on borrowing came into being after numerous municipal bankruptcies in the nineteenth century.

Since World War II municipal bankruptcies have been rare. Cleveland is the only large city to have defaulted on its bonds since the war. There have, however, been a few close calls. In the mid-1970s New York City teetered on the verge of bankruptcy. The city was losing employment, particularly in manufacturing, and there was considerable migration of its middle class to the suburbs. With a total population in the 7 million range the city had a welfare caseload of about 1 million. The city was saved from bankruptcy by a combination of federal guarantees of its debt and the installation of an Emergency Financial Control Board (EFCB) composed of bankers, businessmen, and leaders of municipal unions, among others, which assumed much of the financial authority formerly exercised by the city government. Drastic cuts were made in municipal services and the size of the city work force, and the city skated away from bankruptcy. Since then there has been no serious threat of bankruptcy for the city, and the EFCB is long since gone. But looming budget deficits and the need for draconian budget cuts is a periodic New York City political drama. At this writing the financial affairs of Washington, D.C. are in the hands of an EFCB appointed by Congress. In the 1990s the only major default on municipal bonds was that of Orange County, California. There, the cause was not fiscal stress but simply malfeasance.[7]

Municipal bonds are subject to special tax treatment by the federal government. Interest paid on municipal bonds is exempt from federal income tax. Therefore, the buyers of municipal bonds, whether they be individuals or corporations, will accept lower interest rates than they would on corporate bonds of comparable risk. It is estimated by the federal government's Office of Management and Budget (OMB) that in the late 1990s the annual revenue loss to the federal government through this mechanism was approximately $13 billion.[8] This constitutes a federal subsidy for the entire range of municipal capital expenditures for it reduces the interest that municipalities must pay on the bonds that they issue. It is an inefficient way to subsidize state and local governments because part of the federal revenue loss is captured in the form of higher after-tax income by those who buy municipal bonds. The buyers of municipal bonds are often high-income individuals, because it is taxpayers in the higher tax brackets who benefit most from the tax-exempt status of the interest on municipal bonds.

One key element in the system of municipal bond financing is the system of bond ratings. In the United States there are several companies, of which the two most prominent are Moody's Investor's Service and Standard and Poor, that do municipal bond ratings. The municipal government planning to issue bonds pays one of the bond rating agencies to rate their bonds.

The rating agency examines the municipal government's entire financial situation, including outstanding debt, tax base, tax rates, trends within the municipal economy, and the like, and then rates the bonds. The rating is the company's estimate of the soundness of the municipality's fiscal situation and thus its capacity to repay the bonds. Municipal governments care considerably about their rating because the higher the rating, all other things being equal, the lower interest rate they will have to pay in order to market the bonds. Though the bond rating system is completely nongovernmental and is not required by law, it has become a well-established institution and almost all municipal bonds are rated. Marketing an unrated bond would be difficult because investors would be likely to interpret the lack of rating as a sign that there was significant risk of default.

Most observers would probably agree that the municipal bond system works reasonably well. Municipal governments can borrow in relatively orderly markets to fund public works. This means that municipal governments can make long-term capital spending plans on a fairly predictable basis. However, the system does have its flaws. The federal indirect subsidy (tax expenditure) for municipal bonds is not an efficient one, as noted, and that has been the object of some criticism by students of public finance. There has also been some criticism of the use of revenue bonds to support private economic activity on the grounds that the lowered interest rates constitute a windfall for firms making use of these bonds.[9] Among scholars of the Political Economy school (see Chapter 5) the entire municipal bond system has come in for heavier criticism on the grounds that in some instances banks and other lenders have made inordinate profits in municipal bonds or have exercised undue influence upon municipal governments. Judd and Swanstrom make this case in some detail in connection with New York City's near-bankruptcy in 1976.[10]

Making the Municipal Budget

Every municipality and district has a budget, generally drawn up on an annual or biannual basis. More than any other document, it is a statement of the policies of the municipality because it indicates how much will be spent on what.

The municipal government makes its decisions about taxation and expenditures under a number of constraints. Municipal governments face the conflicting pressures of citizen demands for services on the one hand and citizen resistance to tax increases on the other hand. Municipal governments are also constrained by fears that increasing their tax rates will weaken their competitive position *vis à vis* other municipalities. Note that this is, in effect, the argument that Paul Peterson made in *City Limits,* as discussed in the preceding chapter. In addition to these general constraints there are also some formal legal constraints.

Municipal budgets are divided into an operating and capital portion. The operating budget funds current expenditures, while the capital budget covers assets with a long service life such as roads, bridges, and buildings.[11] The operating budget must be balanced in each year, or on a two-year basis if the municipality uses a biannual budgeting system. All operating expenses must be covered by revenues. Debt service (payments of interest and principal on outstanding debt) must also be covered out of present revenues. Municipal governments cannot borrow to repay previous borrowings. Note that the situation of state and local governments in these regards is very different from that of the federal government, which does not maintain separate operating and capital budgets and which can borrow—and for many years did borrow—substantial sums to finance current expenditures.[12]

Though municipal governments make their own budgets, they are not entirely free to decide what they will and will not spend money on. Both the state and the federal governments impose numerous requirements that municipal governments must meet. For example, if the state education law requires that classes in elementary school have no more than twenty-five students each, then the municipal government or the school district is bound by that requirement. Local governments are also bound by requirements of the federal government. A number of cities, most notably Los Angeles, have spent large sums of money in order to comply with the federal government's air quality requirements under the Clean Air Act.[13] Local governments have spent money to comply with handicapped access to public buildings, as required under the Americans with Disabilities Act (ADA). In fact, many governors and municipal officials have complained vociferously about "unfunded mandates." These are federal requirements that require or "mandate" actions by lower levels of government without providing funds to meet the expenses that the mandates impose.

Generally, the budget is prepared by the executive branch of the municipal government. It thus comes from the office of the mayor, the city manager, the county executive, or whoever is the head of the executive branch. If the municipal government is of substantial size, it may have a separate budget department that prepares the budget and then submits it to the executive branch, which, perhaps with some modifications, submits it to the legislative branch for enactment. In many municipalities the position of budget director is a very powerful one. Each department submits its budget requests to the budget director. Inevitably, these requests will amount to more than can be financed. The fact that the budget director then recommends to the executive branch how much should be allocated to each department and which items in each department's budget requests should and should not be financed gives the budget director substantial de facto power. As is the case with the federal government, it is the legislative body that levies taxes and appropriates funds. Thus, after the executive branch has prepared the budget it must be submitted to a vote by the city council. The budget is a matter of considerable contention at this point, too, for there is no more serious expression of policy than how money will be raised and what activities will be funded.

THE SPECIAL CASE OF PUBLIC EDUCATION

Public education is by far the single largest expenditure for both local governments and state governments. As of the mid-1990s there were about 47 million students in public schools in grades K through 12. Of those 47 million or so five sixths were educated in independent school districts and the remainder in systems run directly by municipal governments. These districts, which are included in the financial totals for local government, can be regarded as quasi governments in that they have some but not all of the powers of government. All have the power to tax and to issue tax exempt bonds. Some have other powers, such as that of eminent domain.

In the mid-1990s about 47 percent of the costs of the public schools was covered by local governments. In the case of the independent school districts there is only one significant source of locally raised revenue: the property tax levied by the school district. In the case of municipal school systems support can come from any revenue source the municipality has, such as property taxes, sales taxes, other business taxes, and user charges. Another 47 percent of the cost of public education came from the states in the form of grants to municipalities and school districts. The federal government was a small player in the financing of public education, providing only about 6 percent of the total funding. Most of that was for a variety of special programs.

The precise mechanics governing the amount of state aid for public education vary from state to state. In general, the amount of aid a district receives is keyed to the number of students a district educates. The figure used may be enrollments, or it may be the number of students in average daily attendance. Typically, aid is given in inverse relationship to the per student property tax base of the district. A common arrangement is for there to be some minimum amount of aid that goes to the district with the largest tax base per student and then, on a sliding scale, less well endowed districts get larger per pupil aid up to some maximum figure.[14] Beyond that there might be some additional funding to meet special needs. For example, a district might get additional funding to help in the education of handicapped students or students whose native language is not English.

In most states spending per student varies substantially from district to district. One big reason for this is the variation in property tax base per student from one district to another. State aid to districts partly redresses this imbalance, but most states do not do so completely. In general, therefore, school districts that have large amounts of commercial activity within them or that have wealthy populations who live in expensive homes are able to provide a substantially more expensive education for their children than are poorer districts or districts without much commercial tax base.

Over the years many people have felt that it was unjust that the amount spent on a child's education should be a function of where the child lived. A number of suits have been brought to force the states to equalize expenditures in all its school districts. Generally, such suits have been based on the "equal protection" clause of the Fourteenth Amendment of the U.S. Constitution (or on comparable provisions in state constitutions). The argument was that disparities in per pupil expenditures and, by implication, in the quality of education violated the principle that all residents of the nation should receive equal treatment under the law. At this writing there is close to a three-decade-long history of litigation on this subject in the state courts. Its general effect has been to push the states toward equalization of per pupil expenditures between districts. The U.S. Supreme Court has never ruled on this issue, and thus there is still considerable variation from state to state.[15] The subject is discussed in more detail in Chapter 16.

IS THERE A LOCAL GOVERNMENT PUBLIC FINANCE PROBLEM?

If we consider local government public finance in the aggregate, it is hard to say that there is a problem. The overall level of public services in the United States is good when considered on a world standard. Our political processes at all levels determine what percentage of the gross national product (GNP) we spend on the services that local governments provide. If we as a society wanted to spend more on public services and less on private consumption, or the other way around, we would be entirely free to do so. It is hard to argue that we are overtaxed to provide adequate public services, for we spend a smaller percentage of our GNP in the public sector than do most other Western nations that enjoy a comparable living standard.

However, when one drops down below the aggregate level and begins to look jurisdiction by jurisdiction, a problem quickly becomes apparent. There is no mechanism that couples municipal need to municipal fiscal capacity. It is this matter of "fiscal disparity" that is considered to be the urban fiscal problem.[16] Because local governments must raise so much of the money that they spend on public services, and because their per capita tax bases vary so much, the capacity of local governments to provide adequate or better levels of service varies greatly. While one local government may be able to provide high-quality services with moderate tax effort, another government may be very hard pressed to provide adequate services at any feasible level of tax effort.[17] One can make the argument that where a large part of the population is poor there is more need for good public services than where the population is prosperous. For example, prosperous people usually do not need public hospitals, except for emergency care. Poor people, by contrast, are less likely to have medical insurance and are thus likely to need the services of public hospitals much more. One could argue that poor children, by and large, need better schooling than do the children of the middle and upper class (see Chapter 16). More often than not, however, it is the municipality that has an above average percentage of population below the poverty line that is also likely to have a below average per capita tax base.

One way to compare local tax bases is to look at the per capita value of real property subject to tax. In Virginia the average figure for the state was $46.7 thousand per capita. In the southwestern tail of the state, part of the Appalachian region, the counties of Dickenson, Lee, Scott, and Wise had, respectively, values of $28.1, $16.3, $15.4, and $21.6 thousand per capita. In the northeastern part of the state, the affluent counties of Fairfax, Loudon, and Prince William, all within the Washington, D.C. metropolitan area, had values of $86.3, $112.4, and $54.3 thousand, respectively.[18] That constitutes a very large disparity in the ability to support public services. To its credit, and perhaps belying Virginia's conservative political reputation, the state legislature has gone far to adjust the pattern of state aid to local governments to attempt to counterbalance these big disparities, particularly in the field of public education. However, no state is able to compensate fully for disparities between local fiscal capacity and local need.

SUMMARY

Municipal finance must be understood in the context of the overall governmental finance structure of the United States. Because of the problem of interstate and intermunicipal competition, states and municipalities must be much more restrained in their taxing behavior than must the federal government. On the other hand, the majority of public service delivery is in the hands of state and local governments. Consequently, we have evolved a system of downward transfers. Local governments' three largest sources of revenue are intergovernmental transfers (primarily from the states), property taxes, and user charges for services such as water and sewerage, refuse collection, and electric power. Because of intergovernmental competition, municipal governments generally make only modest use of sales taxes, and most make no use at all of income taxes. Municipal governments borrow to make capital investments. Municipal bonds (a generic term for the bonds of all units of government below the federal level) are either general obligation bonds secured by the "full faith and credit" of the municipal government or revenue bonds secured by the revenues produced by the facilities that they were used to construct.

Unlike the federal government, state and local governments can borrow only to make capital investments. They cannot borrow in order to meet operating expenses. Municipal governments operate under balanced budget requirements and debt limits that are designed to prevent them from overextending themselves. Though these limits may frustrate municipal officials, they have been successful in that, except for the period of the Great Depression, municipal bankruptcies have been very rare in the twentieth century.

For local governments (this term includes districts) by far the biggest object of expenditure is public education. In recent years about 47 percent of that cost has been paid locally, primarily through the property tax. Another 47 percent has been carried by the states. The federal share was about 6 percent. In most states the aid formulas for school districts are designed so as to favor districts with smaller per pupil property tax bases. This is done to equalize per pupil expenditures between poor and prosperous districts. Though some reduction in disparities is achieved in this way, full equalization in expenditures between districts has generally not been achieved.

NOTES

1. In 1997 the top bracket in the federal income tax was 39.6 percent. The top bracket in most state income taxes is under 10 percent. Only Montana and California exceeded 10 percent in the early 1990s. For details on state income taxes, see Ronald C. Fisher, *State and Local Public Finance,* 2nd ed. (Chicago: Richard D. Irwin, 1996), Chapter 16.
2. Aid for Families with Dependent Children (AFDC) was phased out under the welfare reform legislation enacted by Congress in the summer of 1996. See Chapter 14.
3. In the case of commercial properties assessors may use the income-generating capacity of the property or the cost of replacement adjusted for depreciation rather than comparable sales. Many assessors assess vacant land at a smaller percentage of actual value than they use for housing or commercial development on the grounds that since vacant land yields no income it should not be taxed heavily.
4. John M. Levy, *Contemporary Urban Planning,* 5th edition (Upper Saddle River, N.J.: Prentice Hall, 2000), Chapter 9.
5. Municipal governments can borrow short term to smooth out their cash flow by issuing tax anticipation notes, bond anticipation notes, or revenue anticipation notes, referred to as TANs, BANs, and RANs. But this does not violate the general principle that expenses must be paid out of current revenues.
6. Some municipal governments have gotten around the debt limit by means of "lease-backs." In such an arrangement the local government will encourage a private company to build the facility and will then sign a long-term lease (up to several decades) with the company for the facility. The lease guarantees the revenue yield to the company and thus helps the company to obtain financing. The municipality gets the facility it wants. In that the lease constitutes a long-term obligation of the municipality, just as bonds would, it seems like a transparent circumvention of the debt limit. Nonetheless, the courts have sustained the use of this technique and held that it does not violate debt limits.
7. The county's commissioner of finance used the proceeds of municipal bonds to speculate in bond markets. As long as interest rates fell, bond prices rose, and he was very successful in this regard. Municipal officials turned a blind eye. When interest rates rose, bond values dropped, and the county defaulted on its debt. Orange County is a wealthy county and had the capacity to make the debt good. However, the county's residents in a referendum refused to allow the county to raise taxes to do this. At this writing the ultimate resolution of the issue is still in question.
8. Revenue losses of this type are usually referred to as "tax expenditures"—in effect, expenditures that are made through the tax side rather than the expenditure side of the budget. A tabulation of such tax expenditures is published annually by the Office of Management and Budget and is summarized in the Federal Government Finances chapter of the *Statistical Abstract of the United States.*
9. This practice has been much criticized on the grounds that it serves little public purpose and largely constitutes a windfall for companies. See, for example, Thomas A. Pascarella and Richard D. Raymond, "Buying Bonds for Business: An Evaluation of the Industrial Revenue Bond Program," *Urban Affairs Quarterly* (now *Urban Review*) 18, no. 1 (September

1982), pp. 73–89. In 1990 Congress imposed some limitations on the issuance of Industrial Revenue Bonds, but they are still in widespread use.

10. Dennis R. Judd and Todd Swanstrom, *City Politics: Private Power and Public Policy* (New York: HarperCollins College Publishers, 1994), pp. 327–33.

11. Typically, a capital item is any item that has an expected service life of three or more years.

12. There is a certain logic to this in that most federal debt is held by Americans and thus is an internal debt. Since states and local governments are much smaller, a much larger share of their total debt is held by parties outside their boundaries and thus is external debt.

13. Details of this may be found on Los Angeles Air Quality Management District Web site: www.aqmd.gov

14. For a more detailed discussion of public school finance, see Chapter 18 in Ronald Fisher, op. cit., or Kern Alexander and Richard G. Salmon, *Public School Finance* (Needham Heights, Mass.: Allyn Bacon, 1995).

15. The legal history is complicated and inconclusive. In 1971 in *Serrano v. Priest* the Supreme Court of California found for the plaintiff (Serrano) that the state's system of locally supported public education violated the equal protection clause of the Fourteenth Amendment. It then appeared to proponents of equalization that the courts would soon require that expenditures be equalized across all districts within each state. This was not to be. Some years later the Supreme Court of the State of Texas ruled that every child was entitled to an "adequate education," but there was no constitutional requirement for an "equal" education. The plaintiffs sought to appeal to the U.S. Supreme Court, but the Court refused to hear the case, thus letting the decision stand. As a result the legal situation differs from state to state. For a further discussion of the legal history, see Chapter 2 in Alexander and Salmon, op. cit. It should be noted that it is not just differences in fiscal capacity that cause differences in expenditures; it is also "tax effort." Some municipalities' citizens are much more willing to tax themselves to support public education than are others.

16. This is an old and widely accepted view among scholars of public finance. See, for example, Dick Netzer, "Federal, State, and Local Finance in a Metropolitan Context," in *Issues in Urban Economics*, edited by Harvey S. Perloff and Lowdon Wingo (Baltimore: Resources for the Future, Inc., The Johns Hopkins University Press, 1968), pp. 435–76.

17. One measure of tax effort in this connection is simply the property tax rate. A more comprehensive measure is total tax burden as a percentage of personal income.

18. *Virginia Statistical Abstract*, 1994–5 for year 1991–2.

REFERENCES

Alexander, Kern, and Richard G. Salmon. *Public School Finance*. Boston: Allyn & Bacon, 1995.

Fisher, Ronald C. *State and Local Public Finance*. Chicago: Irwin, 1996.

Chapter

7 | The Economy of the City

The city economy has a central place in this book. How the city economy fares will play a major role in determining whether its population grows or shrinks. How the city economy fares may determine whether a municipal government can pay its bills easily or whether it will lurch from crisis to crisis, facing painful choices about which services to cut to avoid municipal bankruptcy. The state of the city's labor markets—how much and what types of employment they offer—will affect virtually every aspect of the life of its residents, including not just strictly economic matters but also crime rates, family stability, and the entire texture of life in the city. Note that the terms *urban* and *city* are used here generically. They may refer to an actual city or to an entire metropolitan area. When the city is only a part of a larger urban area, the economic mechanisms to be described apply better to the entire urban area than to the literal city itself.

One might think that forecasting the future of a city economy would be easier than forecasting that of the national economy, for the economy of the city is smaller and less complex. In fact, forecasting for a city is much more difficult. How the city economy does will depend in part on how the national economy does. Whatever uncertainties attach to forecasting the national economy also apply to the city economy. In addition, forecasting the future of the city economy involves many uncertainties that do not attach to the national economy—in particular, how well or how badly producers within the city will compete with producers elsewhere.

A MODEL OF THE URBAN ECONOMY

To begin thinking about how the urban economy works we need a model of it. By model we mean a simplified version of the economy that works somewhat as the actual economy does.

The most commonly used model of the urban economy is the export base model.[1] This model has been with us in various versions since the 1920s. Its logic is simple, and it can be constructed from readily available data in a few days, using no mathematics more complicated than elementary algebra. As will become evident, it explains much but also leaves much unsaid.

The model is based upon a simple observation: urban economies are not self-sufficient. No urban economy can be self-sufficient in agriculture and raw materials, nor, as a practical matter, in a full range of manufactured products. Much of the total income earned in the city must leave the city economy to pay for imports. That leakage of income out of the city must be balanced by earnings on exports. For the city to survive, much less grow, it must sell something to the outside world.

In the export base model the economy of the city is divided into an export and a local sector. The export sector brings into the municipality the money that sustains the local sector. Therefore, the performance of the export sector is considered to determine the fate of the entire city economy. In the language of statistics it is the export sector that is the independent variable and the local sector the dependent variable. If the export sector grows, then the economy of the city will grow. If the export sector shrinks, then the entire economy of the city will shrink. Because it is the demand for products exported by producers in the city that determines the fate of the city economy, the export base model is sometimes referred to as a "demand driven" model.

Figure 7–1 shows a very simplified export base model of the city economy. The key assumption of the model is that for every dollar of income earned by households a certain amount leaves the city economy to be spent on imports. In this illustration we assume that for every $1 of income produced in the city 25 cents is spent on imports. One of many simplifying assumptions is that all importing is done by households. In reality, of course, much importing will be done by firms. Another simplification is that the model includes no transactions between firms but only transactions between firms and households These assumptions make presentation of the model simpler but do not change its basic logic.

For the model in the figure we assume that total income generated from all activity in the city is $1 billion. Of that, $250 million (25 cents in every dollar) leaks out of the city economy to pay for imports. This leakage is balanced by $250 million earned on imports. With imports and exports in balance the economy of the city neither grows nor shrinks.

If we divide total income generated in the city by the earnings on exports, we arrive at a ratio referred to as the multiplier. In the above example $1 billion divided by $250 million gives us a multiplier of 4. Every dollar of export earnings supports a total of four dollars of economic activity. In other words, 25 cents' worth of exports will exactly balance the 25 cents' worth of imports that are generated by each $1 of income. If we assume that the

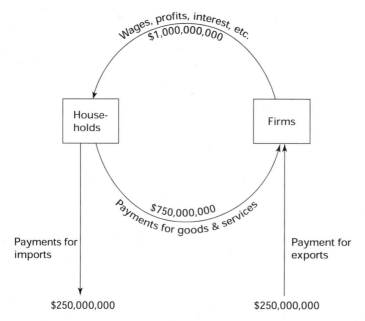

FIGURE 7–1 The Export Base Model. The model assumes transactions between firms and households but no interfirm or interhousehold transactions. For every dollar earned by households we assume that 25 cents is spent on imports and 75 cents is spent with firms in the city. Thus $1 of exports balances the imports resulting from $4 of household income, for a multiplier of 4. A $1 increase or decrease in exports will thus produce a $4 increase or decrease in total economic activity.

multiplier is a fixed number, though different for different cities, we see that as earnings on exports change, the total amount of activity in the city economy will change in the same proportion.

So far, we have described the city economy in terms of money flows. That would be the best way to analyze a city economy. However, it is very difficult to obtain good data on money flows into and out of a city economy. No tariffs are collected at city borders, no licenses are required to export goods and services, and in general, the city economy is completely open to and integrated into the national economy. Instead, as a rough proxy (a stand-in) for money flows we generally use employment. Good, reasonably current data on employment is available for most cities from a variety of sources, including state labor departments.

In the export base model all employment in the city is divided into export sector and local sector. Export sector workers are those who produce for export, and local sector workers are those who produce for consumption within the city. Sometimes the term *basic* is used in place of *export* and *nonbasic* in place of *local*, thus giving us the terminology *basic sector* and *nonbasic sector*.

Who are the export, or basic, sector workers? Clearly, anyone who is engaged in producing a product that is shipped outside the city is an export sector worker. So too, is anyone who produces a service that is sold outside the borders of the city, for the exported service brings money into the city economy just as does an exported product. Thus someone working in an advertising agency in San Francisco on an account for a client in Chicago would be part of the export sector. The good or service does not always have to be delivered outside the municipality for it to be considered export activity. The key question is whether or not it brings in money from the outside. A worker in a hotel that houses guests from out of the municipality is an export sector worker, for that activity brings money from outside the municipality into the municipality.

For many workers, part of their work will be export sector activity and part will be local sector activity. For example, an accountant might spend part of his or her time doing the books for firms whose activity is local sector and part for firms whose activity is export sector activity. In that case, a proper analysis would place the accountant partly in the local sector and partly in the export sector.

Since almost all industries serve both local and export markets, it is necessary to divide employment in each industry into local and export components. A widely used technique is the location quotient. The export employment revealed in this sector-by-sector process is added to arrive at the total export sector employment for the city. A simple example of this technique is shown in the box on page 118.

The model is clearly a great simplification of reality. It ignores money flows into and out of the city economy from sources other than exports or imports. Thus it ignores the role of transfer payments such as from Social Security or pensions, taxes paid by residents and firms to higher levels of government, and grants to municipal governments from the state or the federal government, among others. It also ignores the flow of investment. For example, a city might be growing partly because outsiders are making investments in new plants and equipment, even though those facilities have yet to produce anything for export. The model also assumes that if demand for the city's exports increases, producers in the city will be able to meet that demand and the local sector will also be able to expand as predicted by the model. In other words, the model does not take into account any limitations on the supply side, such as limits on the supply of suitable industrial land or limitations of the city's labor supply. The model takes the multiplier as fixed, but in actuality the multiplier is changeable. If firms in the city begin to produce goods or services that the city formerly imported, then the multiplier increases. In fact, achieving that "import substitution" effect has been an economic development strategy for many places. Perhaps most important, the export base model sheds no light on the capacity of the city to develop new export industries. A look at the history of cities clearly reveals that some have been very successful in replacing their dying industries with new ones, while in other cases the loss of a key industry was a blow from which the city never recovered.[2]

Yet, simplified as the model is, it can be quite useful. It focuses our attention on the key question of competition. The very act of going through the city's industrial and commercial sectors to extract export activity forces us to take a close look at the essential economic anatomy of the city. If the multiplier has been constructed accurately, it will give some indication of how much total employment will change with export sector growth or shrinkage. That, in turn, may help to forecast changes in population, needs for municipal services, changes in municipal revenues and expenditures, changes in traffic flow, and so on.

CALCULATING A LOCATION QUOTIENT

Below are shown calculations to determine the Location Quotient (L.Q.) for the advertising industry in New York City and to determine how many workers in the industry should be considered to be in the export sector. The calculations are done for the year 1990.

Total employment in the United States	117.914 million
Total employment in New York City	3.257 million
New York employment as a percentage of national employment	2.76
Total advertising agency employment in the United States	203,725
Advertising agency employment in New York City	40,121
Advertising agency employment in New York City as a percentage of the national total	19.69
Advertising agency L.Q. for New York City = 19.69/2.76 =	7.135
Export sector employment in advertising $40,121 \times (6.135/7.135) =$	34,496

Sources: National and New York City and employment data are from the *Statistical Abstract of the United States* and the *City and County Data Book,* respectively. Advertising agency employment is from *County Business Patterns,* 1990. All are published by the Department of Commerce, Bureau of the Census.

Notes: The advertising employment numbers are for Standard Industrial Classification 731, which consists of advertising agency employees and miscellaneous advertising workers not elsewhere covered. It does not include many workers who are, in effect, part of the industry—for example, people employed by photographic, commercial art, typography, and other firms that provide services to advertising agencies. Workers in those industries would be divided into export and local sector workers by the same type of process as shown above.

The calculation in the last step, in effect, assigns employment in the sector up to an L.Q. of 1.0 to the local economy and then assigns the portion above 1.0 to the export sector. To find the total amount of export activity in the city and to isolate its export sector, one goes through all the sectors of the city's economy, finds all of those with an L.Q. greater than 1.0, and then totals the amount of export activity in all of those sectors.

OTHER ECONOMIC MODELS

Other economic models are available for the analysis of city and regional economies. In general, they are much more complex mathematically and are usually prepared by consultants who specialize in mathematical modeling. One such model is the input-output model, which provides a much more detailed picture of the interaction between the various sectors of the city or regional economy. For example, the user can simulate a change in export sector activity and then see how that change affects output and employment in each sector of the city's economy. Like the export base model it is a demand-driven model in that it is based on the idea that changes in the city or regional economy occur because of changes in the demand for its export products. In fact, some urban economists have referred to the input-output model as a "highly desegregated" export base model—meaning that although it provides a much more detailed and subtle picture, its underlying philosophy is the same.

There are also econometric models of the city or regional economy. Here the model builder constructs a system of equations, often very complex, that models the past behavior of the economy. The user can then explore possibilities for the future by changing one or more variables and seeing how those changes ripple through the city's or the region's economy.

There are also hybrid models that incorporate elements of both the input-output and econometric approach. A detailed presentation of these more complex models would be out of place in this chapter, but the interested reader can readily pursue them in the urban economics texts cited earlier.

COMPETITION BETWEEN CITIES

The economy of the city exists in competition with the economy of other cities, and its fate depends in large measure on how successfully or unsuccessfully it competes. Though we speak of how well the city competes, most of the competition is actually at the firm level—that is, how well firms in the city compete with firms located elsewhere. That, in turn, takes us to the question of what sort of environment the city provides for commerce and industry.

Some sources of competitive strength or weakness, like location and climate, are totally beyond the city's control. Others, like the physical, educational, and cultural infrastructure of the city, are affected by decisions made by the city government, businesses, and private organizations. In most cases, the effects of such decisions take many years to manifest themselves. We leave the matter of organized economic competition—the municipal economic development program—to the last section of this chapter. Ultimately, virtually everything about a city contributes to its competitive strength or weakness. Below we mention just a few items.

Location is important, particularly as it affects the costs of transportation. That includes the cost of transportation to markets and, usually to a lesser degree, the cost of access to sources of raw materials.[3] It is no coincidence that many of the great cities of North America, Europe, and elsewhere in the world are located at natural harbors or at major transportation breakpoints.

Climate and natural amenities are major factors in determining competitive position. As we become wealthier as a nation, quality of life considerations gain importance relative to pure dollar-and-cents, "bottom line" considerations. Other things being equal, it is easier to recruit employees to work in a location with a pleasant climate and good scenery. Climate and natural amenities have also gained in importance because of the growth of a large retirement-age population with hundreds of billions of dollars of "mailbox income." That has been a major factor in the growth of the Sunbelt. The rapid population growth in many parts of the mountain states, particularly Colorado and Idaho, has been driven in large part by natural amenities.

Infrastructure of all sorts is a major determinant of what types and how much economic activity a city can support. Transportation infrastructure like railroads, highways, and airports is clearly important. The educational establishment of a city is another sort of infrastructure, and one that is becoming more and more important. A major university, particularly one with strength in science and engineering, can be a tremendous economic asset. The two major centers of the microelectronics industry are the Route 128 complex outside of Boston and the larger "Silicon Valley" complex in Santa Clara County, California. They are located where they are in part because of the presence of two major universities, MIT in the first case and Stanford in the second.

When the genetic engineering industry emerged in the early 1980s, it followed a similar pattern. There were three major complexes in the United States. The first was located in and around Boston. A major factor in this case was Harvard University. Much pioneering work in genetics and molecular biology had been done there, and a number of Harvard faculty members were principals in the new firms. Another complex was in the Silicon Valley area, where the location of Stanford was, again, a major factor. The remaining major complex was in Bethesda, Maryland, near the National Institutes of Health, not a university but a major research institution with many universitylike characteristics.

The cultural infrastructure of such items as theaters and museums is important partly because it brings people into the city and creates business for hotels, restaurants, and the retailing and service sectors in general. It also affects the location decisions of firms. When companies are questioned about why they located where they did, a somewhat amorphous factor, "quality of life," is mentioned quite frequently. "Quality of life" issues weigh with the executives who make the decision in a very direct sense of where they themselves would want to live. They also affect firms' location decisions in a more objective, bottom-line way. It is easier to recruit skilled and educated personnel to a firm in a place that they view as being desirable.

The characteristics of the local labor force are a key economic asset—or liability. When firms are questioned about location decisions, labor force considerations almost always appear among the top two or three items.[4] Wage rates are one factor, but often the firm's perception of labor force quality is more important. That item includes job skills and educational backgrounds but also may include less clearly defined characteristics, such as work ethic—do the local people work hard, and are they reliable?

An entrepreneurial spirit and a tendency to innovate and take risks is a great municipal asset. In many cases it enables the municipality to walk away from or even profit from its losses rather than be dragged down by them. In the 1960s, writing about New York City, the urban economist Wilbur Thompson stated:

> . . . . the New York metropolitan area grew by incubating new functions, nurturing them, and finally spinning them off to other sections of the country, all the while regenerating this cycle. The flour mills, foundries, meat packing plants, textile mills, and tanneries of the Post Civil War period drifted away from New York, their place taken by less transport sensitive products, such as garments, cigars, and office work. Currently, New York is losing the manufacturing end of many of its most traditional specialties, as garment manufacturing slips away to low-wage Eastern Pennsylvania leaving only the selling function behind, and as printing splits away from immobile publishing. But New York's growth never seems to falter as the new growth industries are much more than proportionally regenerated in its rich industrial culture.[5]

The quote is several decades old. If written today it might make reference to the Caribbean or Southeast Asia rather than eastern Pennsylvania.

Since then the loss of manufacturing jobs has continued. Many corporate headquarters have moved out, often to the suburbs of the New York metropolitan region. On the other hand, the city has done well in banking, financial services, and many producer services related to world trade.[6] Very recently the city has seen the emergence of numerous small computer graphics firms, mostly located in old loft buildings that in the late nineteenth and early twentieth centuries had housed traditional manufacturing. After World War II the city of Boston lost much of its traditional manufacturing base, but it was able to replace it with high-technology firms in microelectronics and later in biotechnology. The process of loss and regeneration continues. As economic and technological conditions change and as new competitors arise, few cities can count for very long on the same set of leading industries. Whether or not the city continues to prosper will depend heavily upon the ability of its business community to take risks and make innovations that develop strengths in new areas.

The general state of public safety can be a major economic asset or liability. High crime rates drive out retailing and service business activity by frightening customers away. They also discourage business activity by driving up costs for insurance and security. High crime rates may make it harder for firms to recruit workers, particularly for evening shifts. To the extent that crime shrinks the employment base it tends to destabilize families, and that, in turn, is likely to promote more crime. Where there has been large scale civil disorder such as riots and arson, an area may never fully recover. The Watts area of Los Angeles, partly burned out in riots in 1965, has not fully recovered to this date. Whether nor not South Central Los Angeles, which experienced massive burning in the riots following the acquittal of four policemen in the Rodney King case in 1992, will ever fully recover remains to be seen. Not only do such events destroy a portion of the existing business establishment, but they make potential investors very fearful that they will occur again. They may also allow competing areas to forge ahead and gain such an advantage that the damaged area can never catch up.

The municipal and state tax burden is of some concern to firms. Most studies of industrial location decisions place tax burden lower in the scheme of firms' priorities than the market access and labor force considerations noted before. But it is still not trivial.[7] We note that a high-tax situation can feed on itself. If high taxes drive out businesses and thus shrink the tax base, that puts more pressure on tax rates, which, in turn, shrinks the tax base further.

Size itself may be a source of competitive strength. Large places are considered to offer *agglomeration economies*. The argument is that large places offer firms a variety of advantages that smaller places do not. These might include a greater variety of suppliers, a greater variety of customers, and a superior infrastructure, which refers to educational institutions, transportation facilities, a more developed banking system, more extensive financial markets, and the like. One general piece of evidence offered to support the concept of agglomeration economies is that larger cities tend to have higher per capita incomes than smaller cities. That suggests that the larger city is a more efficient economic machine.[8]

The tradeoffs vary from firm to firm. In general, agglomeration economies are thought to be more important for small firms because there are more functions for which they must go outside than in the case of a large firm. Because of the richer business environment of large places, they are thought to provide an "incubator" role for small businesses. To a large firm that has its own law department, accounting department, advertising department, and so on, the agglomeration economies may be of only modest importance. To a three-person firm that has to go outside for all of those services, the agglomeration economies of a large place may be vital. The importance of agglomeration economies may vary between different departments of the same firm, and the firm may divide its operations accordingly. For example, an insurance company might keep its "front office" operation in the center of a major metropolitan area while locating its more routine "back office" activities like claims handling and data processing in a suburban or exurban area where costs are lower.

The matter of size cuts both ways. Urban economists also recognize the existence of diseconomies of scale. A larger place may impose congestion cost, such as traffic delays, on firms. Housing and other living costs may be higher in a large place than a small place, and they show up in higher labor costs. In large places the per capita cost of providing public services may be higher. These costs will show up in higher tax bills. The cost of meeting environmental standards may be higher in a large metropolis than a small town. This expense will manifest itself in higher production costs. Often a firm or an industry will start in a large place because of agglomeration economies—the incubator role noted above. When it gets larger and relatively more self-sufficient, agglomeration economies may become less important to it. In that case it may move out of the large metropolitan area to a smaller place where costs are lower. In manufacturing, this sort of transition is referred to as *the product cycle*. It has been observed in many industries. In recent decades medium-sized metropolitan areas have grown faster than large ones, suggesting that overall the balance between agglomeration economies and diseconomies of scale may lie at an intermediate point rather than the high end of the urban size spectrum.

Localization economies are a variation on the agglomeration economy theme. Firms often benefit from being near other firms in the same industry even though they compete with one another. Firms in an industry cluster share what are, in effect, common resources such as suppliers and providers of specialized services. Unintentionally, they help to train each other's labor forces, for when workers move to another firm in the same industry, they take useful skills and knowledge with them. Particularly in a field in which technology is changing rapidly and knowledge is growing quickly, being in a cluster of similar firms tends to keep a firm and its workers up to date.

One can see the effect of localization economies in a place like Silicon Valley in Santa Clara County, California. An enormous number of semiconductor, software, and related firms are clustered very close together. The localization economies outweigh disadvantages such as having one's employees pirated by competitors or the leakage of trade secrets over an after-hours martini. When the microelectronics industry in Silicon Valley was studied, it was found that firms there brought their products to market faster and achieved more dollars of sales per dollar spent on research and development than did comparable firms elsewhere. In other words, because of the localization economies producers in Silicon Valley are able to utilize resources more efficiently and to develop and bring products to market more quickly than their competitors elsewhere.[9]

The Role of Chance

The existence of localization economies suggests a basic point about urban development and urban competition—that timing and chance may count for a great deal. If localization economies are important in an industry, then whichever place jumps into an early lead will then have the advantage. This will attract more firms to it, giving it a still greater lead. For example, Detroit dominated the U.S. automobile industry for a number of decades and is still very important, though not as dominant as it was. Detroit was and is a good location for automobile manufacture. For example, it is conveniently located with regard to a number of major steel producers. But other cities, such as Cleveland, are equally well located. But no automobile industry ever developed in Cleveland. What made the difference? As a matter of chance, a few of the industry pioneers, such as Henry Ford, happened to be residents of Detroit. And so the industry started there. Once started there, localization economies developed. For example, the city gradually became ringed with subcontractors specializing in brake shoes, bearings, and other parts. The area developed a labor force whose skills fit the needs of automobile manufacturers, and soon it became the most efficient place in the nation, and probably the world, for automobile manufacturing. After some decades the product cycle phenomenon manifested itself, and Detroit, while still a major center, now faces formidable competition from many locations, both in the United States and elsewhere.

Single decisions may also have huge consequences for decades ahead. During World War II civilian automobile production in the United States was halted, and much of the automobile industry, heavily concentrated in and around Detroit, was converted to manufacturing military aircraft. When the war ended, aircraft procurement by the federal government plummeted, and the automobile industry in its haste to begin manufacturing automobiles again showed little interest in continuing its presence in the aircraft industry. Much of the aircraft industry ended up in Southern California.[10] Over the succeeding decades that industry brought many tens of billions of dollars of federal orders for military aircraft into California. This money built local economies by the multiplier process described earlier. Beyond that, and perhaps more important for the long term, it helped to build an enormous base of engineering and manufacturing skills that strengthen the competitive position of the region in many other industries. Had the automobile manufacturers decided to stay in the aircraft business, the economic future of the Detroit region might have been very different and probably much happier. But the profits of manufacturing automobiles for the postwar market were clear to them, whereas the coming of the cold war and the huge demand for military aircraft that it would bring was not.

The preceding examples suggest that although many general principles of urban and regional economics are well understood, predicting the future may be impossible because of the importance of chance events.

COMPETITION FRONTIERS AND THE URBAN HIERARCHY

One of the most basic concepts in location theory is that of the "competition frontier" as shown in panel I of Figure 7–2. The horizontal axis of the diagram represents distance, and the vertical axis represents costs. The costs facing the producer in each city are shown as looking like a wineglass sliced vertically through the center. The stem of the wineglass represents the cost of production, and the side of the glass represents transportation costs. The competition frontier is the point at which the combined cost of production and transportation—the cost at which producers in two different places can deliver the product to the customer—are equal. In the figure one frontier is shown between city A and city B and another frontier between city B and city C. To the left of the first frontier the producer in city A has the advantage. In between the two frontiers the producer in city B has the advantage. To the right of the second frontier the producer in city C has the advantage. Note that all three cities have some area in which they have a total cost advantage even though their costs of production are not the same.

In panel II of Figure 7–2 we show the situation after transportation costs have fallen. The sides of the wineglass now have a flatter slope, and we see that there is now no area in which city B has a total cost advantage. There is just a single competition frontier. Transportation costs (as a share of total costs) vary greatly from product to product, and thus a city does not have one competition frontier but, in effect, a multitude of frontiers for different products and different services.

In many parts of the United States one can see the effects of the sort of process presented in panel II of Figure 7–2. In rural or semirural areas, before the coming of the automobile, there was an economic logic for a pattern of small towns or hamlets spaced perhaps an hour or two apart by foot or by wagon. With the coming of the automobile, travel speeds went up by a multiple of perhaps 10, and the sides of the wineglass in panel II of the figure flattened out. Those places that had some advantage extended their market areas, while other places, no longer shielded from competition by high transportation costs, went into permanent economic decline. The result is a pattern of abandoned hamlets and long-closed crossroads stores in many parts of nonmetropolitan America.

Changes in production costs can also move competition frontiers. In panel III of Figure 7–2 transportation costs are the same as in panel I (same slope), but the producer in city A has reduced its production costs. Perhaps it has achieved this by going to a larger scale of production and thus realizing some economies of scale, or perhaps through adoption of a more efficient technology. One competition frontier has disappeared, and there is again no area left in which the producer in city B has a total cost advantage. If this producer cannot lower either its production costs or its transportation costs, it will have to go out of business, ceding its share of the market to the producer in city A.

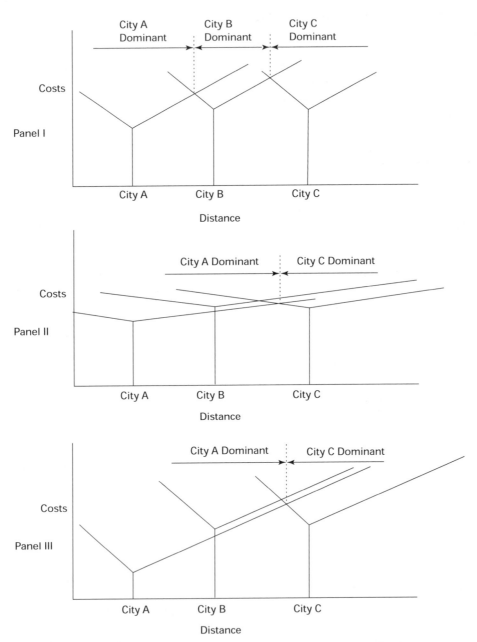

FIGURE 7–2 Competition Frontiers. The vertical lines represent production costs per unit. The sloping lines represent the cost of transportation from the point of production. In panel I each city has an area in which it is dominant (can deliver at the lowest total cost). In panel II transportation costs have fallen while production costs have remained unchanged. There is now no area in which city B is dominant. In panel III we assume that transportation costs are the same as in panel I, but that production costs have fallen in city A. Again, there is no area in which city B is dominant.

The emergence of giant retailers such as Wal-Mart in the United States is a combination of both of the effects just described. Widespread automobile ownership and public investment in highways has reduced the cost of transportation, primarily the time costs of transporting the customer to the store. At the same time, very large retailers are able to achieve economies of scale in purchasing, inventory control, advertising, and personnel training. In terms of the diagram, the stem of the wineglass is shortened and the sides of the glass become less steeply sloped, thus extending the store's competition frontiers and eliminating many smaller competitors.

For goods and services for which there are major economies of scale and for which transportation costs are low in relation to their total value, the competition frontiers of the producer(s) may be very far away. In fact, they may be so far away that the city may have world dominance in that good or service. Thus Amsterdam is dominant in the world market for cut diamonds. Seattle, the home of Boeing Corp., has to itself a large share of the world's market for commercial airliners. Building airliners involves huge front-end expenditures for design, development, and testing. Therefore, there can be only a few producers of them. They can be shipped (in this case, flown) to their buyers for a very small fraction of their cost of production. Thus it is not surprising that one city—really the producer located in that city—can compete anywhere on the planet. The advertising industry in New York City or London reaches far beyond national borders. This is probably not so much a matter of economies of scale within firms as it is of localization and agglomeration economies. The mass of advertising agencies and the various firms that serve them in areas such as law, accounting, photography, printing, graphic design, and market research is apparently more efficient for many types of advertising than are firms in scattered locations. Because the product consists of words and images, shipping costs are not a significant factor.

For other types of goods and services the competition frontier may be very close to home. Where transportation costs are high relative to the value of the product, no one producer can have a very long reach. This is true, for example, of cement. Perishability also limits the size of some firms' competition frontiers. Clearly, no bakery can serve a national market, though a single company with many bakeries might. Most firms that provide personal services have a relatively short reach, not because of the cost of shipping the "product" but because of the time-and-money costs of transportation that the customer faces. The competition frontier of a barbershop in an urban area might extend just a few blocks.

Note that the dimensions of competition frontiers change as technology changes. News is perishable, and it was once clear that no daily newspaper could serve a national market. However, now the *Wall Street Journal,* the *New York Times,* and *USA Today* are national papers. The words and images are produced at one location but then are transmitted electronically to regional printing plants.

A Hierarchy of Cities

The concept of competition frontiers supports the idea of a hierarchy of urban places. In the smallest of places there will only be a few commercial activities. These will be activities for which transport costs are high, for which a small area will provide enough business volume to sustain the activity, and for which there are not great economies of scale. For example, a very small place will have a grocery store. If the place is a bit larger, it may have a variety of other retail and service establishments. In a general way, we can picture a hierarchy of places in which the larger places have most or all of the sorts of business establishments found in smaller places plus some activities not found in smaller places. A town of a few thousand people probably generates enough business to support one or several lawyers who do the sort of legal work that large numbers of people need—such items as wills, house closings, and divorces. A bigger place has the same sorts of law firms and perhaps some firms that handle business and corporate law, items for which the smaller place does not generate enough business to allow such a firm to operate efficiently. A few very large places have the types of law firms previously noted as well as firms that handle still more specialized types of legal practice such as patent law, maritime law, and mergers and acquisitions. Not only does it take a very large area to provide enough cases for such firms, but there are economies of scale accruing to bigger firms. These include specialization of labor, with attorneys becoming extremely specialized in small areas, and the maintenance of specialized law libraries and data bases.[11]

The hierarchy of urban places is clearly in evidence in the real world, where we see a range from the smallest hamlet to a world-class city like New York or London. Understanding the economic forces behind the urban hierarchy suggests that one cannot say that there is an optimal city size. A system with a mixture of place sizes makes far better economic sense and has evolved largely for that reason.

THE GLOBALIZATION OF COMPETITION

In the years since World War II international economic competition has exercised an increasing effect upon U.S. cities. For the United States and many other nations international trade has expanded not just in absolute terms but also as a percentage of the gross domestic product (GDP). For example, in 1960 trade in goods and services represented about 5.2 percent of the U.S. economy. By 1994 that figure had more than doubled to 13.3 percent.[12]

There are a number of well-established reasons for the increase. One is political. Since the end of World War II the major trading nations of the world have engaged in rounds of negotiations under the General Agreement on Trade and Tariffs (GATT), a U.S.-sponsored initiative designed to reduce trade barriers. And the results have been impressive. In the 1930s the average tariff on manufactured goods entering the United States was about 60 percent. By the 1970s that figure was down to about 5 percent, and it is still lower today. In addition to a drastic lowering of tariff walls, there has been some reduction in nontariff barriers to trade.[13] Most recently for the United States there has been the signing of the North American Free Trade Agreement (NAFTA), which almost makes the United States, Canada, and Mexico a single trading area. On the other side of the Atlantic the European Union (EU) has gone far toward producing a free trade area somewhat greater in population and comparable in economic output to North America.

The enormous increase in the speed and decrease in the cost of communications over the last few decades has been a great facilitator of international trade by making it much easier to do business at a distance. There has been a great internationalizing of financial markets. Huge sums of money travel at the speed of light. International money flow, some of it to facilitate transactions and much of it speculative, now exceeds $1 trillion per day. A U.S. company wanting to open a facility in Germany, say, can buy Deutschmarks for dollars instantly by electronic means. If it is concerned about losses should the Deutschmark weaken against the dollar, it can, with equal speed, buy options that hedge against that possibility. An American who has funds in a mutual fund that is invested primarily in the U.S. stock market and who believes that stocks overseas will do better can shift his or her funds to overseas stock markets instantly, very often with a single 800 number call. In short, when it comes to financial transactions, national boundaries have almost disappeared.

Improvements in transportation since World War II have not been as spectacular as those in communications, but they have still been very substantial. Larger and more efficient ships and the advent of containerized freight have greatly decreased the cost of shipping most goods. Airline transportation has improved greatly in speed and reliability and, when measured in real dollars (nominal dollars adjusted for inflation), has become much cheaper over the last several decades. The airfreight industry essentially did not exist before World War II. International one- or two-day package delivery such as that offered by UPS and Federal Express is very new, a creation of improvements in both computer and aircraft technology.

In general, the trends noted earlier—better communications and transportation, the growing ease of making international financial transactions, and the reduction in tariffs and other trade barriers—have made it easier for firms to fine-tune their production processes, doing different parts of the process many thousands of miles apart. A great many, perhaps most, complicated manufactured products like PCs or automobiles tend to be international products in that they have parts and subassemblies made in a number of countries, regardless of what the nameplate says. "Made in . . ." more often would be more accurately rendered as "Assembled in. . . ."

For U.S. cities, immersion in the world market has been a very mixed experience. Seattle benefits from the fact that there is a single world market in commercial aircraft and that Boeing, based in Seattle, is the dominant producer in that market. New York City benefits from international markets in that New York City banks, brokerage firms, law firms, and advertising agencies do business in them. Then, too, for a European or Japanese firm wanting an office on the East Coast, New York is a natural location. Thus the owners of office buildings in Manhattan benefit from the growth of international trade. So, too, do their maintenance workers, albeit to a much lesser degree. However, the same sword cuts both ways. One of New York's traditional industries is garment manufacturing, which is under great pressure from international competition. People in Jamaica, Haiti, the Philippines, and elsewhere can learn to operate sewing machines just as dexterously as can Americans, and wages are much lower in those countries. Even the most inexpensive clothing has a value of many dollars per pound and so can be shipped thousands of miles at a low percentage of its total cost. Therefore, it is not surprising that the United States has lost much garment manufacturing employment in recent years. A very common arrangement is for the clothing producer to split the operation. Design, sales, marketing, and administrative functions stay here. Production goes offshore. Thus the same internationalization of the economy that provides a highly paid job for the young MBA at the currency trading desk of a Wall Street brokerage firm may also push a less-educated garment worker out of a job and onto the unemployment or public assistance rolls.

So far, the effect of the internationalization of the economy has been felt most heavily in manufacturing, for it is the manufactured product that can be put in a box and shipped thousands of miles. As indicated, the effects have been mixed. How much loss of manufacturing jobs in the United States can be attributed to international trade? In 1992 the total value of all shipments by U.S. manufacturers was roughly $3,000 billion. In that same year the U.S. deficit (exports minus imports) on merchandise was about $96 billion, or roughly 3 percent of the total value of manufacturers' shipments. Employment in manufacturing in 1992 was about 18.3 million. Applying the 3 percent figure to the employment figure would suggest that as a very crude "back of the envelope" figure there might have been about 600,000 more manufacturing jobs in the United States in 1992 if the U.S. trade in merchandise had been in balance.[14] That figure is not a huge one for an economy that had a total employment of about 123 million in the same year. But it does mask the fact that some sectors of manufacturing have been very hard hit by the growth of world trade while other sectors of manufacturing have benefited from the growth of the world market.

One side effect of the growth of international trade has been the weakening of labor unions, particularly in manufacturing. Management can, in effect, say to the union, "If you force too expensive a wage and benefit package on us, we won't be able to compete with our foreign rivals and you will put us out of business and you out of a job." Alternatively, management in the face of increased cost pressure from its union might "offshore" some of its production and thus reduce its labor needs in the United States. Or it may be able to do the entire production operation elsewhere and, as noted before, just keep design, marketing, and other nonproduction functions in the United States. The weakening of unions has meant an erosion of well-paying jobs for the person who has, let us say, no education beyond high school or less than a high school diploma.[15] It thus tends to hollow out the middle of the income distribution curve.[16]

The larger question for the U.S. economy in the long run may be the effect of world trade on services and other white-collar work. At present the United States runs a surplus on services. Some services, like haircutting, obviously cannot be exported or imported, but an increasing number of service activities can be. A number of U.S. firms now have programming work done in India, where there is a large supply of highly educated workers and where wages are a small fraction of what they are in the United States. The time differential actually works in favor of the arrangement. The U.S. firm can transmit its programming problem at the end of the business day and often have the solution waiting for it when its workers come in the following morning. Some U.S. hospitals are now having medical transcription done in India for the same reasons. Many clerical functions, such as insurance claims processing, would also appear to be candidates for this sort of "offshoring" or "outsourcing."

Writers of the Political Economy school make the argument that one effect of the growth of international trade is to polarize the populations of many cities by pushing up the wages of people with high-level skills who can compete in the world market while pushing down the wages of less skilled workers.[17] Among members of this school, multinational corporations come in for substantial criticism in this regard. Note that criticisms of this sort are not confined to the Political Economy school. Multinational corporations have also come in for some often similar criticism from some parts of the political Right, as noted in Chapter 5 in connection with former third-party presidential candidate Patrick Buchanan. Ross Perot, a third-party candidate for president in 1992 and 1996 was also sharply critical of both the North American Free Trade Agreement (NAFTA) and multinational corporations that moved jobs across borders. The argument is that driven by purely bottom-line considerations multinational firms open and close plants, hire and lay off workers, and have major effects on the lives of residents and the futures of many cities without having to take those effects into account. If a multinational manufacturer decides to close a plant in Michigan and switch its production to Mexico or Thailand, it leaves behind unemployed workers in Michigan without having to assume any responsibility for the consequences. It has also been suggested that the decision makers in the multinational corporation often have little national allegiance. Instead, they may have more allegiance to the corporation or perhaps to their peers and colleagues located all over the world.

In defending its behavior the representative of the multinational corporation might make several basic points. First, the almost universal opinion of economists is that international trade increases the total output of the nations involved.[18] That is not to deny that it causes pain to some firms and some workers. The executive in the multinational corporation could also argue that by opening plants in developing countries they are increasing incomes in those countries and diffusing manufacturing and other skills around the world. Thus they are a powerful engine for assisting the development of "Third World" nations. He or she might also argue that multinational corporations do not make economic forces so much as respond to economic forces like those created by improvements in transportation and communications. Finally, he or she might ask, given the amount of blood spilled in the twentieth century because of aggressive nationalism, whether having an international business elite that is not very nationalistic might not be a good thing.

INTERPLACE ECONOMIC COMPETITION

The competition between municipalities discussed so far is an implicit competition. It takes place through the actions of individuals and firms within the municipality. There is also an intense competition in which municipal governments are direct and active players. All major cities and a majority of smaller cities as well as a very large number of towns and counties maintain economic development agencies. States are also big players in the economic development game. They all have economic development operations, sometimes operated through departments of commerce and sometimes as separate agencies, such as Virginia's Department of Economic Development. State agencies cooperate with the agencies of municipalities in the entire process, including, in many instances, the matter of grants and tax abatements. When direct expenditures, tax abatements, and operating costs are combined, it is apparent that many billions of dollars are spent by municipal and state governments on interplace economic competition.[19]

Why do local and state governments make such serious efforts both to attract new economic activity and also to hold onto and stimulate the growth of that activity that they now possess? The biggest single reason is labor market conditions. Promoting economic growth tightens up the local labor market, putting upward pressure on wage rates and lowering unemployment rates. Observe the political campaigns of governors, mayors, and county executives, and you will quickly note how heavily their economic record weighs in their campaigns. For the mayor or county executive whose economic development operation can claim to have brought in a major new firm, there is considerable political mileage to be had. If a big employer moves out, the candidate can be belabored with questions beginning with "Why didn't you. . . ." Much the same applies to governors. In 1996 New

York State's three-term governor, Mario Cuomo, was unexpectedly beaten by a substantial margin by a relative political unknown, George Pataki. The main theme of Pataki's campaign was that Cuomo, particularly through policies that favored a high level of public expenditures sustained by high tax rates, was responsible for the state's weak job growth in recent years—that he was responsible for the state's unattractive "business climate."

Fiscal issues also figure heavily in the push for local and state economic development. Most municipal and state governments operate under a condition of some fiscal stress. The same citizens who want good public services also resist tax increases. Promises of tax cuts, or at least resisting tax increases, are a major campaign platform plank in many if not most campaigns at all levels of government. Economic growth holds out the promise of easing the fiscal pressure on local and state governments by expanding the tax base (see Chapter 6).

There are many who benefit from local economic growth. Real estate brokers benefit because more transactions mean more commissions. Landowners and owners of commercial buildings benefit because increasing demand for commercial property pushes up land prices and rents. When increased employment promotes population growth, owners of residential property benefit through higher rents and prices. Bankers benefit from economic growth because it means that they receive more deposits and make more loans. Thus economic growth has many friends within the business community. Note that these points fit very nicely with the "growth machine" hypothesis discussed in Chapter 5.

The competition between municipalities and between states takes various forms. If a firm is thinking about branching or relocating, it is very difficult for the person(s) making the decision to obtain data on such matters as the labor costs, tax rates, utility costs, construction costs, shipping costs, and environmental regulations of perhaps hundreds of places that would be required to make the optimal location decision. Economic development agencies thus use advertising and public relations, backed by large data bases, as part of their selling operation. In the age of the Internet many agencies are opening Web sites such as Ohio's www.Ohiobiz.com. The general view of economic development professionals is that it is not possible using these devices to persuade a firm to move to a location that is bad for it. However, it is very easy to lose a potential firm because it does not know about the advantages that your city or county or state could offer it as a business location. For the same reasons many economic development agencies do a great deal of "direct selling." The product being "sold" is the community as a location for economic activity. The direct selling may be "cold [unannounced] calls" on firms, letters and phone calls to firms, videos about the municipality's advantages mailed to likely prospects, visits by agency personnel to trade shows and conventions where likely prospects may be participating, and so on. Often the sales effort is supported by considerable research. For example, the development agency analyzes the situation of its own municipality and decides what types of commercial or manufacturing activity are most likely to find it a good business environment. Its personnel comb through business directories and other sources to locate firms in those industries and then target their sales efforts to them.

Most economic development agencies make a serious effort to communicate with the business establishment in their own municipality (referred to in the profession as "outreach") both to encourage expansion of those firms and also as a defense against the recruitment efforts of other economic development agencies. Agency personnel make every effort to smooth out government-business relations by doing such things as helping firms in dealing with zoning problems, expediting the issuance of building permits, and shortening delays in making water and sewer hookups.

The community intent upon pursuing economic development will generally try to coordinate its land use planning efforts with its economic development efforts to make sure that it has an adequate supply of developable sites available. That means sites that have adequate width and depth, good road access, and adequate water, sewer, and other utilities.

Last, but far from least, there is the matter of subsidies. These take a multitude of forms. Some are tax breaks. Local governments often offer reductions in property tax rates for new firms. State governments offer a variety of investment tax credits and other offsets against state corporate income taxes. Many local governments will pick up part of the cost of developing a new industrial or commercial site in a variety of ways. The local government may pay part of the cost of site development or acquisition. A very large number of local governments own industrial parks in which they will offer sites for long-term lease or sale at below cost. Hundreds if not thousands of local agencies have built "shell buildings." In this arrangement the local government or its development agency builds the shell of the building and then looks for a firm to lease or buy the building, at which time the interior is finished to meet the needs of the firm. In some cases the local government takes a loss on the lease payments or sales price. In other cases it recovers all of its expenditures. But note that in all cases it is the local government or the agency that takes the risk. It builds the building on speculation. If the building does not sell or lease, it is the municipality's taxpayers who take the loss because it is they who must pay back the loan or pay off the bonds that financed the construction. A great many local and state governments furnish reduced interest rate loans or loan guarantees to support industrial and commercial development.

The amount of subsidy varies greatly. Some industrial and commercial development takes place with no direct public subsidy. Other development can involve huge subsidies. In the mid-1990s IBM and the Japan's Toshiba corporation formed a joint venture to manufacture computer chips and then set about locating a suitable site in the United States. Many municipalities were eager to have the facility. It is relatively "clean" industry. It has that high-tech cachet, and it looks like the sort of operation that might "spin off" many small businesses. Both parent companies are blue chip firms with fine reputations. Manassas, Virginia, about 20 miles west of Washington, D.C., turned out to be the winner in the competition for IBM/Toshiba. The city could not have attracted the firm if it did not have some basic advantages. These include access to the D.C. metropolitan area's large labor force, the proximity of many other high-technology firms, and some quality of life advantages that facilitate the recruitment of personnel. Easy access to many agencies of the federal government and the proximity to the Pentagon and nation's military establishment may also have been factors. So, too, may have been the presence of Dulles Airport just a few minutes away and National Airport within an hour's drive. However, the inherent advantages of the location were not the whole story. The city of Manassas, in conjunction with the state of Virginia, also put up a massive subsidy package. The city offered a $117 million tax abatement package spread out over a number of years. The biggest part of this package was a $96 million abatement of inventory taxes on machinery in the new plant. The state of Virginia put up $48 million. Of this, $38.4 million takes the somewhat unusual form of a direct cash payment to the two companies provided that in years 5 to 10 they meet certain agreed-upon targets for both employment and capital investment.

The plant is expected to employ about 1,200 people when at full operation. Divide that figure into the subsidy package and you get a figure of about $140,000 per job. If you assume a 3 to 1 multiplier, then that figure falls to about $47,000 per job, still a big number. A state development official might argue that, first, the subsidy is being paid out over a period of many years and second, if the state and city did not offer a subsidy the firm would go elsewhere; then, their tax yield on it would be 0. Better to be able to tax something at a reduced rate than nothing at the full rate. To that, you might respond, "But why was it necessary to offer a subsidy at all?" The answer to that is quite simple. It was necessary because competing jurisdictions and competing states offered subsidies. One might ask whether the subsidy package offered was the minimum amount needed to persuade or whether some of it was just a windfall for the company. That is hard to answer. It is not in the firm's interest to reveal the minimum package for which it will settle any more than it is to your advantage to play poker with your cards showing.

The fact that the competition for firms is so intense places a great deal of bargaining power in the hands of firms. In a case that became very well known among economic developers, the state of Illinois put up a $178 million subsidy package to help Sears move a 6,000 worker distribution facility from Chicago to the Chicago suburb of Hoffman Estates.[20] In this case there was no net gain of jobs for the state. Then why did the state do it? The answer was that Sears was unhappy with its Chicago facility and some move appeared inevitable. That, in effect, put Sears in play. Fearing the blandishments of development agencies in other states, Illinois was willing to put up the $178 package to forestall Sear's move. Multipliers run in both directions. Had Sears moved, the total job loss would have been much more than 6,000. From a purely political perspective Illinois' Governor Thompson had little choice in the matter. Had Sears moved out of Illinois he would have been very hard pressed to explain in the next election campaign why he sat idle while the state lost this major employer.

Whether all this competition between places is good or bad when viewed at the national level has been the subject of considerable discussion.[21] At the national level it can be argued that the giving of subsidies distorts firms' location decisions by converting places that are not the inherently most efficient or profitable locations into the most attractive ones by artificially lowering the costs through subsidization. Such a policy is economically inefficient. A counterargument is that those places that need development most will offer the largest subsidy packages and thus render the process efficient.[22] To that counterargument it can be argued that those places that most need development may not be the most effective competitors in the struggle for new business investment.[23] And so the argument goes. Note that even if, on balance, the effects of the competition are negative, that does not mean that some places, like Manassas perhaps, do not come out ahead in the process. This difference between the aggregate effect and some individual effects is not a contradiction. It is no different from saying that, in the aggregate, people who bet on horse races lose money because the race track takes its cut before it distributes the winnings but that some bettors do come out ahead.

Regardless of what one concludes about the efficiency argument, it seems likely that one aggregate effect of the competition is to squeeze local governments financially because it shifts some of the costs of industrial and commercial development from firms to the public. In effect, it partially reverses the normal flow of taxation by causing some funds to flow from the state or city to the firm instead of from the firm to the state or city.

If this competition between places puts a burden on cities and states, why do they not simply agree to not offer subsidies and tax breaks? At least a part of the answer is that it is almost impossible for such an agreement between a very large number of parties to hold for a substantial period of time. The motivation for one party to break the agreement when a particularly attractive prospect comes along is just too great.[24]

SUMMARY

The most commonly used model of the city economy is the export base model. In this model demand for the export products of the city is the determining factor because the economy of the city can grow only if exports grow so as to balance the leakage of money out of the city to pay for imports. Though useful, the model has many limitations. It ignores flows of money due to taxes, transfer payments, and investment from the outside. It also ignores supply-side limitations and the long-term question of whether the city can develop new export industries to replace losses.

Cities compete with each other economically. Some sources of competitive strength include climate, location, infrastructure, "quality of life," and entrepreneurial talent. Size itself can have its advantages, and in this connection we discuss economies of agglomeration and localization. The chapter notes the concept of the competition frontier—the point at which the combined production and transportation costs of a producer in one location equal the combined costs for a producer in another location. Each producer has the advantage on its own side of the frontier. The concept of the competition frontier leads to the concept of a hierarchy of cities extending from the smallest hamlet to a world-class city such as New York or London.

The increasing importance of world trade and the internationalization of financial markets is becoming increasingly important in determining the fate of city economies. World trade has grown as percentage of GDP partly for political reasons, namely the reduction in tariffs and other trade barriers under the General Agreement on Trade and Tariffs (GATT) and the signing of the North American Free Trade Agreement (NAFTA). More important than the political factor, however, have been major advances in transportation and communications technology.

The chapter ends with a discussion of intermunicipal competition. States, cities, and many smaller political jurisdictions mount economic development programs in an intense competition to promote their own growth. These programs employ a range of advertising and marketing, as well as a wide range of subsidies, including loan guarantees, tax breaks, and public assumption of some of the costs of site acquisition and development. In the case of some very large corporate moves or expansions, subsidy packages have gone well past the $100 million mark.

NOTES

1. For an extended description, see an introductory urban economics text such as James Heilbrun, *Urban Economics and Public Policy*, 3rd edition (New York: St. Martin's Press, 1987); Arthur M. Sullivan, *Urban Economics* (Homewood, Ill.: Richard D. Irwin, 1990); Edwin Mills, *Urban Economics* (Glenview, Ill.: Scott, Foresman, 1984) or John M. Levy, *Urban and Metropolitan Economics* (New York: McGraw-Hill, 1985).
2. For a powerful and often-cited criticism of the export base model because it ignores supply-side factors, see Hans Blumenfeld, "The Economic Base of the Metropolis," *Journal of the American Institute of Planners* (now the *Journal of the American Planning Association*) 2 (fall 1955), pp. 114–132.
3. It is widely believed that transportation costs, particularly of raw materials, are decreasing in importance relative to other factors. The argument is twofold. First, manufacturing is coming to constitute a smaller percentage of the total output of the economy. Second, the average value per pound of a manufactured product is increasing as products become more sophisticated. For example, electronic products have a very high per pound value. Even a product like a bicycle has been becoming more complex and lighter in weight over the years. For a general discussion of transportation costs and industrial location see Edgar

M. Hoover and Frank Giarratani, *An Introduction to Regional Economics,* 3rd ed. (New York: Alfred A. Knopf, 1984).

4. For an account of research on the factors influencing the location decision for manufacturing, see Roger Schmenner, *Making Business Location Decisions* (Englewood Cliffs, N.J.: Prentice Hall, 1982). For recent articles, see the periodicals *Area Development* and *Economic Development Quarterly.*

5. Wilbur Thompson, *A Preface to Urban Economics* (Baltimore: Johns Hopkins University Press, 1968), p. 38.

6. Producer services are services provided to other firms rather than to the final consumer. For example, an accounting firm that serves other businesses or a graphic arts firm that does work for advertising agencies would be a producer service. For a discussion of the growth of producer services, see William B. Beyers, "Producer Services and Metropolitan Growth and Development" in *Sources of Metropolitan Growth,* edited by Edwin S. Mills and John F. McDonald (New Brunswick, N.J.: Rutgers, 1992), pp. 125–146. For a general picture of economic change in New York City in recent years, see Saskia Sassen, *The Global City* (Princeton, N.J.: Princeton University Press, 1991).

7. Schmenner, op. cit.

8. Patricia E. Beeson, "Agglomeration Economies and Productivity Growth," in Edwin S. Mills and John F. MacDonald, op. cit. pp. 19–38.

9. Claudia B. Schoonhoven and Kathleen M. Eisenhardt, "Regions as Industrial Incubators of Technology-based Ventures" in Edwin S. Mills and John F. MacDonald, op. cit. pp. 210–254.

10. Wilbur Thompson, *A Preface to Urban Economics* (Baltimore: Johns Hopkins Press, 1965), pp. 45–46.

11. The concept of urban hierarchy is discussed in the urban economics texts cited before. The idea was developed by the economic geographers and location theorists. See, for example, August Losch, *The Economics of Location* (New Haven, Conn.: Yale University Press, 1954).

12. The figure quoted is the average of exports and imports divided by GDP. See Tables 669 and 1319 in the 1995 *Statistical Abstract of the United States.*

13. These items include such items as import quotas, domestic content rules, or product standards and specifications designed to favor domestic producers.

14. Tables 1246 and 1319 in the *Statistical Abstract of the United States,* 1995.

15. By the mid 1990s approximately 15 percent of all U.S. wage and salary workers were unionized, about half the percentage that had been in the years after World War II.

16. The threat to unions posed by international competition is one reason that the unions fought so hard against the ratification of the North American Free Trade Agreement (NAFTA) in 1993. In Congress Republicans voted for it almost in a bloc, and they picked up enough conservative Democratic votes to carry it; but the great majority of Democratic legislators, under union pressure, voted against it even though their own president, Bill Clinton, supported it.

17. Saskia Sassen, *The Global City: New York, London, Tokyo* (Princeton University Press, 1991); Michael Smith, *City, State and Market: The Political Economy of Urban Society* (Oxford: Basil Blackwell, 1988); Manuel Castells, *The Informational City* (Oxford: Basil Blackwell, 1989); or Barry Bluestone and Bennett Harrison, *The Deindustrialization of America* (New York: Basic Books, 1982).

18. This general view goes back to the early nineteenth-century English economist David Ricardo and is referred to as the "principle of comparative advantage."

19. An exact figure is not available. For some idea of the approximate amounts, see John M. Levy, *Economic Development Programs for Cities, Counties, and Towns,* 2nd edition (Westport, Conn.: Prager Publishers, 1990).

20. Robert Guskind, "The Giveaway Game Continues," *Planning* (February 1990), pp. 4–8.

21. Dick Netzer, "An Evaluation of Interjurisdictional Competition through Economic Development Incentives," in *Competition among States and Local Governments,*" edited by Daphne A. Kenyon and John Kincaid (Washington, D.C.: The Urban Institute, 1991).

22. This line of argument depends upon the economist's concept of "externalities." The market can adjust for only those benefits and losses that accrue to participants in the transaction. However, losses or gains (externalities) may also accrue to parties who are outside the transaction. Thus a transaction that is efficient in market terms may not be efficient in broader terms. If the municipality that will experience the most external benefits from having a new industry is willing to make the largest subsidy offer, the situation may be

moved in the direction of greater total benefit when the interests of all are considered. The concept of externalities can be explored further in any textbook on microeconomics.

23. Irene S. Rubin and Herbert J. Rubin, "Economic Development Incentives: The Poor (Cities) Pay More," *Urban Affairs Quarterly* 23, no. 1 (September 1987), pp. 15–36. For a more positive view of the benefits of interplace economic competition, see Timothy Bartik, *Who Benefits from State and Local Economic Development Policies?* (Kalamazoo, Mich.: The Upjohn Institute, 1991).

24. It has been suggested that Congress could lessen the degree of competition considerably by amending the Internal Revenue Service (IRS) code so as to tax firms for the economic development subsidies that they receive. If such subsidies were taxed at high enough rates, they would become much less attractive to firms, and municipalities and states would be less inclined to offer them. Though this idea is attractive to some economists and students of public policy, it has so far awakened no congressional interest.

REFERENCES

Heilbrun, James. *Urban Economics and Public Policy.* New York: St. Martin's Press, 1987.

Mills, Edwin S., and John F. McDonald, eds. *Sources of Metropolitan Growth.* (New Brunswick, N.J.: Rutgers, 1992).

Thompson, Wilbur. *A Preface to Urban Economics.* Baltimore: Johns Hopkins University Press, 1968.

Chapter

8 | Planning the City

We begin by asking, does anyone really plan cities and metropolitan areas, or do they just happen? There is a profession of city planning, and in North America about 70 universities grant a master's degree in city planning, generally either a Master of City Planning (MCP) or a Master of Urban and Regional Planning (MURP). One might be tempted to think of city planning as architecture or civil engineering writ large. Architects draw plans for buildings, and then builders follow them. The buildings tend to resemble the architects' drawings quite closely. Civil engineers make drawings, and then contractors lay pipes and pour concrete more or less as the drawings instruct them to do. However, such a direct relationship between plans and what happens on the ground is not the case with city planning.

POLITICAL REALITIES

In one sense, everything in the city is planned. No one puts a pipe in the ground or pours pavement or builds a house or a commercial building without having done some planning first. In a more general sense, the city or the metropolitan area comes into being as a result of the action of many different and often conflicting economic, political, demographic, and other forces. The planners have a hand in the process, but they are not the only players at the table nor, generally, are they the most powerful players.

Planners, by themselves, are only advisors to government, and they have almost no literal power. Their strength is the strength of their ideas and the support that they can muster for those ideas. For example, the planners can recommend a program of capital investment, but they cannot make it happen by themselves. For roads to be built and sewer pipes to be laid, the legislative body must adopt a capital budget and appropriate the funds. That is a political act. The planners, either the municipality's own planners or its planning consultants, draw up the land use controls. However, land use controls acquire legal force only when the municipality's legislative body passes a resolution adopting them. Again, that is a political act.

Planning decisions often involve very large sums of money for private parties. Land values are affected by capital investments such as roads, highway intersections, public transportation systems, and utility systems. The decision about where to put a highway intersection may affect the value of hundreds of acres of land by thousands or tens of thousands of dollars per acre. Similarly, the location of a metro stop may raise land and property values in the surrounding area by tens or even hundreds of millions of dollars. Those who own property are not likely to be passive about public investment decisions in which they have such a large stake.

For the same reasons, people who own significant blocks of land are not likely to be passive about land use control decisions. Consider the following example. An individual owns 100 acres of undeveloped land. The market for property in that town is such that the most profitable use for that property would be to build condominium apartments on it. If the land could be used for that purpose, it could be sold to a real estate developer for $50,000 per acre, a total of $5 million. However, suppose that the town's land use controls (discussed later in this chapter) prohibit the building of apartments on that site and allow no development more dense than single-family houses on lots that are an acre or more in size. If the use of that land is so restricted, its market value will be $20,000 per acre, or a total of $2 million. In that case the owner of the property has a $3 million interest in whether the land use controls permit apartments or only single-family houses. He or she is likely to exert considerable effort in getting municipal government to zone the parcel in the more favorable way.

Public interest in planning decisions is often very great because such decisions affect people where they live. A change in land use controls in a neighborhood affects what it feels like to live in that neighborhood. It also may alter the values of properties in that neighborhood. For the person much of whose life savings are in the equity (what the property would sell for minus what the person owes on the property) of his or her home, that can be a very important matter. Many suburban communities have been the scene of bitter arguments over whether their land use controls should permit the building of low- and moderate-income housing because residents feared that the children coming from that housing would change the nature of the local schools in ways that affected discipline, academic quality, or their own children's safety. Regardless of the rights and wrongs of such a position, and regardless of whether the fears are in fact realistic, it is easy to understand why people become very aroused and politically mobilized when they think the welfare of their children is at stake.

Economic competition between municipalities may introduce conflict into the planning process. Assume that the city's economic development department has been working for months to encourage a major manufacturing firm to locate within its borders and that, in fact, the city is willing to offer some large tax breaks and other assistance to make this happen. However, the company wants to build its plant in an area that the municipal planners think should be used for other purposes, or in a manner that citizens fear will create serious traffic congestion, or in a way that members of the local chapter of the Sierra Club are convinced is environmentally unsound. The seeds of political conflict are clearly present.

Most citizens think they know something about the substance of planning, and, indeed, they do. Planning involves the neighborhood they live in, the streets they drive on, the public facilities they use, the location and layout of the shopping center they patronize, or the office or industrial park in which they work. Therefore, when it comes to planning issues, citizens tend not to defer to the "experts" but to be very active participants in the political process that surrounds planning. More than one planner has come home from a public meeting feeling a bit abused and pummeled.

There is a strong antiauthoritarian streak in the U.S. political character, going back at least to the Revolution. The American planner who visits, say, Great Britain, the Netherlands, or Scandinavia will quickly observe that the public there seems to be much more deferential to the planners and to public officials in general. In many European nations there is a tendency for people to feel that they have met their civic responsibility by voting and that after the election it is the responsibility of the politicians and public servants to get on with the business of governing without further supervision.[1] Americans are much more likely to view both their elected officials and career public servants with considerable suspicion, look over their shoulders at frequent intervals, and rarely give them the benefit of the doubt.

Finally, the same planning decision looks very different to different people. Urban Renewal (see Chapter 10) looked to some like tearing down slums and replacing them with good housing and bright and shining new commercial development. But to other people it looked like "putting me out of business" or "destroying my neighborhood" or "putting me out on the street." The amount of political conflict it generated was enormous.

For the above sorts of reasons planning decisions often take place in a highly political and contentious environment. The scene can often resemble a big dog fight, and generally the planners are far from the biggest or fiercest dogs. One might wonder if planning decisions might not be better if planners did not have to be responsive to political bodies and if they could make decisions based solely upon their own professional expertise. It is probably a rare planner who has not pondered this from time to time, but such would not be compatible with our system of democratic governance. Ultimately, in a representative democracy, the decision-making power of government must be vested in the citizens' elected representatives and not in a group of unelected experts, no matter how competent or well-intentioned those experts might be.

A BRIEF HISTORY OF CITY PLANNING IN THE UNITED STATES

In the colonial period the biggest of cities, such as New York, Philadelphia, and Boston, were, in current terms, the size of big towns. And their growth rate had been modest. New York City took over a century to grow to its Revolutionary era size of about 30,000. In the colonial period municipal governments had considerable power to control how land was used within their borders. A number of cities started as royal grants to individuals, and thus the grantee had very considerable power to plan the city and see that it developed at least somewhat as planned. Savannah, Georgia, began as a grant to James Oglethorpe, who laid out an orderly and gracious street pattern, complete with a number of small parks. Some of this pattern persists to the present day. Philadelphia began in a somewhat similar way with a grant to William Penn.[2] Growth pressures in the postcolonial period were greater in Philadelphia than in Savannah, so less of the original pattern is to be found there than in Savannah.

The Revolution, of course, ended the process of royal grants. More important, the Constitution provided very strong guarantees for private property rights. The Revolution had been, in large measure, a rebellion against what the colonists thought was the excessive and arbitrary exercise of royal authority. It was only natural that the Constitution should severely limit the power of government to tell individuals what they might or might not do with their own property.[3] Since most property was privately owned, limiting the power of government to tell individuals how they might use their property limited the ability of a municipal government to plan.

As discussed in Chapter 2, many nineteenth-century cities grew with great speed. Local governments had little power to plan and little expertise in planning. In many places the watchword was growth, and any attempt to plan in a way that seriously diverted or slowed growth would have met with great resistance. A great many cities were laid out on a gridiron pattern, often regardless of whether or not this best suited the topography of the site. The reason was that gridiron plans are easy to do and they facilitate the subdivision and sale of land. If you look at a present-day map of Manhattan, you will note that the southernmost tip of the island (the original point of settlement) shows an irregular street pattern that had evolved from the time of the Dutch settlement until the early nineteenth century. But north of that and covering the great majority of the island's land area is a rectangular grid that was laid down on the entire remainder of the island in the early nineteenth century. The only exception to this absolutely regular, rectangular scheme is Broadway. This was the old post road from the lower tip of the island to

Albany, and since it was already in place and in use it had to be incorporated into the new plan.

What planning there was in the early nineteenth century tended to focus on commercial areas and was largely devoted to improving the competitive position of the city. For most of the city, municipal governments laid down very simple street plans and then let market processes determine both to what use land would be put and also how intensely that land would be used.

In the second half of the nineteenth century, pressures built to plan and to impose some public control on growth. The living conditions of the poor made it clear that some planning for housing was needed. As cities became more densely built up, it became apparent that some public action was necessary to provide public open space. When significant numbers of Americans began to travel to Europe in the post–Civil War period, they began to appreciate good urban design and to think that Americans could do much better than they had been doing in the design of public spaces and public buildings. In short, in the latter part of the nineteenth century the motivation to plan grew and the beginnings of modern city planning began to appear.

This chapter does not provide a history of urban planning in the United States, but the reader can find one in a number of other places.[4] However, we note two major themes here. First, municipal governments realized that they could shape the development of the city through capital investments—where they built roads, bridges, public water and sewer lines, and public buildings; where they acquired land for parks and playgrounds; and how they laid out such public spaces as civic centers. It is generally considered that the first modern city plan in the United States was that done for the city of Chicago in 1909.[5] Its focus was public capital investment—the building of roads and bridges, the construction of new rail facilities (Union Station), improvements to waterways (the Chicago River), the development of the city's lakefront, and the acquisition and development of many thousands of acres of parkland. That theme—shaping the municipality by the expenditure of public funds on publicly owned lands—has remained a major theme of planning to the present time.

A second theme emerged in the late nineteenth century. There began a long struggle, fought out in the courts, to give governments some power to impose controls on how privately owned land is used. Most urban land in the United States is privately owned, and most residential and commercial buildings are erected on private land with private funds. If government has no power to control what is done on private property, its capacity to shape the form of the city or town or metropolitan area is severely limited. In fact, one reason that the plan for the city of Chicago focused almost exclusively on the capital expenditures was that at that time the right of government to exert much control over the development of privately owned land had not yet been clearly established. This right was gradually established in a series of court cases beginning in the late nineteenth century and stretching out over a period of several decades. This chapter will not tell the story in any detail but will briefly explain the central constitutional issue involved.

The Fifth Amendment of the Constitution states: ". . . nor [shall any person] be deprived of life, liberty or property, without due process of law; nor shall private property be taken for public use, without just compensation."[6]

It has always been clear that private property could be taken for public use but that if this was done the property owner had to receive "just compensation" for the property taken. The taking of property can be done under the government's right of "eminent domain." This is a power that government obviously needs. If government did not have the right to take property, one property owner could stop the building of a highway just by refusing to sell. Even so, when government takes property it must either reach a negotiated settlement with the property owner or it must condemn the property and then pay the owner a sum of money that has been determined in court to be the fair market value of the property.

Taking property and then paying the owner the fair market value is a very different matter from imposing regulations without a change in ownership. For in the latter case the municipality may be imposing an uncompensated loss on the property owner. To understand how regulation can impose a loss on the property owner, just consider the land use example given previously. The land has one value if used for apartments and a much lower value if it can be used only for single-family houses on big lots. If land use controls (regulation) prohibit apartments and allow only the single-family houses, the difference between the price of the land in the two different uses is the loss imposed on the owner. The legal question that took so long to resolve was this: Does imposing that loss constitute a "taking" of property?" That question—what constitutes a "taking" of private property—is at the heart of the legal issue about government's right to exercise control over the use of private property; for if a "taking" has occurred, then government must compensate the property owner. And that would make public control over the use of private property extremely expensive and complicated.

The position that emerged after numerous court cases from roughly the 1880s to the 1920s was that government did have the right to restrict the use of private property, as in the example above, without having to pay compensation. In other words, some reduction in the value of the property due to regulation did not necessarily constitute a "taking." The definitive case is *Village of Euclid v. Ambler Real Estate,* generally referred to in the planning literature as *Euclid v. Ambler,* decided by the Supreme Court in 1926.[7] The general position taken by the courts over the years has been that government may impose reasonable restrictions on the use of private property under the rubric of the "police power" without such action constituting a "taking" and therefore without compensation being required. "Police power" simply means the power of government to take actions to safeguard the health, safety, and the public welfare in general. Control over the use of privately owned land can be justified much as we justify speed limits or rules that prevent us from parking in front of a fire hydrant. Though the general principle that governments can regulate the use of private property without having to compensate the owners is long established, the exact amount that government can do is often a matter of dispute, and many attorneys earn their livings litigating land use control conflicts.

THE GOALS OF PLANNING

The goals of the plan will vary from one municipality to another, but some of the commonly found goals might be:

Health. The goal is to achieve a pattern of development that promotes public health by such means as providing for safe water supplies, making possible adequate sewerage treatment, and keeping residential development separate from industrial or commercial activities that produce pollution or other health hazards.

Safety. This might include such matters as seeking a street pattern that minimizes accidents and provides as much separation as possible between pedestrian and vehicular traffic. It might mean minimizing flood hazards through protection from flooding or by preventing people from building in flood plains. In some areas it might mean urban design that reduces the risk of crime by minimizing sites where muggings and robberies can take place out of sight.

Circulation. This means a street system and in some cases public transportation facilities that enable people to go where they want to go expeditiously and efficiently.

Efficient provision of public services. This means locating public facilities in a way that permits them to serve their designed function effectively and at reasonable cost. This is true whether we are discussing public schools, parks, museums, or the municipal solid waste facility.

Economic goals. This would mean, at a minimum, land use and capital investment planning that provides an adequate amount of land that is properly zoned, served by appropriate roads and utilities, and otherwise amenable for the development of industrial and commercial facilities. The municipality might be motivated primarily by a desire to provide jobs for its unemployed. Alternatively, it might be motivated mainly by a desire to expand its tax base and thus hold down its property tax rate. Or it might be motivated by a mixture of factors. At this time, economic development is a major item on the agenda of many municipal governments.

Housing. In many municipalities housing not only represents the largest single land use, but it often involves more land than all other uses combined. Planning for housing in a growing community might simply involve providing adequate road access and utilities and zoning enough land for residential use. It might also involve some plans for public participation in the provision of housing for those who cannot afford adequate housing without some assistance.

Downtown renewal. If businesses have been moving from downtown to outlying areas and if few people are going downtown to shop anymore, the municipality may make revitalization of the downtown a part of its plan. That might include steps like improving the street pattern, creating a pedestrian mall, making loans to downtown businesses for facade improvements, or providing a downtown parking structure.

Historic preservation. In many municipalities, preserving historic buildings or historic neighborhoods is a goal. This may be done strictly out of a love of the past, but it may also be done in part in recognition that historic districts can bring tourism dollars into the local economy. The goal may be accomplished by zoning, by controls on how owners of historic buildings may or may not modify their properties, and by financial incentives to preserve buildings in their original condition.

Growth management or growth control. If the municipality has been growing more rapidly than its population likes, or if it fears that this soon may be the case, a goal of the master plan may be to limit growth either to some annual percentage or to some ultimate cap.[8]

Environmental quality. The municipality may be concerned with preserving blocks of open space in their original condition, to protect what it sees as ecologically fragile areas from development, or to achieve a pattern of land use that affords its residents easy access to unspoiled areas. These goals may be pursued through land use controls, through public acquisition of parkland and other open space, or by public capital investment for such items as water treatment.[9]

The above are common goals but they are far from a complete list. Not all communities follow the same path. One municipality that faces substantial unemployment and a weak tax base might actively court growth. An affluent town that has experienced considerable growth might try to deflect or limit growth. There are often overlaps between goals presented above. For example, the downtown revitalization goal might be part of a larger economic development program. It might also be tied in with the municipality's housing goals or with historic preservation goals.

THE TOOLS OF PLANNING

A city government has two main ways of implementing the plans that its planning agency has developed and that its legislative body has adopted. These are capital investment and land use controls.

Capital Investment

Capital investments in infrastructure such as roads, bridges, water mains, sewer lines, airports, mass transit facilities, parking structures, parklands, and the like are generally the most powerful means that a municipality has to shape its own pattern of development. The location of roads determines what areas can be developed because no development can happen without some road access. Intensive development, whether commercial or residential, requires a high level of road capacity. Comparable comments can be made about investment in mass transit facilities. Parking facilities likewise contribute to accessibility and are key ingredients in many downtown plans.

Water and sewer lines are essential if there is to be intensive development. If public water supply and sewer lines are not present, development must be served by wells and septic tanks. That generally limits residential development to single-family houses on fairly large lots.[10] Commercial development is also sharply limited by the absence of public water and sewer service.

Public land acquisition is a major shaper of the municipality. When land is acquired for a park it is unavailable for residential or commercial use and thus channels and reshapes the flow of development.[11] Some public capital investments act as magnets for development. For example, an airport may attract hotels, conference centers, businesses that make heavy use of airfreight, and companies that provide services to the aviation industry. Many municipalities have shaped the pattern of industrial location by using public funds to develop municipally owned industrial parks.

Public capital investments such as those noted above last for decades and exert a continuing and powerful effect upon the pattern of development. It is the experience of most planners that when economic forces created by public capital investment are in sharp contradiction to the land use pattern permitted by land use controls, sooner or later the controls change.

Land Use Controls

Subdivision regulations. These are one of the older and more important types of controls. In most municipalities before land can be subdivided (broken up into plots that can be sold separately) the property owner must meet a number of requirements. Requirements include minimum street widths, the connection between the subdivision's street pattern and that of the municipality, storm water runoff control, the provision of water and sewer lines, and easements for utility lines.[12] Subdivision requirements pertain primarily to residential development.

Zoning laws. These are the best known of all land use controls. Zoning laws work in the following manner. A zoning map that divides the municipality into a number of zones is drawn up. The map is drawn with sufficient precision so that there is no doubt about in which zone(s) each parcel of property is located. The zoning ordinance then defines in considerable detail exactly what type and what intensity of development are allowed in each zone. For example, the ordinance might specify that for an R-20 zone single-family houses are permitted on lots of 20,000 square feet or more. It might also specify that the lot must be at least 100 feet wide, that the house be set back at least 30 feet from the building line and at least 20 feet from the side yard and rear yard line, and so on. It might also specify that doctors' and dentists' offices are permitted in houses or that some nonresidential uses are permitted in the zone. For example, many residential zones permit churches. The ordinance might specify that in the C-1 commercial zone stores may not cover more than 50 percent of the lot area, that there must be so many feet of setback from front, side, and back lot lines, that the structure may not have a height of more than 25 feet, that there must be at least one parking space on the site for every 500 square feet of floor space, and so on. Exactly which commercial uses are permitted and which are not permitted will also be specified. The ordinance will also specify how its provisions are to be enforced, and it will generally also specify how its provisions may be appealed. For example, many municipalities have a zoning board of appeals (ZBA) to which a property owner can appeal for relief from some provision of the zoning ordinance.

Site plan review. Some zoning ordinances will specify that for developments over a certain size not only must the development meet all the specific provisions of the ordinance but that it also must meet an overall design review. Site plan review generally applies to commercial or mixed use (commercial and residential) development.

The above is not a complete list of types of land use control but covers the most commonly found types. Controls may also be imposed on matters of architectural taste and historic preservation.

The Pros and Cons of Zoning

Zoning has been the object of much controversy and criticism since it became widespread in the 1920s. There are clearly many positive things to be said about it. It makes it possible for municipal governments to avoid the juxtaposition of incompatible land uses. For example, it prevents someone from opening up a noisy facility like a Go-Kart track in a residential area. It can be used to prevent excessively dense development that overloads the street system and causes congestion. It can be used to prevent a builder from erecting a building that casts adjacent buildings in a perpetual shadow and thus destroys much of their value. More generally, it is an instrument of community design that lets the planners or the urban designers specify what uses and how much of each use is permitted in the various parts of the city. It can thus achieve a more harmonious pattern of uses than would happen were development left purely to market forces.

Zoning has also been subjected to criticism on many points. One long-running criticism is that zoning often produces an excessive separation of land uses. In the 1960s Jane Jacobs argued that very often the most lively and desirable areas in cities were those areas of the city that had developed before zoning and that contained a very fine-grained mixture of commercial and residential uses.[13] For example, a zoning ordinance and map that specify that a large area shall have only residential uses is a prescription for dullness. Not only that, but it may also be a prescription for danger, because much of the time there will be few people out on the street and thus the area may be one that invites street crime.

Though Jacobs wrote entirely about cities, similar arguments can be made for the suburbs as well. In recent years a "neotraditional" planning movement has developed. Members of this movement, sometimes also referred to as "the new urbanism," make similar arguments about the suburbs. They argue that by zoning large blocks of land for a single use we create a dull and inconvenient land use pattern. If you live in an R40 zone (single-family houses on building lots of at least 40,000 square feet), you cannot walk to the corner grocery store because the zoning does not permit grocery stores in R40 zones. Then, too, the spacing of houses on lots at least 200 feet wide spreads things out so much as to discourage walking for most purposes. The result is extreme dependence upon the automobile for most daily activities. Andre Duany, the best known of the neotraditional designers, argues that suburban zoning is a major cause of suburban traffic congestion because the separation of land uses makes constant use of the automobile a characteristic of suburban life. He and other neotraditionalists note that children too young to drive must be driven everywhere because different activities are so spread out—a reduction in the child's autonomy and a great inconvenience for the parent. Similarly, old people who may have the strength and energy to walk but not the visual acuity to drive lose their independence in such places. The neotraditionalists advocate a move back to older principles of town planning that involve a much finer-grained mixture of land uses and an emphasis upon design for the pedestrian rather than for the automobile.[14]

Perhaps the sharpest criticism of zoning has been over the matter of "exclusionary zoning," generally in the suburbs. Many suburban communities adopted zoning codes that greatly limited the types of housing that could be built there. Specifically, many suburban zoning ordinances prohibited the building of multifamily housing, so that the only type of housing that could be built was the free-standing, single-family house. Many ordinances went further than this by requiring large minimum lot sizes as well. A few went still further and also mandated a minimum house size, expressed as the minimum number of square feet of floor space. The effect of such requirements is to elevate the prices of new housing in a number of ways. The free-standing, single-family house is inherently more expensive to build than garden apartments or row houses. Beyond that, large lot zoning raises land costs because more land is required per unit of housing. Large lot zoning elevates construction costs because building on a larger lot means higher grading costs and greater expenditures on roads and utilities simply because of the greater spacing between houses. Finally, because large lot zoning reduces the total number of housing units that can be built in a municipality, it exerts a general upward pressure on the prices or rents of much if not all of the housing stock in the municipality, not just on new single-family housing.

Why then, would municipalities do this? One reason is the fiscal issue mentioned earlier. An expensive house is assessed higher and therefore at any given tax rate yields more property tax revenue. Another reason that opponents of such zoning point to is an exclusionary motive. It prevents people with lower incomes from being able to move into the municipality. Opponents then go on to argue that the segregation by income caused by exclusionary zoning also produces segregation by race. For several decades median family income for Blacks in the United States has been approximately three fifths that of Whites (see Chapter 13). If a municipality uses zoning to limit its housing stock to expensive single family housing, the difference in incomes almost assures that the number of Blacks living there will be small.

The issue of exclusionary zoning has been fought out in the courts for many years. Some suits have been brought by developers who have a financial interest in that they want to be allowed to develop land more intensively. Some suits have been brought by organizations such as the National Association for the Advancement of Colored People (NAACP) that represent minority groups and some by coalitions of both interests. In general, the effect of numerous suits and appeals going back to the mid-1960s has been to limit the ability of municipal governments to practice exclusionary zoning. The courts have overturned a number of zoning ordinances that they found to be unduly restrictive and have forced many municipalities to make some provision in their zoning ordinances for low- and moderate-income housing. They have also required a number of municipalities to consider regional housing need in the making of municipal plans.[15] The courts have recognized that if a large number of municipalities design their zoning and other land use controls to exclude those of lower and middle income—each municipality arguing that those who are excluded can find housing elsewhere—the net effect will be a regionwide shortage of housing for such people. However, court decisions on land use do not generalize as widely as decisions on some other subjects, in part because each community, each parcel of land, and all of the other particulars are not entirely the same from one case to the next. Although there have been many decisions in state courts, there has been no decision on the subject in the U.S. Supreme Court. Though much constrained by the courts, exclusionary zoning is far from banished from the suburban scene.

Zoning is an evolving institution. Not only does it change because of court decisions but it is also subject to modification by planners and municipal governments. In general, zoning has been becoming more flexible and more subject to negotiation in recent years, partly in response to the recognition of some of its faults noted earlier.[16]

THE PLANNING PROCESS

Most cities, as well as many counties and towns, have planning departments. Generally, the planning department is a part of the executive branch of the municipal government. A typical arrangement is as follows. The planning department is headed by a commissioner who is a political appointee nominated by the mayor or city manager and confirmed by the city's legislative body. Often the person selected must have some formal credentials as a planner, such as a master's degree in the subject or some years of professional experience.

The staff of the agency is not politically appointed, but rather is civil service. Candidates for jobs as planners must meet educational and experience requirements, such as a planning degree and so many years experience, and must take a civil service examination. In a large city the planning agency may be big enough so that it can be organized into a number of sections. There might be one section that handles zoning and other land use control issues. Another section might do long-range planning, another might do capital projects review, and still another might do planning-related research. In a small municipality the planning staff may be too small for any specialization, and the planner or planners will be jacks of all trades, doing whatever is necessary. Both large and small agencies from time to time make use of planning consultants, particularly for specialized types of work such as traffic and environmental studies. In a very small municipality there may be no full-time planner at all. When the municipality needs planning, it will hire a planning consultant firm to do a specific piece of work, such as drawing up a master plan.

The planning commissioner will report to the mayor or city manager and may also report to the city council. In many cities, the planning commissioner may also report to a planning board. This is a lay board, a group of citizens who serve without pay, or for a nominal sum, on an advisory basis. Typically, these citizens are nominated by the head of the executive branch and confirmed by the legislative body. Their function is to help make the planning department aware of and responsive to the will of the citizens of the city. How influential the planning board is varies greatly. In some cases, the board is little more than a rubber stamp. In other cases the board may play a very active role, both in influencing the actions of the planners and also in mobilizing public support for the initiatives of the planning department.

A simplified and idealized planning process would be as follows. The municipality's planning department draws up a master plan for the municipality. This includes a general vision of the municipality's development, expressed in some generalized land use maps and supporting documents. It also draws up the zoning map and zoning ordinance that supplement and flesh out the generalized land use plan. In addition, it also develops or helps to develop a long-term capital facilities plan that shows what roads, sewer and water systems, public facilities, and the like are to be provided and also gives a rough schedule for their provision. The plan is drawn up with a great deal of public participation from the very beginning. As the plan develops the planners will present it at public meetings and give the public substantial opportunity to comment. Generally, the law requires substantial public participation. Beyond that, for the plan to be implemented it must have substantial political support. The public is much more likely to support the plan if it has had a hand in producing it.

The plan and such supporting documents as the zoning ordinance are adopted by the municipality's legislative body, and as the years pass, that body appropriates the funds necessary to carry out the necessary public investments. Inevitably, things will not work out exactly as planned. Therefore, the plan is reviewed periodically and necessary readjustments are made.

A FEW COMPLICATIONS

The above is a very simplified and idealized view of the planning process. A few complications follow.

Though government sets the stage for the development process through the use of its capital budget and land use controls, it is not in sole control of events. Land use controls, in effect, tell people what they may do on privately owned land. Or, if you say that in their absence all things would be permitted, then controls tell property owners what they may not do. In this way land use controls shape development. However, they cannot make development occur. The municipality can zone land for industrial development, but it cannot compel anyone to invest on that spot. It can zone for office parks, but it cannot compel builders to construct office parks.

Similarly, the municipality can spend its money to provide highway access and utilities in a way in that it believes will stimulate desirable development. That does not compel any private party to come forth and make the hoped-for investment. In one municipality where growth pressures are weak, land zoned for commerce and industry (or housing) and provided with all the requisite utilities may sprout nothing but weeds year after year. In another municipality where growth pressures are very strong, growth may occur at a pace that the municipality can barely handle. Municipal officials, rather than seeking to promote growth, may be deluged with calls about traffic jams, inadequate public utilities, and public schools that don't have enough classrooms for this year's enrollments.

At present, a great deal of development occurs through a negotiated process. Consider a very typical sort of situation. City officials are pleased that Acme Manufacturing, Inc., has announced plans to build a $50-million-dollar facility in their town at which several hundred people will be employed. The manufacturing process is a clean one, so that there are no serious environmental problems, and calculations done by the town government indicate that the facility will pay more in taxes than it will cost in additional services. It is possible that the firm just happened to find a site with the right utilities, the right traffic access, the right site geometry, and the right zoning through contact with an industrial real estate broker and has decided to move in without consulting the town. But that scenario is unlikely.

The more likely scenario is that there have been extended negotiations between town and firm. The firm may have wanted some modifications in the zoning of the site. It may have needed the town to extend laterals from its main water and sewer lines. Perhaps it needed the town to add a turning lane and a stoplight in front of the plant entrance. In return, the firm may have made some concessions to the town. Perhaps the firm needs only 50 acres of the site's 63 acres, and so it agrees to donate those less usable 13 acres at the back to the town for an extension of the town park. It may agree to such design requirements as the planting of an extra buffering strip, so that the plant will be barely visible from the road, or some other site design feature that the town wants. There may be some subsidy of the development by the town, perhaps as infrastructure investments on the site or perhaps in the form of property tax breaks. In order to secure these the firm may have agreed that it will have invested so many dollars in the site by a certain date, will employ so many people by another date, and will repay some of the subsidy if it fails to meet these conditions—an arrangement called a "clawback" by economic developers.

The point is that there is a negotiated process. Who gets most and who gives most depends upon the details of that transaction—who is the more skilled bargainer and who wants what most. If the town is hungry for development while the firm has a choice of many other good locations, the town may offer big property tax breaks and other concessions to the firm. If the town is doing well anyway and the firm, for whatever its reasons, is very eager to locate there, the town may offer no subsidy and take a very inflexible stance about such matters as making adjustments in zoning.

In the case of many large real estate developments, whether commercial, residential or mixed use, the developer approaches the municipality, often with a "master plan" for the new development, and a process of negotiation ensues. In this case the planning process described earlier becomes reversed. The planning for, in some cases, hundreds of acres and hundreds of millions of dollars' worth of construction is not done by the municipality's planners or planning consultant but by the developer. Rather than make plans, the municipal planners act as the judge of plans made by others. In effect, the role of the city's planners is to represent the city's interests in the development process.

Though a municipality has a master plan and envisions itself as developing in a particular pattern, events may not always permit it to do so. When the municipality is confronted with a large development proposal that does not fit into its master plan, it then may have to choose between turning the development away or making major changes in its plans. How it reacts to the proposal will vary from place to place and proposal to proposal. Do the citizens like or dislike the new proposal? How highly does the municipality value new jobs and new tax revenues versus peace and tranquillity? How powerful are the construction unions that support the proposal for the jobs it will provide versus the environmentalists who want to preserve what they claim is a precious and sensitive area? Suppose the proposal to build a 300-acre mixed use development looks fairly good to the municipality, but there are a few things about the proposal that it really does not like. The developer's representatives indicate that they are not in a position to compromise much. If they do not get just about everything that they have asked for in the way of new roads, utilities, and rezonings, plus some generous property tax abatements, they will walk away. After all, they say, there are lots of other municipalities that would like all the jobs and new tax revenues. Are they bluffing, or do they really mean it? At this point in the process, skill as a poker player might be more useful to the town's negotiator(s) than anything one learns in planning school.

Private communities (see Chapter 9), some of which may cover thousands of acres, generally originate with a single development proposal. They do not represent a filling in of the existing municipal master plan at all. And they may change the shape of the municipality, often a county, into something very different from anything its citizens or planners ever envisioned. All of the above comes back to the point that the actual planning process contains a great deal of uncertainty and compromise.

THE MULTIPLE JURISDICTION PROBLEM

About 70 percent of the U.S. population lives in a metropolitan area, which means that the real city in which they live is made up of many governments. There will be the government of the central city or cities, governments of smaller cities within the metropolitan area, county governments, and town governments. There will be quasi governments, such as school districts, as well, and their boundaries may or may not correspond with municipal boundaries. Some years ago Robert Wood wrote a book about the governmental structure of the New York metropolitan region. Its title, *1400 Governments*, expressed the basic situation succinctly.[17] The 1400 included the government of New York City and a number of other cities, about fifteen county governments, hundreds of town and village (a type of political subdivision in New York State) governments, and a mass of quasi governments.

Coordinating this mass of governments is not simple. Land use controls in the United States generally reside either at the county level or, more commonly, with the smallest unit of government, such as a town within a county. There is no mechanism to coordinate them. Some municipalities coordinate land use planning with their neighbors, and some do not. The fact that municipalities are often in economic competition with each other complicates the situation. A variety of organizations have been developed to bring about intermunicipal coordination on planning matters. A number of regions have regional planning agencies. The federal government has tried, and succeeded to some degree, in encouraging intermunicipal cooperation by requiring such cooperation for the receipt of some types of federal grants. For example, approval by the regional planning agency may be required before a municipal government can receive federal funds for, say, expanding its water supply system. Many metropolitan areas have councils of government (COGs) as described in Chapter 4. These seek to coordinate actions of their constituent governments. Typically they have very little power. To the extent that they affect the course of events it is by persuasion and by brokering agreement. Often, intergovernmental cooperation is best where the scale of what must be done absolutely necessitates cooperation. Thus cooperation is likely to be best over large issues like the metropolitan highway network, water supply and sewerage treatment facilities, and the like. It is not nearly as good over land use planning.

In many metropolitan areas the situation is complicated by the inclusion of parts of more than one state in the metropolitan area. Thus the Washington, D.C., metropolitan area includes a number of counties in Virginia and Maryland as well as the District of Columbia. The Philadelphia metropolitan area includes parts of Pennsylvania, New Jersey, and Delaware. Most of the Chicago metropolitan area is in Illinois, but part of its southern portion extends into Indiana. And so on. The multistate situation takes an already complex situation and makes it still more complex by adding more players and more interests.

SUMMARY

For most of the nineteenth century, city planning in the United States was very limited. Plans generally focused upon economic growth and land development. The first modern city plan is generally considered to be the plan for Chicago, done in 1909. It emphasized public capital investment in roads, bridges, and structures and the acquisition and development of public open space. During the late nineteenth century and early twentieth century a series of court cases, culminating in *Euclid v. Ambler* in 1926, established the right of government to exercise some control over the use of privately owned land without having to pay compensation to property owners. Today, the primary tools of the planner are public capital investment and land use controls, of which the best known is zoning. A common arrangement for the municipal planning department is for it to have an appointed commissioner supported by a professional staff hired through civil service. Generally, the planning department reports to the mayor or city manager and often to the city council as well. In some cases it may also report to a lay planning board. The municipal plan is generally developed with a substantial amount of citizen input, both because of legal requirements and because without significant public support a plan has little chance of being implemented.

City planning involves decisions that may have large financial consequences for developers and property owners and that may have important consequences in the daily lives of the municipality's residents. Thus it is necessarily a highly political process, and many planning decisions are made after considerable amounts of negotiation.

NOTES

1. For a discussion of the difference between U.S. and British political culture in this regard, see J. Barry Cullingworth, *The Political Culture of Planning* (London and New York: Routledge Inc., 1993), particularly Chapters 13 and 14.
2. For a history of colonial era American city planning, see John Reps, *The Making of Urban America* (Princeton, N.J.: Princeton University Press, 1965).
3. For a discussion of how the revolution changed American attitudes toward authority in many different forms, see Gordon S. Wood, *The Radicalism of the American Revolution* (New York: Vintage Books, Random House, 1991).
4. A short history of planning in America from colonial times to the present can be found in John M. Levy, *Contemporary Urban Planning*, 4th edition (Prentice Hall, 1997), Chapters 3

and 4. A much more detailed history can be found in Mel Scott, *American City Planning since 1890* (Berkeley: University of California Press, 1971).

5. For a detailed account of the plan for the city of Chicago, see Robert L. Wrigley, Jr., "The Plan of Chicago," in Donald A. Krueckeberg, ed., *Planning History in the United States* (Rutgers University Press, 1983).

6. This is reinforced by the Fourteenth Amendment, which states in part, ". . . nor shall any State deprive any person of life, liberty or property without due process of law; nor deny to any person within its jurisdiction the equal protection of the laws."

7. See Chapter 5, "The Legal Basis of Planning," in Levy, op. cit., or Mel Scott, op. cit. chapters 2 and 3.

8. For an overview of growth management, see Chapter 15 in Levy, op. cit. For more detailed discussion, see John M. DeGrove, *The New Frontier for Land Policy: Planning and Growth Management in the States* (Lincoln Land Institute, 1992); or Douglas R. Porter, *Understanding Growth Management* (Washington, D.C.: Urban Land Institute, 1989).

9. For an overview of environmental planning, see Levy, op. cit. Chapter 16. For an annual summary of environmental legislation and policy as well as data on air pollution and other measures of environmental quality, see the annual reports of the Council on Environmental Quality, U.S. Government Printing Office, Washington, D.C.

10. The public health hazard is the possibility that leakage from septic tanks will contaminate the groundwater that is brought up from wells. The exact number of housing units per acre that can be supported by septic tank disposal varies with soil characteristics. Where soil characteristics are favorable, lot sizes of somewhat less than an acre may be feasible. Where the soil does not drain well, the minimum safe lot size for development in the absence of a public water system may be several acres.

11. Kevin Lynch, in a classic book on urban design, *The Image of the City* (Cambridge: M.I.T. Press, 1960), refers to park boundaries as "hard edges." Because the land is in permanent public ownership, it constitutes a permanent barrier to development, a permanent edge that defines the pattern of development.

12. An easement is a provision that grants the public some right of access to or use of private land. For example, an easement might be granted for a right-of-way for water and sewer lines.

13. Jane Jacobs, the *Death and Life of Great American Cities* (New York: Vantage Books, Random House, 1961). Though Jacobs is not a planner, the book is quite possibly the most influential book written on planning in the last 50 years.

14. See *The New Urbanism*, edited by Peter Katz (New York: McGraw-Hill Book Co., 1994) and Andre Duany, *Towns and Town-Making Principles* (Harvard University Press, 1991).

15. The best-known zoning litigation in recent years has been a series of cases collectively known as the Mt. Laurel [N.J.] Cases. An account of them can be found in Levy, op. cit.

16. See Chapter 9 in Levy, op. cit.

17. Robert C. Wood, *1400 Governments: The Political Economy of the New York Region* (Cambridge: Harvard University Press, 1961).

REFERENCES

Eisner, Simon. *The Urban Pattern*, 6th ed. New York: Van Nostrand Reinhold, 1993.

Garvin, Alexander. *The American City: What Works, What Doesn't*. New York: McGraw-Hill, 1995.

Levy, John M. *Contemporary Urban Planning*, 5th ed. Upper Saddle River, N.J.: Prentice Hall, 2000.

So, Frank S., and Getzels, Judith, eds. *The Practice of Local Government Planning*. Washington, D.C.: International City Managers Association, 1986.

Chapter

9 | Housing: Part 1—An Overview

In this chapter we provide some basic facts about the physical state of housing in the United States, the mechanics of housing stock change, and how housing is financed and taxed. In the following chapter we turn to housing problems and housing policy.

HOW WE ARE HOUSED

By world standards, Americans are well housed. For example, the average American occupies close to twice as much residential floor space as the average person in a number of other prosperous, industrialized nations.[1] In large measure this is because of public policies that favor investment in housing, particularly owner-occupied housing.

Table 9-1 presents a general picture of the U.S. housing stock. Note that about two thirds of all housing units are owner occupied, a substantially higher percentage than in most other Western democracies. Note also the preponderance of single-family housing.

One might suspect from the similarity between the numbers for single-family units and owner-occupied units that the terms mean almost the same thing, but this is not the case. There are about 10 million single-family houses occupied by renters at any given time. Conversely, there are about an equal number of owner occupiers who live in multiunit structures. In a great many two- and three-family units, the owner occupies one unit and rents out the other. There are also many owner occupiers in larger multiunit condominium or cooperative buildings. Condominiums and cooperatives are discussed later in the chapter.

TABLE 9-1 The United States Housing Stock (figures in millions except where indicated)

Total units (1996)	113.3
Seasonal (1996)	3.2
Year-round (1996)	109.2
Occupied units (1996)	100.5
Owner-occupied units (1996)	65.4
Renter-occupied units (1996)	35.0
Units in structure (1990)	
1 (detached)	60.4
1 (attached)	5.4
2	4.9
3 and 4	4.9
5–9	4.9
10–19	4.9
20–49	3.9
50 or more	4.4
Mobile home or trailer	7.4
Other	1.1
Median number of persons per owner-occupied unit (1990)	2.40
Median number of persons per renter-occupied unit (1990)	2.04
Median number of persons per room, owner-occupied unit (1990)	0.45
Median number of persons per room, renter-occupied unit (1990)	0.59
Median existing single-family house price (1995)	$112,900
Median new single-family house price (1995)	$133,900
Median contract rent for existing unit	$n/a
Median contract rent for new unit (1995)	$654
Rental vacancy rate (1995)	7.6 percent
New units authorized (1995) (figures in thousands)	
1 unit in structure	999
2 units in structure	33
3 or 4 units in structure	32
5 or more units in structure	269
Manufactured housing (not included in above figures)	354

Sources: The 1995 figures are from various tables in U.S. Housing Market Conditions, U.S. Department of Housing and Urban Development, Office of Policy Development and Research, May, 1996. The 1990 figures are from the Census of Housing, CH-1-1, Vol. 1, Table 15.

Notes: The category of single-family houses includes both free-standing houses and row houses, sometimes termed attached houses or townhouses. Within the free-standing category are both houses built on site and mobile homes—that is, houses that are built in factories and then trucked to their permanent site. Although mobile homes (also called manufactured homes) are not included in the building permit data, they are included in the "1 unit in structure" category higher up in the table if they meet local building codes. The figures in the table do not include group quarters such as college dormitories and military barracks.

In the decades since World War II the U.S. housing stock has increased faster in percentage terms than has the U.S. population. Note the small number of people per unit in both owner-occupied and renter-occupied units. The table shows a total of 3.2 million seasonal homes. That number is more than triple the number for 1970. Its rapid growth is one indicator of increasing affluence for at least part of the population.

In general, the U.S. housing market is not particularly tight. Note the rental vacancy rate of 7.6 percent in 1995. To be counted in the vacancy rate, a unit not only has to be physically vacant but also available to be rented. An apartment that is physically vacant but has been rented and is simply awaiting its new occupant would not be counted. Housing economists generally consider a vacancy rate of 5 percent to be sufficient to permit easy mobility and give renters or buyers an adequate amount of choice. In that sense there is no generalized housing shortage in the United States, though there are shortages in some places.[2]

The Improvement in Housing Quality

Housing quality, to the extent that it can be accurately measured, has been rising in the United States. For example, the average new single-family house has been getting larger over the years even though household size (the people occupying one housing unit) has been declining. In 1970 36 percent of all new single-family houses had 1,200 square feet or less of floor space. By 1993 the comparable figure had dropped to 9 percent. Conversely, in 1993 the number of houses with over 2,400 square feet of floor space had more than doubled to 29 percent from the 1970 figure.

Several decades ago the Bureau of the Census attempted to assess housing by having its enumerators rate housing using words like "deteriorating" and "dilapidated." Ultimately, the bureau decided that such terminology was too subjective, and the effort was dropped. But two somewhat more objective measures, whether a housing unit has complete bathroom facilities and complete kitchen facilities, have been retained, and they both show an increase with each decennial census. Another quality index, though it does not measure the physical soundness of housing, is overcrowding. The Bureau of the Census rates a unit as "overcrowded" if it has more than 1.0 occupants per room. By this measure, too, the U.S. standard of housing has been rising in recent decades.

Table 9–2 breaks down the figures on owner/renter status and on type of structure, using the basic Bureau of the Census geography. As you would expect, the percentage of owners and the percentage of single-family houses is smallest in central cities and highest in nonmetropolitan areas. However, even in the central cities there are almost as many owner as renter households, and single-family units account for more than half of the total housing stock. Though the big apartment house may symbolize central city

TABLE 9-2 Housing Type and Owner/Renter Status by Place

Place	Percentage of units owner occupied	Percentage of units renter occupied	Single-family units as percentage of all units
Metropolitan areas	61.8%	38.2%	66.7%
Central city	49.0%	51.0%	52.7%
Outside of central city	71.0%	29.0%	76.9%
Nonmetropolitan	72.4%	27.6%	86.7%

Source: Census of Housing, General Characteristics of Housing, CH-1-1, Vol. 1, Table 15.

housing, the single-family house actually makes up a much larger share of central city housing. If one adds to the single-family housing figure structures with 2, 3, or 4 units in them, one has then accounted for about 68 percent of all housing units in central cities.

Grouping all central cities together conceals a wide range of differences. Toward one end of the spectrum, only 16 percent of Boston's housing stock is made up of single-family units, and about 69 percent of all households rent. Toward the other end of the spectrum, in Phoenix, Arizona, single-family housing makes up about 70 percent of the total housing stock, and about 59 percent of all units are owner occupied. In general, cities whose main growth has been more recent and that are developed in a low-density, automobile-oriented pattern are more likely to have relatively larger amounts of single-family housing and higher percentages of home ownership.

Who Pays the Bill?

One salient point about the U.S. housing stock is the extent to which it is privately built and privately owned. Over 98 percent of the housing is owned privately, either by the party who occupies it or by a landlord. The overwhelming mass of it was built on privately owned land and was built for profit.

The U.S. situation is quite different from that of many other nations. In many Western European nations a large percentage of the total housing stock is government owned. Adequate housing is viewed as a right or entitlement and so is provided publicly, often with a heavy subsidy behind it. A large government presence in the provision of housing is part of the European "social democratic" model. For example, in Germany, the Netherlands, Scandinavia, and other parts of Western Europe a very substantial percentage of the population lives in publicly provided housing, generally referred to as "social housing," for which the rent covers only part of the actual cost. In Great Britain the government presence in the housing market is smaller than on the continent, but still much larger than in the United States. Some millions of British households occupy "council housing," as publicly supplied housing in Great Britain is called. Whether the European or the U.S. model is better can be argued. The positive side of the European social democratic model is a higher standard of housing for people of low or modest incomes. The negative side is that to pay for that part of the cost of social housing not covered by rents, as well as the more generous social services "safety net" in general, the total burden of taxes is a much larger percentage of the gross domestic product (GDP) than it is in the United States. As the economists are fond of telling us, "There is no such thing as a free lunch."

This difference in the way housing is provided stems from an ideological difference. In contrast to most of the nations of Western Europe, the U.S. has never had much of a socialist movement. To the American body politic, massive public provision of housing looked too much like socialism. We grudgingly agree to let government provide housing or some assistance in obtaining housing on the free market for some of the poor, and that is as far as we will go. There is, however, a large indirect government presence in the rest of the housing market, as discussed later in this chapter.

THE MECHANICS OF HOUSING STOCK CHANGE

Housing enters the inventory by the obvious act of being constructed. It leaves the inventory by being demolished (usually to make way for new structures), by burning down, and sometimes by being abandoned. The latter is sometimes followed by or preceded by fire and is often followed, sooner or later, by demolition. Some units also enter the housing stock by being converted from nonresidential to residential use. For example, in a number of cities old manufacturing loft buildings that are no longer marketable as sites for manufacturing have been converted to residential use. Some housing leaves the residential category by being converted to a commercial use, such as the house that is converted to a professional office.

If one just looks at the housing stock over a brief period, its distribution looks fixed. If one takes a longer view, that is not the case. Like modeling clay, the housing stock is capable of plastic flow and gradually changes form under pressure. Consider some of the pressures.

The Effects of Increasing Demand

Consider a moderate income neighborhood with a housing stock of moderate quality in which, not surprisingly, rents and house prices are moderate. Suppose that, for whatever reason, demand for housing in this neighborhood goes up. Perhaps it goes up as a function of population growth in the city. Or perhaps because of commercial growth downtown, a number of younger, affluent couples decide it is a convenient place to live. Under the pressure of increasing demand house prices and rents begin to rise. Landlords who own rental units there begin to spend more money on repairs and remodeling because they see that there is money to be made in offering more attractive units at higher rents. They do not worry about sinking money into their rental properties because they see that the prices of rental properties are rising and they know that they will recoup their investment when they sell. This is sometimes referred to as a "neighborhood effect," meaning that the value of a property is powerfully affected by what happens to its surroundings.

A similar process occurs in the owner-occupied part of the housing stock in the same neighborhood. A certain percentage of the owner-occupied housing stock is sold each year. As prices rise the buyers tend to have, on average, higher incomes than the sellers. They have a tendency to improve the properties they buy. They, too, do not worry about sinking money into their properties because they see housing prices rising and know that they will get their money back when they sell. And given the strong demand, they know that they will not have trouble selling if and when they decide to do so.

As prices continue to rise the value of the land under buildings rises, and at some point the land becomes so valuable that it is worthwhile for investors to buy older properties and pay the cost of demolition simply to obtain building lots. Redevelopment occurs, and the average age of buildings in the area declines. The only people who do not benefit are some of the original renters who may be priced out as rents rise. The original owners, of course, are delighted because they make nice capital gains when they sell their now more valuable properties. Again, notice the neighborhood effect. If you own a modest property in this rapidly improving neighborhood, you do not have to do much to make a profit here. All you have to do is wait for a while and then sell.

The Effects of Decreasing Demand

Now consider the same neighborhood if demand for housing there declines. It may decline for any of a number of reasons. Perhaps employment downtown has fallen, reducing the demand for residence. Or perhaps a great deal of new housing has been built in nearby suburban areas, and many of the people who would have been buyers or renters here have now moved out to the suburbs.

As demand weakens, rents decline, or at least they do not keep up with increases in landlord's costs. As a result, landlords' profit margins decline, and after a time some of them are operating at a loss. One way for landlords to keep their cash flows positive, at least for a time, is to "disinvest" in the building. That means spending less on maintenance and repair than is necessary to maintain the quality of the building. Disinvesting compromises the long-term future of the building, but if the landlord thinks that the building is doomed anyway—the "neighborhood effect" again—it may be the most sensible thing to do. As the building's cash flow diminishes, the owner may not have the ability to maintain the building in decent condition even if he or she wants to do so. The situation tends to feed on itself. As the quality of the building declines, it tends to attract poorer and poorer tenants. Not only does the landlord sign leases at lower rents, but the number of rent delinquencies rises. Thus, actual rent collections fall by more than just an examination of the leases would show.

Under these circumstances the market value of the building declines. At some point the landlord's equity—what the building is worth on the market minus the debt (mortgage(s) on the building)—may become negative. At that point the landlord may simply abandon the building. In most cities it is illegal to abandon a building, but that does not mean it is not commonly done. A variation on the abandonment theme is arson. In that case a troublesome building is converted some night, albeit illegally, into a check from the insurance company.

Similar processes may operate in connection with owner-occupied properties. As the owner sees the market value of the house shrinking, he or she is less willing to put money into it, so its quality declines. The property owner may be pushed into selling by the fear that if he or she does not get out now, prices will only go lower. As properties come to be owned by poorer and poorer people, there may be more houses in arrears on property taxes and mortgage payments, and houses may be foreclosed by the city or the banks.[3] Housing abandonment may show up in the owner-occupied as well as the renter-occupied part of the housing market. New investment in the neighborhood slows down and may ultimately cease, for what investor wants to buy in a declining neighborhood?

The above, when it goes to the extreme, is the basic story of slum formation. Even if the landlord does not want the property to deteriorate, he or she may not have much choice about it. When one hears the term "slumlord," one may think of a fat cat squeezing big profits from a mass of slum properties. In fact, many owners of slum properties are "mom and pop" operations and are neither highly profitable nor backed by vast financial resources.[4]

The ultimate driving force is failing demand. Demand for residence there may fall for any number of reasons. It may be that the older housing in the area cannot compete with newer housing types that most people regard as being more attractive. A turn-of-the-century tenement, even if very well maintained, is not a very attractive housing type by most people's standards. Demand may shrink because of declining job opportunities. Adverse social conditions, in particular street crime, will shrink the demand for housing in an area. The effect is likely to be circular. As increasing street crime drives out the remaining middle-class and working-class population and much of the employment that the buying power of those classes sustained, rates of poverty and unemployment go up. That, in turn, is likely to exacerbate the crime problem. One may think of slums as overcrowded places, in part because of the image of overcrowded tenements in the turn of the century. In actuality many slum neighborhoods are characterized by declining populations and many partially vacant or abandoned buildings; when conditions get bad enough, everyone who can get out does so.

Some years ago it was widely believed that the problem of slums was largely a problem of the physical condition of housing. This view was one of the assumptions behind Urban Renewal, the federal program discussed in the following chapter. The more modern and comprehensive view is that the physical condition of the housing is largely a reflection of social and economic forces.

The Filtering Process

The previous section described what are essentially neighborhood effects—things that happen to the individual building largely because of where it is located. Neighborhood effects apart, housing often goes through a "filtering" process as a matter of age. Specifically, over time it passes from more to less prosperous hands, whether it be owner- or renter-occupied housing. One reason is simply that new housing, by most people's standards, is usually better housing than old housing. Not only does housing age physically, but our standards for housing change. The average house built in recent years is larger than the average house built several decades ago. New technologies like central air conditioning are easily installed in new houses but are often difficult to "retrofit" to older housing. Without subsidy new housing cannot be built for the lower portion of the income distribution curve (mobile homes are a partial exception to this rule). In fact, one reason that new housing cannot be built for people in the lower part of the income distribution curve are the zoning and building codes discussed previously. These codes guarantee that new housing will be good housing (matters of taste excepted), but by imposing a variety of site and structural requirements on builders, they also guarantee that it will not be cheap housing. Note that the basic idea of filtering is not unique to housing. Automobiles filter too. People of modest means do not drive new Cadillacs, but some of them do drive used Cadillacs.

Gentrification

Though downward filtering is the usual situation with housing, it is not always the case. Neighborhood effects can force the housing filter to run in reverse. Where this effect is pronounced enough to cause the neighborhood to take on a clearly upper-middle-class tone, it is sometimes referred to as "gentrification," from the word *gentry*. In most large cities one can find "gentrifying" areas. In this situation we observe high levels of investment in both the restoration of old buildings and the construction of new ones. Rents and house prices rise, and the area becomes a venue for real estate speculation. People buy properties partly in the expectation of further price rises.

An example of a gentrifying neighborhood in New York City is Greenwich Village. Part of its appeal is location. It is a quick subway ride or a half hour's walk from New York's financial district to its south and from the midtown Manhattan business district to its north. And the village, with its maze of old streets dating back to the days of Peter Stuyvesant, has considerable charm. For many people it is a very "in" and trendy place. As a result an old four-story brownstone building on a 25 by 100 foot lot may sell for the better part of $1 million. And many such houses, 100 or 150 years old, that look quite plain on the outside are splendidly and expensively restored inside. In other parts of the city buildings of comparable age and the same original structure may be slum properties.

Many municipal governments are delighted with the process of gentrification. The increased property values mean increased property tax collections. The wealthier population is also likely to contribute more to the city's sales tax revenues and in the case of the few cities that have an income tax, to those revenues as well. The wealthier population is also likely to require less of the city in the way of social services. For these and similar reasons many municipal governments will do whatever they can to assist the process of gentrification. However, no social process is without its downside and its detractors. Some advocates of the poor have complained about the process of gentrification and urged municipal governments to resist it on the grounds that rising values and hence rising rents displace poor people and may destroy functioning neighborhoods. If an investor buys a deteriorated apartment house in a gentrifying area, guts it, rebuilds it to a much higher standard, and then rents the units in it for three times their original rent, or markets it as a condominium or co-op, what happens to the original tenants after they get their eviction notices? Will they be able to find adequate accommodations elsewhere in the city's housing market or not?[5]

HOUSING FINANCE

A house is the largest purchase that most people ever make. For that reason only about 13 percent of all houses are bought for cash or a cash equivalent such as another property in trade. The other 87 percent are bought, in part, with borrowed money. This is hardly surprising. In 1995 when the median house in the United States sold for about $113 thousand, the median family income was somewhat under $40,000. Most people simply do not have that much cash available, particularly in the prime home-buying years. Nor, if they did, would they necessarily want to tie it all up in the purchase of an asset that cannot always quickly be sold. The sale of housing, probably more than any other good, is sensitive to conditions in the credit markets. Whether large numbers of construction workers are putting in overtime or whether they are collecting unemployment insurance is very dependent on the availability of loans to home buyers.

The mortgage is the basic credit instrument for buying a house. A mortgage is essentially a long-term loan that is secured by the house itself. If the owner of the house does not make the required payments on the mortgage, the mortgage lender may go through a legal procedure and take the property back (foreclose) from the owner.[6]

A Typical House Financing

Below we illustrate a typical house financing. Assume that the house costs $125,000 and that the buyer has $25,000 in cash to be used as a down payment on the house. The buyer intends to borrow the other $100,000 on a 30-year mortgage with an interest rate of 7 percent. We also assume that property taxes on the house will be $180 per month and that insurance will cost another $20 a month.

Mortgages are generally written as "level debt" instruments. You make the same size payment each month over the entire life of the mortgage. At the beginning when you owe the entire amount—in this case, $100,000—most of your payment will be interest on the remaining amount that you owe. As time passes and you reduce the amount that you owe, the interest component of your payment shrinks and the amount that goes to reducing (amortizing) the principal rises.

When you go to the bank to apply for this $100,000 mortgage, the loan officer checks a table in a "mortgage book" or uses a computer program and sees that to pay off $100,000 in 30 years (360 payments) at 7 percent interest you will need to make monthly payments of $665.70. The changing relationship between interest and principle is shown in Table 9–3.

As you can see, for a loan of this duration and at this interest rate, interest payments amount to considerably more than the principal amount of the loan. Note, also, that the bulk of the principal payments are made toward the end of the loan. In fact, at the midpoint of the loan, after the 180th pay-

TABLE 9–3 Principal and Interest Payments on a 30-Year, $100,000 Mortgage at 7 Percent

Payment number	Interest paid	Principal paid
1	$594	72
180	$442	224
360	$4	662

Total payments = $665.70 × 360 = $239,652
  Total principal payments: $100,000
  Total interest payments: $139,652

ment, you will still owe approximately three fourths of the original $100,000. Because interest is such a large part of the total mortgage payment, the cost of buying a house is extremely sensitive to interest rates.

Will the bank be willing to make the loan? Most banks have a rule of thumb for the ratio of the borrower's income to the amount of the monthly payment. Here the monthly payment is $665.70 for the mortgage itself plus $200 for insurance and taxes. Let us say the bank requires that the monthly payment, in this case $865.70, be no more than 28 percent of monthly income, a typical sort of requirement. In that case they will require a monthly income of $3,092 or $37,104 per year. The bank will probably also want to see some history of continuous employment. The one instance in which they may be willing to lend if you do not have the income or sufficient employment history is if someone else who does have the income, say a parent, is willing to co-sign the mortgage. That means that the other party is obligated to pay should you fail to pay.

What happens if you decide to sell the house? At the closing (the time when the house changes hands) you must pay to the bank the remaining principal (the unpaid balance of the loan). This stipulation is written into the mortgage agreement, and the bank's attorney or other representative will usually be present at the closing to see that such payment is made.

In the example above we used a down payment of 20 percent, and, indeed, down payments in the 20 to 25 percent range are very common. It is also possible for some people to buy with much smaller down payments. The instrument that makes this possible is mortgage insurance. The insurer guarantees the lender that in the event of default on the mortgage the insurer will pay off the unpaid balance. There are private insurers and there are also federal agencies that will provide mortgage insurance, notably the Federal Housing Administration (FHA). The insurance premium is packed into the monthly mortgage payment as perhaps a quarter percentage point higher interest rate than would be the case with an uninsured mortgage.

The Origins of Modern Home Financing

The long-term housing finance described above was not always available in the United States. Rather, it originated during the Great Depression as a series of acts of federal policy. To the extent that federal policies gave millions of Americans something they very much wanted, namely the chance for homeownership, at very small cost to the federal government, we would have to say that federal policy was very successful.

Until the mid-1930s—the depths of the Great Depression—financing a house was a much more difficult matter than it now is. Typically, banks would not lend more than 50 percent of the cost of the house, and generally they would not lend for longer than five years. Both the big down payment and the short duration were required by banks to protect themselves from the risk of default by the borrower. Very often the loan would be structured so that the buyer paid off only a small part of the loan over its life, leaving a large "balloon" to be paid off at the very end. That meant that the home-buyer then had to hope that he or she could then find another lender to refinance. As one writer notes, the old melodrama with the villain twirling his mustache and threatening to throw out the hapless widow and her children onto the street unless she gives in to his unspeakable demands had its origins in this bit of financial reality.[7] The above circumstances kept many people from homeownership, and in the 1920s and 1930s substantially more households rented than owned.

The Federal Government and Mortgage Insurance

In the mid-1930s the federal government changed the situation drastically by the very simple expedient of offering mortgage insurance through the Federal Housing Administration (FHA). The federal government's goals were twofold. One was the direct objective of opening up homeownership to more people. The other goal was to stimulate the national economy by encouraging residential construction.

The basic idea of mortgage insurance was very simple. The homebuyer paid a small premium that went into a fund that indemnified banks for the occasional default. The cost to the federal government was minimal because the premiums were paid by the homebuyers. Once the risk of default was under control, banks were willing to lend for 25 or 30 years and often with down payments as low as 10 percent. One might ask why, given that banks have always had the option of foreclosing in the event of a default, they would care that much about mortgage insurance. One answer is that foreclosure is a time-consuming legal procedure. Another reason is that in a weak real estate market, such as was common in the Great Depression, the bank might not be able to dispose of the property once it had acquired it through foreclosure. The prospect of being saddled with numerous properties that it might have considerable difficulty in selling or renting was hardly an attractive one to banks.

The effect of the program was modest during the sluggish years of the Great Depression, but the effect after World War II was very large and persists to the present. In 1995 the FHA insured over one half million new mortgages with a total value of about $48 billion.[8] After World War II the Veterans Administration (VA) began to insure mortgages for veterans, making it possible for them to buy houses with down payments as small as 5 percent and in some cases with no down payment at all. Huge numbers of younger people who had adequate income but little or no savings could now become homeowners.

In the years after World War II the federal government also moved to facilitate mortgage lending in another way—by creating secondary mortgage markets. This takes a word of explanation from the bank's perspective. Even though the mortgage is insured against default, the bank still faces what is

Levittown, Long Island, NY, under construction in the late 1940s. Prosperity, federal mortgage insurance, and pent up demand from the Depression and war years fueled the post war suburban housing boom.

generally referred to as an "opportunity cost" or "investment" risk. Let us say that interest rates are low and the bank writes you a 30-year mortgage at 7 percent interest. The money that they lent you is now tied up for a long time at a low interest rate. Now, assume that interest rates go up so that the bank could lend the same money out at 9 percent if only it had the money. However, the bank cannot make you prepay, and the odds are that you will not want to prepay a low-interest loan during a period of high interest rates. That difference between what the bank is earning on its money that you have and what it could get for that money if only they had it instead is the opportunity cost.

The secondary mortgage market is a place where the issuers of mortgages, banks, can sell mortgages. If the bank that issued a mortgage decides after a time that it has better uses for the money tied up in a mortgage, it can sell the mortgage and get its money out now. This thus reduces the opportunity cost risk. The two biggest federal agencies in the secondary mortgage market are the Federal National Mortgage Association (FNMA, pronounced "Fannie Mae") and the Government National Mortgage Association (GNMA, pronounced "Ginnie Mae"). Another effect of these agencies is to bring additional money into mortgage lending by linking mortgage markets to the stock market. One way that these agencies get money to buy mortgages is by issuing securities to the investing public. This process of "securitizing" mortgages enables investors to put money into mortgage lending without having to have any direct connection with the issuing of mortgages. For example, an individual can buy securities issued by Fannie Mae or Ginnie Mae directly or through a mutual fund. By linking the mortgage lending to the "investing public," these federal agencies make a great deal more money available for investment in housing.

The federal policy described above has made homeownership much easier and more widespread, exactly as intended. It has also reshaped the map of America in a way that was not intended or anticipated. By stimulating homeownership these programs also promoted suburbanization because so much owner-occupied housing has been built in the suburbs. The federal role in mortgage financing stands as one of the most important pieces of federal urban policy—perhaps even the most important—even though these programs really had no specific intent vis à vis city-suburb relations.

THE TAXATION OF HOUSING

Federal tax policy also has major effects on the housing market, both in how it treats property tax and how it treats mortgage interest payments. Because of favorable tax treatment, millions of homeowners view their houses as not only physical shelters but also as tax shelters.

The property tax, as noted in Chapter 6, is a mainstay of local government finance. By the end of the 1990s local property tax collections in the United States totaled over $200 billion. Regardless of whether you own or you rent your housing, you pay property taxes. But the manner in which you pay them is quite different.

If you own the house in which you live you pay the tax explicitly (whether you send the check yourself or whether the bank that holds your mortgage sends it for you). When you file your federal and state income tax returns, if you itemize those returns, you can take the property taxes you paid as a deduction against your federal and state taxable income. Suppose that you are in the 28 percent tax bracket for federal income tax purposes and that you paid $1,000 in property taxes. In that case your federal taxable income is lowered by $1,000 and your federal tax bill by $280 (28 percent of $1,000). This favorable tax treatment for homeowners was estimated to be worth about $15.7 billion in 1996.[9] It could be regarded as a $15.7 billion subsidy for homeownership. If so regarded, it is one of the biggest federal housing programs, though there is no actual program but only a few words in the Internal Revenue Service (IRS) code that permit this deduction for homeowners.

A comparable situation prevails in regard to mortgage interest. If you own your home you pay it explicitly. If you rent you pay it implicitly because mortgage payments are a cost that your landlord must cover. The homeowner who files itemized income tax returns deducts mortgage interest from his or her federal and state taxable income. The renter cannot do so. Mortgage interest payments can amount to large sums of money. Recall the mortgage financing example in Table 9–3. In the first month alone interest was $592, and for the first year it was about $7,000. For an owner in the 28 percent bracket, and using the $7,000 figure as an approximation, deducting that interest from federal taxable income would reduce the owner's federal tax bill by $7,000 × .28 or approximately $1,960. There would also be a smaller reduction in state income tax as well.

For 1996 the federal government's Office of Management and Budget estimates the value of that special tax treatment as being worth about $54.2 billion. If that were a housing program, it would be by far the federal government's largest housing program.

If you rent you also pay property taxes in that one of your landlord's major expenses is property tax and that expense will appear implicitly in your rent. As a rule of thumb property taxes are about one fourth of total expenses for residential rental property. Thus the property tax that you pay through your rent is not a trivial sum. In most cases, you are also paying mortgage interest in that your landlord probably does not own the property free and clear but has a mortgage on it. However, because you are paying these taxes and interest payments indirectly, you cannot deduct them from your federal income tax. Thus there is no tax incentive for renting comparable to the tax incentive for owning.[10]

A look at the history of the federal tax treatment of owner-occupied housing suggests that it is largely accidental. The 16th Amendment to the Constitution, ratified in 1913, gave the federal government the authority to tax incomes, and the actual taxation of incomes began in 1916. From the beginning, taxes paid to subnational units of government and interest were deductible. But for a long time the federal income tax was not the major force in American life. In fact, for its first several decades the minimum income at which one started to pay income taxes was sufficiently high that most American families paid none at all. With the coming of World War II, federal expenditures climbed, income tax rates increased, and the great majority of the population became taxpayers. With these changes, the federal tax system became a major force in housing markets and remains so to the present time.

The tax treatment of owner-occupied housing, both with regard to property taxes and mortgage interest, exerts a very powerful pull toward home ownership. The implicit $15.7 billion subsidy for property taxes and the $54.2 billion implicit subsidy for mortgage interest dwarf all the explicit federal housing programs combined. The favorable tax treatment for owner-occupied housing not only explains a large part of the lure of the single-family house, but also explains much of the popularity of cooperative apartments and condominiums. As noted previously in connection with mortgage financing, anything that promotes widespread homeownership will, indirectly, favor suburbanization.

RECENT TRENDS IN HOUSING

Table 9–4 shows housing units authorized for 1995. It is reasonably typical of recent years. The table is based on building permit data.[11]

In the table, note the predominance of single-family units and also the regional differences. The table actually understates the predominance of single-family construction because mobile homes do not require building permits and therefore do not appear in the totals. Once in place they function as single-family homes. The term "mobile" is a bit misleading. Most mobile homes are mobile exactly once—during the trip from the factory to the site at which they are installed. Though they are constructed so that they can be lifted off the foundation and trucked again, most never are. Despite the similarity in name, they should not be confused with house trailers or with motor homes. If the mobile home figure were added to the other figures, the total amount of housing (permits and mobile homes shipped)

TABLE 9–4 Building Permits Issued in 1995 (figures in thousands)

Total	1,333.0
1 unit in structure	999.1
2 units in structure	33.3
3 or 4 units in structure	32.0
5 or more units in structure	286.6
Mobile homes shipped to dealers (permit not required)	354
Permits by metropolitan/nonmetropolitan location	
Inside MSAs	1,109.8
Outside MSAs	223.2
Permits by region of country	
Northeast	123.0
Midwest	291.9
South	587.0
West	331.1

Source: U.S. Housing Market Conditions, Department of Housing and Urban Development, Office of Policy and Research, 1997, pp. 11 and 49.

Notes: Mobile homes do not have to meet local building code standards but rather must meet HUD standards and so are not included in the permit totals. The mobile home figure is not actually the year's total but is the last quarter's figure converted to an annual rate.

would be almost 1.7 million units, of which about 1.35 million units would be single family. The regional figures are also distorted a bit by the exclusion of mobile homes. More mobile homes are placed in the South than in the rest of the nation combined. For example, in 1995 195,000 mobile homes were placed in the South, compared with 14,000 in the Northeast, 56,000 in the Midwest, and 41,000 in the West. Thus the table understates the growth of the housing stock in the South relative to the rest of the nation.

One trend that does not show up in Table 9–4 is the increase in condominiums. Condominium construction began in the 1960s and continues to be strong. A condominium is a particular form of home ownership. If you own a condominium apartment, you own your unit plus a proportionate share of the common facilities. If your unit is one of 50 units and is an average value unit, then you also own 2 percent of the common facilities. Condominiums can be built in any physical form, such as free-standing single family units, row houses, garden apartments, or high-rise apartment buildings. Regardless of the physical form, the condominium offers its owners the tax advantages of homeownership, namely, the deductibility of property taxes and mortgage interest. That favorable tax treatment is one of the big reasons for their popularity. In an area where the economics of the housing market favor multifamily structures, the condominium is one way in which the apartment dweller can get the same tax benefits as the owner of a single-family house. In cities many condominiums come into being not by new construction but by conversion of apartment houses from rental to condominium status. One driving force behind this is tax treatment. When the property owner converts the building from rental status to condominium status, he or she sells not only a physical asset, the apartment, but also something intangible but valuable, a different tax status. Therefore the same physical structure may be worth a great deal more as a condominium than as a rental property, and this accounts for much of the motivation to convert.

The Growth of Private Communities

Perhaps the most important housing trend in the United States in recent years has been the growth of private communities. In 1975 there were 340,000 housing units in private communities. By 1990 there were more than 5.9 million units. The number has grown rapidly since then.[12]

A private community is one in which one must join a community association and agree to abide by its rules as a condition of buying property in it. Private communities occur in a large number of types. Originally, many were built as retirement communities, and a great many continue to be built as such. In recent years, however, a very large number have been built for working-age populations as well. Some are quite exclusive, intended for a very affluent population. Others are aimed primarily at a middle- or upper-middle-income population. None are aimed at the lower part of the income distribution curve simply because, mobile homes excepted, it is not economically possible to build unsubsidized housing for people of less than average means.

Some private communities offer a relatively urban lifestyle. Others offer an exurban or almost rural lifestyle. Some may be closely linked to developed areas in the larger municipality. Others provide considerable physical and social isolation from the municipality in which they are built. Some private communities are open like the rest of the municipality in that anyone can enter them, even though the community may have facilities like pools or golf courses whose use is restricted to residents and guests. Other private communities are gated, with the entrance restricted to residents, guests, and tradesmen. In that way they are very different from the rest of the municipality.

The private community is generally not built in conformance with the existing municipal plan. Rather, the developer of the private community approaches the municipality with a "master plan" for a new community. Then, after some or perhaps very extensive negotiations, the municipality will rezone and otherwise replan part of its land area. The private community is then built within the larger municipality in accordance with this new plan. For this reason the terms private community and planned community are almost synonymous. In most cases the private community remains a part of the municipality in which it is built. In some cases, when the private community becomes substantial in its own right, it will break off from and become a political subdivision by itself. One example is Reston, Virginia, which began as a municipality within Fairfax County and is now incorporated as the city of Reston with a population in the 50,000 range.

Private communities are rarely built in the central parts of metropolitan areas because large blocks of undeveloped land are not available. Rather, they tend to be built in the suburban or exurban parts of the metropolitan area. Retirement communities are often built entirely outside of the metropolitan developed area because commutation to work is not an issue.

What does development as a private community offer that ordinary development within the existing municipal plan does not offer?

For the developer it offers the opportunity to sell an entire package rather than just a house or a group of houses. Housing, some retailing and service facilities, recreational facilities, some natural amenities, and whatever else is included are all together as part of a unified design. And that design can be aimed at a particular segment of the market. The community can be given a theme. For example, many private communities have been designed and marketed as golf communities. The housing is wrapped around one or more golf courses, and it is marketed to people for whom that is very important. The developer then markets the community as a package that offers a certain lifestyle. Combined in the package, the elements of the community may sell for more than they would as separate elements. Some attractive design features can be incorporated easily in a new design. For example, both Reston and Columbia, as do many other planned communities, have a system of paths to separate bicycle and foot traffic from automobile traffic. This feature is not confined to the United States. The British planned community of Milton Keynes has an extensive system of bicycle paths such that it is possible to go virtually anywhere in the community by bicycle without ever crossing an automobile road at grade. Such systems are difficult to "retrofit" into an existing development pattern and are extremely unlikely to be as good or as complete as if planned for from the beginning.

The private community is likely to be a more homogeneous place than the average city or town or county if for no other reason than the price of housing in it acts as a filter. In addition, its particular features tend to attract people with similar tastes. There is no question that physical safety is a big selling point for the private community. Within the general class of private communities the fastest growing category is the gated community.

For the municipality the private community may offer a variety of attractions. If it appears that the average housing unit in the new community will carry an above average assessed value, the municipality is likely to conclude that the planned community will yield more in tax revenues than it will cost in additional services. Many private communities provide a variety of services themselves that are provided with public funds elsewhere in the municipality. These services include such items as recreational facilities, street maintenance, trash pickup, and security. That adds to the private community's fiscal attractiveness to the municipality in which it is built. If the plan for the private community includes a certain amount of commercial development, that will make the private community more attractive to a municipal government that is interested in economic development. If the municipality's planning department or board of legislators is sensitive to good design, the idea of planning a large area *de novu* may be attractive on design grounds alone.

The rapid growth of private communities speaks very clearly for the market's positive verdict on them. Do they also have a downside?

Some critics fault them for producing too much social homogeneity. Housing prices in the community will sort the population by income, and the mix of amenities it offers may sort by taste as well. In an older community or an established municipality there is likely to be more of a mix of housing prices and rents and thus a more varied population. That homogeneity may be exactly what many of the residents of the private community want, but the critic may find the result very dull. Writing about Green Valley, Nevada, located about 20 miles from Las Vegas, one writer states:

> Real estate agents peddle Green Valley as a place for families, a community where people have returned to basic values—flagrant code phrases offering escape from the fear and threat not only of high rolling Vegas but of modern life in general. Banking on the American Nevada Corporation [The firm that started Green Valley] to impose the desired controls and restraints, thousands of pilgrims to this master-planned paradise ultimately sign mortgage contracts and stay.[13]

Later in the same article he observes,

> All of Green Valley is defined . . . by CCRs [covenants, conditions and restrictions]. . . . Every community has some restrictions on matters such as the proper placement of septic tanks . . . but in Green Valley the restrictions are detailed and pervasive, insuring the absence of individuality and suppressing the natural mess of humanity. Clotheslines and Winnebagos are not permitted; for example, no fowl, reptile, fish, or insect may be raised; there are to be no stereo speakers, horns, whistles, or bells. No debris of any kind, no open fires, no noise. . . .

The resident, on the other hand, may not characterize it as dull but as safe, relaxing, and congenial. Note that Guterson's comments are very similar to those made of the suburbs by many social critics.

It has been argued that the growth of private and, especially, gated communities is divisive socially. It lets those people who can afford to buy into such a community walk away from the rest of America. Speaking specifically of gated communities, Edward Blakely, a professor of planning, states:

> They create physical barriers to access. And they privatize community space, not just individual space. . . . When offices and retail complexes are placed within walls, the new developments create a private world. . . . This fragmentation undermines the very concept of civitas—organized community life.[14]

One could, indeed, live in one of the larger private communities and have very little to do with the society outside. The community might provide for most or all of one's social needs and most of one's recreational, shopping, and personal service needs, as well as, quite possibly, provide one's place of employment. Therein lies the fragmentation of which Blakely speaks.

One could stretch the argument by saying that if a large part of the middle class that can afford to buy into a private community does so, it would leave the remainder of urbanized America as a residual for those who cannot afford the private community. Can we expect that those who have taken care of their civic needs through the mechanism of the private community will care very much about what happens to less affluent people in the cities? Will they be willing, for example, to be taxed heavily to pay for an array of urban social services that they and their children make little use of? This is like the argument against school vouchers (see Chapter 16).

There are, of course, counterarguments. One very important one is that if one believes in a high degree of personal freedom then one must accept that people may sort themselves out. If we believe in consumer choice in clothing and automobiles, should we be against consumer choice in communities?[15] One might also note that there is now a great deal of de facto segregation by class and race in most U.S. cities. The choice is not between the private community on one hand and the completely integrated society on the other.

SUMMARY

By world standards, and even by those of most developed nations, U.S. standards of housing are high. In the decades since World War II the housing stock of the United States has increased much faster than the population, and thus the number of persons per household has fallen. About two thirds of the housing stock is owner occupied, and about 60 percent of it consists of single-family units. Even in central cities, single-family housing makes up slightly more than half of the total housing stock. In contrast to a number of European nations, privately owned, built-for-profit housing makes up over 98 percent of the total housing stock.

Because a house represents several years of income for most purchasers, the housing market is highly dependent upon credit. The introduction of mortgage insurance by the federal government in the 1930s promoted a major increase in home ownership and was one of the major forces contributing to the post–World War II suburban housing boom. The trend toward home ownership and the single-family house was and is also powerfully aided by the very favorable tax treatment that the federal government affords to owner-occupied housing.

The chapter discusses the effects of increases and decreases in the demand for housing upon the housing stock and notes the importance of "neighborhood effects." It notes that housing generally filters downward with the passage of time but that increases in demand in particular neighborhoods can cause the filtering process to run in reverse—the "gentrification" phenomenon.

The chapter closes with a note on what may be the most important housing trend of recent years, the growth of private communities.

NOTES

1. For example, in the mid-1980s the average American occupied an estimated 654 square feet of residential floor space. Comparable figures for Great Britain, the Netherlands, and Japan were 377, 333, and 302. See Willem van Vliet, *International Handbook of Housing Policies and Practices* (Westport, Conn.: Greenwood Press, 1990), p. 29.
2. In the economist's meaning a shortage occurs when there are people willing to buy at the prevailing price who cannot find a unit to buy. That is different from the noneconomist's meaning, which might be that there are not enough units available at what the speaker considers to be an acceptable price.
3. Foreclosure is a legal procedure by which property is transferred to a creditor because of unpaid debts. Many cities have acquired ownership of considerable amounts of older housing because of unpaid property taxes. Banks acquire properties because of unpaid mortgage debt.
4. For a detailed presentation on who owns slum properties, see George Sternlieb, *The Tenement Landlord* (Rutgers University Press, 1969), and subsequent edition, *The Tenement Landlord Revisited.*
5. For case studies of gentrification in the United States and an extensive bibliography on gentrification, see Elvin K. Wyly and Daniel J. Hammel, "Modeling the Context and Contingency of Gentrification," *Journal of Urban Affairs,* (summer 1998). For a discussion of

British experience, see Nick Bailey and Douglas Robertson, "Housing Renewal, Urban Politics and Gentrification," *Urban Studies,* 34, no. 4 (April 1997), pp. 561–78.

6. Local governments can also foreclose on properties that are in arrears on their property tax payments. For that reason banks that hold mortgages generally require that your mortgage payment to them include money for taxes. They put this money into an escrow account and then pay your property taxes for you. This assures the bank that if it has to foreclose you will be up to date on your taxes and they will not find the municipal government ahead of them in seeking to foreclose on the property. Generally they will also require that your payment to them include fire insurance. Thus if the house burns down the insurance will be available to pay off the mortgage and thus leave the bank unharmed.

7. Carter F. McFarland, *Federal Government and Urban Problems,* (Boulder, Colo.: Westview, 1978), p. 117.

8. *U.S. Housing Market Conditions,* Department of Housing and Urban Development, Office of Policy and Statistics, 1997, Tables 14 and 16.

9. This type of preferential tax treatment is referred to as a "tax expenditure" in that it comes from the tax code but has much the same effect as if it came from the expenditure side of the budget. The value of various tax expenditures by the federal government are estimated annually by the Office of Management and Budget. The figure quoted is taken from a summary of these estimates in Table 518 in the *Statistical Abstract of the United States,* 116th edition, 1996.

10. Periodically it is suggested that the tax code be changed to permit renters to take deductions for the property taxes and mortgage interest that they implicitly pay through their rent. This would enable rental housing to compete on a more even footing with owner-occupied housing and should work in favor of those cities of which a large part of the total stock is rental. Though the idea seems simple and fair, it has never made any headway politically, and no legislation on its behalf has been introduced in Congress.

11. Before a house, whether single family or multifamily, can be built, a building permit must be issued. This means that the municipality's building inspector has determined that the plans are in conformance with the municipality's building codes regarding plumbing, electricity, fire safety, and the like and that the housing is also in conformance with the municipality's land use controls, such as its zoning ordinance and subdivision requirements. Because filing a permit involves the payment of fees, people do not file for permits unless they are reasonably sure that they will actually build. Thus permits are a very good source of housing data.

12. Some data on private communities can be obtained from the Community Associations Institute in Alexandria, Virginia. The 1990 figure is from Clifford J. Tyreese, ed., *Community Associations Factbook,* 1993.

13. David Guterson, "No Place Like Home," *Harpers* (November 1992), pp. 55–63.

14. Edward Blakely, "Viewpoint," *Planning* (January 1994), p. 46.

15. It has been argued that a multiplicity of small communities, by offering the "consumer" of municipal services a wide range of choices, improves the market for residence just as a wide range of products improves the market for consumer goods. This idea was first stated by the economist Charles Tiebout in a very widely cited article, "A Pure Theory of Local Expenditures," *Journal of Political Economy* 64 (October 1956), pp. 416–24. It is discussed in many publications in urban economics, urban politics, and public finance. Though private communities were rare when Tiebout wrote and are not mentioned in the article, private communities are Tieboutian in that they represent a very fine dividing up of the supply side of the housing market to suit a great multiplicity of tastes.

REFERENCES

Pozdena, Randall. *The Modern Economics of Housing.* New York: Quorum Books, 1989.

Chapter

10 | Housing: Part 2— Public Policy

The previous chapter laid out some basic mechanisms in housing markets. In this chapter we turn to public policy directed specifically to housing, beginning at the municipal level.

Municipal governments have a major effect upon the quantity, type, and condition of their housing stock. They exercise this effect primarily by (1) regulation and (2) public capital investment in infrastructure.

Zoning and other land use controls discussed in Chapter 8 specify what types of and how much housing can be built in each of the zones on the zoning map. Thus, land use controls can have a powerful effect on what an area looks like and what it feels like to live in it. Because controls affect both the types of housing that can be built and the quantities that can be built, they can have a significant effect upon house prices and rents.[1] Because different types of housing typically attract different segments of the population, the types of housing that the zoning code permits or rules out can shape the population pattern of the municipality. For example, in a suburban situation 100 single-family houses are likely to contain many more school-age children than will 100 apartments. Thus a decision about housing type is indirectly a decision about the age structure and school population of the municipality. Because the prices and rents of different housing types vary greatly, decisions about what types of housing may be built are also, indirectly, decisions about who is able to live in the community.

The quality of housing is regulated in a number of ways. Virtually all municipalities have building codes that specify standards that a house must meet. Before a house can be erected, the building inspector must determine that its plans meet the building code with regard to plumbing, electrical, structural, and other requirements. As the building is put up there may be periodic inspections to see that it actually does meet those standards. For a large residential building such as a high-rise apartment house, there will be many inspections before the building is complete. Most municipalities also have a housing code that applies to completed buildings. If the building does not meet the standards of the housing code, it may be denied an occupancy permit, in which case it cannot be occupied. It cannot be rented or sold and it may have to be vacated if presently occupied. Many older, deteriorated buildings have been demolished because the cost of bringing them "up to code" exceeded what their market value would have been. It must be noted, however, that housing codes are often not as fully enforced as building codes. Often, it is simply not feasible. Most building inspectors will hesitate to revoke an occupancy permit if it will throw a large number of tenants in substandard housing out on the street. Building and housing codes go back to the reform movement of the post–Civil War period and the tenement house acts of the time. Like zoning, building and housing codes are an exercise of the police power.

Housing cannot be built just anywhere. It must have road access, and for more than very low densities it must have water supply and sewer connections. It also must have public facilities such as schools and firehouses. Public capital investment provides the framework upon which the municipality's housing supply develops. As is the case with zoning, public capital investment is not a sufficient condition for the growth of the housing stock. But it is a necessary condition. In a growing municipality public capital investment is likely to be a much more powerful force than any regulatory actions. New roads and new utilities, by opening land up for development, create powerful market forces. Because roads and water and sewer pipes last for decades, their cumulative effect can be very great. By contrast, regulatory policy is always subject to change. And it is the experience of most planners that when powerful economic forces collide with regulations, such as zoning laws, sooner or later the regulations are modified.

Most local governments have neither the will nor the fiscal capacity to make major direct investments in housing. However, many local governments do invest limited amounts of money, often community development funds, as discussed later in this chapter, in the improvement of low- and moderate-income housing. For example, one common practice is the making of low-interest loans for the rehabilitation of low-rent housing or the rehabilitation of low and moderate-income owner-occupied housing. This sort of direct investment is far less important overall than either regulatory policy or public capital investment.

The Role of the States

In general the states are much smaller players in the housing game than are the other two levels of government. Unlike local governments the states are not intimately involved in the control of land use nor in the matter of providing the physical infrastructure, such as water mains and local roads, that forms the framework upon which the housing stock develops. Unlike the federal government the states do not play a major role in mortgage markets or in structuring the tax environment in which investment in housing takes place. The states also do not spend nearly as much as the federal government in the direct subsidization of housing. However, there has been some state participation in the support of low- and moderate-income housing, often through the provision of low-interest loans to subsidize construction. In New York State, for example, some thousands of middle-income apartments were financed at low interest rates under the state's Mitchell-Lama program. States also play some regulatory role in housing in that many municipalities use a standard state code as their building code. Finally, in recent years we have seen a growing state role in large-scale land use planning. For example, the state of Oregon makes use of urban growth boundaries to try to limit urban sprawl. This necessarily has effects upon where housing is built, what type of housing is built and upon land and housing costs. The state of Vermont through its Act 200 growth management plan seeks to preserve the state's rural and small-town flavor by restricting growth in some areas. That will divert some growth to other areas and will thus have some effect upon housing markets within the state and perhaps in adjacent areas of other states.[2]

FEDERAL HOUSING POLICY

As described in the previous chapter, the federal government has had an enormous effect on housing through its presence in the housing finance market and also through the way in which the federal tax code treats owner-occupied housing. Here we turn to particular federal programs. These programs have been targeted at particular places, particular types of housing, and particular segments of the population. Their effects, though important, are much smaller than those of the federal government's systemwide tax and mortgage market policies. Below is a chronological account of some of the major federal efforts in housing.

The federal presence in housing markets began with the Great Depression. A substantial part of the urban population had been badly housed even in the prosperous 1920s. With the coming of the Great Depression, residential construction had declined by an almost incredible 95 percent from 1929 to 1933. There was thus no immediate prospect that the private market was going to be able to meet the nation's growing housing needs. The unemployment rate was about 25 percent. Clearly, there was a need to stimulate the economy in almost any way possible. To meet both housing and employment needs the Public Works Administration began to engage in slum clearance projects and build public housing. That program lasted only a little while before a Supreme Court decision put the PWA out of the housing business on the grounds that the building of housing did not meet the test of an established public purpose for the federal government.

Then, under the Housing Act of 1937 the federal government turned to a system in which the federal government would fund local housing authorities, which would do the actual building and operating. The usual arrangement was for the federal government to meet most of the capital costs of public housing while local governments met a substantial portion of the operating costs. Rents paid by tenants generally covered only part of the operating costs. Most of the million-plus units of public housing in the United States were built under this general sort of arrangement. Local governments also subsidized public housing in an indirect manner. As a publicly owned structure, a public housing project is not required to pay property taxes. The municipality, however, must provide services for its population, such as educating the children who live there.[3]

At first, public housing worked well. It provided good quality housing at low cost in a nation in which large numbers of people were out of work. In the Depression years it attracted a broad mix of tenants. This situation persisted through World War II and for a few years afterwards because of housing shortages resulting from low rates of residential construction during the Depression and war years. Then, the situation changed.

> But by 1955 a significant change had occurred. Because of sustained national prosperity and low unemployment, the Jimmy Carters [the family of President Jimmy Carter lived in public housing for a time after the war] of the country no longer needed public housing as a temporary way station. In addition, the massive migration of poor Blacks from the rural South to the cities was well under way. Increasingly, public housing became the haven of rural Blacks, the culturally deprived, the broken families, the welfare recipients, the permanent poor. Social prejudice produced bitter resistance to public housing projects and turmoil within them. As a result it was difficult for local housing authorities to find sites on which to build. Where sites could be found, the land was expensive. Expensive land made high rise construction an economic necessity. Too many public housing projects became concentrations of culturally deprived families packed into large, tall structures—an environment ill-suited for normal family life (what mother can supervise the play of her children from the twelfth floor) and very conducive to the disruptive behavior encouraged by the anonymity and monotony in which the deprived families lived.[4]

As McFarland notes, the large, high-rise design was very dysfunctional for public housing, though it often works very well for other types of housing—witness the million-dollar selling prices of high-rise co-op apartments at some of Manhattan's more stylish addresses. But the real source of failure was the crowding of so many people with so many serious problems into one place. One of the more striking failures of public housing was the Pruitt-Igoe project in St. Louis. This is the way Tom Wolfe described its last days:

Respectable folk pulled out even if it meant living in cracks in the sidewalks. Millions of dollars and scores of commission meetings and task-force projects were expended in a last ditch attempt to make Pruitt Igoe habitable. In 1971, the final task force called a general meeting of everyone still living in the project. They asked the residents for their suggestions. It was a historic moment for two reasons. One, for the first time in the fifty-year history of worker housing, someone had finally asked the client for his two cents worth. Two, the chant. The chant began immediately: "Blow it . . . up. Blow it . . . up. Blow it . . . up!" The next day the task force thought it over. The poor buggers were right. It was the only solution. In July of 1972, the city blew up the three central blocks of Pruitt Igoe with dynamite.[5]

Not all public housing has been a failure. Many projects, particularly smaller ones in smaller places, have succeeded in providing adequate housing for very poor people. But the overall record, particularly in the big cities, has been discouraging. In the 1980s and 1990s Chicago's Cabrini Green housing project became notorious as one of the more frightening and dangerous places in America to live. At this writing it is being replaced with low-rise units. To those who derided "social engineering," public housing provided a handy supply of rhetorical ammunition. For planners and architects perhaps the biggest lesson of public housing was that good architectural design by itself was not sufficient. The Pruitt-Igoe complex had been designed by the renowned architect Minoru Yamasaki and had actually won a design award from the American Institute of Architects (AIA). But while its architectural design was good, its sociological design was bad. Crowding together large numbers of poor families, the great majority of them female headed, and many of them with little or no permanent connection to the labor market, turned out to be a disaster.

Rebuilding the Cities with Urban Renewal

Concern with housing also led to the initiation of the largest direct federal intervention in urban affairs in U.S. history—a program titled Urban Renewal. Though the program is now over it has left a major mark on hundreds of cities and on U.S. urban policy in general. It had some successes and some failures, and it stands as an object lesson in how difficult it can be to design social policy that does what is wanted and does not have all sorts of side effects that are not wanted.

The idea for Urban Renewal was conceived during the Great Depression and rested on the simple observation that it was much easier for a developer to build a substantial project in an outlying area than it was to do so in a developed urban area. There were (and are) two basic reasons for this.

The land assembly problem. In most cities land was subdivided into small parcels. That means that even one city block might have a dozen or two different owners. For the developer who would like to acquire the entire block to put up, say, one large apartment house, getting title to the whole block could be a major problem. The titles of some parcels may be "clouded," meaning that they have legal problems that make it difficult or impossible to say with absolute certainty who really does own them. Then, there is another problem as well. Even if all the titles are legally clear, one holdout can block the project or demand ten times the market value of his lot, thinking that the developer, having purchased all the other lots, is over a barrel.

The residual value problem. In a built-up area new construction usually must be preceded by demolition. For the developer to obtain land in a fair market transaction, he or she must pay the owner what the existing structure is worth plus the value of land under it. Even if the building is obsolete, as long as it produces some stream of revenue it has some value for which the owner must be paid. The developer must also absorb the cost of demolition and clearance. By contrast, in outlying areas land tends to be owned in much larger blocks, and there is likely to be little or no development on it.

The plan conceived by federal officials at the end of the Great Depression was quite simple. "City Realty Corporations" would use their powers of eminent domain to solve the land assembly problem. Recall that private property can be taken for public purposes as long as the property owner receives fair compensation for it. To pay condemnation awards, clearance costs, and other expenses the City Realty Corporations would receive some aid from local governments and substantial subsidies from the federal government.

The plan was put on the back burner during World War II but was enacted into law in the Housing Act of 1949. The main goal was to improve the housing stock of the city by demolishing deteriorated old housing and building good new housing. The planning and the developing was to be done by Local Public Agencies (LPAs). These would draw up plans, assemble sites, make site improvements (new street patterns, grading, storm drainage, etc.) and then market the sites at well below cost to developers who would build the new housing within the framework of the LPA's plan. Basically it was a slum clearance plan.

The idea was simple and the intentions were good, but the realities were more complicated. In a typical project a plan was drawn up and land was acquired. The land and the buildings on it were acquired through voluntary sale when possible and through eminent domain and condemnation if not. Then renters, homeowners, and businesses were given notice to vacate. After that came the demolition phase. When demolition and clearance were complete, site improvements were made. Then the cleared sites were marketed. After that, construction of new buildings began. From the time old buildings were vacated to the time that new buildings were ready for occupancy a considerable number of years might pass. For example in White Plains, New York, the time between clearance and the time that the site had been substantially redeveloped was about a decade.

In principle, clearance could have been done a bit at a time, followed by a little building, followed by a little more clearance, and so on. But projects were generally not done that way. It was more economical to do the clearance all at once, or at least in a few big pieces. Then, too, from the administrator's point of view a big clearance operation at the beginning made political sense. After the ground was all cleared there was no going back. Whereas, if clearance was done a bit at a time, a project could always be canceled in midcourse if it met too much opposition.

Thus a program designed to solve housing problems also created them. When substandard, low-rent inner-city housing was demolished in large numbers, it tightened up the rest of the city's low-rent housing market, pushing up rents and pushing down vacancy rates. New housing would ultimately appear on the Urban Renewal site, but that might be many years later. In some cases the new housing was public housing or other subsidized housing. In other cases it was luxury housing—a sort of forced gentrification—that the original residents would never have been able to afford. What was intended as a housing program also became a dehousing program for the urban poor. In a very powerful attack on Urban Renewal Martin Anderson wrote:

> The people are poor. A great many of them are Negroes and Puerto Ricans. Good quality, conveniently located housing is scarce; good quality, conveniently located housing for $50 or $60 a month is [recall that this was written in the 1960s] almost impossible to find. It is difficult to picture hundreds of thousands of low income people, many of them subject to racial discrimination, moving from low quality into higher quality housing at rents they can afford. And then, one might ask, why if all this good housing at low rents is available, didn't they move before urban renewal nudged them along?[6]

Studies of people displaced by urban renewal showed that most of them moved relatively short distances and often found themselves in housing not that different from that from which they had been evicted. With a little bad luck a person could be displaced by urban renewal more than once. Urban renewal destroyed many neighborhoods, and a neighborhood is more than just buildings. It is also a web of connections between friends, relatives, businesses and their customers. When residents are scattered and businesses closed that web is destroyed. Because urban renewal projects were usually sited in older parts of the city where housing was most deteriorated and, therefore, rents were low, its impact fell disproportionately on minority group members. This fact did not go unnoticed, and Urban Renewal was sometimes sardonically referred to as "Negro Removal."

After the program had been operating for a while it became apparent that local governments and the federal government often had different ideas and goals for urban renewal. From the federal perspective urban renewal was primarily a housing program. But for many local governments it appealed to them more as an economic development tool, and if their urban renewal program had no housing element at all that might suit them fine. Suppose a small city in a metropolitan area cleared a few blocks that was, say, a mixture of small business establishments and old, deteriorated housing, and replaced it all with new commercial buildings. From the municipal perspective that might be very satisfactory. It eliminated its slum housing problem and added new jobs to its economy and new "ratables" to its property tax base. What could be better? The population forced out of the old housing wouldn't disappear from the face of the earth, but if they moved into adjacent municipalities they were now someone else's problem. From the federal perspective, of course, that was not solving a housing problem, it was just relocating it. Local governments had to compromise with the federal government to some degree because they wanted project money. The federal government also had to compromise. The federal official whose task it was to fund projects had to compromise with local officials if agreement was to be reached. With the passage of time the program took a more commercial turn and many projects were largely commercial.[7]

Because of the displacement of population and the impact on neighborhoods, public opposition to the Urban Renewal program mounted, and in 1973 Congress terminated the program. At that time the Congressional Research Service, studying the program, found that as of 1971 the following had been accomplished. More than 2,000 projects had been done on about 1,000 square miles of urban land. On those 1,000 square miles about 600,000 housing units had been torn down and about 250,000 units built in their stead. There had been constructed about 120 million square feet of public floor space (schools, municipal hospitals, and other public buildings) and about 224 million square feet of commercial floor space. At an average density of 500 square feet per worker, that meant workplaces for perhaps 600,000 employees. The 1973 study caught many urban renewal projects after the clearance phase was over but while the construction phase was underway. Thus the final totals for both residential and nonresidential construction in urban areas are undoubtedly much larger than the numbers given above. Though no new projects were started after 1973, work on projects that had been "in the pipeline" in 1973 continued for many years afterward.

In retrospect, what can be said about the program? The human costs were bigger than anticipated and bigger than society was willing to tolerate. As a housing program, its original purpose, Urban Renewal was not a success. As a program for commercial revitalization it did much better. The big infusion of federal capital permitted many cities to make the changes they needed to have a chance of competing with their suburbs. White Plains, New York, noted before, was a suburban county seat with a population of about 50,000. Urban Renewal funds were used to clear many acres immediately adjacent to downtown and replace an old, congested street pattern more suitable to horse and wagon than the automobile with a few wide, one-way streets that linked the core of the city to a nearby interstate. Ultimately, the urban renewal area and immediately surrounding areas sprouted office buildings that contain thousands of jobs, and a major retailing center that competes very strongly with nearby suburban shopping centers. Without the federal funds and the major surgery of urban renewal there is no way that such commercial success would have been possible. For the low-income population and a number of small businesses displaced by Urban Renewal, the experience was a negative one. But from the vantage point of the city government, looking at the economic situation of the city as a whole and being very concerned about the city's ability to compete for jobs and retail sales, the project was an outstanding success. Stamford, Connecticut, is thriving as an urban center in the suburbs. Its success, too, is largely due to urban renewal. Part of New York City's strength as a cultural center is rooted in Lincoln center, which was built on an Urban Renewal site. The center provides many jobs directly, and it indirectly provides the demand to sustain a large number of jobs in stores, restaurants, and hotels. Much of Boston's waterfront redevelopment was made possible by Urban Renewal. So, too, was much of Baltimore's Inner Harbor redevelopment, a major economic asset for a city fighting a difficult battle to survive in competition with surrounding suburban areas.

COMMUNITY DEVELOPMENT—A "KINDER AND GENTLER" APPROACH

In 1974, a year after Congress terminated the Urban Renewal program, it passed the Housing and Community Development Act of 1974, which, with subsequent amendments, stands as a major part of federal urban policy to the present time. Under the program municipalities get federal grants on the basis of a formula that counts population, age of housing stock, and poverty. The funds may be used for a very broad range of purposes. They can be used for infrastructure, for building or rehabilitating housing, for commercial development, and for many purposes that do not involve "bricks and mortar," such as public health and daycare. The regulations specify that the major share of community development funded construction or services must be for the benefit of "low and moderate income" persons. They also require that before decisions can be made about the spending of community development (CD) funds citizens must be informed and must have a chance to comment on pending decisions. The regulations also specifically require the involvement of "low and moderate income people" and "minority group members." These requirements very clearly are an outgrowth of the Urban Renewal experience and the citizen resistance and anger that it provoked. The regulations also specify that CD funds not be used to substitute for funds from other municipal sources (like property taxes). That is, they are not to be used for tax relief. Rather, they are to fund projects or activities that would not otherwise be undertaken.

In housing, the community development approach has emphasized rehabilitation and preservation, rather than clearance and massive new construction as did Urban Renewal. Community development programs have funded infrastructure and other improvements in declining neighborhoods. Many community development programs have offered low-interest loans for rehabilitation to low-income homeowners and to owners of properties rented to low- and moderate-income tenants. One often cited example of a community development approach to housing preservation is Baltimore's Urban Homesteading program. Over the years the city has come into possession of many old row houses, sometimes because of abandonment and sometimes as a result of foreclosure because of nonpayment of taxes. The city has offered these properties at no cost to people who agree to restore the property to the standards of the city's building and housing codes. If the building is brought "up to code" within the specified time, the title [ownership] of the building then passes from the city to the occupant. The "homesteader" has thus acquired the building for the cost of bringing it up to code. That cost may be purely monetary—money spent on contractors—or it may include a substantial amount of the occupant's labor, so called "sweat equity." So far, the program has worked very well. It improves building quality, fills abandoned buildings with occupants, and stabilizes neighborhoods because the new owners, having invested money and labor in their rehabilitated row houses, now have an important stake in what happens in their neighborhoods.

HOUSING SUBSIDIES

Providing adequate housing for those who do not have sufficient income to obtain it unaided on the private market has long been a preoccupation of the federal government. The most direct way to do this is for government itself to provide housing. The provision of public housing was discussed earlier. As shown in Table 10–1 there are over 1 million public housing units in the United States today. However, the building of additional public housing was stopped many years earlier. The sociological problems noted earlier were one reason. The second reason was the very high per unit cost. The federal government then switched to programs that did not involve direct governmental provision and that generally involved much lower per unit costs.

The term *project-based rental housing* refers to subsidies given to builders to lower the cost of constructing apartment houses. In return for receiving the subsidy the builder would agree to limit the occupancy of the building to tenants under a certain income limit and also agree to limitations on how much rent he or she would charge.[8] Tenant-based subsidies go through the tenant. A typical arrangement might be that households under a certain income would receive a payment that paid the difference between the rent on

TABLE 10-1 Direct Government Provision of Housing, 1993

Total U.S. housing stock	113,000,000
All subsidized housing	4,054,000
Public housing	1,138,000
Project-based rental housing	1,716,000
Tenant-based rental housing	1,200,000

Source: Data supplied by Office of Policy Development and Research, Department of Housing and Urban Development.

an apartment and 30 percent of the household's income. There would be limits on how expensive a unit the household could rent to prevent excessive expenditures per household.[9]

In addition to the federally subsidized units listed in the table there is also some state-subsidized housing. But the number of states that have housing subsidy programs is small, and the number of units quite limited. Only a minority of those whose incomes would qualify them for housing subsidies actually receive them. Note that the total number of units in the table is less than 4 percent of the U.S. housing stock. Critics of U.S. housing policy are quick to point out that the federal government's direct expenditures on housing for low- and moderate-income households are much smaller than its indirect expenditures on owner-occupied housing through its favorable treatment under the federal tax code.

THE PROBLEM OF HOUSING SEGREGATION

Segregation in housing has been a fact of American life for many decades. In the wake of the Civil Rights revolution of the 1960s both the federal government and many of the state governments have taken steps to redress that problem. Below, we discuss some of those steps. After that, we turn to the question of why the problem of housing segregation has been such an intractable one.

The Civil Rights Act of 1968 outlawed a variety of discriminatory practices in the sale and rental of housing. The act makes it illegal to discriminate against any person in the selling or renting of property on the basis of "race, color, religion, or national origin." For example, if a property owner advertised an apartment for rent or a house for sale, it would then be illegal for the owner to turn away someone who makes a bona fide offer on the basis of race or any of the other characteristics just noted. A bona fide offer is one that meets the asking price and is made by someone who has the financial ability to make good on that offer. The courts have held these provisions to also ban "racial steering." A real estate broker who made a practice of show-

ing some neighborhoods only to Whites or only to Blacks would be in violation of the law. The act also makes it illegal to discriminate on the basis of
terms and conditions. That is, it would be illegal to attempt to charge a different rent or price to Blacks than to Whites.

The act also bars discrimination in housing finance. This is important
because most people cannot become homeowners if they cannot borrow
money. Under the act if a bank were to approve mortgage loans for Whites
while denying loans to Blacks in equal financial circumstances and seeking
to buy comparable properties, it would be in violation of the law.

The act bans "redlining." Under this practice banks had refused to lend
money in some neighborhoods where they believed conditions exposed
them to a high risk of default. They justified this practice on the basis of their
fiduciary responsibility to their stockholders and depositors. The counterargument, and the one that convinced Congress to ban redlining, is that by
starving an area for real estate finance the banks greatly enhance the
prospects for further deterioration—that drawing a red line around an area
sets in motion a self-fulfilling prophecy. Congress was also concerned that a
disproportionate number of redlined areas were minority areas and thus
redlining constituted de facto racial discrimination.

Finally, the act also banned the practice of "blockbusting." In this technique unscrupulous real estate brokers would panic White homeowners with
warnings that the neighborhood was about to turn Black and therefore the
White homeowners should sell quickly before their house values were driven
any lower. If the trick worked, there would be a wave of panic selling at well
below true market value. The brokers who started the panic would then buy
up houses at bargain prices and then resell them at substantial profits after
the panic was over. One reason for outlawing this scam is that it tends to
make neighborhood integration impossible. Once the White owners have
fled, the block is likely to turn solidly Black and the chance of achieving an
integrated neighborhood through a gradual process is gone.[10]

In 1978, largely to put some legal teeth behind the antiredlining provisions of the Civil Rights Act of 1968, Congress passed the Community Reinvestment Act (CRA). In Senate hearings on the act ten years later Senator
Dixon explained the act this way:

> What does CRA do? First, it makes crystal clear that federally regulated or in-
> sured lenders have an affirmative obligation to make loans in their communi-
> ties. The loans naturally must be sound, as Arthur Burns [a former chairman of
> the Federal Reserve system] said, taking that into account. The first requirement
> of a banker is to meet the credit requirement of his service area.
>
> Second, the CRA requires regulators to rate the lender's reinvestment and to
> take this evaluation into account when deciding to approve or deny an applica-
> tion to change banking operations.[11]

That second item gives the federal government considerable power over
banks because it can deny requests for mergers or expansions if the bank's

pattern of lending shows evidence of redlining or discrimination. Beyond that, the act has made it possible for a variety of community groups and advocacy organizations to bring lawsuits seeking to stop mergers and acts on the grounds that the bank has not met its obligations under CRA. The community advocate might argue that this power to twist the banker's arms through the threat of litigation is all to the good because redlining and discrimination in lending still exist and, at least in the last several years, bank profits in the United States have been very good. The banker might argue in rebuttal that redlining and discrimination in lending are now relatively rare and the CRA opens up a certain opportunity for a bit of legal extortion. The director of a community organization appears in the banker's office with a request for a loan to one of the organization's projects and, subtly or otherwise, indicates that such a loan would certainly cause the community organization to forget about bringing a CRA-based lawsuit to prevent that merger the bank is contemplating. The banker thinks that making the loan in question violates his or her notions of a prudent exercise of fiduciary responsibility, but he or she also knows that lawsuits are expensive, they can produce lots of unpleasant publicity, and one can never be sure how they will come out. So perhaps the path of least resistance, all things considered, is to make the loan.

Clearly, in the matters of race and ethnicity, as well as, to some degree, of neighborhood, the federal government has made a very substantial effort to level the playing field in regard to the sale, rental, and financing of housing. We should also note that many states have open-housing laws that parallel at least parts of the federal legislation.

The Persistence of Housing Segregation

One of the most frustrating elements of the U.S. housing situation has been the persistence of a high degree of de facto segregation of Black and White Americans despite all the steps just described. The problem appears to be most severe in the large cities of the Northeast and North Central regions of the nation and somewhat less severe in the South and West.

Sociologists and geographers who have studied segregation often make use of a segregation index, which is easily constructed from census data. To construct one for any group of people who are enumerated by the census, the investigator constructs a data base that shows, for each census tract or block group (a subdivision of the census tract), its total population and the number of people of the group under study who live in it. Then the investigator calculates what percentage of the group under study would have to be moved so that the group would constitute the same percentage of the population in each tract or block group. If the group is more or less evenly spread, the segregation index will be relatively low because few members of the group would have to move for the group to be distributed in a completely even pattern. If, at the other extreme, the group is heavily concentrated in a few tracts or block groups and absent in others, then the index will be very high. Generally, the indexes are structured to have a range of 0 to 100, corresponding, respectively, to complete evenness or randomness of distribution to complete segregation. Now that census data is available in computerized form, the indexes for a large number of cities can be computed very quickly.

The group that has been studied most and that generally shows the highest index is Blacks. A study of 232 metropolitan areas done after the last two decennial censuses showed a 1980 index of segregation for Blacks of 68.8 and a 1990 index of 64.3 1. The 1980 figures for a number of cities in the Northeast, including New York, Chicago, and Boston, were in the 80 percent range.[12] The figures for Blacks are very high. For example, figures for Hispanics and Asians in the same study were in the low 40s for both years.

What accounts for the high degree of de facto housing segregation among Black Americans? Next, we examine a number of factors.

Income disparity. For the last several decades the median family income of Blacks has been approximately three fifths that of Whites. That differential handicaps Blacks in the competition with Whites for more expensive housing and, all other things being equal, would cause Black Americans to be overrepresented in older urban areas and underrepresented in the suburbs.

Social scientists who have studied the matter of residential segregation have concluded that the income effect is important but, by itself, not sufficient to explain the phenomenon in its entirety. W. A. V. Clark, in reviewing a number of studies, mostly done with 1980 census data, concludes that between "30 and 70 percent of racial separation is attributable to economic factors."[13] (Note that the spread that he gives is very large and that the data behind it is old.) One reason for believing that the residential segregation of Blacks cannot be explained primarily in income terms is that Blacks with high incomes are, statistically, almost as segregated in terms of residence as are poorer Blacks.[14] If the segregation of Blacks were predominantly an income effect one would expect that well-to-do Blacks would be much less segregated than poor Blacks. But, at least as of 1980, this was not the case.

The tipping point phenomenon. Surveys of White Americans have shown that prejudice against Black Americans appears to be declining and that with the passage of time larger percentages of the White population are comfortable living in integrated neighborhoods. However, the same surveys also show that the integrated neighborhood that many Whites find acceptable is one that still has a substantial majority of Whites. Many Whites express comfort with a neighborhood that has, say, 10 or 20 percent Blacks but express discomfort when the percentage of Blacks rises much higher. By contrast, many Blacks indicate that that they would be comfortable with a 50–50 Black-White ratio. The difference in comfort levels between Blacks and

Whites is a prescription for instability. The result is the "tipping point" phenomenon. A formerly White neighborhood begins to integrate, and for a time the process goes along at a modest pace. When the tipping point is approached, Whites begin moving out in large numbers and the neighborhood soon returns to a one-race status, this time all Black instead of all White. Its brief period as an integrated neighborhood is over. The tipping point phenomenon is one reason why there is less segregation, as measured by segregation indexes, in many Western cities. The Black populations of most western cities are small percentages of the total city population. Therefore, there is not enough Black population to push many neighborhoods up to the tipping point, and so they remain integrated. It is the existence of the tipping point phenomenon that made the now illegal "blockbusting" technique work. If Whites as a group were willing to live as a minority in integrated neighborhoods, it would not have been possible for unscrupulous real estate brokers to panic White residents.

Discrimination in sale and renting. Although discrimination in the sale and rental of housing is now illegal, some still goes on. For example, real estate brokers direct Black buyers or renters to predominantly Black neighborhoods and steer them away from predominantly White neighborhoods. The steering phenomenon has been extensively examined in "audit" studies. The investigating agency sends out both Black and White investigators who present themselves as prospective buyers or renters. By observing how investigators who are apparently similar except for race are treated by brokers it is possible to estimate the amount of discrimination that there is in the marketing of housing. Studies done in the 1980s in a number of metropolitan areas showed a considerable amount of discrimination by brokers.[15] Studies done for the Department of Housing and Urban Development (HUD) in the late 1990s still showed such discrimination, but at somewhat lower levels than earlier studies. How powerful the effect of such discrimination is can be argued. Assume that in a given suburb 50 percent of all real estate brokers engage in steering potential Black home buyers away from predominantly White areas. This figure is roughly in line with studies done in the 1980s. Given that many prospective homebuyers go to two or more brokers in the course of their search, it may well be that this form of discrimination is not overwhelmingly powerful.

Discrimination in mortgage lending. As discussed earlier in this chapter, there is no question that in decades gone by there was massive discrimination against Blacks in mortgage lending. Such discrimination would promote housing segregation by keeping Blacks out of suburban areas composed primarily of owner-occupied housing. The question is whether or not such discrimination, though illegal, still exists. Studies have shown that Blacks are rejected for mortgages at somewhat higher rates than Whites. This would appear to represent racial discrimination. Or is there another explanation? Those who argue that there is little discrimination make the following argument. If lenders were systematically discriminating against Blacks, then to get a mortgage the least-qualified successful Black applicant would necessarily be better qualified than the least-qualified successful White applicant. Successful Black applicants would, on average, be more qualified (better credit risks) than would be successful White applicants and therefore would default on their mortgages less often than would Whites. In fact, however, mortgage default rates for Black mortgage holders are no lower than for White mortgage holders. This would suggest that there is no evidence of systematic discrimination. This argument is no different from saying that if for some strange reason college admissions offices were to discriminate against left-handed students, then the average left-handed college student would have a better high school record than the average right-handed college student. To this argument based on default rates there are, in turn, counterarguments, and at this writing the matter does not appear to be entirely settled.[16]

Self-segregation. Studies conducted in the 1980s indicated that the great majority of Blacks would prefer integrated neighborhoods. In recent years, however, there has been some doubt about whether this finding is entirely true. Prince Georges County in Maryland, lying just to the east of the District of Columbia, offers a clear illustration of this. The Washington, D.C., metropolitan area has a large Black middle class that could afford to penetrate many largely White housing markets in the Washington, D.C., suburbs. Nonetheless, much of that affluent Black population concentrates in Prince Georges County. An article profiling the county quoted the demographer William H. Frey as saying:

> As an increasing number of black Americans head for the suburban dream, some are bypassing another dream—the dream of an integrated society. These black Americans are moving to *black* upper and middle class neighborhoods, usually pockets in counties that have a white majority. [italics in original]

The article also quotes some residents of such Black enclaves in the county:

> We always wanted to make sure our children had many African-American children to play with. . . . We always wanted to be in a community with a large number of black professionals, and to feel part of that community. We never really felt like we were part of Fairfax [a county bordering the District of Columbia on the west].

Another resident, taking a more militant note, stated:

> I think the integration of black folks in the 60s was one of the biggest cons in the world. . . . You want to call me a separatist, so be it. I think of myself as a pragmatist.[17]

To the extent that some de facto segregation is self-segregation, a part of it is undoubtedly a positive preference for being with others of one's own group. Some, too, is undoubtedly a matter of fear, whether that be fear of unpleasantness and rejection or fear for the safety of one's person and property. Incidents of violence over housing integration are much rarer than they once were, but they are still not unheard of.

Side effects of public policy. The siting of public housing has often been cited as one cause of de facto segregation. Almost all public housing built in the United States has been built in poor areas. If a large percentage of the population of a poor area is Black and if most of the people who rent units in the public housing are also Black, the effect is necessarily to increase the amount of de facto segregation. Little if any public housing is now being built, but the effects of decisions made long ago are still with us. Why, one might ask, was public housing concentrated in poor areas? There are two very clear reasons for this. One is that such housing was put where it appeared to be needed. The other reason, probably the more powerful one, is political. Public housing was built where it was politically acceptable. And that meant not in prosperous neighborhoods.[18]

A certain amount of residential segregation has also been produced inadvertently by attempts to combat school segregation. For example, when in 1973 a federal judge ordered busing to integrate the Boston public schools, the number of white families with school-age children in Boston plummeted. The schools had to comply with the order. However, families could void the order for themselves simply by moving across the city line into the Boston suburbs, and they did this in large numbers. The result was to leave Boston a much more segregated city than it had been before (see Chapter 16 for details).

How much the situation of de facto segregation changed during the 1990s is not clear at this writing. It will become clearer early in the 21st century after there has been time to analyze data on race and residence from the year 2000 census. It is clear, however, that the situation of de facto segregation is a reflection of many larger forces in our society. Major change is much more likely to come from underlying social forces than from further changes in public policy, for the legal "leveling of the playing field" has largely been accomplished.

THE ROLE OF NONPROFIT ORGANIZATIONS

Nonprofit organizations are also part of the urban housing picture. Often, they are more cost effective than government. They are less tied by rules, they may benefit from a great deal of free labor, and because they are grounded in a system of belief they may be better motivators of behavior.

One such nonprofit housing effort is the Nehemiah project of the East Brooklyn Congregations (EBC), a group of Catholic, Episcopal, Lutheran, and other churches located in the East New York section of Brooklyn. The primary goal of the program is to provide owner-occupied, single-family housing for low- and moderate-income people. The effort is capitalized by funds raised from the church congregations. To money supplied by EBC is added a no-interest loan from the city of New York, which must be repaid only if and when the buyer sells the house. The organization builds townhouses and sells them to eligible buyers on a nonprofit basis. As of the early 1990s the Nehemiah project (named after the Old Testament prophet who helped rebuild Jerusalem) had built over 1,000 houses in East New York and was working on plans to build in other depressed sections of the city as well.[19]

According to its director, the program had three basic principles:

1. Housing was allocated to eligible people on a first come, first served basis.
2. The units were concentrated enough to produce a neighborhood effect.
3. The buyer is required to live in the house, not simply buy it as an investment.

So far the program has not only opened up the opportunity of homeownership to people who would not otherwise have been able to afford it, but it has gone far to reduce crime and stabilize neighborhoods. Like the Urban Homesteading program noted earlier, the Nehemiah program achieves part of its effect by giving residents a stake in the future of their community. The program has improved the quality of public services in the neighborhoods in which it has built by a policy of continuous cooperation with the police department and other city agencies.

Another non-profit organization that has built a large amount of single family housing in both urban and non-urban areas is Habitat for Humanity. By eschewing profit, receiving some philanthropic support, and using a great deal of volunteer labor the organization is able to build at well below market cost. Its most prominent spokesman, and volunteer worker, is former President Jimmy Carter.

SUMMARY

Local governments have powerful effects upon housing markets through regulation and through capital investment. Regulations include zoning, subdivision requirements, and other land use controls, as well as building codes and occupancy codes. Capital investment in roads, water and sewer supply, and public facilities forms the basic skeleton upon which the housing stock of the municipality develops.

The largest direct federal intervention in housing markets was the federal government's Urban Renewal program authorized under the Housing

Act of 1949. Intended as a housing program, Urban Renewal used the power of eminent domain and large federal subsidies to overcome the problems of land assembly and absorption of the residual value of existing structures. The intention was to place cities on an equal competitive basis with suburban areas. Though many Urban Renewal programs were successful from a commercial point of view, they exacted a high human cost in terms of population displacement and neighborhood disruption. In 1973, in response to citizen protest, Congress canceled the program. In 1974, largely as a replacement for Urban Renewal, Congress passed the Housing and Community Development Act. In general, community development efforts take a gentler approach than Urban Renewal. There is much more emphasis on rehabilitation and less emphasis on large scale clearance and rebuilding.

The chapter notes the use of housing subsidies by the federal government. Altogether, the federal government subsidizes about 4 million units of low- and middle-income housing, somewhat less than 4 percent of the total housing stock.

Since the 1960s the federal government has taken numerous steps to level the playing field in the rental and purchase of housing. The Civil Rights Act of 1968 banned discrimination in the sale and leasing of housing and also outlawed the practices of redlining and blockbusting. The Community Reinvestment Act (CRA) of 1978 put teeth into the antiredlining provisions of the Civil Rights Act by giving federal banking regulators the power to compel banks to invest a substantial amount of their deposits in their own service areas. Since the 1960s many states have enacted their own fair housing laws, which supplement the federal legislation.

Despite legal prohibitions on discrimination in the sale and rental of housing and on redlining and mortgage lending there still remains a high level of de facto housing segregation. The possible causes discussed were the Black-White income differential; the "tipping point" phenomenon; persisting (though illegal) discrimination in the marketing, selling, and rental of housing and in mortgage lending; and, finally, voluntary self-segregation.

The chapter concludes with a note on the role of nonprofit organizations in the provision of low- and moderate-cost housing. These organizations, many of them church based, have often been very successful.

NOTES

1. In principle, an inexpensive house could be built on a large lot. In fact, however, a builder who pays a great deal for a building lot is very unlikely to put a low-cost structure on it. Therefore, large-lot development tends to be expensive development. Then, too, in a development in which houses are widely spaced, the per house cost of roads and utilities is higher than if houses are closely spaced.
2. For a summary of various state land use and growth management plans, see John M. Levy, *Contemporary Urban Planning* 5th ed. (Upper Saddle River, N.J.: Prentice-Hall, 2000), Chapter 15.

3. Public housing projects in some cases may make payments in lieu of taxes (sometimes referred to as PILOTs) to municipalities or school districts, but these payments, at best, will cover only a fraction of the costs of providing the project's occupants with public services.

4. Carter M. McFarland, *The Federal Government and Urban Problems* (Boulder: Westview, 1978), p. 131.

5. Tom Wolfe, *From Bauhaus to Our House*, (New York: Farrar, Strauss, & Giroux, 1981), p. 82.

6. Martin Anderson, *The Federal Bulldozer* (Cambridge: MIT Press, 1964), p. 64.

7. Jewell Bellush and Murray Hausknecht, eds., *Urban Renewal: People, Politics, Planning* (New York: Anchor Books, Doubleday, 1967), especially pp. 3–17.

8. Such subsidies are often termed "supply side" subsidies because they go to the supplier of the product—in this case, the rental apartment. The best-known supply side subsidy was the Section 208 program, which provided money to reduce builder's interest costs to as low as 1 percent.

9. This type is often called a "demand side" subsidy because it is given to the demander—that is, the buyer. The best-known supply side housing subsidy was the Section 8 program.

10. George R. Metcalf, *Fair Housing Comes of Age* (New York: Greenwood Press, 1988), pp. 86–7.

11. Hearings before the Committee on Banking, Housing, and Urban Affairs, United States Senate, Second Session, March 22 and 23, 1988.

12. Reynolds Farley and William H. Frey, "Changes in the Segregation of Whites from Blacks During the 1980s: Small Steps Toward a More Integrated Society."

13. W. A. V. Clark, "Residential Segregation in American Cities: A Review and Interpretation," *Population Research and Policy Review* 5, no. 2 (1986), pp. 95–127.

14. Douglas S. Massey and Nancy A. Denton, *American Apartheid* (Cambridge: Harvard University Press, 1993), p. 86.

15. Massey and Denton, op. cit. Chapter 4.

16. *Cityscape: A Journal of Policy Development and Research,* published by HUD's Office of Policy Development and Research, devoted the February 1996 issue (vol. 2, no. 1) to this question. See "Mortgage Discrimination and FHA Loan Performance" by James A. Berkovec, Glenn B. Canner, Stuart A. Gabriel, and Timothy H. Hannan, and replies and commentary by Yinger et al.

17. David J. Dent, "The New Black Suburbs," *New York Times,* Magazine section (June 14, 1992), pp. 18–25.

18. For a description of how the Chicago public housing agency chose sites back in the 1950s, see Edward C. Banfield, "Ends and Means in Planning," *International Social Science Journal* 11, no. 3 (1959). For an account of the siting of public housing in Yonkers, N.Y., its link to the question of de facto segregation in the public schools, and history of litigation pertaining to that, see John M. Levy, *Contemporary Uban Planning,* 5th edition and earlier (Prentice Hall, 2000), Chapter 7.

19. "Church Group Wins City's Help in Brooklyn Housing Drive," *New York Times,* (August 18, 1985); p. A43; and Peter Galuszka, "Letter from East New York," *Business Week* (May 25, 1992), pp. 17–22.

REFERENCES

Anderson, Martin. *The Federal Bulldozer.* Cambridge: MIT Press, 1964.

Koebel, C. Theodore, ed. *Shelter and Society: Theory, Research, and Policy for Non-Profit Housing.* Albany, NY: State University of New York (SUNY) Press, 1998.

McFarland, Carter M. *The Federal Government and Urban Problems.* Boulder: Westview Press, 1978.

Wilson, James Q., ed. *Urban Renewal: The Record and the Controversy.* Cambridge: MIT Press, 1966.

Chapter

11 | Melting Pots, Mosaics and Salad Bowls

O ne image of America, and particularly of the city, has been the melting pot. Based largely on the experience of immigration from Europe in the nineteenth and early twentieth centuries, there formed an image of an America that quickly amalgamated newcomers into a universal nation. People's ethnicities went from being central to their lives to being merely interesting facts about their ancestry. A family might spend a generation, or maybe two, in an ethnic neighborhood, where their mother tongue was spoken and where there was continuity with the culture that they had left behind. But then in the normal course of events the children or the grandchildren would move out into the larger society in every sense—vocationally, educationally, residentially, and socially. There was in years gone by a certain force of social consensus behind this picture. The public schools saw it as their duty to teach immigrant children English as rapidly as possible. Bilingual education (noted later in this chapter and discussed in detail in Chapter 16) had not been heard of and would have seemed very strange to the turn-of-the-century public school teacher or principal. In eastern cities like New York that received large numbers of immigrants, settlement houses and immigrant aid societies saw it as part of their mission to "Americanize" new immigrants as quickly as possible in matters of language, dress, and behavior.

But this melting pot vision is not universally held. An alternative vision is that of the mosaic. In this view the country appears as a mosaic, and each group is one tile in that mosaic. A variation on that theme is the salad bowl metaphor. The pieces of the salad are all tossed in together, but each piece remains separate and recognizable.

In the United States there is considerable disagreement over the melting pot versus mosaic issues, both in regard to what is likely to happen and in regard to what is the right public policy. Canada, which in proportion to its population (about one ninth that of the United States) admits more legal immigrants than does the United States, has opted for the mosaic view. When immigrants become naturalized as Canadian citizens, they are encouraged to retain the ethnic or national identities that they brought with them to Canada. We should note that Canada, for historical reasons, has a weaker national identity than does the United States. For example, there is nothing in the United States at present that corresponds to pressure for Quebec separatism in Canada.

DOES IT MATTER?

Which of these two views one inclines to is likely to affect how one feels about many current issues. It may, as explored in the next chapter, affect one's views on immigration. If your picture of America is the melting pot, you may view large scale immigration very calmly. If you take a mosaic or salad bowl view, you may see large scale immigration as a prescription for group conflict and endless quarrels about who gets what jobs, what places in college admissions, and so on. You may look at scenes of ethnic conflict in other parts of the world—and feel much angst about our demographic future. On the other hand, if you prize diversity of ethnicity and race for its own sake, you may favor high levels of immigration specifically in order to make the nation more diverse and reduce the majority status of Americans of European ancestry.

One is more likely to favor affirmative action if one sees America in mosaic or salad bowl terms. Affirmative action programs, to varying degrees, necessarily contain the notion that if you are a member of a "protected" group you have some rights or entitlements as a member of that group rather than as a free-floating individual. If you see all group boundaries as rapidly dissolving in the melting pot, then the case for rights and entitlements based on group membership is less likely to appeal to you than if you see group boundaries as relatively permanent.

If you like the vision of America as a melting pot, you are likely to take a dim view of bilingual education. If you like the mosaic vision and want to see America continue as a mosaic, you may favor bilingual education in the hope that it will keep alive languages other than English and thus help to keep alive non–English-speaking subcultures.

Many local and congressional voting districts have been designed (opponents of the process would say "gerrymandered") to more or less guarantee election of Black candidates, following the passage of the 1982 amendments to the Voting Rights Act.[1] This has been done by drawing district lines in such a way as to produce districts with Black majorities, often producing very strange shapes in the process. It is much easier to make a case for this practice if you adhere to the mosaic vision rather than the melting pot vision. In fact, it is very hard to see how one can justify it from a melting pot position.

In a similar vein, it has been proposed that municipal governments adopt various proportional representation schemes to enable minorities to elect minority candidates. For example, instead of having, say, seven city councilmanic districts each of which would elect one representative by majority vote, all seven candidates would be elected at large and each voter would have seven votes. The voter would be able to cast one vote for each of seven candidates, or seven votes for one candidate, or any other combination. Thus minority voters by concentrating their votes would have a better chance of electing one of their own members than under the district system. Such a scheme does not pose the constitutional issues of the special district. In fact, proportional representative voting schemes have been used occasionally in U.S. municipal elections. The question is simply whether or not it is a good idea.[2] From the mosaic position, clearly, it looks like a much better idea than it does from the melting pot position.

MELTING POT OR MOSAIC—WHAT DOES THE DATA TELL US?

How much or how little melting is occurring? If one wanted to find one statistic to gauge the amount of melting that was or was not taking place, what statistic might one use? One obvious choice would be intermarriage. Marriage is, for a great many people, the most intimate of all their relationships; moreover, it is unambiguous: one either is or is not married.

We begin with the so-called "White ethnic" groups. Good data group by group is not available, but there is one statistic that is highly suggestive. Most the groups referred to as White ethnics have either Eastern European origins, such as Russian, Polish, Czech, Hungarian, or Rumanian, or Southern European origins, such as Italian or Greek. Thus most came from countries where the predominant religion was Catholic, either Roman or Greek Orthodox. In 1990 about 28 percent of Catholics who were married had nonCatholic spouses.[3]

For someone of, say, Italian ethnicity who marries a non-Catholic the odds are fairly high that the marriage partner is not Italian—that the out-of-religion marriage is also an out-of-ethnic-group marriage. And, of course, the Catholic-to-non-Catholic intermarriage rate does not catch the many marriages of those with the same religion but of different ethnic groups. In short, the data suggests that the intermarriage rate for White ethnic groups is high. Note that data on intermarriage looks different when cast in terms of persons than it does when cast in terms of marriages. If you expressed the above statistic in terms of marriages, then for every 100 Catholics there would be 28 marriages involving one Catholic and one non-Catholic and 36 marriages involving two Catholics ($28 + 2 \times 36 = 100$). Thus, although 28 percent of Catholics are married to non-Catholics, 44 percent of marriages involving Catholics are religiously mixed marriages. Another way to consider the matter of ethnic mixing is to look at census data. The 1990 census asked respondents to indicate their ancestry. Replies covering 222 million people out of the 1990 population of 249 million reported 497 million ancestries.[4]

In recent years rates of intermarriage have also been very high for American Jews. Among Jews who got married in the period 1970 to 1990, 54 percent married other Jews and 46 percent married non-Jews.[5] The present rate of out-marriage is believed to be 50 percent or more. The history of this rate is typical for many other ethnic groups. Very briefly, the big Jewish immigration to the United States occurred in roughly the period from 1890 to 1910. As late as the 1950s over 90 percent of all Jews who were married were married to other Jews. In the 1960s the picture began to change, and the rate of intermarriage climbed rapidly. What accounts for the big change? Much of it may be just acculturation and its various effects—feeling more at home in the larger society, moving out of ethnic neighborhoods into more mixed neighborhoods, moving from a few big cities like New York and Chicago into other locales where Jewish populations are small, sending one's children away to colleges where most students are not Jewish, and so on. What many think is a substantial reduction in anti-Semitism in the United States in the years after World War II may also be a factor. If one had looked at the Jewish population up to some time in the 1950s, one might have been persuaded that the mosaic was the right model because, judging by marriage statistics, very little melting was taking place. But at present, the melting pot is working so vigorously for American Jews that many who want to see Jews survive as a distinct group in American society now worry that intermarriage in America's open society will do what centuries of persecution in other lands could not.

Among Native Americans marriage across racial lines is more common than marriage inside the race. In 1990 only 40 to 41 percent of Native Americans who were married were married within the group. Almost 60 percent were married outside the group, primarily to Whites. These figures may seem surprising if one pictures Native Americans as living on reservations where one would assume rates of intermarriage would be very low. But in 1990 only 22 percent of Native Americans lived on reservations or other specially designated lands.[6]

The data for Asians at this writing is from 1980. In that year the percentage of members of some Asian ethnic groups who were married outside their own groups were: Chinese 14.4 percent, Filipino 22.2 percent, Indian 15.4 percent, Japanese 21.3 percent. In general, those members of the group born abroad had much lower intermarriage rates than those born in the United States. For example, among Chinese Americans born in the United States 37.6 were intermarried, versus a figure of only 8.2 percent for those born outside of the United States. For Filipino Americans the intermarriage figure for those born in the United States was 60.4 percent, while for those born abroad it was 12.9 percent. Part of the difference is undoubtedly the acculturation effect, and part is that many of those born abroad were already married when they arrived in the United States. For Asian Americans who married out of their own ethnic group, by far the largest source of partners was White Americans. The second largest source was Asians of another ethnicity.[7] Present-day intermarriage figures are probably higher.

Hispanic Americans

It has been suggested that perhaps the Hispanic experience may turn out to be somewhat different from that of other ethnic groups for the following reason. Consider the European immigrant to a major U.S. city, say circa 1900. As a member of a particular ethnic group he or she generally was a part of a small ethnic and linguistic minority within the city. Even if the immigrant lived in a tight ethnic neighborhood, a walk of a few blocks would generally take him or her out of that neighborhood and into another realm with a different ethnicity and another mother tongue. Even if "minorities" made up the majority of the city's population, the immigrant had to learn English in order to function outside his own neighborhood.

The situation may be somewhat different for Hispanics simply because there are sections of the United States in which Hispanics make up a sufficiently large part of the total population that the Hispanic is not in an ethnic or linguistic minority. This is particularly true in Texas, Arizona, New Mexico, and California—states that were part of Mexico until the Mexican War. Where that is so, the pressure to acculturate and to make the linguistic transition may be smaller. Also, for many Hispanics or Latinos in the Southwest the mother country is just an automobile or bus ride away rather than across an ocean. That, too, may tend to slow assimilation.

The outcome for Hispanics vis à vis the melting pot versus mosaic question may also be affected by the matter of bilingual education, a process in which the schoolchild studies English as a foreign language but is educated in other subjects in his or her mother tongue. By far the biggest language of bilingual education in the United States is Spanish. Many people who take an integrationist or melting pot stance oppose bilingual education on the grounds that it tends to retard the learning of English. However, many Hispanic or Latino advocacy groups such as La Raza (The Race) favor it as a preserver of the mother tongue and cultural identity.

On the other hand there is also some evidence that the Hispanic population of the United States is following a path not very different from that of many European immigrants of the turn of the century. A study by Gregory Rodriguez at Pepperdine university shows a rapid movement into the middle class by Hispanics in the Los Angeles area. He defined middle-class economic status as family income above $35,000 and concluded that about half of the families of Hispanics born in the United States and about a third of those born outside the United States had reached this status. He also noted rapidly rising rates of homeownership among Hispanic families. He noted that for many Hispanic families middle-class economic status, often achieved by having several wage earners in the family, often preceded sending children on to higher education.[8] That pattern of economic progress first, followed by large-scale participation in higher education, has been common to many immigrant groups in the United States—for example, Italian Americans.[9] If Hispanics follow a similar scenario, economic progress will be followed shortly thereafter by more general integration into every facet of U.S. society.

In 1998 voters in a California referendum, Proposition 227, decisively supported the ending of bilingual education in the state. The outcome was not a surprise, but the very considerable support that Proposition 227 had among Hispanics was not expected. Writing in the aftermath of the election, Richard Rodriguez stated:

> The paradox is that Latinos as a political force will diminish as the United States becomes more culturally Latin American. Precisely as California becomes more Mexican (more Mestizo), a distinct Latino political agenda will become impossible to sustain because we Californians will be too mixed, too intermarried to entertain separate racial/ethnic categories.[10]

So far as can be told from limited data the rate of intermarriage between Hispanics and non-Hispanics is moderate. In 1994 there were for every existing three marriages between Hispanics in the United States approximately one marriage between a Hispanic and a non-Hispanic.[11] But that statistic leaves much in doubt. First, the data includes many Hispanics who were married to other Hispanics before arriving in the United States. Then, too, if the Hispanic experience is similar to that of many other ethnic groups, the current rate of intermarriage is probably higher than the "inventory" figure above suggests.

Black Americans

The situation with Black Americans is more problematical. The intermarriage rate for Blacks is much lower than for the groups noted above, but it is not trivial either. And it has been rising. In 1993 12.1 percent of all first Black marriages involved a White partner. In 1970 the figure was only 2.6 percent.[12] It is not hard to think of reasons for the increase. The general lessening of segregation and, particularly, the integration of educational institutions and workplaces, has meant more opportunities for Blacks and non-Blacks to meet. The great migration of Blacks from the South to other parts of the country has thrust many Blacks into an environment where they are a minority and necessarily encounter more Whites. Then, too, legal barriers have been ended. For example, many southern states had "antimiscegenation" laws that made marriage between members of different races a criminal act. It was only in 1967 that the Supreme Court in *Loving vs. Virginia* ruled these laws unconstitutional. The rising intermarriage rate may be a harbinger of more general intregration to come.

On the other hand, one of the most eminent American sociologists, Nathan Glazer, states:

> But there is a great exception [to the integration of racial and ethnic groups]. If intermarriage is taken as key evidence for powerful assimilatory forces, then Blacks are not subject to these forces to the same degree as others. Hispanic groups and Asian groups, despite the recency of immigration of so many of them, and thus the greater power of family and group attachment, show rates of intermarriage approaching the levels of Europeans. Blacks stand apart, with very low rates of intermarriage, rising slowly. They stand apart too in the degree of residential segregation. Thirty years of effort, public and private, assisted by anti-discrimination law and a substantial rise in Black earnings, have made little impact on this pattern.[13]

To the above quote Glazer adds other indices of separation. For example, he notes the persistence of Black English as a separate dialect.[14] Were the melting pot working strongly for Black Americans one would expect linguistic convergence, but linguists see little evidence of this happening. In fact, the strength of the Ebonics movement suggests just the opposite.

This writer makes no claim to be able to predict whether or not Blacks will follow a path somewhat like that of many immigrant groups or whether a high degree of separatism will remain. But from both an urban and a national perspective, few future questions are more important for the nation's future.

SUMMARY

The chapter begins by contrasting the *melting pot* and the *mosaic* images of American society. We note that which view one takes may affect one's position on a number of current issues such as immigration, affirmative action, and bilingual education. Most of our information on questions of race, ethnicity, and national origin is collected and analyzed by the Bureau of the Census.

The chapter suggests intermarriage rates as a measure for judging the degree of "melting" between groups. It notes very high rates among various European ethnic groups and for Native Americans, moderate rates for Asians and Hispanics, and relatively low rates for African Americans. The chapter ends with some speculation about the melting pot versus mosaic question with regard to two large American ethnic groups, Latinos and Blacks.

NOTES

1. This practice has been sharply reduced by the Supreme Court's 1995 decision in *Shaw v. Reno* [Janet Reno, Attorney General of the United States].

2. For arguments in favor of such systems, see Lani Guinier, *The Tyranny of the Majority: Fundamental Fairness in Representative Democracy*, (New York: Macmillan, 1994).

3. Bernard Lazerwitz, "Jewish Christian Marriages and Conversions 1970 and 1990," *Sociology of Religion*, (winter 1995), pp. 433–444. (The data doesn't take into account divorces and remarriage, just present status.)

4. *Social and Economic Characteristics of the Population* vol. 1, Table 26 (Washington, D.C.: Bureau of the Census, Department of Commerce, 1990).

5. Lazerwitz, op. cit.

6. Claudette E. Bennett, Nampeo R. McKenny, and Roderick J. Harrison, "Racial Classification Issues Concerning Children in Mixed Race Households." Unpublished data from the 1990 census presented at the April 1995 annual meeting of the Population Association of America.

7. Sharon M. Lee and Keiko Yamanaka, "Patterns of Asian American Intermarriage and Marital Assimilation," *Family Studies* 21, no. 2 (summer 1990).

8. "Latinos in California: The Next Italians," *The Economist* (December 14, 1996), pp. 28–30.

9. See the chapter on Italian-Americans in Thomas Sowell, *Ethnic America* (New York: Basic Books, 1981).

10. Richard Rodriguez, "El Futuro: The New California," *Washington Post* (June 6, 1998), op. ed. page.

11. Marital Status & Living Arrangements, Current Population Reports, Series P20, No. 484 (Washington, D.C.: Bureau of the Census, Department of Commerce), Table A4.

12. *Time* (July 8, 1996), p. 16.

13. Nathan Glazer, *We Are All Multiculturalists Now* (Harvard University Press, 1997), p. 120.

14. Glazer, op. cit. p. 135.

REFERENCES

Glazer, Nathan. *We Are All Multiculturalists Now.* Cambridge: Harvard University Press, 1997.

Sowell, Thomas. *Ethnic America.* New York: Basic Books, 1981.

Massey, Douglas, and Nancy A. Denton. *American Apartheid, Segregation and the Making of the Underclass.* Cambridge: Harvard University Press, 1993.

Chapter

12 | The Controversy over Immigration

T he city has been the great receiver of immigrants throughout U.S. history. Just as the immigrant may be transformed by his or her experience in the city, so too may the city be transformed by the fact of immigration. The visitor to New York several decades ago would have seen an essentially biracial city—a White majority and a relatively small Black minority. Today, the visitor sees a multiracial city in which non-Hispanic Whites, the "Anglos," are no longer the majority but rather the largest minority in a city in which no one group constitutes a majority. The change has been wrought by immigration, for the city has absorbed vast numbers of immigrants, primarily from the Caribbean and from Asia. And there is no aspect of the city, whether it be culture, cuisine, politics, or labor markets, that has not been powerfully affected. While most large cities of the Northeast and North Central regions have lost population in the last several decades, New York has not. Why? Because each year over several decades the 100,000 or so native-born Americans who have moved out of the city have been replaced by an approximately equal number of new Americans (New York, in absolute numbers, has received more immigrants than any other U.S. city). Miami, once a predominantly Anglo city, is now a thoroughly bilingual city and, in the words of Joel Garreau, the "capital of the Caribbean" with a huge Hispanic (primarily Cuban) population.[1] Los Angeles, the recipient of large amounts of immigration from Mexico and from Asia, is demographically a radically different place than it was several decades ago.

A HISTORY OF U.S. IMMIGRATION

U.S. policy toward immigration will have major effects on how many of us there are and who we are. It is not surprising that it is the object of considerable controversy. Before considering the arguments we turn to a brief history of U.S. immigration. Table 12–1 summarizes immigration to the United States since 1821.

A few decade-to-decade changes are worthy of note. The big jump from the decade of the 1830s to the 1840s was in large part due to the inauguration of transatlantic steam service, making the trip quicker and safer and also opening up the United States to immigration from Southern Europe. The falloff from the decade of the 1900s to the decade of the 1910s is largely due to World War I (1914–1918). Much of the sharp drop from the 1920s to the 1930s was due to immigration quotas imposed during the 1920s. This ended the era of essentially unrestricted immigration. Some of the drop is also attributable to the Great Depression and the high levels of unemployment in the United States during the 1930s. World War II (1939–1945) held back immigration in the decade of the 1940s. Some of the big increase from the 1970s to the 1980s is due to the Immigration Reform and Control Act (IRCA) of 1986. This act made it possible for illegal immigrants who had been in the

TABLE 12–1 Legal Immigration to the United States by Decade

1991–1995	5,230,000
1981–1990	7,338,000
1971–1980	4,493,000
1961–1970	3,322,000
1951–1960	2,515,000
1941–1950	1,035,000
1931–1940	528,000
1921–1930	4,107,000
1911–1920	5,735,000
1901–1910	8,795,000
1891–1900	3,688,000
1881–1890	5,246,000
1871–1880	2,812,000
1861–1870	2,314,000
1851–1860	2,598,000
1841–1850	1,713,000
1831–1840	599,000
1821–1830	143,000

Source: Figures for 1981–90 and 1991–95 are from the *Statistical Abstract of the United States,* 117th ed., Table 8. Previous figures are from *Historical Statistics of the United States* as summarized in *U.S. Immigration in the 1980s,* edited by David E. Simcox (Boulder: Westview Press, 1988).

Note: The 1991–94 figure is somewhat inflated by the inclusion of some illegal immigrants who became legal immigrants under the provisions of IRCA (1986) discussed subsequently in the chapter. If they are subtracted, the rate for the first several years of the decade would be about 800,000 per year. Then, if we add back in an estimated net illegal immigration of perhaps 300,000 a year, we would have a total in the range of 1 million per year.

A SHORT HISTORY OF U.S. IMMIGRATION LAW

1882. The Chinese Exclusion Act almost completely banned immigration from the Orient. For others the United States continued to offer essentially open immigration except in the case of persons with communicable diseases or criminal records.

1921 and 1924. The Quota Act of 1921 and the Immigration Act of 1924 ended open immigration by establishing a national origins quota system based on the distribution of national origins recorded in the 1890 census. The effect was both to sharply reduce total immigration and to favor immigrants from Great Britain, Germany, Ireland, and other parts of Northern Europe.

1965. The Immigration and Nationality Act Amendments increased the total number of immigrants allowed and also abolished the national origins system established in the 1920s. The amendments also established family unification as the largest single basis for admission.

1980. The Refugee Act of 1980 established political refugees as a distinct group. Previously, refugees had been periodically admitted, particularly in the years immediately after World War II, on the basis of particular legislation applying to a particular group.

1986. The Immigration Reform and Control Act (IRCA) permitted illegal aliens who could prove a history of sustained residence in the United States from January 1, 1982, to apply for citizenship without penalty of law. The act also contained some relatively weak provisions designed to make it more difficult to employ illegal aliens.

1990. The Immigration Act increased the total number of legal immigrants permitted and instituted a small immigration lottery system (run through U.S. consulates and Embassies) to diversify the immigrant stream by permitting some people in for reasons other than family reunification, labor market qualifications, or refugee status.

1996. The Illegal Immigration and Reform and Immigrant Responsibility Act (PL 104-208) took steps to reduce illegal immigration through greater expenditures on enforcement and stronger criminal sanctions that would make it easier to deport people who are illegally in the United States. The bill as signed made no change in legal immigration.[2]

United States for a specified time and could document this to become legal immigrants and begin the process of becoming citizens. Large numbers of illegal immigrants took advantage of this opportunity. Thus part of the immigration figure for the 1980s is made up of people who had been in the United States for a number of years.[3]

Table 12–2 shows the changing pattern of immigration to the United States for several selected years. Note the shift from Northwestern Europe to other parts of Europe and emergence of large amounts of immigration from Asia and other parts of the Western Hemisphere.

Behind much of the European migration to America was the Industrial Revolution, for it promoted massive increases in population and at the same time, through the mechanization of agriculture, drove large numbers of people off the land.

> Imagine a map of Europe. Across this map a time line traces the evolution of the Industrial Revolution. From a point in the British Isles in the late eighteenth century the line crosses to the low countries and Germany in the mid-nineteenth century and to eastern and southern Europe in the late nineteenth and early 20th centuries. Across the same map a second line traces the chronological evolution of migration to the United States. As it happens, the two lines are almost precisely congruent—migration came principally from the British Isles in the eighteenth and early 19th centuries, then mainly from Germany, and finally from the great watersheds of the Vistula and the Danube and the mountain ranges of the Apennines and the Carpathians to the south and east. . . . The congruence of those lines is not coincidental. Industrialization, in this view, is *the* root cause and the most single powerful variable explaining the timing, the scale, the geographic evolution, and the composition of the great European migration.[4]

TABLE 12–2 Sources of U.S. Legal Immigration for Selected Years

Year	Total	Northwest Europe	Central Europe	Eastern Europe	Southern Europe	Asia	Americas
1850	369,980	228,148	78,901	46	1,228	7	15,768
1900	448,572	85,212	133,354	97,639	108,495	17,946	5,455
1970	373,326	24,743	23,056	2,193	60,661	90,215	161,727

Source: Historical Statistics of the United States, Vol. 1, p. 105 and following.

Notes: Despite its apparent precision, the data for 1850 and 1900 should be taken only as indicative, for there are a number of gaps in it. The year 1970 was substituted for the year 1950 in the sequence to avoid the distortion of refugee admissions following World War II. The very low figure for Eastern Europe in 1970 reflects the extremely restrictive emigration policies of the Soviet Union at that time. Northeastern Europe includes Great Britain, Ireland, Scandinavia, Belgium, Netherlands, Luxembourg, France, and Switzerland. Central Europe includes Germany, Poland, Czechoslovakia (now the Czech Republic and Slovakia), the former Yugoslavia, Hungary, and Austria. Eastern Europe includes the territory of the former USSR, the Baltic countries, Romania, Bulgaria, and the European part of Turkey. Southern Europe includes Italy, Spain, Portugal, and Greece. Asia includes Asia Minor, Asia and the Indian subcontinent, and the Pacific. The Americas include the entire Western Hemisphere.

TABLE 12-3 Place of Origin of Legal Immigrants, 1995, by Continent and Selected Country (figures in thousands)

All countries	720.5
Europe	128.2
Former Soviet Union	54.5
Poland	13.8
Asia	267.9
Philippines	51.0
China	35.5
Vietnam	41.8
India	34.7
Korea	16.0
North America	231.5
Mexico	89.9
Dominican Republic	38.5
Cuba	17.9
Jamaica	16.4
Haiti	14.0
Canada	12.9
El Salvador	11.7
South America	45.7
Columbia	10.8
Peru	8.1
Guyana	7.4
Ecuador	6.4
Africa	42.5
Ethiopia	7.0
Nigeria	6.8
Egypt	5.6

Source: Statistical Abstract of the United States, 1997, 117th edition, Table 8, p. 11.

Notes: "North America" includes Mexico and what is generally referred to as Central America. Countries are listed in descending number of immigrants received.

The above quote does not explain everything about nineteenth- or early twentieth-century immigration. People also come to the United States for reasons of family reunification, as political refugees, because they find American culture attractive, because they have technical skills or entrepreneurial talents that they believe will find more scope in America than at home, and for many other reasons. But it does explain a great deal.

In the post–World War II period, immigration has increasingly come from this hemisphere south of the Rio Grande and from Asia and the Pacific. Much of the impetus behind this is the same as that behind European immigration in the nineteenth century—massive population growth that can be accommodated neither in the countryside nor in urban labor markets. Table 12–3 shows the detailed pattern of immigration for 1995.

The recent shift in the origin of U.S. immigrants, however, is not just the result of changing demographic and economic forces. It is also, to a substantial extent, the result of public policy. The most important policy change was the Immigration and Nationality Act Amendments of 1965. As shown in the box on page 211 the amendments abolished the national origin quotas that had prevailed since the 1920s and, in effect, placed most visa applicants in a common pool. In addition, it allotted most of the openings for visas for purposes of family reunification. The effect of these two changes was to shrink European immigration and to drastically increase immigration from poorer and faster growing parts of the world—notably this hemisphere south of the Rio Grande and Asia. The "common pot" approach reduced the percentage of Europeans by ending their favored status. The family unification provisions, clearly done for humanitarian reasons, also disfavored Europeans because the mass of European immigration had been some decades back. Thus family links across the Atlantic no longer existed in large numbers. Whether or not it was foreseen by Congress in 1965, the family reunification emphasis had the effect of creating endless chains. The relative who enters the country for purposes of family unification, when he or she becomes a citizen, can then seek to bring over other relatives who, when they become citizens . . . and so forth. In effect, then, those groups who had come through the door in large numbers shortly prior to 1965 were largely able to hold their positions through the family reunification mechanism.

Other elements of policy should also be noted. The Immigration Control and Reform Act (IRCA) of 1986 allowed persons here illegally to apply for citizenship if they could document their presence here over a period of years.[5] Despite the term "control" in the act's name, the effect was probably to accelerate immigration by creating more citizens who had close relatives in other countries. It is also possible that granting the amnesty once creates an expectation that it will be done again, thus possibly encouraging more illegal immigration.

Another factor in accelerating immigration is a provision of the Fourteenth Amendment of the U.S. Constitution that grants birthright citizenship. Therefore, any child born here, even the child of someone who is here illegally or is just passing though on a tourist visa, is automatically a citizen. Though Americans take birthright citizenship for granted, it is almost unique to America. If an American citizen gives birth while visiting in Germany the child does not become a German citizen, but the child of a German citizen temporarily in the United States does have the option of U.S. citizenship. Birthright citizenship was provided for in the Fourteenth Amendment (ratified in 1868) for a very good and specific reason—to prevent Southern states after the Civil War from disenfranchising newly freed slaves by ruling them to be noncitizens. That reason is now moot, but the practice cannot be changed short of a constitutional amendment.

The United States experiences substantial illegal immigration. Estimates generally place the net figure (moves in minus moves out) in the range of several hundred thousand per year. The gross movements may be up to several million persons a year. Much of the illegal immigration occurs across a single border, the Rio Grande. And in fact, much of that occurs over a few relatively short stretches, most notably in the San Diego area. The driving force behind it is clear. Mexico's birth rate is 70 percent higher than that of the United States, its unemployment rate is high, and its per capita income is between one sixth and one seventh that of the United States. There is not another long border anywhere in the world where the economic and demographic contrast is quite so sharp.

One might ask, why we do not greatly curtail illegal immigration? Part of the answer is really a matter of political culture. As a nation of immigrants and descendants of immigrants we have not had the will to stop it. One can even see this in the commonly used terms "undocumented alien" or "undocumented worker," for the term "undocumented" has a very different feeling than "illegal" has, though the meaning is the same. And, truthfully, it is hard not to have a mixture of sympathy and admiration for someone who may put his or her life at risk crossing a border illegally to seek a better life. Coming in without papers is clearly a legal crime, but most of us do not see it as a moral crime.

Because so much illegal immigration to the United States comes in across the Rio Grande, a disproportionate part of the total illegal population in the United States lives in the Southwest. The Bureau of the Census' low estimate for "undocumented immigrants" resident in the United States was 3.5 million for 1994. The figure includes both those who crossed the border illegally and those who came legally but then overstayed their visas or permits. Of the 3.5 million, the Bureau of the Census estimates that 1.32 million were in California and 462 thousand were in Texas. Thus slightly over half were in just the two states bordering the Rio Grande. It is not surprising that political pressure to control illegal immigration has been strongest in California, as discussed at the end of the chapter. Of all illegal residents, the Immigration and Naturalization Service (INS) estimates that about 39 percent are from Mexico. El Salvador is a distant second with slightly under 10 percent.[6]

Finally, the U.S. legal system tends to make our borders more porous to immigration than one might expect simply from reading the provisions of our immigration laws. In general, people cannot be deported from the United States without some form of due process. And for some time backlogs for hearings have stretched out for many years. For someone overseas who is desperate to come to the United States and faces a wait of many years for a visa, the most expeditious thing might be to come on a visitor's visa and simply overstay it. With any luck it would be many years before the case came up, and the individual would be legally entitled to stay until that time.

A SPECTRUM OF VIEWS ON IMMIGRATION

In bureaucracies and businesses it is sometimes said that "personnel is policy," meaning that personnel decisions are the most important policy decisions the organization makes, even if they are not called policy decisions. Who we are and what we are as a nation has been and will be powerfully shaped by our national "personnel" decision—who we admit and how many we admit.

The Bureau of the Census periodically produces projections of the U.S. population.[7] Their middle range projection shows the population climbing from about 263 million in 1995 to about 394 million in 2050. That projection assumes present rates of fertility and mortality and *immigration*.[8]

The same reports notes that if from 1995 on the United States were to experience zero net immigration, the 2050 projected population would be 314 million, approximately *80 million* less. Note that zero net immigration is not the same as no immigration, since people do emigrate too. As a rough estimate, if we admitted about 200,000 immigrants a year, we would be in a condition of zero net immigration.

As a nation we are very conflicted on the subject of both legal and illegal immigration, and often opinions on those subjects do not fall out in a predictable manner across the political spectrum. A range of opinions on immigration policy follows. It is not this writer's intention to take a position, but simply to present some commonly made arguments.

In a Fourth of July editorial, the *Wall Street Journal* stated:

> Four years ago today we offered an alternative [to current immigration policy]. We wrote 'If Washington still wants to do something about immigration, we propose a five word constitutional amendment: There shall be open borders.'
>
> We added, 'Perhaps this policy is overly ambitious in today's world, but the US became the world's envy by trumpeting this kind of heresy.' A policy of liberal borders is no more or less radical than the notion that a democracy founded in a new, wild world could become the envy of all nations.
>
> Our support of more immigration isn't entirely for the benefit of immigrants alone. This nation needs the rejuvenation that waves of new Americans bring. Latins, Vietnamese and West Indians are the new Irish, Italians and Poles. We must guard against slipping into the self-satisfied view that we are good enough as is, no need apply or trespass on the American experiment.[9]

The reader might be surprised to see such a "liberal" view in such a "conservative" publication, but the fact is that business, both large and small, has often taken a relatively permissive view on immigration. Ideologically, notions about free markets and free movement of goods across borders have at least a superficial kinship with the free movement of people across borders. Then, too, immigrants expand the labor supply and thus exert some downward pressure on wages. They also, of course, constitute new customers. Traditionally, organized labor, despite its more "liberal" stance on many social and economic issues, has been anti-immigration precisely because of its presumed effects on wages. The restrictive immigration legislation of the 1920s came to pass in part because of lobbying by labor unions.

Slightly less permissive, but still favoring more immigration than we now receive is the economist Julian Simon.[10] Simon is not concerned about overpopulation at either the world or the national level. He takes the position that the planet and the nation can sustain a population much larger than we now have. In this regard he is very much at odds with the environmental movement. He argues that natural resources or natural resources per person do not count for very much. Look how prosperous Japan or Switzerland is, and what natural resources do they have? In his view there is only one really important resource and that is the human brain. A bigger population means more ideas, more inventions, more solutions to problems. In short, population is itself a resource to be sought. He does favor what he terms "designer" immigration. He would select at least somewhat for people with special skills, talent, or higher education. Incidentally, a number of countries including Canada and Australia do select in exactly that way. They would argue that by so doing they are increasing the productivity and quality of the labor force and thus contributing to their own prosperity.

The advocate of increased immigration for the United States might note that in many parts of the country the economic contribution made by immigrants is very clear to see. In Silicon Valley (the Santa Clara county area south of San Francisco), for example, numerous high-technology firms have been started by immigrants, and immigrants constitute a substantial share of the area's highly skilled labor force. As a professor at an institution that accepts a large number of foreign students into its graduate programs, this writer observes that many of them, particularly Indian and Chinese students, choose to remain in the United States after receiving masters' and doctoral degrees. It seems unquestionable that these highly motivated and highly talented individuals will be a long-term asset to the U.S. economy.

At the other end of the spectrum there are many who would cut immigration back drastically. For example, the Federation for American Immigration Reform (FAIR) would cut legal immigration back from its current level of approximately 1 million to perhaps 300,000 per year. They would do that by "a moratorium on all immigration except spouses and minor children of U.S. citizens and a limited number of refugees." Given that there are always some people emigrating, often to the nations from which they came, that would reduce net immigration to close to zero.

Arguments for a drastic cutback in immigration are numerous. Some environmentalists oppose large scale immigration simply because it expands the population and thus puts pressure on resources, open space, and the like. Consider the Bureau of the Census population projections cited earlier—a population of 394 million in the year 2050 if immigration (both legal and illegal) continues at the rates that prevailed in the mid-1990s, compared with 314 million had net immigration dropped to zero in the mid-1990s and remained there until 2050. The additional 80 million people might be expected to occupy an additional 30 million or so housing units and drive, perhaps, an additional 60 million or so motor vehicles. If current per capita petroleum use remained the same, the United States would consume another 200 million or so gallons of oil a day. The largest metropolitan area in the United States is the New York area—the city itself and fifteen surrounding counties in parts of three states— containing about 18 million people. The 80 million person difference would be in terms of population, housing, economic activity, and the like—the equivalent of between four and five additional New York metropolitan areas.

Many who oppose large scale immigration make use of a labor market argument. They point out that under the present immigration rules the majority of immigrants come from less developed countries, Mexico being the largest single source. The majority of such immigrants come in with a relatively low level of skills and education. That is not in any way a comment on their long-term potential, but it does mean that most of them enter the U.S. labor market at its low wage end.[11] Therefore, they have very little effect on the wages of lawyers and systems analysts but may have substantial effect on the wages of taxi drivers, fast-food servers, gardeners, janitors, and other occupations that do not require substantial education or great fluency in English. If immigration leaves the wages in higher-paid occupations more or less unchanged but pulls down the wages in lower-paid occupations, it necessarily increases the degree of wage inequality in the United States. They argue that high rates of immigration, legal or illegal, put a burden on the poor, whether they are citizens or recent immigrants, by pushing down wages and pushing up unemployment rates in the labor markets in which the poor must compete.

Some have argued that immigration makes it more difficult for the United States to resolve its racial problems because it specifically hinders Black economic progress. The argument is that in areas where there are large recent immigrant populations, the immigrants often displace Blacks from much potential employment. Writing about the situation in Los Angeles, where there is both a large Black population and also a large and very fast growing Latino population, one writer stated:

> If you live here, you don't need the General Accounting Office [of the federal government] to bring you the news. The almost total absence of black gardeners, busboys, chambermaids, nannies, janitors, and construction workers in a city with a notoriously large pool of unemployed, unskilled black people leaps to the eye. According to the US Census, 8.6 percent of South Central Los Angeles residents were unemployed in 1990, but another 41.8 percent were listed as "not in the labor force." If the Latinos were not around to do that work, nonblack employers would be forced to hire blacks—but they'd rather not. They trust Latinos. They fear or disdain blacks. The result is unofficial but widespread preferential hiring of Latinos—the largest affirmative-action program in the nation, and one paid for, in effect, by blacks.[12]

The same writer argues that a similar phenomenon occurred early in this century. Southern Blacks migrating northward to greater personal freedom and industrial and commercial employment collided with immigrants from Southern and Eastern Europe in the labor markets of New York, Chicago, Philadelphia, and other northern cities. By and large, employers favored the Europeans.

> By an irony that I find particularly cruel, Latino immigration may be doing to American blacks at the end of the twentieth century what European immigration did to them at the end of the nineteenth.

At the almost opposite end of the spectrum from the "There shall be open borders" position of the *Wall Street Journal* is the writer Peter Brimelow. He is not quite at the other end of the spectrum because he would not ban all immigration. He would, however, reduce immigration very sharply and base the criteria for admission largely on labor market qualifications. He would also shift the quota arrangements back to favoring Europeans. Ironically, Brimelow is himself an immigrant. He came to the United States as a young man from Great Britain in the 1960s, remained, and became a citizen. Though he makes the sorts of economic arguments noted above, his larger argument is essentially cultural. He asserts that he is not a racist, and would probably assert that he is not an "ethnicist" or a "classist" if such words existed. Because those who hold views like Brimelow's are vulnerable to the charge of being racists, bigots or "nativists," many of them may be inhibited about expressing them. Thus such "politically incorrect" views are likely to be more common than one would suspect from, say, a casual reading of newspapers. Among those who supported Proposition 187 in California (see next section) were no doubt many who are in general agreement with Brimelow. Partly for that reason, Brimelow's position is worth describing.

He starts with a vision of what it means to be a nation that is quite different from what we might call the multicultural vision. He does not see a nation as a mix of peoples who simply agree to abide by a common set of rules or procedures. He does not think that what has been called a "universal nation" has much chance of long-term survival. Rather, he has what many would consider to be a much more parochial vision of nationhood.

> But, essentially, a nation is a sort of extended family. It links individual and group, parent and child, past and future, in ways that reach beyond the rational to the most profound and elemental in human experience.[13]

He views the United States as an essentially European nation that has been, each year since the immigration legislation of 1965, becoming less so. And in this transition he sees the seeds of much conflict and unhappiness, and he regards our present course as the most extreme folly.

He asserts that, by and large, multiracial and multiethnic societies do not work very well, and he cites numerous cases. One such case is the friction in Belgium between French-speaking Walloons and the Flemish (who speak a dialect of Dutch). Another is English-French conflict in Canada. (In 1996, the year after Brimelow's *Alien Nation* was published, a referendum in predominantly French-speaking Quebec came within a percentage point of voting to secede from Canada.) Czechoslovakia in 1993 split along ethnic lines into the Czech Republic and Slovakia. But those are the relatively happy cases for they were bloodless. The disintegration of the Soviet Union, though partly a result of the economic failures of communism, was also in large measure the result of ethnic conflict that has been far from bloodless.[14] Ethnic conflict has bedeviled Northern Ireland for decades and has been marked by hundreds of bombings and shootings. In what was until recently the nation of Yugoslavia ethnic conflict has led to genocide on a scale not seen in Europe since World War II. Were Brimelow writing now he might mention the horrifying ethnic violence in Rwanda.

He thus asks why we should have an immigration policy that daily makes us more diverse racially, ethnically, and culturally. As he puts it:

> The onus should not be on critics of immigration policy to explain their motives. Instead, supporters of current policy must explain why they wish to transform the American nation as it had evolved by 1965 [the year in which the national origins basis for admissions was dropped and replaced by family unification criteria].[15]

THE PRESENT STATE OF PLAY

As one might expect, the conflict over immigration policy has reached its height in California, for the state receives the largest numbers of both legal and illegal immigrants. In November, 1994, voters in California passed by a large majority Proposition 187, designed to slow the flow of illegal immigration into the state. The proposition would have barred the children of illegal immigrants from attending public schools, barred people illegally in the United States from using public higher education facilities in the state, and would have cut off illegal immigrants and their dependents from all public health care except in emergencies. The effects would have been massive. For example, it is estimated that there may be as many as 400 thousand children in the California schools who are in the United States illegally. The proposition, both before and after passage, generated a great deal of heat. Its proponents referred to it as "Save Our State" and saw it in exactly those terms. Its opponents saw it as a monument to bigotry and nativism, and they characterized it that way. Because the measure would have forced school officials, social service workers, and health workers, in effect, to play the role of police by verifying that people were here legally before providing them with services (like admitting children to the public schools), many of them stated publicly that they would not obey the law. As it happened, the courts shortly after ruled the amendment unconstitutional and the matter was not put to the test.[16] But the overwhelming passage of the amendment clearly showed the strength of public sentiment in California.

On September 30, 1996, President Clinton signed into law a bill (PL 104-208) to restrict illegal immigration.[17] The bill authorized the hiring of additional border guards and Immigration and Naturalization Service agents, funded the construction of additional fencing along the U.S.-Mexico border near San Diego, simplified and speeded up various deportation and exclusion procedures, and increased criminal penalties for immigration law violations. The original legislation that came out of the joint committee of Congress was considerably stronger, and it also included some measures that would have made some types of legal immigration more difficult. However, the provisions pertaining to legal immigration were dropped in the final maneuvering before signing. Much of the push for the legislation came from Republicans and conservative Democrats. Opposition to much of the legislation came from the President and liberal Democrats, notably Senator Kennedy. One provision the bill lacked was language that would impose serious controls on the employment of illegal immigrants. That provision was blocked by a coalition of civil libertarians and business interests. By failing to turn off the magnet that attracted many illegal immigrants, the potential effectiveness of the law was greatly compromised.

There seems little doubt that the United States will retain its attractiveness to millions of people in more densely populated and less prosperous parts of the world. Whether the United States will slow down the rate of immigration or whether we have entered an age in which high rates of immigration will become a permanent part of American life remains to be seen. Regardless of where one comes out along the "open the borders" to "severely restrict immigration" spectrum, one can readily acknowledge that there are few if any public policy decisions that will have more effect upon urban America than what the United States chooses to do about immigration policy in the decades to come.

SUMMARY

This chapter begins with a brief history of U.S. immigration. We note the rise in the rate of immigration across the nineteenth century and the peak flows in the decade from 1900–1910. In the twentieth century we note the transition from essentially open immigration to the sharp reductions in the 1920s. In the post–World War II period, immigration to the United States gradually accelerated, so that at the present time the rate of legal immigration, in absolute numbers, is comparable to the peak flows at the turn of the nineteenth century. The pattern of U.S. immigration was radically changed in 1965 by the amendments to the Immigration and Nationality Act. These amendments abolished the national origins quotas that had favored Europeans and also made family reunification the primary grounds for immigration. In the early nineteenth century the majority of immigrants came from Northern and Western Europe. In the late nineteenth and early twentieth century the majority of immigrants came from Southern and Eastern Europe. At the present time the largest numbers of immigrants come from Asia and from this hemisphere south of the Rio Grande. We also note the substantial amount of illegal immigration, not known precisely but estimated at a net annual figure of approximately 300,000.

The chapter presents a range of views on immigration from the essentially open-door policies advocated by the *Wall Street Journal* and the economist Julian Simon to the restrictionist policies advocated by the Federation for American Immigration Reform (FAIR) and by Peter Brimelow. In 1996 the United States moved to slow the rate of illegal immigration with the passage of PL 104-208, which mandated increased expenditures on border control and tighter legal sanctions against illegal immigration.

NOTES

1. Joel Garreau, *The Nine Nations of North America,* Boston: Houghton Mifflin, 1981.
2. *Congressional Quarterly,* September 28, 1996, p. 2756; and October 5, 1996, p. 2865. *PL* means public law, and 104 refers to the 104th Congress.
3. Jason Juffras, *The Impact of the Immigration Reform and Control Act on the Immigration and Naturalization Service* (The Rand Corp., for the Urban Institute, 1991).
4. David M. Kennedy, "Can We Still Afford to Be a Nation of Immigrants?" *Atlantic Monthly,* (November 1996), p. 58. Italics are in original.
5. See David E. Simcox, *U.S. Immigration in the 1980s* (Boulder: Westview Press, 1988), for a detailed description of the act.
6. *Statistical Abstract of the United States,* 116th ed. (1996), Table 10.
7. Current Population Reports, Series P. 25, no. 1130, *Population Projections of US by Age, Race, Sex and Hispanic Origin,* (Washington, D.C.: Bureau of the Census, February 1996).
8. To a demographer a projection is a mathematical procedure based on certain assumptions. As long as the mathematics is done correctly, a projection cannot be said to be wrong. This is different from a forecast, which is the demographer's estimate of what will happen. Unlike projections, forecasts can be wrong.
9. "The Rekindled Flame," *Wall Street Journal* (July 3, 1990), p. A10.
10. Julian Simon, *The Economic Consequences of Immigration* (New York: Blackwell, 1989).
11. This statement may sound as though it contradicts the previous comments about Silicon Valley and high technology, but it really does not. Immigration is not a single stream but rather many streams. For example, the percentage of adult immigrants who have less than a high school diploma is much higher than the comparable figure for the U.S. population. On the other hand, the percentage of immigrants who have Ph.D.s is also higher than the comparable percentage for the U.S. population.
12. Jack Miles, "The Struggle for the Bottom Rung: Blacks vs. Browns," *Atlantic Monthly,* (October 1992), pp. 41–52.
13. Peter Brimelow, *Alien Nation: Common Sense about America's Future* (New York: Random House, 1995), p. xix.
14. Daniel P. Moynihan, *Pandemonium: Ethnicity in International Politics,* Oxford, (Oxford University Press, 1993).
15. Brimelow, op. cit. p. 119.

16. Kenneth R. Noble, "California Immigration Measure Faces Rocky Legal Path," *New York Times* (November 11, 1994). See also Drummond Ayres, Jr., "Curb on Aliens Dims Dreams in Hollywood," same issue, p. A28. Note that the court's decision may have been fore-shadowed by the Supreme Court's ruling in 1982 in *Plyler v. Doe* that found that Texas could not cut off funds to school districts that admitted students illegally.
17. "As White House Calls Shots, Illegal Alien Bill Clears," *Congressional Quarterly* (published weekly) (October 5, 1996) pp. 2864–66. See also pp. 2756–7.

REFERENCES

Simcox, David E. *U.S. Immigration in the 1980s,* Boulder: Westview Press, 1988.

Chapter

13 | Poverty—the Background

overty is far from an exclusively urban problem. However, it is a very important urban problem. The greater concentration of poverty in central cities has not always been the case in the United States. In 1959, the first year for which good income data is available (from the 1960 census), central cities had only 83 percent of their proportionate share of the nation's poor. At present they have about 142 percent of their proportionate share. Poverty rates in central cities, as Table 13-1 shows, are on average about twice that in the parts of metropolitan areas outside the central city.

A number of the causes of the urbanization of poverty have been discussed earlier in this book. One big factor has been the combination of technological and economic forces that promoted the suburbanization of the more affluent population and of much employment. In particular, the loss of manufacturing, goods handling, and other blue-collar employment from central cities has made many urban labor markets difficult places for people without the education and skills needed in the "postindustrial" economy. The great internal migration of the rural poor caused by the rapid mechanization of agriculture (see Chapter 3) also contributed to the problem. In some cities massive immigration, discussed in Chapter 12, may have been another factor.

For both cities and for the poor, the concentration of the poor in the cities is a serious problem. Consider the situation first from the perspective of the city. Large numbers of poor people impose a serious fiscal strain on the city because such a population will necessarily cost more in services than it will return in tax revenues. The city can raise taxes to cover the costs, but higher tax rates make the city less attractive as a business location and as a place of residence for wealthier individuals. The smaller tax base increases the pressure for further tax increases, which tends to shrink the tax base further in a self-perpetuating cycle.

TABLE 13-1 Percentage of the Population below the Federal Poverty Line by Place of Residence, 1993

United States	15.1
Metropolitan areas	14.6
Central cities	21.5
Part of metropolitan area outside central city	10.3
Nonmetropolitan areas	17.2

Source: Income, Poverty, and Valuation of Noncash Benefits: 1993, Bureau of the Census, Series P60–188, 1995, p. xvi, Table C.

Beyond the fiscal effect there is a difficult-to-quantify but nonetheless real social effect. Many people, whether upper class, middle class or working class, have a real aversion to living near the poor. One may decry this, but that does not make it less so. One reason for this aversion is that the poor, most of whom are not members of the "underclass," and the underclass tend to occupy the same space.

Some years ago, the journalist Ken Auletta broke the underclass into four main groups:[1]

1. The passive poor, among whom are many long-term welfare recipients
2. Street criminals
3. Hustlers: people who earn their livings in marginal ways, some legal and some not
4. The traumatized, including alcoholics, drug addicts, bag ladies, and deinstitutionalized mental patients

Seeking a statistical criterion for defining underclass neighborhoods by census tract, two researchers, Mincey and Weiner, used the following four items available in the census:[2]

1. Male detachment from the labor force
2. Percentage of households receiving public assistance
3. Percentage of households headed by women with children
4. Teenage high school dropout rates

This definition and Auletta's definition are not precisely the same. But either one will take you to the same neighborhoods.

Much of that aversion of the nonpoor to living close to the poor is fear of the underclass and, in particular, fear of street crime. Many of the non-underclass poor have exactly the same fears. But unlike more prosperous people, they do not have the income to move away. People who have school-age children may avoid living near concentrations of the poor because they do not want their children going to school with the children of the underclass, both for fear of violence and for fear that their children will not get a good education. Acts like aggressive panhandling (see the note on squeegeemen in Chapter 15) decrease the attractiveness of neighborhoods or business locations near large concentrations of poverty. In short, the presence of a large underclass population prompts out-migration of the nonpoor and makes it much harder for the city to compete with suburban and non-metropolitan areas.

For the poor, living in situations of concentrated poverty exposes them to many more risks, such as that of violent crime, and also decreases the chance that they and their children will be able to rise out of poverty. For reasons discussed in the next chapter, large concentrations of poverty tend to have a self-perpetuating or "culture of poverty" effect. If a large, poor population places great stress on the city's finances, the poor may suffer even more because of a decrease in the quality of social and public services.

MEASURING POVERTY

Most of our data on poverty comes from a single source, the Bureau of the Census. The decennial census asks some millions of households about their income in the previous year. Thus there is extensive data for all years ending in 9. In between, smaller samples give us updates on trends since the last decennial census. For example, the 1993 data in Table 13–1 comes from a sample of about 60,000 households done in 1994.

The Bureau of the Census sets a "poverty line" that varies by household size and then determines whether each household filling out a questionnaire is above or below that line. For 1993 the poverty line or threshold was $7,363 for a one-person household, 9,414 for a two-person household, and 11,522 for a three-person household. The poverty line ranged up to $29,529 for a household with nine or more members. It is an absolute rather than a relative standard. When it was developed in the 1950s, the Bureau ascertained that poor people spent about one third of their income on food. It then developed cost figures for a nutritionally adequate diet for various household sizes and multiplied by three.[3] Since then, the figure has been adjusted each year to compensate for the effects of inflation.

The poverty figures produced by the Bureau of the Census are based on cash income as reported by people responding to census questions. These figures do not count noncash benefits as income. For example, if someone lives in subsidized housing, the value of that subsidy (the difference between the rent the person pays and what it actually costs to provide their housing) is not counted as income. Similarly, medical care through Medicaid (a program that provides medical care for low-income people under the age of 65) is not counted as income. Therefore, the published figures overstate real poverty to some extent. For example, in 1994 the Bureau of the Census counted about 34.4 million people as poor. However, it estimated that if the cash value of various forms of assistance such as food stamps, free medical care under Medicaid, and housing subsidies were counted as income, the number of poor would fall to about 25.6 million.[4] Saying how much aid from various sources really reduces poverty is difficult. One reason is that even though we may know exactly how much the aid costs to deliver (its "price"), it is difficult to say how much it is worth to the recipient.[5]

Census data on income are problematical in another way too. For 1993 the Bureau of the Census estimated that without cash transfers that are counted as income—for example, Social Security—about 56.4 million people would be under the poverty line. But if the transfers did not exist, people's behavior would not be the same. For example, if Social Security did not exist, many people of retirement age would have saved more in other ways, and some would, no doubt, have worked longer before retirement. Therefore, the actual number below the line would probably have been less than 56.4 million. The point is that estimating poverty and estimating the effects of public policy upon poverty is a complicated matter, and the published figures should be taken only as a very general indication of the situation.

Note that for the first decade shown in Figure 13–1 the percentage of the population in poverty declined sharply. Since the end of the 1960s the percentage of the population under the poverty line has shown little systematic change. Thus as the population of the nation has grown, the number of people in poverty has risen. The poverty rate tends to rise during recessions and fall as employment picks up. For example, the poverty rate fell consistently during the sustained economic boom of the 1990s. But these cyclical changes are not large.

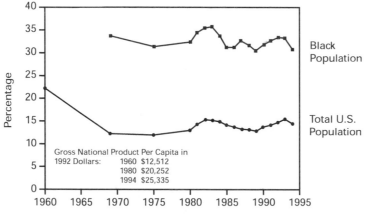

FIGURE 13–1   Percentage of Persons below Federal Poverty Line, 1960–1994

Source: Statistical Abstract of the United States, 1996, 116th edition, Table 730 and earlier years.

In 1994 the poverty rate for Blacks was a little more than two and one half times the rate for Whites. That ratio has changed relatively little over the time period shown in Figure 13–1.

WHY HASN'T THE POVERTY RATE DECLINED?

The behavior of the U.S. poverty rate since about 1970 raises a puzzling question: Why has it not declined? The poverty rate is computed against an absolute rather than a relative standard. As average income rises, one would expect the poverty rate to decline. The United States has become considerably more prosperous in the last quarter century. In 1992 dollars, per capita gross national product (GNP) in 1973 was $18,412. By 1993, measured in the same dollars, it was $24,728, an increase of 34 percent. One might reasonably expect a very substantial decrease in the poverty rate. But as Figure 13–1 shows, it did not happen.

To begin, we can rule out a few explanations that one commonly hears. The failure of the poverty rate to fall was not a result of inflation, for all figures are adjusted for inflation before the rate is calculated. It was not because the U.S. economy was unable to create jobs. In the last several decades the U.S. economy has created jobs at a remarkable pace. For example, from 1970 to 1995 the number of jobs grew from 79 million to 125 million, roughly a 46 percent increase. During the same period the population grew from 216 million to 263, a roughly 22 percent increase. Employment, measured in percentage terms, grew twice as rapidly as population. The percentage of the total population that was employed grew from 57.4 percent to 62.9 percent.[6]

A small part of the failure of the poverty rate to decline may be partly explained by an increase in inequality in wages over the last few decades. Various reasons have been advanced for this. One is that with the shift to the postindustrial economy the productivity and therefore the wages of workers with specialized skills have increased relative to the wages of less skilled workers. One piece of evidence often cited for this effect is the percentage difference between the wages of college graduates versus high school graduates. This difference has been increasing in recent years.

Another factor in the increase in wage inequality has been the decline in manufacturing employment as a percentage of total employment. Historically, industries like steel and automobiles have been an important source of well-paying jobs for people without higher education. One reason for the shrinkage of manufacturing jobs as a percent of total jobs has been that productivity in manufacturing has risen faster than in the economy generally. Thus, as manufacturing remains the same approximate percentage of the gross national product (GNP), it must shrink as a percentage of total employment.[7] Another factor in the relative shrinkage of manufacturing employment has been the growth of world trade. A certain number of manufacturing jobs have been lost to outsourcing (the overseas production of parts of the finished product) and importing. Members of the Political Economy school discussed in Chapter 5 are quick to point to the growth of multinational corporations in this regard.[8] Regardless of the causes, the relative weakening of manufacturing has resulted in a thinning out of the middle of the wage distribution curve. In the last several decades labor union membership has shrunk relative to total employment. That has probably also contributed to the decline in blue-collar wages because weaker unions are less able to drive hard bargains with management. As noted in Chapter 11, the competition from immigrant labor in some labor markets may drive down wages for some types of lower-skilled work while leaving wages for highly skilled work relatively unaffected.[9]

All of the above contributes to a situation in which we have increases in both the numbers of high earners and the number of low earners and some erosion of middle-income wages. However, the fact is that the modest increase in wage inequality that we have seen in the last several decades is simply not sufficient to account for the failure of the poverty rate to fall, though it may be a part of the explanation.

This leaves us back where we started. As a society we produce considerably more goods and services per person than we did, say, two decades ago. And more of us have jobs than was previously the case. Then why has the percentage of the population living in poverty not declined? In his inaugural address in 1961 President Kennedy, speaking about the matter of economic growth, used the phrase "a rising tide lifts all boats." The economic tide has been rising, but not all boats have risen. To answer that question we need to know a little bit about exactly who is poor.

The Structure of Poverty

Who you are by age, by race, and perhaps most important, by family structure greatly affects the odds on whether or not you are poor. Table 13–2 shows rates for the entire population by age.

Poverty rates are highest for children, a matter discussed subsequently. The rate falls to a minimum for the 45 to 54 age group, which, at least for men, typically represents the years of peak earnings. Note also that poverty rates for those 65 and over are below the average for all ages. Several decades ago poverty rates were higher for those 65 and over than for any other age group simply because most older people are not employed. But poverty rates among older individuals have been brought down drastically by a single federal program, Social Security. The average retired worker receiving Social Security gets somewhat more than $700 a month. While not a vast sum, it is sufficient to lift many millions of retired persons from below to above the poverty line. Social Security has been a very successful antipoverty program for those of retirement age.

TABLE 13-2 Poverty Rates by Age, 1993

Age Group	Percentage below the Federal Poverty Line
Total	15.1
Under 18	22.7
18–24	19.1
25–44	12.2
45–54	8.5
55–59	9.9
60–64	11.3
65 and over	12.2

Source: Current Population Report, Series P.20, No. 484, Bureau of the Census.
Note: Poverty is computed by household. The figure for children thus means the percentage of all children who live in households below the poverty line.

The poverty rate is somewhat lower for persons in families than for the total population. Recall that a family is defined as two or more people living in the same household and related by blood, marriage, or adoption. Poverty rates are higher for isolated individuals and for unrelated individuals sharing households than for families. Within the category of families there is considerable variation by race and ethnicity, as shown in Table 13–3.

There is also a great deal of variation in poverty rate by family structure. The differences between families of married couples and families with no husbands present are shown in Table 13–4.

It is hardly puzzling that husband-and-wife families have lower poverty rates than female-headed (meaning no husband present) families. Men still earn more on average than women. Then, too, if there is no male present, there is a good chance that the requirements of child care will prevent the woman from being able to work full-time or, perhaps, to work at all. Changes in family structure take us to the heart of the problem, as will become apparent.

TABLE 13-3 Poverty Rates for Persons in Families by Race and Ethnicity, 1993

Group	Poverty Rate in Percent
White	9.4
Nonhispanic White	7.6
Black	31.3
Asian & Pacific Islander	13.5
Hispanic	27.3

Source: See Table 13–2.

TABLE 13-4 Poverty Rates in Percent by Family Structure, 1993

All families	12.3
Husband-and-wife family	6.5
Female head, no husband present	35.6

Source: See Table 13–2.

Changes in Family Structure

One cannot assign a precise date to the beginning of a social trend. However, roughly some time in the early 1960s attitudes toward the family began to change, and the number of one-adult families, of which about nine tenths are female headed (ie., no male adult present), began to climb sharply. This change goes far to explaining why greater average prosperity has not reduced the poverty rate and why the Black-White poverty rate gap has shown little sign of closure. It also goes far to explain why poverty rates are substantially higher among children than among the total population. Table 13–5 shows one indicator of changing attitudes to the family.

The upturn in births outside of marriage, as you can see, is very large. Something happened in America in the 1960s, for the rate doubled across that one decade and then just kept rising.

You might consider how very counterintuitive was the increase in births outside of marriage. Assume that you could be transported back in time to 1960 with no knowledge of events since then. You are asked to assume that by the end of the 1960s an essentially fail-safe (if used as instructed) birth control device will be on sale in every drugstore in America. You are also told to assume that in the 1970s the Supreme Court will legalize abortion. You are then asked what you think will happen to out-of-wedlock births. The obvious answer would be that they will decline. There will be fewer accidental pregnancies. And of the accidental pregnancies, more will

TABLE 13-5 Percentage of All U.S. Births outside of Marriage, 1940–93

Year	Percent
1940	3.5
1950	3.9
1960	5.3
1970	10.7
1980	18.4
1990	28.0
1994	32.6

Source: Statistical Abstract of the United States, 117th edition, 1997, Table 97 and earlier editions.

be terminated by abortion. The things you were asked to assume came to pass. By the end of the 1960s birth control pills were in such common use that they were referred to simply as "the pill." In 1973 in *Roe vs. Wade* the Supreme Court legalized first-trimester abortion throughout the United States. But what any reasonable person would have predicted is exactly what did not happen. Out-of-wedlock births as a percentage of all births increased by a factor of six between the beginning of the 60s and the early 90s.

With the massive increase in out-of-wedlock births, as well as some increase in divorce and separation rates, the number of female-headed families began to climb, and the ranks of those in poverty increasingly came to be composed of women without husbands and their children. The changing composition of the poverty population is shown in Table 13–6.

In 1959 when family structure was more intact than it was soon to become, only 20 percent of all families in poverty were female headed. The predominant poverty family was a two-parent family, and in a great many cases the male worked. He just did not earn enough to pull the family above the poverty line. By 1993 the heads of more than half of all families in poverty were female. This change in the composition of the poverty population was so pronounced that in the 1980s it developed its own term in the social science literature—the "feminization of poverty."

The weakening of the traditional family structure and the great increase in the number of families headed by females goes far to explaining how it was possible for the nation's per capita income to increase so much and for employment to increase so rapidly without producing a decrease in poverty. The big employment increases largely represented an increase in women's labor force participation rates. In fact, the increases in total employment could not have come about without increased participation by women in the labor market. However, much of the increased national wealth produced by the increase in the number of working women was captured by the growing number of two-income families. At the same time that the number of two-income families was climbing, the number of families without a male earner was also climbing. As the nation became wealthier, the number of poor, female-headed families also rose. Just as the distribution of wages and salaries has become more unequal, so too has the distribution of family income.

TABLE 13–6 Structure of Families below the Poverty Line, in Percent

	1959	1976	1993
Husband-and-wife family	76	47	41
Female head, no husband present	20	50	53
Other	4	3	6

Source: Current Population Reports, Series P. 60, nos. 115 and 124, and Series P. 20, no. 484, Bureau of the Census.

Note: The "other" category includes households headed by males with no wife present.

Much of that increase has been due to the changes in family structure just described.

Changes in family structure also go far to explaining another puzzle about income and poverty. Since the Civil Rights revolution of the 1960s all sorts of legal and customary barriers to the progress of Black Americans have been torn down. Affirmative action has replaced anti-Black discrimination across large stretches of American life. Universities that 40 years ago discriminated against Black applicants now compete with each other for Black students. Corporations whose middle and upper reaches were once a White male preserve now retain "diversity consultants" to help them find minority workers and nurture their careers. This is not to say that there is now no prejudice and discrimination but only that many barriers to Black economic progress have been removed. And this has facilitated the development of a large Black middle class in the last 30 or so years. However, since the late 1960s the Black-White gap shows no consistent trend toward closure. In 1959 the median family income of Black families was 53 percent that of White families. By 1969 it had risen modestly to 61 percent of the White figure. In 1979 it was back to 57 percent. By 1989 the 1990 Census showed it to be down a point to 56 percent. The latest available current figure, 1994, showed it to be back up to 60 percent, about where it was 25 years earlier.[10]

One explanation for the persistence of the income gap lies in the realm of family structure. The changes in family structure discussed above occurred with much greater force in Black America than in White America, and the prevalence of female-headed families is much greater in the Black population than the White population. Another way to say it is that marriage as an institution is more threatened among Blacks than among Whites. For example, in 1990 about 73 percent of all White women had been married by age 30. Among Black women the comparable figure was only 45 percent. Among that portion of the Black population that has been able to take advantage of the improvement in civil rights and the opening up of formerly closed-off opportunities in education and the professions, there has been great progress. But among a substantial portion of the Black population it would appear that those gains have been largely canceled out by a fragmenting of family structure. If one examines income data for Blacks and Whites and computes an index of inequality for each group, one finds that inequality is greater among Blacks than among whites. One commonly used index is the income of the 75th percentile divided by that of the 25th percentile. The larger the number, the more unequal is the distribution of income within the group. Among Black families the 75th percentile earns about 3.7 times as much as the 25th percentile. For White families, the corresponding figure is considerably smaller, about 2.6.[11] That greater inequality is consistent with the explanation that one part of the Black population has been pulled down economically by family structure effects while another part of the Black population has been very successful at taking advantage of opportunities that barely existed for Blacks before the Civil Rights revolution.

Poverty and the Urban "Ghetto"

The poverty problem for urban areas presents itself in starkest terms in what have come to be called "ghetto" areas. The word *ghetto* comes from medieval Europe and literally refers to sections of European cities to which Jews were confined, typically surrounded by a wall. The word itself is believed to come from an Italian word for iron, a reference to the location of the city of Venice's ghetto close to a foundry.[12] But in modern America the term has been used for poor, inner-city neighborhoods, usually with large Black or, sometimes, Hispanic populations. Ghetto areas make up only a small part of urban America, both in terms of land area and also in terms of number of residents. However, names like Watts, South Central Los Angeles, the South Bronx, and Bedford Stuyvesant are well known and, particularly for people who do not live in central cities, may form much of their image of the city. Using the criteria noted earlier in the chapter, Mincy and Weiner placed the population in all underclass neighborhoods in 1990 at about 2.7 million. Of that population about 57 percent was Black, 20 percent Hispanic, another 20 percent non-Hispanic White, and about 3 percent "other."[13]

One scholar who has looked very closely at the question of ghetto poverty and has influenced views of the ghetto as much as anyone is the sociologist William J. Wilson. Formerly of the University of Chicago and currently at Harvard, Wilson did his work in Chicago. Wilson's most recent book, *When Work Disappears: The World of the New Urban Poor,* is largely derived from his work in Chicago's "black belt," a group of contiguous Black neighborhoods in central Chicago.[14]

Wilson points out that urban areas have always had concentrations of poor people. Indeed, the areas that he studied have always contained large numbers of poor people, a great many of whom were what are called "the working poor." What he sees as new in these areas is not the presence of poverty, but the disappearance of work.

> By "the new urban poverty" I mean poor, segregated neighborhoods in which a substantial majority of individual adults are either unemployed or have dropped out of the labor force entirely. For example, in 1990 only one in three adults ages 16 and over in the 12 Chicago community areas with ghetto poverty rates [40 percent and over] held a job in a typical week of the year. . . . But Chicago is by no means the only city that features new poverty neighborhoods. In the ghetto census tracts of the nation's one hundred largest cities, there were only 65.5 employed persons for every hundred adults who did not hold a job in a typical week in 1990. In contrast, the non-poverty areas contained 182.3 employed persons for every hundred of those not working. In other words, the ratio of employed to jobless persons was three times greater in census tracts not marked by poverty.[15]

The long-term disconnection from the labor force is a much more serious problem than is poverty. It alienates people from the larger society. It attacks the economic roots of marriage and causes marital breakup or prevents marriage in the first instance. In particular, if the male cannot furnish a substantial share of the support for a family, he has no economic role in the family. In effect, the main thing he can offer his wife is more children whom he cannot support. And this disconnection has a self-perpetuating property: The child brought up in a family in which the adults do not work does not have much of a role model for his or her own participation in the world of work. If the neighborhood is filled with other families in which most adults do not work, then he or she also does not get encouraging messages about work from the larger environment. Wilson attributes a large share of the problems of the ghetto—crime and drug and alcohol abuse—to the disconnection from work and the resulting shattering of family structure.[16]

Wilson points out that many ghetto neighborhoods are characterized by declining populations and vacant apartments and abandoned buildings. They generally have many fewer small businesses than in their better days. That is not surprising, for an area characterized by shrinking population, low incomes, and a high level of street crime is not an attractive place to invest. That lack of small businesses, in turn, deprives ghetto residents of the kinds of job opportunities that would be found in other neighborhoods. A lack of legitimate jobs tends to draw more young men into criminal or marginal hustling activities. The presence of large amounts of illegal activity, particularly drug-related activity that generates a lot of cash, creates a bad set of motivations and expectations. When young drug dealers are driving BMWs, a certain number of adolescent boys will decide that the legitimate entry-level jobs that they might be able to get pay only "chump change." It is a very different set of observations from those a young boy would make in a prosperous suburb when most of those who drive the BMWs are doctors, lawyers, systems analysts, and others, who, for the most part, stayed in school and played it straight. As Wilson notes in connection with employer attitudes, many employers are extremely reluctant to hire anyone who gives a ghetto street number as a home address. Some of that may be just prejudice, though as Wilson notes, some of the employers expressing it are themselves Black. But part of it is simply that the ghetto environment tends not to breed the attitudes toward work that employers seek.[17] In short, the absence of work can breed attitudes about work that further shrink the supply of legitimate work.

We should note that the relationship between family structure and social order, and particularly the effects of the absence of large numbers of fathers, has long been observed. Three decades ago Daniel P. Moynihan wrote:

> From the wild Irish slums of the nineteenth-century Eastern seaboard, to the riot-torn suburbs of Los Angeles [a reference to the 1965 Watts riots], there is one unmistakable lesson in American history: a community that allows a large number of young men to grow up in broken families, dominated by women, never acquiring any stable relationship to male authority, never acquiring any

rational expectations about the future—that community asks for and gets chaos. Crime, violence, unrest, disorder . . . that is not only to be expected; it is very near to inevitable. And it is richly deserved.[18]

By the last line, "And it is richly deserved," Moynihan was saying that the nation that fails to deal with the problem has only itself to blame. That statement implies that the solution to the problem is there if only we as a nation have the will to apply it. In subsequent writings he has admitted that it is far from clear that we know what to do and that in the past social scientists and politicians had more faith in our ability to do successful "social engineering" than was justified by our knowledge and understanding.[19]

To return to Wilson's view, the core of his position is that work opportunities for ghetto residents have shrunk because of overall changes in the U.S. economy. It is this drying up of job opportunities that is at the root of family breakup and the problems that flow from it. He notes many of the facts presented in Chapters 3 and 6, such as the loss of manufacturing and goods handling jobs from the central cities. He observes that many of the jobs in the postindustrial economy require levels of education not possessed by many ghetto residents, and in this connection he points to problems in many inner-city schools. He also notes that many of the jobs that ghetto residents might be able to hold are now out in the suburbs, and that these jobs are hard to reach or even find out about if one does not have a car.

Because he sees the problem as starting with the availability of work, his policy prescriptions lay heavy emphasis on public expenditures for job creation and also for job training and education—a "domestic Marshall Plan," in his words. In short, he sees much of the task as bringing jobs within reach of the very poor and also making the very poor better able to compete on the job market.[20] He places little faith in the private sector to perform this task of returning work to the inner city, and so he necessarily argues for a very large federal role in performing the task. As will be in the apparent in the next chapter, much of what he suggests is highly reminiscent of the "war on poverty" begun under President Lyndon Johnson.

Whether Wilson's view that the root of the problem of ghetto poverty is structural—due primarily to changes in the economy that have caused a mismatch between the amount and type of work available and the potential ghetto labor force—has been the subject of considerable dispute. Some feel that he has diagnosed the problem correctly.[21] Others argue that he ignores important social and political factors.[22]

SUMMARY

In the last several decades the poverty rate in central cities relative to the rest of the nation has risen. Among the causes for this have been the relocation of manufacturing, retailing, and other economic activity out of central cities and the migration of more prosperous residents from central city to suburb or exurb. We also noted the effects of the massive migration of the rural poor to central cities following the rapid mechanization of agriculture in the 1950s and 1960s.

Poverty rates are measured by the Bureau of the Census using an absolute standard. Given the substantial increase in real (inflation adjusted) per capita income in the last several decades, one would expect the poverty rate to have declined considerably, but this has not happened. A major reason that the poverty rate has not fallen has been a very large increase in the number of single-parent (usually female) households. This has resulted in what has been termed by social scientists as the "feminization of poverty." The poverty rate of Black Americans bears about the same relationship to that of White Americans that it did before the Civil Rights revolution of the 1960s. Much of the persistence of this gap is attributable to the above changes in family structure which occurred with particular force in Black America. Finally, we noted the problem of "ghetto" poverty and William J. Wilson's argument that it is largely a product of structural changes in the urban economy.

NOTES

1. Ken Auletta, *The Underclass* (Random House, HE, 1982), p. 43.
2. Robert B. Mincey and Susan J. Wiener, "The Underclass in the 1980s: Changing Concept, Constant Reality" (Washington, D.C.: The Urban Institute, 1993). Summarized in Anthony Downs, *New Visions for Metropolitan America* (Washington, D.C.: The Brookings Institution, 1994).
3. Mollie Orshansky, "Counting the Poor: Another Look at the Poverty Profile," *Social Security Bulletin*, Social Security Administration (January 1965).
4. See Table 740 in the *Statistical Abstract of the United States*, 1996, 114th ed.; and *Current Population Report* P60, No. 189, Bureau of the Census.
5. For an insight into the complexities of attempting to estimate how much an item of aid-in-kind is worth to the recipient, see Timothy Smeeding, "Alternative Methods for Valuing Selected In-Kind Transfer Benefits and Their Effect on Poverty," technical paper # 50, U.S. Department of Commerce, Bureau of the Census (March 1982).
6. One might wonder how it is possible for employment to rise so much more rapidly than population. The answer is that while the labor force participation rate for men has not changed very much for several decades the participation rate for women has risen dramatically. For example, in 1994 the labor force participation rate for women ages 25 to 55 was about 75 percent. The comparable figure for 1970 was about 50 percent. For details see Table 615 in the 1996 *Statistical Abstract of the United States* and Table 348 in the 1973 edition.
7. Manufacturing employment in the United States has fluctuated within the 18 to 20 million range for the last several decades without showing much of a long-term trend. But it has been shrinking steadily when measured as a percentage of total employment, which has been growing.
8. See, for example, Saskia Sassen, *The Global City: New York, London, Tokyo* (Princeton University Press, 1991); Michael P. Smith, *City, State and Market: The Political Economy of Urban Society* (New York: Basil Blackwell, 1988); and various works by Manuel Castells.
9. One might think that this effect would show up only in metropolitan areas that had received substantial immigration. But it may spill over to other areas if immigrant workers displace native workers who then move to other labor markets. See John Cassidy, "The Melting Pot Myth," *New Yorker* (July 14, 1997), pp. 40–43.

10. Table 718 in the 1996 *Statistical Abstract of the United States* and comparable tables in earlier editions.

11. Calculations by author from 1994 census data.

12. Joseph Telushkin, *Jewish Literacy* (New York: William Morrow, 1991), p. 191.

13. Mincey and Weiner, op. cit.

14. Alfred A. Knopf, New York, 1996.

15. Wilson, op. cit. p. 19. The term *labor force* includes both those who are employed and those who are actively seeking work.

16. This theme is also explored in a previous work by Wilson, *The Truly Disadvantaged* (University of Chicago Press, 1987). See especially Chapter 3.

17. Wilson, op. cit. Chapter 5.

18. Daniel P. Moynihan, "How the Great Society 'Destroyed the American Family,'" *The Public Interest* (summer, 1992), pp. 53–64. The quote is from his article in *America* in March 1965.

19. See, for example, his *Miles to Go: A Personal History of Social Policy* (Harvard University Press, 1996).

20. For an exposition of Wilson's policy views, see the last chapter in *When Work Disappears*.

21. For two favorable reviews of *When Work Disappears*, see "Jobless and Hopeless," by Sean Wilentz, *New York Times Book Review* (September 29, 1996), p. 7; and "What the Poor Need: Jobs, Jobs, Jobs," by Keith H. Hammonds, *Business Week* (October 7, 1996), p. 20.

22. For an unfavorable review of Wilson's argument, see Fred Siegel, "Jobless, Not Hopeless," *Wall Street Journal*, (September 1996), p. A15. Siegel's argument is based largely on the findings in Roger Waldinger's *Still the Promised City? African Americans and New Immigrants in Post Industrial New York* Cambridge: Harvard University Press, 1996. He notes that Waldinger's book documents the relative success of many new immigrant groups in New York's labor markets despite weaker educational qualifications and less familiarity with English than is the case for American Blacks. Therefore, he argues that other forces are at work.

REFERENCES

See Chapter 14.

Chapter

14 | Poverty and Public Policy

As noted in Chapter 13, the failure of the poverty rate to decline in the face of several decades of rising per capita income and rising employment is puzzling. It is more puzzling when we contemplate how much the nation has spent on fighting poverty since the 1960s.

A BRIEF HISTORY OF ANTIPOVERTY PROGRAMS

At the beginning of the 1960s the United States did not have anything that could be considered a national antipoverty program. In fact, the elimination of poverty was not really on the national political agenda at all. It simply was not an objective of government. We had a limited number of programs left over from the Great Depression that were intended to help people in temporary trouble not of their own making—the "worthy poor." For the temporarily unemployed there was unemployment insurance, a combined federal and state effort. For poor women with children and no husband there was Aid for Families with Dependent Children (AFDC), also a joint federal-state effort that in most states provided very modest levels of assistance. The job-creation programs of the Great Depression, like those of the Work Projects Administration (WPA), had been terminated early in World War II when job shortages turned to labor shortages under the pressure of wartime mobilization. There were miscellaneous federal and state programs for small groups of people in special circumstances, and there was private philanthropy. There was no widespread consensus for a general effort to eliminate poverty beyond the idea that the federal government should do what it could by means of macroeconomic policy to maintain a generally high level of economic activity.

But in the early 1960s the mindset of many in leadership positions, whether in government, the media, academe, or major philanthropic organizations such as the Ford Foundation went through a rapid change.[1]

One element of the new view was that we should not make a sharp distinction between the "deserving" and the "undeserving" poor. Rather than seeing poverty as largely the result of individual luck, decisions, attitudes, and behavior, we should see the existence of poverty primarily as a failure of the larger social system. If the roots of poverty are primarily systemic rather than individual, that suggests a major role for government. Make the right array of jobs available to the poor. Give the poor the job training to hold those jobs. Help people with health problems, housing problems, and child care problems that get in the way of their working. Give remedial education to people who have been poorly educated. Give those at the bottom of the heap a bigger voice in society so that they do not feel helpless. If some people are the objects of discrimination, then ban that sort of discrimination. In effect, open the door and you will see the poor walk through it by the millions.

The idea that government, primarily the federal government, could, in effect, make war against poverty and defeat it germinated under President John F. Kennedy, but little was actually done about it during his administration. President Kennedy was assassinated in November of 1963 and succeeded in office by his vice president, Lyndon B. Johnson. As president, Johnson seized upon the idea. Using the mantle of Kennedy plus his own great ability in dealing with the Congress, he pushed through a mass of legislation in a short time. That he saw the elimination of poverty as a doable feat of social engineering was clear. In addressing the Congress in 1964 he stated:

> It [the war on poverty] is right, because it is wise, and because for the first time in our history, it is possible to conquer poverty.[2]

In the summer of 1994 Congress passed the Economic Opportunity Act (EOA) and also set up the Office of Economic Opportunity (OEO) to coordinate it. The initial thrust of the program was not to give money, but to give people the means to work their way out of poverty. Kershaw quotes OEO's first director, Sargent Shriver, as saying proudly, "We don't give handouts," and OEO personnel as saying, "Our middle name is opportunity" [from EOA]. And, indeed, the initial set of programs fitted the slogan "A hand up, not a handout" fairly well. However, in the next several years a number of pieces of legislation that also provided direct aid and had less of a self-help character were passed. What had been a more tightly targeted attack on poverty from the self-help side became an assault on all fronts at once. A partial listing, not in chronological order, of the legislation of the 1964–67 period follows.

The Economic Opportunity Act (EOA) provided for setting up Community Action Programs (CAPs) in every major city and many smaller cities and towns to provide a variety of neighborhood services in areas such as health, employment, recreation, child care, and housing. Before the end of the 1960s there were well over 1,000 community action agencies across the United States. The watchword for the CAP was "maximum feasible participation" for the poor, and the act required that the CAP's board of directors must include the poor. One goal was to mobilize the poor and increase their political awareness and participation or, in today's jargon, to "empower" the poor. Community action programs also provided thousands of jobs for community activists and organizers, further helping to mobilize the poor. It had long been known that the poor were often unable to have their day in court because of the cost of legal services. Before the end of the 1960s about 1,700 attorneys in 800 community action agencies were providing the poor with free legal services.

A number of well-known programs that exist to the present time were begun as community action programs. To help children from poor families get off to a better start in school, the EOA initiated the Head Start program, which provides a variety of preschool programs to give its enrollees a better chance of doing well when they begin school. Another is the Job Corps, which provides job training in a residential setting to disadvantaged youth. Still another was the war on poverty's domestic equivalent to the Peace Corps, Volunteers in Service to America (VISTA).

Across the 1960s the Aid to Families with Dependent Children (AFDC) program which had been started during the Great Depression was made more generous and, in several ways, more reasonable and humane. For example, prior to the 1960s most states had a "man in the house rule" that made the family ineligible for assistance if a man lived permanently in the house, and social service agency personnel sometimes made "midnight raids" to determine if the rule was being violated. That indignity was first restrained by administrative action in the Department of Health Education and Welfare (HEW), the predecessor of the present Department of Health and Human Services (HHS), and then ended altogether by the Supreme Court in 1968 in *King v. Smith*. After that, the presence of a man in the house could not serve as the basis for terminating aid to a woman and her children. In the early 1960s aid was structured so that every dollar a woman made by working would result in the loss of one dollar of AFDC. That rule was changed to allow women to keep a modest amount of earnings without a one-to-one loss. Beyond these changes in rules, funding was increased and benefit levels raised.[3]

Large sums were appropriated for manpower training targeted to the poor, with an emphasis on youth. The Manpower Development and Training Administration (MDTA) began funding such programs in the early 1960s. Probably the best known of the programs begun under MDTA is the Job Corps, a residential training program for disadvantaged youth. MDTA was supplanted by the Comprehensive Employment and Training Act (CETA) in 1973. That program provided both training and jobs in the public sector in large quantities. CETA was replaced in 1983 by the Jobs Training Partnership

Act (JTPA), which had more of a private sector focus and remains the federal government's number one job training program to the present time. Like CETA, JTPA is targeted to people with histories of poverty and unemployment. Literally millions of trainees have passed though CETA and JTPA since their inception.

The federal food stamp program was initiated in 1965. It comes close to being a national public assistance program. Food stamps can be used directly only for food and a few related items. However, when the stamps cover all or part of a household's food expenses, money that would have been spent on food is liberated for other uses. In that sense the stamps are a close equivalent to cash. In some poor neighborhoods stamps can be exchanged at a discount for cash, albeit not legally. The program started small and grew steadily. By the early 1990s about 9 million households containing about 29 million persons received stamps. A very large percentage of families receiving AFDC also received food stamps.

In 1965 Congress also enacted the Medicaid program to provide medical care for "medically indigent" people under the age of 65. (Medicare, not a means-tested program, provides care for persons over 65). Essentially "medically indigent" means low-income people without medical insurance. Medicaid also started small but grew rapidly. By 1994 federal and state expenditures on Medicaid totaled over 140 billion and reached about 25 million people. Next to Social Security it is the largest entitlement program in the United States. About three fifths of its cost is paid by the federal government and the remainder by state and local governments on a matching basis pursuant to federal regulations. As with food stamps, virtually anyone eligible for AFDC was also eligible for Medicaid.

Beginning in the 1960s the federal government assumed an increased role in assisting low-income people with their housing costs, as discussed briefly in Chapter 9. By the mid 1990s, federal expenditures for housing assistance were in the $20 billion range and benefited approximately 11 million individuals in 5 million households.[4]

Many of the efforts to end discrimination in housing and mortgage lending (see Chapter 10) had their origins in the mid and late 1960s. So, too, did legislation to end discrimination in hiring. Affirmative action became federal policy (and also policy in many corporations and nonprofit organizations such as universities) in the late 1960s. The Voting Rights Act of 1965 put voting procedures in Southern states under federal supervision so as to prevent local officials from disenfranchising Black voters. All of these measures were components of Lyndon Johnson's vision of the Great Society, for all addressed issues of fairness and justice, and all sought to attack barriers to the full participation of disadvantaged groups in American life. To the extent that discrimination and lack of political voice handicap a group's economic progress, they in an indirect sense also were elements of the war on poverty.

The programs described above are far from a complete listing. The point is that since the 1960s there has been a massive effort to help the poor—a mixture of direct income transfers, services in kind, training, and the removal of legal and social barriers to the progress of minority group members.

Saying exactly why the nation suddenly decided to make war on poverty in this wide-angle way may not be possible, but some causes stand out. One basic factor was that since the end of World War II the U.S. economy had done very well. Employment and per capita income had both grown at an impressive pace. Thus it appeared that we had the resources to "end the paradox of poverty amidst plenty." Another reason was a triumphant feeling coming from our success in World War II. It seemed that if, as a nation, we set our mind to a task we could accomplish great things in short order. Perhaps another reason for the timing of the war on poverty was that it took a while after World War II for the nation to realize that some places and some segments of the nation were not enjoying the general national prosperity. After 15 years of more or less continuous postwar economic growth, that fact was becoming very clear. Then, too, there may have been some idiosyncratic reasons. For example, it has been claimed President Kennedy, when campaigning in West Virginia in 1960, was shocked by the extent of the poverty he saw in small Appalachian towns. A very widely read book by the socialist writer Michael Harrington made the poverty of bypassed places and poor subgroups of the population much more visible than it had been before.[5] The Civil Rights movement of the 1960s made Black Americans much more assertive than they had ever been before about demanding change. At the same time it made many Whites much more aware of the problems of Black America and also made many of them feel a sense of guilt about how America had treated and was treating its Black population. That favored the passage of legislation designed to help poor people, of whom a more than proportionate share were Black.

Still another factor that pushed along the war on poverty was that in the 1960s many of the problems of Black America moved north. The post–World War II mechanization of agriculture displaced a large percentage of the southern rural Black population in the space of a few years, and much of that population, often desperately poor, moved to northern cities. That made it much harder to think of problems of poverty and unemployment among Black Americans as just southern rather than national.

The specific series of events that got many people's attention was the waves of rioting that hit northern and western cities in the 1965–68 period. The first major riot was in the Watts section of Los Angeles. Like many others, the triggering event was a minor incident. A Black motorist was stopped by a White policeman on suspicion of driving drunk. A crowd gathered and harsh words were exchanged. Words led to blows. The ensuing riot took six days to contain, and when it was over 33 people were dead, close to three thousand arrests had been made, 15,000 national Guardsmen were sent in to augment the Los Angeles police force, and much of the commercial area of Watts was burned out.[6] Across the 1965–68 period, riots occurred in Boston, Buffalo, Cairo (Ill.), Cincinnati, Detroit, Grand Rapids, Hartford, Jersey City,

Milwaukee, New Haven, Newark, New York, San Francisco, South Bend, Wichita, and Youngstown, among other U.S. cities. Most of the riots were not quite so destructive as the Watts riot, but at least two others, Newark and Detroit, matched it in scale and numbers of dead and injured.

These urban riots were a frightening portent. Terms like "civil war" and "urban guerrilla warfare" were used frequently. The whole scene, complete with sniping and Molotov cocktail throwing, was unnerving to a nation that was at that very same time seeing scenes of the Viet Nam war on the evening news. The riots were more or less confined to ghetto neighborhoods, often by strenuous police and National Guard efforts, but after each it was not clear that this would necessarily be the case the next time.

The consensus view of the riots was that at base they were a symptom of poverty, high unemployment, and racial discrimination and that if we were not going to have endless riots and maybe worse, base conditions had to be fixed. Martin Luther King, for example, expressed the position that riots had to be controlled when they occurred, but that such short-term measures would be useless unless the root causes were addressed. President Lyndon Johnson took the same view, as did most of the political mainstream. For a few years thereafter, the epidemic of urban riots made it easier to wring antipoverty appropriations out of Congress, for clearly something had to be done.

We should note that nothing like the 1965–68 epidemic of urban riots has occurred since. One reason, quite apart from any successes of social policy, may simply be that most places that had the basic conditions did experience a riot in that period. It became very apparent after the riots that the overwhelming price was paid by the Black and, in some cases, Hispanic populations in the ghetto areas. Riots frightened White America, but it was not White America that felt most of the pain. It was the ghetto populations who represented most of the dead and injured, who represented most of those who were arrested, and whose jobs were lost when businesses were burned out and not reopened. That sad lesson, no doubt, inhibited future rioting. When rioting occurred in South Central Los Angeles after the 1992 verdict in the Rodney King case it was thought that it might set off a wave of riots in other cities.[7] But that did not happen.

A DISAPPOINTING OUTCOME

Unfortunately, victory was not to be had in the war on poverty. In fact, victory was almost as elusive as it was in the Vietnam War that was going on at the same time. The poverty rate declined considerably during the 1950s and through much of the 1960s. Then, in the late 1960s, it leveled off, and since then no further progress was made (see Figure 13–1). In other words, the decline seemed to end just about the time the "war on poverty" got into high gear.[8] This coincidence did not go unnoticed.

Not only were the income statistics disappointing, but the war on poverty also began to show unexpected side effects. The following is one example. The 1960s were a generally prosperous period in U.S. economic history. Economic growth was rapid, and at the end of the decade unemployment was substantially lower than it had been at the beginning of the decade. Yet the number of people receiving AFDC had more than doubled across the decade. That hardly squared with the "a hand, not a handout" rhetoric of the "war on poverty." A variety of factors contributed to the increase. One was that somehow the psychology of the poor about taking assistance was changing. As the poor became mobilized and provided with legal services, more of them came to demand (and litigate for) all the benefits to which they were legally entitled. And many who worked in public assistance and other antipoverty programs came to see the extension of benefits as a desirable goal. A widely cited book on poverty and public assistance published in 1971 concluded with these words:

> In the absence of fundamental economic reforms, [a massive increase in the role of government in the economy], therefore, *we take the position that the explosion of the rolls is the true relief reform*, that it should be defended, and expanded. Even now, hundreds of thousands of impoverished families remain who are eligible for assistance but who receive no aid at all.[9] [Italics are in the original.]

Without arguing the question of whether Piven and Cloward were right or wrong in their judgment about the issue, it is clear that expansion of the welfare rolls was hardly the goal that the poverty warriors of the Kennedy and Johnson administrations had visualized. Nor was it a result that pleased the majority of the public who had supported the War on Poverty. As it became evident that large expenditures for the war on poverty were not succeeding in reducing poverty, at least as measured by the Bureau of the Census, skepticism among many of its advocates and former advocates mounted. At a more nitty gritty political level, growing expenditures on public assistance provoked a powerful backlash. For example, the idea that federal funds paid the salaries of Community Action Program (CAP) lawyers who then represented clients who sued public welfare agencies to secure more benefits simply incensed many people. The surprisingly strong third party candidacy of the segregationist governor of Georgia, George Wallace, in the 1968 presidential elections was in substantial part a backlash against welfare and the expansion of the welfare state. It was at about that time that the mythical "welfare queen" driving her Cadillac downtown to pick up her public assistance check entered American folklore and political oratory.

Gradually, a very skeptical conservative view of the poverty problem and of the public efforts to alleviate it developed and in time came to displace the older liberal view as the "conventional wisdom." That conservative view culminated in the "welfare reform" legislation passed by the Congress in 1996 and discussed at the end of this chapter.

Did We Dig Ourselves into this Hole? The Conservative View

As indicated, a conservative reaction to the Great Society and the War on Poverty was not long in coming. There was the political reaction noted above. But there was also a more intellectual reaction from sociologists, political scientists, economists, policy analysts, and administrators. In a fair number of cases those who expressed disillusion about the prevailing policy were former believers. Disillusion with the results of the War on Poverty helped to make conservatives out of some former liberals and progressives.

The essence of the conservative view is very simple. Conservatives took the position that the War on Poverty as well as other forms of assistance to the poor set up a system of perverse incentives. They argued that removing the stigma of poverty—the old distinction between the "worthy" and the "unworthy" poor—and providing more generous benefits encouraged family breakup and out-of-wedlock births. Conservatives suggested that when AFDC benefits plus food stamps plus Medicaid, and perhaps plus housing subsidies as well, added up to more than the wages of a low-skilled worker, the low-earning man began to lose his function as a husband. That attacked the very roots of marriage among the less educated and those with minimal job skills, for public assistance in its various forms made a better and more reliable provider than a low-earning man. The conservative's prescription was very simple: It was to cut back the whole apparatus of the welfare state, what is often called the "social safety net." The most influential early academic proponent of this view was the political scientist Charles Murray. In a very influential book published in 1980 he proposed:

> . . . scrapping the entire federal welfare and income-support structure for working-aged persons, including AFDC, Medicaid, Food Stamps, Unemployment Insurance, Worker's Compensation, subsidized housing, disability insurance, and the rest. It would leave the working-aged person with no recourse whatsoever except the job market, family members, friends, and public or private locally funded services. It is the Alexandrian [after the story of Alexander and the Gordian knot] solution: cut the knot, for there is no way to untie it.[10]

He called the above a "thought experiment," and whether he would really do it all if he had the power to do so is not known. Writers often state an argument in extreme form to sharpen the point and to get peoples' attention. But the general conservative analysis has, as of this writing, triumphed politically. What was a radical view from the right is now the "conventional wisdom," not in academe, but in the political world.

The argument made by Murray and other conservatives was given a boost by the unexpected results of a large social science experiment done by the federal government. From 1970 to 1976 the Department of Health, Education, and Welfare financed a series of experiments in which about 4,800 families were provided with guaranteed annual incomes for three years. One such experiment was SIME (for Seattle Income Maintenance Experiment) and another was DIME (for Denver Income Maintenance Experiment).[11] One result of the experiment was that the provision of a small regular income reduced the average number of hours worked per family by the equivalent of several weeks of full-time work per year. Apparently, the recipients took some of their new income in the form of increased leisure, exactly the sort of rational economic behavior that the conservative's arguments called for. What was worse, the recipients' rate of divorce and separation increased. The experiments' designers had thought that traditional welfare payments that were restricted to female-headed households were destabilizing but that the guaranteed annual income payments that were not restricted in that way would help to stabilize marriages. But that turned out not to be the case. Rather, the results seemed to jibe with the conservative view that part of the function of a marriage is economic, and that when economic necessity is removed the marriage bond is weakened. Needless to say, conservative writers made good use of the unhappy results of the income maintenance experiments.

During the 1992 presidential campaign Bill Clinton, tapping into a wellspring of public disillusion with welfare, promised to "end welfare as we know it." Little happened in the next two years, but then, in 1994, the Republican party gained control of both houses of Congress and began a push for "welfare reform." The centerpiece of their effort was an end to AFDC. The first welfare reform bill was passed in early 1996 but vetoed by President Clinton, who claimed it was simply too harsh. A somewhat milder version was passed in the summer of 1996 and signed by the President on August 22, 1996. Its provisions went into effect July 1, 1997. The delay in implementation was provided to give the states time to adapt their systems to it. The bill had solid Republican support but split the Democrats. More conservative Democrats generally supported it while many liberal Democrats opposed it. Among those opposing the bill were The Children's Defense Fund, headed by a longtime Clinton friend, Marion Wright Edelman, the National Organization for Women (NOW), the Coalition for a Feminist Majority, and the Council of Catholic Bishops. The feminist opposition was understandable in that most recipients of AFDC are women and children. The Bishops opposed the bill partly because they saw it as violating Catholic social teachings on the matter of charity. Several high-ranking Clinton appointees in the Department of Health and Human Services (HHS), including the Assistant Secretary for Planning and Evaluation, Peter Edelman, resigned in protest over it.[12]

The most important feature of the bill was that it abolished AFDC. That was replaced by block grants to the states, which the states had considerable discretion in spending. States were required to place a certain percentage of their welfare caseloads in jobs or face cutbacks in their block grants. In addition, no person was to be permitted to receive public assistance for more than five years across their entire lifetime. States were permitted to adopt an even stricter lifetime limit, and a number of states subsequently went to two- and three-year limits. The bill provided increased funding for child care, intended to assist AFDC mothers in being able to work. That was part of the carrot. It also contained a cutback in appropriations for food stamps. That was part of the stick. The clear intent of the bill was to give the population now dependent upon public assistance a very powerful push towards employment, both by assisting them in obtaining work and making life without work much less attractive.

By 1999 conservatives, and some liberals as well, were pleased with the results of welfare reform. The dire predictions of mass homelessness had not come to pass. Studies in several states indicated that large numbers of former welfare recipients had found jobs, albeit low paying ones for the most part. Between 63 and 87 percent of former welfare recipients had held jobs for at least some time after the termination of their benefits, and between 61 and 71 percent were employed at the time that they had been surveyed.[13] Some critics noted that welfare reform was enacted when unemployment rates were low and that subsequently rates had fallen further, reaching a three decade low of 4.2 percent in mid-1999. They thus argued that it was not clear that the welfare to work transition would go nearly as well in less fortunate economic circumstances. Some noted, too, that the reforms had not reduced poverty very much. The reforms simply caused some income from government to be replaced by income from employment. To this, the conservative supporter of welfare reform might reply that the primary goal of reform was not to reduce poverty statistics, but to bring long term welfare recipients back into the labor market. In that regard, there seemed little doubt as of 1999 that the reforms had succeeded.

A WIDER PERSPECTIVE

Liberals, like William J. Wilson, cited in the previous chapter, lay much of the problem of family breakup and its many consequences, particularly in the poorest sections of our society, on an inadequate supply of suitable jobs. Liberals advocate more public intervention, especially in regard to job creation and job training, as a remedy. Conservatives lay much of the blame at the feet of what they consider to be failed social policy, and they call for less government intervention. At the risk of great oversimplification, we might say that the liberals had their turn in the 1960s and 1970s. The conservatives are having their turn now. Whether the conservatives will do better or worse than the liberals in providing long term solutions to the poverty problem remains to be seen.

If the biggest issues connected with poverty policy are those involving family structure, are there larger issues to be thought about? Clearly, family structure has gone through major change in the last three decades or so and, as noted, not just in the United States. Were changes in family structure largely caused by social policy, or are there larger social forces at work, making such changes inevitable regardless of public policy? One of the moral and emotional bases of the traditional family over the centuries has been religious belief. Are there basic changes of attitude in that area that have affected family structure? How much of the change in family structure has to do with the "sexual revolution" of the 1960s and an increase in the availability of sex without long term commitment? Certainly, for at least some males, an environment in which it is possible to have an active sex life outside of marriage will make marriage a less attractive arrangement. In an age of sexual liberation the game between the sexes gets played much more by male rules than it did in a more straightlaced age. How much of the change is related to a more "me centered" culture, as epitomized by phrases like "do your own thing" and "pull your own strings"?

We pose these questions by way of saying that perhaps some change in family structure, or maybe much change in family structure, is due to larger trends in our society that would have occurred regardless of public policy. The answer to that question cannot be known with certainty unless there is a parallel universe in which we can rerun the last three decades without the Great Society and the War on Poverty programs and their related social policies.

Perhaps, also, basic technological changes that affect wealth, life, and the nature of work can explain much of the change in the family. One feminist writer argues that if you had been around early in this century and had known that three very basic changes were coming to American society, you could have predicted that major changes in the relationship between men and women and hence in the structure of the family were inevitable.[14] These changes are:

1. increased life expectancy,
2. a decrease in the average number of births per woman across her lifespan, and
3. a decrease in the relative importance of physical strength in the labor market.

The first two changes would seem to reduce the percentage of people who mate just once for life. The second and third change reduce the economic dependence of women on men, and that, in turn, weakens the economic side of marriage as we know it. These things have all come to pass throughout the Western world, and we note that the family is changing throughout the Western world. For example, the increase in the percentage of out-of-wedlock births since the 1960s that occurred in the United States is very closely paralleled by increases in Great Britain.[15] Other nations in Europe have also experienced large increase in out-of-wedlock births.[16] But does that prove that the changes Genovese notes are the cause of the change in family structure? Not necessarily, for we also note that the welfare state has made its appearance throughout the Western world in the last several decades. Perhaps, as Murray and other conservatives might argue, that is a more powerful cause. Or perhaps not. We end this chapter on that note of uncertainty because the reality is uncertain.

SUMMARY

The chapter begins with an account of the program called the War on Poverty that began under the Johnson Administration in the mid 1960s. Among the initiatives of this period were the Office of Economic Opportunity (OEO), a variety of job training and job creation programs, the community action program (CAP), Medicaid, food stamps, and liberalization of the Aid for Families with Dependent Children (AFDC) program. The war on poverty was begun under the assumption that with sufficient funding and an array of well-designed programs, poverty in the United States could essentially eliminate poverty. This hope was not realized. At just about the time that the war on poverty got underway, the poverty rate in the United States stopped declining, and since that time it has moved up and down with the business cycle but shown no long-term trend toward further decline. Conservative critics of the federal government's policy programs argued that these programs set up perverse incentives that actually made the problem worse by reducing work incentives and fostering family breakup. This criticism culminated in the welfare reform legislation of 1996 that returned much of the responsibility for public welfare to the state through the mechanism of block grants, set limits on the time that any individual could remain on public assistance, and generally shifted the emphasis of public welfare from income support to job training and employment. As of 1999, the nation has seen a substantial movement of people from public assistance into employment.

NOTES

1. Daniel P. Moynihan, *Maximum Feasible Misunderstanding* (New York: Macmillan, 1969). The title is a play on the requirement for the "maximum feasible participation" of the poor in community action programs.
2. Joseph P. Kershaw, *Government Against Poverty* (Washington, D.C.: The Brookings Institution, 1970), p. 24. The book offers an excellent summary of the early years of the "War on Poverty" and its various programs. The war on poverty was the centerpiece of what Lyndon Johnson referred to as "The Great Society," his agenda for completing the work of Franklin Roosevelt's New Deal, begun during the Great Depression of the 1930s.
3. Benefit levels varied greatly from state to state because the funding was done on a federal-state matching basis. Generally, the lowest levels were in southern states.
4. For statistics such as those cited above, see Section 12, Social Insurance and Human Services, in the *Statistical Abstract of the United States.*
5. Michael Harrington, *The Other America: Poverty in the United States* (New York: Macmillan, 1962).

6. For an account of the Watts riot and the national reaction to it, see the *New York Times* from August 12 to 18, 1965, or another major newspaper, such as the *Los Angeles Times*, for the same period.

7. Rodney King was a Black man stopped by Los Angeles police after a high-speed automobile chase. In the course of his arrest King was seriously beaten by the four arresting officers, who were videotaped in the act. The tape was then repeatedly played by a local TV station, creating great outrage in the Black community. When the officers were acquitted by a predominantly White jury in the nearby community of Simi Valley, a riot comparable in scale to the Watts riot of 1965 followed. Some time later the officers were retried in another court by federal prosecutors for violating King's civil rights. Two were convicted and served prison terms.

8. Many benefits like food stamps and Medicaid are not counted as income. Thus many of those who were statistically below the poverty line after the war on poverty were, in terms of living standard and health, better off than they would have been without it.

9. Frances Fox Piven and Richard A. Cloward, *Regulating the Poor: The Functions of Public Welfare* (New York: Pantheon Books, Random House, 1971), p. 348.

10. Charles Murray, *Losing Ground: American Social Policy, 1950–1980* (New York: Basic Books, 1984), p. 227. Politically, Murray is best identified as neoconservative. Distinguishing between conservatives and neoconservatives on the basis of a specific issue is hard to do, in part because on many issues the neoconservative view has become standard conservative doctrine. One general difference between the two groups is that many neoconservatives started out on the political Left and after becoming disillusioned made the journey to the political Right. Another difference in degree if not in kind is that the neoconservatives as a group were relatively more concerned with social and value issues and less concerned with purely economic issues than many traditional conservatives. The founding father of neoconservatism is generally considered to be the writer Irving Kristol. See his book *Neoconservatism*, (New York: The Free Press, 1995). The quarterly political magazine, *The Public Interest*, is probably the best periodical source on neoconservative thought across a range of social, economic, and political issues.

11. For an early account of the experiments, see Philip K. Robbins et al., eds. *A Guaranteed Annual Income: Evidence from a Social Experiment* (New York: Academic Press, 1980).

12. Peter Edelman, "The Worst Thing That Bill Clinton Has Done," *Atlantic Monthly* (March 1997), pp. 43–59. For a general liberal argument against cutting back assistance to the poor, see Herbert Gans, *The War Against the Poor* (New York: Basic Books, 1995).

13. Judith Haveman, "Most Adults Find Jobs after Leaving Welfare," *Washington Post*, May 27, 1999, p. A1.

14. Catherine Fox-Genovese, *Feminism Without Illusions* (University of North Carolina Press, 1991).

15. Charles Murray, "The British Underclass," *The Public Interest* (spring 1990), pp. 4–28.

16. David Popenoe, "Family Decline in the Swedish Welfare State," *The Public Interest*, (winter 1991), pp. 65–88. For a Swedish response to Popenoe's article, see comments by Sandqvist and Andersson in the fall 1992 issue, pp. 114–122.)

REFERENCES

Moynihan, Daniel Patrick. *Miles to Go: A Personal History of Social Policy*, Cambridge: Harvard University Press, 1996.

Murray, Charles. *Losing Ground: American Social Policy 1950–1980*, New York: Basic Books, 1984.

Noble, Charles. *Welfare as We Knew It*, Oxford: Oxford University Press, 1997.

The Politics of Welfare Reform, Norris, Donald F. and Thompson, Lyke eds., Sage: Thousand Oaks, CA., 1995.

Rochefort, David A. *American Social Welfare Policy*, Boulder: Westview Press, Div. of Harper-Collins, 1985.

Schanberg, Eric D. *Poor Policy: How Government Harms the Poor*, Boulder: Westview Press, Div. Harper Collins, 1996.

Chapter

15 | Crime and the Criminal Justice System

Few if any forces have more effect on the nature and quality of urban life than crime, particularly crime that involves violence or the threat of violence. How one feels in the city is very much a function of the state of public safety. Do you feel relaxed, or do you feel tense and wary out on the street? Do you come and go as you please, or do you adjust the when and where of your life to the fear of crime?

The fear of crime exerts a powerful force on the geography of many metropolitan areas. There is no question that fear of crime has been a force behind the migration to the suburbs. Crime affects the location of industry both between cities and also within cities. "Quality of life" issues, of which personal safety is a major one, rate heavily in almost every study of industrial and commercial location. Crime and safety affect people's decisions about where to shop and where to go for entertainment. That, in turn, affects which areas thrive and which experience disuse and decay.

The "tipping point" phenomenon discussed in Chapter 10 in connection with residential segregation is also largely a manifestation of fear of crime. Were crime not an issue, we would be much further down the path toward the goal of a truly integrated society.[1]

The growth of private communities noted in Chapter 9, a trend that is reshaping the form of many metropolitan areas, has been driven partly by fear of crime. Their developers have no illusions about this, for personal security features very prominently in their advertising. And in percentage terms, the fastest-growing category of private community is the most safety conscious type—the gated community.

THE GEOGRAPHY OF CRIME

Table 15–1 shows rates of violent crime by type of place. Note that on average rates are higher in urban areas than in suburban or rural areas.

TABLE 15-1 Rates of Violent Crime by Type of Place, 1995 (figures per 100,000 of population)

United States	684 .6
Metropolitan statistical areas	774.4
Cities with populations over 250,000	1,564.3
Suburban counties	449.1
Rural counties	253.0

Source: Uniform Crime Reports, Federal Bureau of Investigation, U.S. Department of Justice, Washington, D.C., 1995 edition.

Note: These statistics are based upon crimes known to the police. The data in the book are compiled by the FBI from the reports of local police departments. The actual number of offenses is higher because not all offenses are reported. Violent crimes as summarized in the *Uniform Crime Reports* consist of four categories; murder and nonnegligent homicide, forcible rape, robbery, and aggravated assault.

Crime rates vary greatly from city to city. In 1994, Honolulu was at the low end of a compilation of big city crime rates, with only 287 violent crimes per 100,000 residents. At the other end of the spectrum was Newark, New Jersey, with 3,840 violent crimes per 100,000 residents. Major cities were strung out all along the continuum, with concentration in the 1,500 to 2,500 range.[2] Within any sizable city there are wide variations in crime rate from one part of the city to another, and most residents are generally well aware of them.

SOME BACKGROUND ON THE CRIMINAL JUSTICE SYSTEM

The maintenance of law and order in the public realm is primarily a function of local government. Of the more than 800 thousand people employed by law enforcement agencies, about 85 percent are employed by local governments. We used the term "public realm" to distinguish between these employees and the even larger number of privately employed security guards and related personnel.

Most people prosecuted for crimes are prosecuted by local governments and tried in municipal courts. The decision about whether to prosecute is essentially up to the municipal prosecutor or district attorney and is based on many factors, including the severity of the offense and the likelihood of obtaining a conviction. For every case that comes to trial, about six are settled by plea bargain. In that case the defendant's attorney and the prosecutor agree on the terms of the sentence, and the defendant pleads guilty. Typically, plea bargains occur where the evidence is sufficiently strong that there is little doubt about the outcome. The defendant gets some reduction in the severity of the sentence, and the municipality avoids the expense of a trial.

Of those arrested for a felony offense, only a minority are actually incarcerated. In the late 1980s the results of 100 arrests broke down as shown in Table 15–2.

Rejection or diversion may occur because the district attorney does not think there is sufficient evidence to obtain a conviction or for other practical or administrative reasons. "Dismissed or otherwise not prosecuted" may mean that the judge throws out the case for some reason—a witness fails to show up or the defendant has been arrested while awaiting trial on this charge and will be prosecuted on another charge instead, or some other reason. Of those diverted to the juvenile justice system, some may serve time in a juvenile facility.

Of those incarcerated in the United States on any given day, about one third are in jails run by municipal governments. Typically, jails hold people sentenced for a year or less and people awaiting trial in jail either because they were denied bail or because they could not post bail. The great majority of the remaining two thirds are held in state prisons. About 5 percent of all persons incarcerated are in federal prisons.

Crime, Youth, and Gender

Crime is, to a large extent, a young man's game. Over 90 percent of those sent to prison are male, and a very large portion of both violent crime and property crime is committed by young males. Figure 15–1 shows the age distribution of people arrested for violent crime. For violent crime the peak age is 18 and for property crime the peak age is 16.

TABLE 15–2 Typical Resolution of 100 Felony Arrests, 1988

Total arrests	100
Sent to juvenile justice system	35
Brought to district attorney	65
Rejected or diverted	20
Accepted for prosecution	45
Dismissed or otherwise not prosecuted	10
Prosecuted	35
Acquitted in trial	2
Pleaded guilty without trial	30
Found guilty in trial	3
Released on probation	14
Incarcerated	19
Jailed (usually less than one year)	11
Imprisoned (usually more than 1 year)	8

Source: Brian Forst, "Prosecution and Sentencing," in *Crime*, edited by James Q. Wilson and Joan Petersilia (San Francisco: ICS Press, 1995), p. 364.

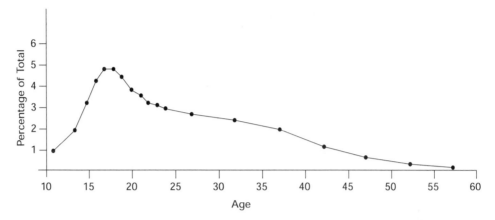

FIGURE 15–1   Violent Crimes Committed by Males, Percentage of Total by Single Year of Age, 1996

Source: Uniform Crime Reports for the United States, Federal Bureau of Investigation, Government Printing Office, Washington, D.C., 1996, Table 39.

Notes: The figure presents single-year data for ages 15 through 24. The other ages were grouped, 10–12, 13–14 and in 5-year intervals beginning at age 25. Points plotted for grouped years are for the midpoints of those groups.

The prison population is older on average than Figure 15–1 would suggest because many first offenders, particularly for property crime, receive probation (a suspended sentence). Then, too, repeat offenders generally get longer sentences for the same offense than those being sentenced for the first time. Even so, the prison population is a relatively young one. In 1991 about 22 percent of all state prison inmates were under 25, and almost 68 percent were under 35.

TRENDS IN CRIME

As Table 15–3 shows, crime rates in the United States rose very rapidly in the 1960s and 1970s and then more slowly during the 1980s. Early in the 1990s the crime rate began to dip and continued to drop through 1999. But as of the late 1990s it was still several times higher than it had been in 1960.

The Growth of the Prison Population

Table 15–4 shows the trend in incarceration since 1960. Note that from 1980 to 1996 the jail and prison population of the United States tripled, a rate that far outstripped the increase in the crime rate. Since the last year shown in the table, 1996, the total number of people incarcerated on the average day has continued to rise, reaching 1.8 million in 1999.

TABLE 15-3 Reported Crime in the United States, 1976–1995 (per 100,000 residents)

Year	Violent	Property
1960	137	900
1970	364	3621
1980	597	5,353
1990	732	5089
1991	758	5140
1992	758	4903
1993	747	4738
1994	714	4660
1995	684	4,593

Source: *Uniform Crime Reports for the United States,* Federal Bureau of Investigation, U.S. Department of Justice, Washington, D.C., 1996 and earlier years.

Note: Violent crime in the table above consists of murder and nonnegligent homicide, forcible rape, robbery, and aggravated assault. Nonviolent crime in the table is the sum of burglary, larceny, motor vehicle theft, and arson. Because not all crimes are reported to the police, victimization surveys show higher rates for some offenses.

In the 1970s and 1980s we clearly became more punitive. Beyond a general tendency to punish the same array of crimes more severely, we also increased prison populations substantially as a consequence of "the war on drugs." At present about one third of federal prisoners and about one fourth of state prisoners are incarcerated for drug-related offenses. Two decades ago drug offenders constituted about one tenth of all prisoners.

Table 15-4 Incarceration in the United States, 1950–1996

Year	Total Number of Persons Incarcerated in Selected Years
1960	349,000
1970	257,000
1980	502,000
1990	1,146,000
1993	1,365,000
1996	1,631,000

Sources: Figures, rounded to the nearest 1,000, are from 1993 and earlier from *Statistical Abstract of the United States,* 1996, Table 354 and earlier editions.

Notes: The figures are for a given day, so the number of persons spending some time in the system across the year is substantially larger. The figures do not include persons in juvenile institutions. The figures are totals not adjusted for population size and thus show a higher rate of increase than they would if given in terms of rate per 100,000 as are the figures in the previous table.

If we add to the more than 1.5 million persons incarcerated on any given day those people on probation, parole, or under indictment (charged with a crime and awaiting trial) we get a total of about 5 million.[3]

In 1995 the total adult male population of the United States over the age of 18 was between 93 and 94 million. That means that about 5 percent of the adult male population on any given day was in some way under supervision of the criminal justice system, and about 1.5 percent were actually locked up. Of the male population between 18 and 35, at least 3 percent were locked up on any given day, and about 10 percent were under some degree of supervision. By both world standards and the standards of our own past, those are very big numbers.

ARE WE A MORE CRIMINAL NATION?

The United States locks up about four to five times as many people per 100,000 inhabitants as do Britain, Canada, Australia, and Germany and about seven times as many per 100,000 as the average European country.[4] In fact, there is no First World nation with a higher incarceration rate than the United States. One might think that this is because the United States is inherently a much more criminal nation than others, and the United States does have that image. In reality, that image is, at best, a half-truth.

As compared to other industrialized nations, U.S. crime rates appear to be generally similar—with one big exception. Exact international comparisons are difficult because of differences in reporting rates for many crimes and, in some cases, different definitions of crimes. With that caveat the data shows that for many crimes of violence rates in the United States are not radically different from those in many other Western countries. Our rate for robbery is toward the high end of the range (robbery differs from theft in that it involves force or the threat of force), but our rate for forcible rape is reported as lower than in Canada, Australia, or what used to be West Germany (the figures come from before German reunification). For property crimes our rates are also in the same general range as many European nations. Our reported total property crime rate is actually lower than that in Australia, Canada, England, West Germany, the Netherlands, and Sweden. For automobile theft, to note one major property crime, our rate is above that of Canada and the Netherlands but below that of Australia, Britain, and France.[5]

The one exception to this general picture of U.S. ordinariness is the crime of homicide. There, we are in a category of our own. For example, in 1984 our rate was 7.9 per year per 100,000 of population. Some comparable figures are Canada 2.7, England and Wales 1.1, France 2.3, Netherlands 1.2, Sweden 1.4 and Switzerland 1.1. You are actually more likely to be the victim of burglary in Sweden than in the United States. But, statistically, you are more than five times as likely to be murdered in the United States.

Why is our murder rate so exceptional? A big part of the U.S.-world difference comes down to a single cause—the widespread availability of guns. The presence of a gun converts many incidents that might otherwise be lesser crimes into homicides. For example, someone who is shot in the course of a crime has a much higher probability of dying than someone who is stabbed or hit with a blunt instrument. A fight that might never be reported to the police at all may be converted to a homicide if one participant has a gun. About two thirds of all homicides in the United States are committed with guns. Where juveniles are involved (either as victims or as perpetrators) about nine tenths of all homicides involve guns.

Murder makes up a very small portion of all crimes, and murderers make up a small percentage of all prisoners. The difference in incarceration rate is thus in large measure due to the fact that we punish a wide range of crimes, particularly property crimes and drug offenses, more strictly than do other nations. However, it may be that the high U.S. rate of homicide has a great deal to do with U.S. attitudes and policies towards crime in general and thus indirectly leads to a higher overall incarceration rate. In particular, the nature of homicide in the United States has changed somewhat in recent years. Until recently the majority of homicides involved people who knew each other. To a substantial degree, homicide was a "crime of passion," particularly within families and between spouses. In that regard, it was not that threatening to the general public. At present, however, about 55 percent of all homicides involve strangers. That is very threatening and contributes to a very tough public attitude towards crime in general.

CHANGING ATTITUDES ABOUT IMPRISONMENT

With the increase in the crime rate, shown in Table 15–3, American policy with regard to imprisonment began to change. For most of the twentieth century the idea of rehabilitation played a major role in our thinking about imprisonment. True, prisons were there to deter and to keep dangerous people separate from the larger society, but they were also there to help rehabilitate people. In fact the root of the word *penitentiary* is *penitent,* which the dictionary defines as "feeling or expressing remorse." In the 1960s and early 1970s most people sent to prison were sent on indeterminate sentences. The minimum to maximum range of the sentence was quite long, and the actual release was dependent upon the decision of the parole board. Presumably, when the board deemed the person safe to release, the person was released. Most prisoners were paroled well before their maximum time had been reached. In the 1970s, attitudes began to change, and in time that change was reflected in public policy.

Several factors were behind the change in perception. First, there was fear and anger about an increasing rate of crime, particularly crimes of violence. Then, too, studies of programs that were intended to rehabilitate pris-

oners generally showed very disappointing results.[6] If prisons could not rehabilitate and parole boards could not accurately determine who would and
who would not repeat their crimes, what role was left for jails and prisons?
The obvious answer was punishment and incapacitation. Punishment would
deter the prisoner himself from committing more crimes after he was released, and it would deter others by example. The term *incapacitation* simply
refers to the fact that that people cannot commit offenses against society
while they are sequestered from society.

The granting of parole has now been abolished or much reduced in
most states (though many people previously granted parole are still subject
to its requirements), and the indeterminate sentence has largely been replaced by sentences of relatively fixed length. The state of Virginia, for example, abolished parole and the indeterminate sentence with a so-called
"truth in sentencing" policy that requires convicted persons to serve at least
85 percent of the time to which they are sentenced.

Mandatory minimum sentences and sentencing guidelines have become commonplace. In the mid 1990s political pressure for "three strikes
and you're out" laws grew, and a few states, including California, adopted
them. Such laws provide for a mandatory life term without parole upon conviction of a third violent offense. After a hiatus of many years, executions
have resumed in the United States.[7] In 1997 the Supreme Court let stand a
state law that permitted sex offenders who had served their sentences and
who were still deemed dangerous to be sent directly to psychiatric institutions rather than being freed. In brief, the nation's attitude toward the matter of punishment became increasingly hard-nosed.

The electoral politics of crime began to change under the pressure of rising crime rates. At one time toughness on crime was a Republican issue. In
fact, George Bush's 1988 landslide victory over Michael Dukakis occurred
partly because Bush was able to portray Dukakis as soft on crime with the aid
of the Willie Horton incident.[8]

But President Clinton made sure that he would not be vulnerable on
the Right by taking a hard-line stance from the beginning. In his 1992 campaign he proudly noted that in his terms as governor of Arkansas he had
signed a number of death warrants. And he has been a hard-liner ever since.
Just as forty years ago no politician wanted to be open to the charge of being
"soft on communism," no politician today wants to be open to the charge of
being "soft on crime."

Part of the more punitive stance of the nation toward crime may be due to
the media. Crime holds people's attention, and it is inexpensive to cover. A
local TV station can cover it simply by listening in on police calls and sending
a news van if one sounds promising. And crime gets prominent billing. It has
been said of local TV news coverage that "if it bleeds, it leads." Then, too, crime
is entertainment, and shows like "NYPD Blue" give a sense that we live in a
crime-saturated society. To the extent that media coverage focuses our minds
on crime, it may contribute to shaping a more punitive policy on crime.

HAS DETERRENCE WORKED?

Has imprisoning more people reduced the amount of crime? The liberal, skeptical of our tougher stance on crime, might argue that all during the 1960s, 70s, and 80s we were locking up more people and yet the crime rate kept rising. Clearly, he or she might argue, imprisonment does not stop crime. The conservative might agree that imprisonment does not attack the root causes of crime but argues that had we not imprisoned as many people as we did there would have been still more crime. Not all criminals are irrational at all times, and so deterrence must have some effect. He or she could argue that even if studies of prisoners show that deterrence has not been very effective with them, that hardly proves that prisons do not deter. Prisons necessarily contain those who were not deterred. Perhaps many thousands are deterred by fear of punishment and so are not in prison to be studied.

Possibly more important than deterrence is the incapacitating effect of imprisonment. If someone is kept in prison for many of his most crime-prone years, is it not reasonable to believe that he will commit fewer crimes in his lifetime than if he were free for the entire time? This should be so even if the possibility of return to prison exercises no deterrent effect upon him whatsoever.[9]

James Q. Wilson argues that the high rate of incarceration in the United States has indeed reduced the crime rate to well below what it would be under a softer policy. Thus he supports our tougher stance. He cites the difference between U.S. and British experience as evidence.

Twenty years ago the crime rate in Great Britain, for virtually all offenses, was much lower than in the United States. At present, the British homicide rate is still much lower than that of the United States, but for many other offenses the British have now caught up with us or passed us. For example, British rates for both burglary and automobile theft now exceed U.S. rates. Furthermore, British rates are still rising, while U.S. rates (at least through 1999) are declining. Wilson attributes the difference to a different policy regarding imprisonment. The British government was and is basically anti-imprisonment except for the most serious offenses.

> The Criminal Justice Act of 1967 required that sentences not in excess of six months be suspended unless the offender was a violent one. A Parole Board had been created with the power to release from prison offenders who had served one third of their sentences. These policies had their effect. In 1968, about three fifths of all inmates were released from prison after having served only four months. In 1972, a new Criminal Justice Act weakened the 1967 commitment to suspended sentences but still recommended them, urging judges to reserve prison terms for only the most serious offenders. The British government was strongly committed to the idea of noncustodial treatment. It helped create the system of community service orders which allowed offenders to do work in the city instead of spending time behind bars.[10]

British policy would appear to be in some ways more "enlightened" or "progressive" and certainly more humane than the increasingly punitive U.S.

approach. But, if Wilson is correct, the less "enlightened" U.S. view has offered the larger society more protection. He argues that Britain has taken a softer approach because for a variety of political reasons the British government has so far not had to be very responsive to the will of the British public. Nevertheless, if the rate keeps rising and public anger builds, we may in time see Great Britain making a U-turn and following the American model.

One can argue the question of whether, and if so by how much, the United States has cut crime by locking up so many people. It is hard to believe that tougher policies have not produced some reduction, but we do not know that with complete certainty. We do know, however, that incarceration policy is complicated and that policies may produce very different effects than intended. Consider the following example.

Joe Blow, age thirty-five, has just been convicted of his third violent offense, a mugging. Unfortunately for him, he did it in California, and he gets the mandatory sentence of life without possibility of parole. He is a very bad guy, and an angry public might consider that he has only himself to blame. Fast-forward twenty-five years. Joe is now sixty, much calmed down, and in a state of depression about the fact that he is likely to end his days in a prison geriatric ward (there are some now and there probably will be more). At this time a federal judge finds that the California prison system is so overcrowded that conditions in it subject prisoners to "cruel and unusual" punishment, which is prohibited by the 8th Amendment. The court orders the system to reduce the number of inmates. Someone will have to be released.

Joe would be a good candidate for release. Prison has not made him a nicer person, but at sixty he is not likely to go back to a life of street violence. However, he cannot be released because of his mandatory sentence. Instead, someone young enough to be his grandson and much more dangerous, but who is not in on a mandatory sentence, gets early release. Alternatively, California judges, understanding that the prison system is in a jam may act against their own better judgment and give probation instead of prison time to some eighteen-year-old first-time offenders who are just beginning their criminal careers. In either case toughness in sentencing has actually made the streets more dangerous.

The above scenario is not that fanciful. There have been court-ordered releases, and in some cases nonviolent offenders in prison on mandatory drug sentences have been held while more violent inmates have been given early release. One such well publicized release occurred in Florida.

Consider another situation. We noted that about 3 percent of the U.S. male population age eighteen to thirty-five is incarcerated at any given time (roughly 1 million out of 30 million). That percentage is several times as high for the Black population and may be an order of magnitude higher in some urban ghettos. One reason that it is higher is because of sentences for possession of crack, which appears to be the preferred form of cocaine in the inner city. In the mid 1990s federal sentencing guidelines mandated five years without parole for possession of five grams (there are 28 grams in an ounce) of crack. The same guidelines mandated five years for 500 grams (over a pound) of powdered cocaine. The reason for the disparity was that crack was widely believed to be more dangerous form of the drug. Whether or not that is correct, the result has been that large numbers of young Black men have gotten long sentences for possessing very small amounts of crack. Earlier we noted the very high rate of female-headed families and out-of-wedlock births in ghetto neighborhoods. Putting young Black men away in large numbers for possessing small amounts of crack certainly contributes to the marriage squeeze in the ghetto discussed by William J. Wilson (see Chapter 13). We also know that there is a strong statistical association between single-parent households, out-of-wedlock births, and crime. Is it possible that putting away large numbers of young men for possession of small amounts of crack will actually increase the crime rate some years from now through the family structure mechanism just suggested? Then, too, a five year prison sentence in early adulthood, in addition to all its other impacts on the indivudal, leaves that person with a prison record that is likely to be a serious handicap in the job market. When that happens to masses of young men, will it also have long term effects on family structure? The above questions suggest that apparently simple policies may have complicated unintended and unwanted effects.

It is not surprising that within the Black community there has been much protest about what many consider to be legal and police practices that result in higher rates of black incarceration. The difference in the treatment of possession of crack versus powdered cocaine discussed above is one such issue. Many Blacks and black organizations have complained that police stop Black motorists much more frequently than they stop White motorists in similar situations. This alleged practice has been satirized as stopping people for the offense of "driving while black." A number of black groups have pushed for the keeping of records on the race of drivers stopped to document the practice. Most police departments deny that their officers engage in the practice.

Whether a person is convicted in court, and what sort of deal they strike if they choose to plead guilty rather than go to trial, is heavily dependent on the quality legal representation that they have. A defendant who can afford to retain counsel is likely to be better represented than a defendant who is represented by a court appointed attorney, though this was not always the case. Because poverty rates are higher among Blacks than Whites, it could be argued that in this regard the legal system is somewhat tipped against Blacks, though the direct issue here is not race but wealth and income.

TRENDS IN POLICING

The high rate of incarceration may be the reason for the recent drop in crime rates. There are other plausible explanations as well. One candidate for the honor is better police work. And, indeed, many police commissioners and mayors will make this claim.

Until perhaps two decades ago it was uniformly understood that the main function of the police was to apprehend criminals. If a police department was confronted with both serious crime and also minor crime and disorder, the logical course of action was to focus its resources on serious crimes. If serious crime is going unpunished, why spend scarce time dealing with kids who do graffiti or with winos who irritate passersby but do not commit serious offenses? Consistent with the emphasis on catching criminals, many police departments shifted manpower from foot patrols to patrol by car, for the latter seemed more efficient at the task. However, not everything that is obviously commonsensical turns out to be correct, and this older view has been the object of much rethinking and much change in police practice.[11] A big part of that change has been an emphasis on "community policing."

A major element of the community policing philosophy is that an important role of the police is the prosaic matter of maintaining public order. The idea is that when small antisocial acts and minor infringements on public order are allowed to take place they create a climate that gradually leads to more serious acts. They intimidate the public, they keep law-abiding people off the streets, and they embolden criminals. The honest citizen who is constantly annoyed by small unpleasantness and minor threats loses faith in the ability of the authorities to protect him or her from larger offenses. And the criminal or would-be criminal gets the idea that the police and the community are no longer in control and so is encouraged to push the limits into the realm of serious crime. Wilson and Kelling have referred to this as the "broken window" effect. A window remains broken for a while, and gradually people come to think that no one cares and that no one will do anything. So more windows get broken, and gradually people come to perceive the street as a disorderly and maybe a dangerous place. Soon it is only dangerous people who go there voluntarily. The appearance of danger has produced the reality of danger.

New York City experienced a considerable decline in crime of all types beginning in the early 1990s, and both its mayor and police chief attribute much of the reduction to an increase in community policing efforts. One part of the new approach has been to go after minor offenses against public order. For example, a few years ago virtually every subway car in the city's system was covered with graffiti. Some of it was not bad to look at and some may even have had artistic merit. But the message that car after car covered inside and outside with graffiti gives to the subway rider is very simple—it is not the authorities who are in control here; it is the kids with the spray cans. The city has attacked the problem both by going after the kids with the spray cans and by cleaning the cars. It seems like a minor matter, but it makes the subways feel safer, and it establishes a different feeling about what is and is not acceptable.

The city also made a big push against "squeegeemen," a New York term that may need explanation. You pull up to a stoplight and for the next minute you can move neither forward nor backward. A rough-looking fellow with an unfriendly expression on his face splashes some soapy water on your windshield, squeegees it off, and then holds out his hand for a tip. Waving him off won't stop him from doing it. You don't have to give him a tip, but if you don't perhaps he will walk away with one of your windshield wiper blades in his hand or maybe he will test the paint job on your car by banging his bucket on it a few times. It is a very minor form of extortion, and it trashes the quality of city life just a bit. If the police drive off the squeegeemen, it makes the streets feel a bit safer and pleasanter. And it tells you and everyone else that the police are in control.[12]

For similar reasons the police have made a big push against aggressive panhandling, though that effort has gotten tangled up in the courts. Specifically, the legal issue is whether the panhandler's asking you for money is an exercise of his right to free speech that is deserving of First Amendment protection.

The crackdown on minor offenders has also had another payoff. Crime is part of a larger continuum of antisocial behavior. The person who commits felonies is also likely to be generally antisocial and to commit minor infringements that, in themselves, would never get anyone a day in jail. The New York City police department began a campaign against fare beaters—people who jump over the subway turnstile rather than paying. When caught, fare beaters are taken down to the police station and fingerprinted. That is clearly an excessive sanction against the basically law-abiding person who was in a desperate hurry, reached the turnstile, and then realized that he didn't have any change. But it also turns out that that a surprising percentage of fare beaters are wanted for more serious offenses. In 1991 New York's Police Commissioner William J. Bratton was quoted as saying that of every six persons stopped for fare beating, one was either carrying a weapon or was wanted on a warrant for another crime. Fare-beating arrests have also cracked serious cases that might otherwise have gone unsolved.

> When New York City police arrested 22-year old John Royster on June 12, the day after he bludgeoned to death 65-year old Evelyn Alvarez, owner of a Manhattan dry cleaning store, the quick solution of the killing seemed a miracle. Royster was not on probation or parole and had no felony record. . . . What led the police to him were . . . fingerprints on record from his sole arrest three months ago when he had been booked and fingerprinted for attempted fare beating on the subway.[13]

Another aspect of community policing has been the attempt to coordinate a variety of city services to produce a more orderly environment. For example, police departments have coordinated with housing departments to arrange for repairs and cleanups. That does not sound as if it bears any relationship to the matter of crime; but apparently it leads to a sense of greater order, and that begins to affect behavior. Where housing conditions have been improved by such interagency efforts, crime rates have fallen.[14]

Part of the community policing approach has been an increase in the number of foot patrols or, in some cases, bicycle patrols. One reason for that shift is that the officer on foot does better with maintenance of order problems, such as disorderly conduct, public intoxication, or aggressive panhandling. Another reason is that the officer on foot or bicycle constitutes more of a presence on the street and is likely to develop better rapport with citizens. In a similar vein the community policing approach favors meetings with groups of residents and visits with residents to understand their concerns and get their ideas about what needs to be done. One direct way that better citizen-police rapport pays off is that citizens are more willing to come forward with information, which is the way that most crimes are solved.

The community policing approach is still relatively new, and it is not without administrative and other problems. For example, the policeman who gets to know large numbers of people on his beat also has more chances to be corrupted. But so far the community policing approach looks very promising.

HARDENING THE TARGET

Some reduction in the crime rate may also be due to various defensive measures against crime. There is no fixed number of crimes that are fated to occur. Much crime is opportunistic—for example, a mugger who at that moment sees a vulnerable-looking person in an isolated location. As crime has become more common, so too have all sorts of defensive measures against it. An apartment complex might be designed so that it has no unobservable spaces that would be good for assaults or robberies. Shrubbery will be kept low and adequate lighting provided for the same reasons.[15] Shopping centers increasingly have private security forces. An increasing number of businesses are located in office and commercial parks where isolation from the municipal streets and controlled access make it easier to provide security. The private community, or even the apartment house with a twenty-four-hour doorman is a deterrent to crime. According to the political scientist John J. DiLulio,

> Most serious debate about crime trends concerns the "crime numerator"—the daily supply of street criminals, juvenile and adult, who are not stopped by whatever means from finding victims.
> But crime also has a "denominator"—the daily supply of potential crime victims, young and old, who are not protected by whatever means from becoming victimized. Beyond any reasonable academic or ideological doubt, the crime denominator has been *shrinking*. [Italics are in original.]
> . . . By 1992, for example, an estimated 32 million Americans, or 12 percent of the population, lived in common interest developments (CIDs)—condos, co-ops, gated communities, elderly only villages, and so on. Today as many as 50 million people are living in CIDs.[16]

Crime and the Economy

Another reason for the decrease in crime rates since the early 1990s may be the state of the U.S. economy. After the end of the 1991–92 recession the economy entered into a prolonged upswing. By 1999 the unemployment rate had fallen to a little over four percent. Some reduction in the crime rate is probably due to improved labor markets. However, if the long-term relationship between crime and unemployment is a reliable guide, it is unlikely that this factor accounts for more than a small part of the recent decrease in crime.

Crime Rates and Birth Rates

For all the reasons discussed previously—more incarceration, better policing, hardening the target—we have experienced a substantial drop in the crime rate in the 1990s. As shown in Figure 15–1 criminal activity peaks at an early age. In 1977, when the eighteen-year-olds of 1995 were being born, there were 3.33 million births in the United States. By contrast, in 1990, when the eighteen-year-olds of 2008 were being born, there were 4.15 million births in the United States. It is not that births per woman went up but that the number of women in the childbearing years went up—the so-called "echo of the baby boom." It remains to be seen whether that coming increase in persons in the most crime-prone years will reverse the decline in crime that we have seen since the early 1990s.

PERSPECTIVES ON CRIME

Below are described very briefly three different perspectives on crime. Though presented as separate, one's own view might include some elements of all of them.

The Classical and Retributive Model

At present the United States seems committed to a straightforward approach to crime—making policing as effective as possible and incarcerating large numbers of people. The model by which we operate is classified by C. Ray Jeffery as a composite of the Classical Model and an older Retributive model.[17]

The classical elements in it include the principles that the punishment should be proportionate to the offense, that the accused is entitled to due process, that people are not punished retroactively ("no crime without law"), and that for a person to be judged guilty of a crime there must have been criminal intent. In the classical view the primary purpose of the criminal justice system is the protection of society. He argues that our present system also includes a substantial amount of retribution—that we punish out of anger. For example, it has been argued that one reason for permitting the death penalty is the satisfaction or sense of justice or closure that it gives to the family of the victim. That sounds fairly close to the idea of retribution, though cast in more positive terms. Note that behind the idea that it is just to punish criminals (as opposed to the idea that we do it for strictly practical reasons) is the idea of free will—the criminal of his own free will has made a choice and should be held accountable for it. If, on the other hand, one believes that peoples' behavior is determined by forces beyond their control, then one may still favor punishment for practical reasons; but it is hard to justify it on abstract moral grounds. The point is that questions of philosophy or perhaps theology are not far below the surface of policy toward crime.

The Sociological View

Another perspective on crime is the sociological one. In the sociological view differences inherent in individuals receive relatively little attention and the focus is on social forces and social conditions. A sociologist seeking to explain changes in the crime rate over time might look at such factors like poverty, unemployment, changes in income inequality, and rates of residential mobility. Similarly, a sociologist seeking to explain changes in the prison population over time would look at society-wide social and political variables. The predominant instrument of such studies is the multivariable statistical analysis.[18]

If one reads sociologists of a Marxian bent, one will read much about class conflict and about the role of crime control as a more general form of social control to maintain the interests of the dominant class(es). The criminal becomes part of a system, and crime can be understood only in system terms.[19]

The sociological model, as noted, suggests that the real attack on crime must come at the level of the whole society. It has the theoretical weakness that in focusing so intently on the big picture it slights the disciplines of biology and psychology. That seems like an especially serious weakness at the present time when knowledge in biology and in the physiological side of psychology is expanding so rapidly.

The Medical Model

Another perspective is one that examines individuals in detail to understand who is likely to commit crime. A substantial amount of data exists on this matter. Below is a mixed bag of findings as just a sampling from a very large body of material. An early childhood history of aggressive behavior is a powerful predictor of adolescent and adult criminal activity. Being the victim of child abuse is correlated with adolescent and adult criminal behavior. Low cognitive and verbal skills as indicated by low IQ scores or low scores on the Armed Forces

Qualification Test (AFQT) are another powerful predictor. Some studies of adopted children have shown that the criminal history (or lack thereof) of the biological parent is a better predictor of the child's behavior than is the history of the adoptive parent, suggesting some sort of inherited influence. Abnormal electroencephalographs (EEGs) and histories of head trauma are correlated with criminal histories. So, too, are histories of perinatal (around birth) trauma, presumably because of some sort of damage to the central nervous system. Low levels of the neurotransmitter serotonin seem to be correlated with a propensity toward aggression and impulsiveness.[20]

The findings that there are observable differences between individuals that can predict the probability of criminal behavior might take us to a very different view of crime policy than either the sociological view or the dominant view noted earlier. For one thing it attacks the free will notion. If someone with an abnormal EEG, a history of childhood head trauma, and a low serotonin level has a history of violence, just how much is he to be blamed? Maybe we have to incarcerate him as a matter of public safety, but that is another matter. Beyond the question of moral guilt (as opposed to legal guilt), findings like those noted above point toward a medical model for reducing crime. At-risk persons would be identified early in life and treated in the hope of heading off a criminal career. The Jeffrey book cited above is very much a brief for a medical model of crime control.

But the medical model, too, has its problems. For one thing, genetic explanations of behavior are deeply offensive to many people. One reason is that in years gone by genetic theories were identified with terrible racism. The subjugation of Blacks in America and the genocide of Jews in the Nazi period were both rationalized with all sorts of claims about genetic differences.[21] Understandably, then, the word *genetic* sets many people's teeth on edge. In fact, any sort of biological determinism at all can do that. The advocate of the medical model may protest that he or she is interested only in differences between persons and that minor average differences between groups of people, if they exist at all, are absolutely irrelevant. But such disclaimers may or may not avail.[22]

Another problem with the medical model is a legal one. In our system we punish people for their acts. We do not punish them for their thoughts or their propensities. Identifying people who we think are potential criminals before they have broken the law and intervening in their lives to prevent them from doing what we think they might someday do, but cannot say for sure that they will do, takes us into a very problematical legal area.

This writer suspects that one way or another the medical model will make some progress just because of the very rapid advance that we are now seeing in psychopharmacology. For example, suppose a drug that can control aggression or impulsiveness as well as Prozac can control depression is developed. There will be many people who want to see it used—including some of the people whom it might keep out of prison. But whether a full-blown medical model will ever compete with our present model remains to be seen.

SUMMARY

On average, violent crime rates are more than three times as high in large cities as in suburban counties and about six times as high in large cities as in rural counties. The task of law enforcement falls primarily to local governments, for they employ the great majority of law enforcement personnel, and it is local governments that prosecute most offenses.

From 1960 to 1990 the rate of violent crime in the United States increased by a factor of about five. Since then, the crime rate has fallen substantially, but it is still several times as high as it was in 1960. From 1960 to the present the number of persons incarcerated has increased greatly. On an average day in 1999 the number of incarcerated in the United States was approximately 1.8 million.

Our rate of violent crime is generally similar to that of many other industrialized nations, with the single exception of homicide. For that crime the U.S. rate is several times as high. One reason for this disparity is the greater availability of guns in the United States.

In recent years the United States has taken a more punitive stance on crime, placing more emphasis on deterrence and incapacitation and relatively less on rehabilitation. Parole and the indeterminate sentence have largely given way to fixed terms as our faith in rehabilitation has weakened.

Three possible causes of the recent drop in crime rates are discussed. One is the deterrent and incapacitation effect of incarcerating so many people. A second is the improvement in policing, particularly the "community policing" techniques. A third factor is what John J. DiLulio has called "hardening the target," defensive measures taken by individuals, communities, and businesses.

The chapter closes with three different views of crime: (1) the classical and retributive model, which emphasizes legal procedures and punishment (the primary model in use at present); (2) the sociological model, which emphasizes the effects of social forces and conditions; and (3) the medical model, which emphasizes neurological, biochemical, and other factors particular to the individual.

NOTES

1. Allan E. Liska and Paul E. Bellair, "Violent Crime Rates and Racial Composition: Convergence over Time," *American Journal of Sociology* 101, no. 3 (November 1995), pp. 578–610.
2. Complied from *Crime in the United States* as summarized in Table 313 of the *Statistical Abstract of the United States*, 114th edition, 1996.
3. Probation is a suspended sentence subject to supervision and revocation. Parole is release from prison by decision of the parole board prior to completion of sentence. Parolees, too, are under some degree of supervision and may be sent back to prison for violation of the terms of their parole.
4. "Crime in America," *The Economist* (June 8, 1996), pp. 23–25.
5. James Lynch, "Crime in International Perspective," in *Crime*, edited by James Q. Wilson and Joan Petersilia (San Francisco: ICS Press, 1995), pp. 11–38.

6. C. Ray Jeffrey, *Criminology: An Interdisciplinary Approach* (Englewood Cliffs, N.J.: Prentice-Hall, 1990), pp. 120–22.
7. This became possible because in the 1970s the Supreme Court reversed itself and determined that the death penalty did not violate the Eighth Amendment prohibition of "cruel and unusual punishment."
8. Horton, a Massachusetts prisoner serving a life sentence, was let go on a weekend release and promptly went on a crime spree. The Bush campaign did a very effective job of hanging Horton around Dukakis's neck.
9. Alfred Blumstein, "Prisons," in Wilson and Petersilia, op. cit. pp. 387–419. The article not only contains estimates of how much prison deters crime but also indicates how difficult it is to make such estimates reliably.
10. James Q. Wilson, "Criminal Justice in England and America," *The Public Interest* (winter 1997), pp. 3–14.
11. The seminal article for the new view is by James Q. Wilson and George L. Kelling, "The Police and Neighborhood Safety," *Atlantic Monthly* (March 1982), pp. 29–38. See also a subsequent article by the same authors, "Making Neighborhoods Safe," in the same magazine in February 1989, pp. 46–52.
12. Not everyone agrees with this policy. An advocate for the homeless might tell you that if a desperate person cadges some change this way we should allow it, not repress it. The same has been said about panhandling, and similar arguments have been made about squatting by the homeless. A policing policy that focuses on public order will necessarily confront us with hard choices and situations that are not win-win situations.
13. Jackson Toby, "Reducing Crime: New York's Example," *Washington Post* (July 23, 1996), op. ed. page.
14. Wilson and Kelling, op. cit.
15. See Oscar Newman, *Defensible Space*, New York, Macmillan, 1972.
16. John J. DiLulio, "A More Gated Union," *The Weekly Standard* (July 7, 1997), p. 8.
17. Chapter 4 in Jeffrey, op. cit.
18. For an example of such a study, see David Jacobs and Ronald E. Helms, "Toward a Political Model of Incarceration: A Time Series Examination of Multiple Explanations for Prison Admission Rates," *American Journal of Sociology* 102, no. 2 (September, 1996), pp. 323–357.
19. For an example of this orientation see John F. and James L. McCartney, *Criminology: Power, Crime and the Law* (Homewood, Ill.: The Dorsey Press, 1977).
20. R. J. Herrnstein, "Criminogenic Traits" in Wilson and Petersilia, op cit. pp. 39–64. See also Chapters 10 through 13 in Jeffrey, op. cit.
21. For an account of some early misuses of ideas about heredity, see Daniel J. Kevles, *In the Name of Eugenics; Genetics and the Uses of Human Heredity* (New York: Alfred Knopf, 1985).
22. In the mid 1990s a conference under National Institute of Health (NIH) auspices was planned to explore research on biological correlates of behavior. It was canceled after a storm of protest. One of the leading protesters was the NAACP, which feared that somehow something would come out of the conference that would stigmatize Blacks. Their position, right or wrong, is very understandable given the history of the subject.

REFERENCES

Wilson, James Q., and Joan Petersilia, eds. *Crime.* San Francisco: ICS Press, 1995.

Gray, Mike. *Drug Crazy.* New York: Random House, 1998.

Chapter

16 | Public Education and the City

Education, if we judge by dollars spent or number of people employed, is by far the largest activity of local and state government. About 40 percent of all local government expenditures are for education in grades K through 12, and over half of local government employees, roughly 6 million out of 11 million, are in education. Teachers, about 4 million, make up by far the largest category of government employees, whether at the local level or for all levels of government combined. For many people, perhaps most people, their most sustained and important contact with government is their experience with public education, first as students and then as parents.

Few if any aspects of local government and state government performance are the objects of as much concern and contention as public education. And that concern is entirely understandable. We live in a highly competitive society in which there is considerable social mobility, both upwards and downwards. How a child does in school and what school does or does not do for a child both greatly affect a child's life chances. The U.S. economy and the types of jobs it offers are changing rapidly. It is only natural that we are concerned about whether children are getting in the public schools the skills they will need in the emerging "information age" or "postindustrial" economy.

In Chapter 15 we discussed the ghetto neighborhoods in connection with the work of William J. Wilson. The future of many children brought up in such neighborhood will depend in part, perhaps in very large measure, on their experience in school and whether they emerge from school with a set of marketable skills and the attitudes that enable them to use those skills.

The schools are a great mirror of society, reflecting who we think we are and what we think we should be doing. Virtually all our social problems and our disagreements with each other over matters of politics, morality, and religion are reflected in concern and controversy over public education.

THE PUBLIC SCHOOL SYSTEM

Public education began as a local endeavor in the Colonial period in the United States. Towns and cities gradually began offering public education for their residents and then, after a time, began to require that all children within their boundaries receive some schooling, though not necessarily in the public schools. The first compulsory attendance law was passed in Massachusetts in 1852.

> Every person who shall have any child under his control, between the ages of eight and fourteen years, shall send such a child to some public school within the town or city in which he resides, during at least twelve weeks, if the public schools within that town or city shall be so kept. . . .[1]

The present system evolved from a mass of local origins in the 50 states, and to this day public education is largely the responsibility of local government. Local control of public education is a venerable U.S. tradition. This is a very different situation from that in a nation such as France, where there is a national curriculum and local schools carry out policy established by the national educational department in Paris. About five sixths of all public school students in the United States attend schools operated by school districts, which are separate, quasi-governmental organizations. In most states school district board members and supervisors are directly elected, giving the district considerable political separation from municipal government. As noted in Chapters 4 and 6, a school district is considered a quasi-governmental body because it has some but not all the powers of government. The most important of these powers is the power to tax.

About one sixth of all public school pupils attend schools that are run directly by municipal governments. This is the case in a number of larger cities such as New York and Chicago.

As of the late 1990s about 45 million children went to public schools, and about 9 million went to private schools. These figures are for grades K through 12 and exclude higher education. Of the 9 million in private schools, somewhat over 3 million were in Catholic parochial schools and smaller numbers in other denominational schools. In recent years there has been a large increase in the percentage of children attending schools run by Fundamentalist Protestants. There has also, not included in the above figures, been a substantial increase in the percentage of children schooled at home. The driving force behind the growth in home schooling has been religious. Note that though all states require that children be schooled, no state can require that said schooling must take place in a public institution. This was established by a Supreme Court decision in 1925 overturning an Oregon law that would have required all children in the state to attend public school through the eighth grade.[2]

Decision-making power in public education is divided. Considerable power regarding such matters as curriculum and teacher hiring resides at the local level. This is true whether public education is provided by a separate school district or directly by a municipal government. However, districts and local governments are bound by state education law, so that the state may impose requirements on curriculum, the length of the school calendar, minimum criteria for teacher hiring, maximum number of children per class, and similar matters. In Chapter 4 we noted that substate governments are "creatures of the state" (Dillon's rule), and this principle applies to the provision of public education as well as to any other function of local government (or quasi-governmental entity such as a school district). Private schools, whether religious or secular, are also subject to regulation by state education departments.

The states and local governments and districts are also subject to some regulation and control by the federal government. Federal control is established partly by making funding contingent upon the recipient's (state or local) meeting certain federal guidelines. Federal control is also established directly by federal legislation. For example, the Americans with Disabilities Act (ADA) passed by Congress defines disability and establishes standards for the accommodations that must be made for disabled persons. A parent who believes that his or her child is not being suitably treated under provisions of the act can, in the ultimate extreme, take the matter to court. In 1997 the Clinton administration moved to institute a system of national achievement tests for elementary and high school students. It was strongly opposed by many conservatives, who saw in it a step toward a standardized national curriculum and hence a lessening of local control over public education.

Because public education is close to home and because it has such powerful effects upon the lives and life prospects of children, it is inevitably a source of controversy. Some controversy is about how to achieve goals upon which we all agree, such as teaching children to read well. For example, is phonics the most effective method of teaching reading in the early grades? But there is also considerable controversy about what we should be teaching children, particularly in the realm of values and attitudes. Conservatives and liberals will disagree about what we should teach children about our history. Should textbooks present the opening and settling of the American West in triumphant and admiring terms or as a holocaust for Native Americans? Should a world history course treat the cold war as a triumph of democracy over totalitarianism or as a struggle between morally equivalent antagonists? If the schools provide instructions on contraception, is that simply being sensible by teaching teenagers how to do safely what many of them will do in any case, or is that encouraging them to commit what many Catholics and Fundamentalist Protestants regard as a serious sin? There is much room for disagreement about what attitudes schools should communicate about life and about our society and its history.

The very rapid growth of private schools operated by Fundamentalist denominations, as well as the rapid growth of home schooling, has been driven largely by disagreements over values. The parent who takes his or her child out of public school and enrolls the child in Christian school is most often doing so over value questions—taking the child out of what he or she considers to be a completely secular environment and placing the child in an environment that communicates the parent's attitudes about religion, about sex, about family, and the like. What some have referred to as the "culture war" in the United States is partly fought out over issues of educational policy.

THE TASK OF THE PUBLIC SCHOOLS

In many ways the task of the schools has become more difficult in the last several decades. One urban school principal whom the author interviewed indicated that he felt the biggest problems that the schools faced were those connected with poverty and the effects of racism. After a pause he added a third category, family problems, saying that at times he felt like "a pseudo parent, a pseudo social worker, and a pseudo health worker."

How might the situation look to a city school principal or school superintendent? He or she has no control over the composition of the student body. Every child is entitled to an education. Some children arrive for kindergarten or first grade from family situations that have prepared them well for school. They started before birth with good prenatal care, they come from stable, loving family situations, they have been read to and talked to a great deal, and they are otherwise ready to be educated. Other children are not, starting with absence of adequate prenatal care. Some of them will have involuntarily consumed a certain amount of cocaine or cannabis or alcohol or nicotine while still in utero, and some of that consumption may show up in later years in reduced ability to concentrate or learn or in behavioral problems. Because of the changes in family structure discussed in Chapter 13, an increasing percentage of children are likely to come from troubled family situations that contribute to poor performance and behavioral problems.

This writer attended the New York City schools several decades ago. Had someone then asked me whether I felt safe in school, I probably would have wondered why anyone would ask such a strange question, for it had never occurred to me not to feel safe. Many of the city's schools today have security guards and metal detectors, and no child in such schools would be startled by such a question today. Clearly, a child who is fearful in school, or fearful about the trip to or from school, is not in a calm, relaxed mood suitable for focusing on the subject matter. Society quite literally brings its problems to the doorstep of the public school and demands that the school deal with them.

Schools must cope with large numbers of students who come from non–English-speaking households, a problem that is exacerbated by the high rates of both legal and illegal immigration. Because of lower rates of immigration in periods up to the 1930s through 1950s, it is a much bigger problem than it was several decades ago. However, it must be noted that the public schools faced an equally large if not larger language problem at the end of the nineteenth century and the first two decades of the twentieth century.

We have expected the schools to solve at least one problem that the adult society has not been able to solve. In particular, we have expected the schools to solve the problem of integration. By and large they have not been able to do so, and we are now backing off from that demand, as discussed later in this chapter. We have not solved that problem with respect to housing, as noted in Chapter 10. Nor have we solved it in all of our voluntary and community associations. As has been noted by many, Sunday morning may be the most segregated time of the week in the United States. But we have expected the schools to solve it.

In some ways the task of the schools has been made more difficult because we have become a more humane society. At one time high schools would force pregnant students to drop out. Now we realize such a policy is cruel and counterproductive for the student, so some schools now provide day care and classes in parenting. Most of us would think that it is the right thing to do, but it is another instance of the school system taking on the burdens of the larger society. Some years ago one would see few seriously handicapped children in the public schools. The schools were free to turn away students whom they believed they could not educate. Current law stipulates that every child is entitled to an education and that if the child has a disability, whether physical, cognitive, or emotional, that child is entitled to a program of study adjusted to that disability. The fact that we do this speaks well of the United States as a society. But it can be a heavy burden for a school system. We have made a commitment to mainstreaming.[3] Mainstreaming is done, in part, in pursuit of the praiseworthy goal of social egalitarianism. It also may make the task of the classroom teacher more difficult. It can also be extremely expensive, sometimes to the extent of providing an additional teacher for a single child.

How Much Can the Schools Do?

We expect a great deal from our schools. Many educators would tell us that we expect more than is reasonable and then "bash" the schools when they do not meet those expectations.[4]

In 1964, pursuant to section 402 of the Civil Rights Act, the U.S. Commissioner of Education commissioned a study to explore the facts

> . . . concerning the lack of availability of equal educational opportunities for individuals by reason on race, color, religion, or national origin in public educational institutions at all levels in the United States, its territories and possessions, and the District of Columbia.

The result, delivered two years later, was the massive study, *Equality of Educational Opportunity,* which soon became known by the name of its principal author as simply "The Coleman report."[5]

The report detailed differences in school systems in such matters as expenditures per child, types of instruction available, class size, qualifications of teachers, and similar variables. It also detailed the degree of de facto segregation that then existed in the United States. Many of the findings surprised no one, for the wide disparities in funding and facilities, as well as the very high degree of de facto segregation, were common knowledge. The purpose of the report was to provide the details so that we could take steps to deal with these disparities. But one finding of the report was something of a shock to many. Coleman's massive statistical analysis of data from some 4,000 public schools flew in the face of the then-conventional wisdom and was very disappointing. The finding was that differences between schools (expenditures per pupil, teacher's qualifications, types of courses offered, and the like), in a statistical sense, "explained" only a small part of the differences in student achievement from one school to the next. Family background variables explained a much larger share of the variation than did anything within the control of the schools.

> It is known that socioeconomic factors bear a strong relation to academic achievement. When these factors are statistically controlled, however, it appears that differences between schools account for only a small fraction of difference in pupil achievement.

Of the school variables that had some effect, one of the biggest if not the biggest variable was simply who attended the school.

> Finally, it appears that a pupil's achievement is strongly related to the educational backgrounds and aspirations of the other students in the school.[6]

That last variable is, at most, only partially within the control of a school system. School busing, magnet schools, and school choice can affect the composition of the student body to some degree.

The Coleman report, whose general conclusions seem to have stood the test of the next three decades fairly well, was a frustration to many for it suggested that there is only a limited amount that any educational reforms are likely to achieve. Note that the report in no way minimizes the importance of education as such. It only found that differences between schools did not seem to have a major effect on differences in pupil achievement.

ISSUES IN PUBLIC EDUCATION

Given the large public expenditures on public education, the importance of education to one's life chances, and the extent to which questions of educational policy involve basic values, it is not surprising that public education is a source of major controversy. In this section we examine several of the current controversies.

The Controversy over School Financing

Much of the funding for public education comes directly from the municipality or school district. This can lead to very large disparities in the amount spent per child from one school system to another. In the case of districts there is basically one source of locally raised revenue, the property tax. A district with a large property tax base per pupil can, with the same tax rate, raise more per child than a district with a small property tax base per child. In general, though it is not always the case, districts with wealthier populations have larger tax bases per child. If the schools are funded directly by the municipality, there is more than one source of local revenue; but there are also many other demands on those revenues, and the wealthy municipality is generally able to allocate more per child than can the poor municipality.

More often than not, more money will be spent on the education of children from prosperous than from poor families unless major steps are taken to achieve equality of funding. If such equalization is not achieved, the child who has the advantage of being born into a prosperous family then gets the further advantage of having a better-funded education. In 1971 the Supreme Court of California found in *Serrano v. Priest* that such disparities in expenditures per child violated the equal protection clause of the 14th Amendment (". . . nor deny to any person within its [the state's] jurisdiction the equal protection of the laws").

> We have determined that this funding scheme [reliance on the local property tax] invidiously discriminates against the poor because it makes the quality of a child's education a function of the wealth of his parents and neighbors. Recognizing as we must that the right to an education in our public schools is a fundamental interest which cannot be conditioned on wealth, we can discern no compelling state purpose necessitating the present method of financing. . . . [S]uch a system cannot withstand constitutional challenge and must fall before the equal protection clause.

For a time it looked to the advocates of school financing reform that the system of school finance based upon the local property tax was doomed and would have to be replaced by a more egalitarian system. But this hope was quashed in 1973 when the Supreme Court of the United States ruled in *Rodriguez v. San Antonio* that the equal protection clause did not require that spending per child be equalized from one district to another. It determined that it was sufficient if all children received an "adequate" education. Since then, advocates of equalized spending have pursued their cause on a state-by-state basis, often looking for and basing their appeals on provisions of state constitutions rather than the U.S. Constitution. The results have been mixed.

In some states successful suits have been followed by changes in the financing system so that disparities in per child spending have been drastically narrowed. A wide variety of equalizing schemes have been used. Their common element is that, one way or another, they involve skewing state aid to schools districts so as to favor poorer districts.[7]

In other states litigation is in progress or has been so recent that changes in the system have not yet been implemented. For example, in March 1997 the Supreme Court of the State of Ohio found that the disparities in per pupil spending, resulting from heavy reliance on the property tax, violated the state's constitution. Unless there is an appeal to the U.S. Supreme Court that reverses the decision, some reform in Ohio's school financing system will be inevitable. However, the nature of that reform is not yet evident. In May of 1997 the Supreme Court of New Jersey found that disparities in spending per district violated a provision of the state constitution that all children in the state be provided with a "thorough and efficient" education. It ordered the state to provide sufficient funding to bring the spending of a group of poorer districts up to the level of New Jersey's wealthier districts.[8] The Ohio and New Jersey situations are greatly different in degree. In Ohio the highest spending district spent about three times as much per pupil as the lowest spending district. Thus equalization might deliver very substantial gains to the poorer districts. In New Jersey the gap was quite small, approximately $7 thousand per pupil in the poorer districts compared to approximately $8 thousand per pupil in the wealthier districts. There, the effects of equalization will probably be slight.

How much effect complete equalization of expenditures would have on the performance of less affluent districts and on the performance of the most troubled inner-city schools is not clear. As noted, the Coleman report of 1966 showed that school performance, as judged by items like standardized tests, was affected to only a small degree by educational expenditure and much more by family background and other factors beyond the control of the schools. Studies since then have generally supported Coleman's findings. But it may be that that programs carefully aimed at specific problems and specific target populations of children would show significant effects. One could argue that we should go past equalization and spend much more per child in poorer districts and inner-city neighborhoods to attempt to counterbalance the special burdens of children from poverty backgrounds. Whether or not that is correct, it is not likely to happen, for it is hard to see where the political force to make it happen would come from.[9]

The Controversy over School Busing

In 1954 in *Brown et al. v. Board of Education of Topeka,* the Supreme Court of the United States ruled that legally segregated schools violated the equal protection clause of the 14th Amendment and were unconstitutional. In doing so it reversed the 1890 *Plessy v. Ferguson* decision, which had held that "separate but equal" facilities were constitutional. The Supreme Court found in 1954 that "separate but equal" was a contradiction in terms—that separate facilities were inherently unequal even if identical in every detail of funding, physical facilities, and the like.

> Does segregation of children in public schools solely on the basis of race, even though the physical facilities and other "tangible" factors may be equal, deprive the children of the minority group of equal educational opportunities? We believe that it does. . . . To separate them [school children] from others of similar age and qualifications solely because of their race generates a feeling of inferiority as to their status in the community that may affect their hearts and minds in a way unlikely ever to be undone.[10]

At the time of the decision, the national situation on legal segregation of the schools was mixed. Seventeen states and the District of Columbia required segregated school systems, the requirement generally being written into the state constitution. These states were primarily the states that had composed the Confederacy in the Civil War. Sixteen states, mostly in the Northeast and North Central regions of the nation, prohibited segregated schools. Eleven states, mostly in the West, had no specific legislation on the subject and generally had such small Black populations that the question was moot. Four states allowed the matter to be decided by local option.

The decision banned de jure segregation and left it up to the affected states to work out the details of ending the legal segregation of their schools. The decision was met with compliance in some places and dogged resistance in others. It was not until well into the 1960s that legal segregation had ended. But that, as it turned out, was not the major issue. The decision was silent on what turned out to be the much more difficult issue of de facto segregation. The decision made it absolutely clear that school districts and municipal governments could not take any steps to cause schools to be segregated. But it did not speak to the question of whether anything needed to be done about schools that were segregated not by intent but just by accident of geography. For example, it did not address the issue of whether anything needed to be done if one school was overwhelmingly Black and another overwhelmingly White simply because of who lived in which neighborhood. And that, in fact, was the situation for the majority of schools outside of those states that had legal segregation.

The question of de facto segregation was addressed in a series of decisions in the 1960s that, in effect, extended the reach of the Brown decision so as to achieve de facto desegregation. The instruments used by the courts were two. First, courts required that school catchment area lines be drawn so as to achieve a mixing of the races in schools. But that worked only in a limited number of cases, so there was a second and far more controversial remedy—busing to achieve integration. It should be noted that busing had long been used, especially in rural areas, simply to get children to the nearest school. In the South it had also been used to achieve segregation, taking both Black and White children past the nearby school of the "wrong" color to a more distant school of the "right" color.

In the 1960s school busing to achieve integration became common throughout the United States, often in places that had never before seen a school bus. For example, through the 1950s and into the 1960s New York City children went to the elementary school and high school in the district (catchment area) in which they lived. The city's population density was sufficiently high that, in general, the area for an elementary school was sufficiently small so that no location within its district was more than a few blocks away from the school. In fact, a very large number of elementary students walked home for lunch and then walked back to school. The areas for high schools and junior high schools were larger, often covering several square miles, and so many students got to them by public transportation. The city's only contribution to their transportation was to give students reduced fares on the city's subways, buses, and trolleys. In the 1960s the city began busing to achieve integration. Because there were large areas that were predominantly White and large areas that were predominantly Black, children often had to be bused quite long distances, and the trips were often very time consuming. The situation was similar in many other cities.

Brown vs. Board of Education had been greeted with general approval in the United States outside the South. For example, the historian Arthur Schlesinger Sr. was quoted as saying

> The Supreme Court has finally reconciled the Constitution with the preamble of the Declaration of Independence [all men are created equal and endowed by their creator. . .].[11]

By contrast, busing to achieve integration never enjoyed anything like the public support that the ending of legal segregation did. The situation is somewhat parallel to that with nondiscrimination legislation and affirmative action. The great majority of the population expresses support for making it illegal to discriminate, but a much smaller percentage, when polled, expresses support for affirmative action. Support for dealing with the de jure issue was much broader than support for engineering the elimination of the de facto situation.

Why was the support for busing so much weaker? One reason was simply geographic. The Northerner could regard *Brown v. Board of Education* as purely a Southern issue since his or her own state had long made intentional school segregation illegal. On the other hand, the decision to pursue the elimination of de facto segregation had personal impacts. It might mean that his child would no longer go to a neighborhood school and might spend two hours a day on a bus. Rural folk had long been used to seeing their children bused off to consolidated schools, but in most cities the neighborhood school, generally within easy walking distance, was an old and prized institution.

A whole complex of relationships—the local PTA attended by one's friends and neighbors, children walking home from school with their friends, the school as part of the neighborhood—was wiped out if a child was bused to another part of the city. What could shatter the comfort level of a parent more than having his or her child bused to a neighborhood five miles away to satisfy the numerical requirements for integration imposed by a judge? To a person of modest means the judge's decree might look like class discrimination. Here was a federal judge, a well-educated, affluent fellow, maybe from an old, prominent family, perhaps living in an upscale, predominantly White suburb, with enough income to send his children to private school if he so chose, deciding that an ethnic working-class and middle-class population must do what he, himself, would not have to do. Even if the parent on an abstract level sympathized with the goal of busing, it might still look to the parent as though the child were paying a heavy personal price for the service of an abstract legal or political principle. And, of course, many northern parents did feel racial prejudice.

The desegregation of the Boston schools was a case in point of what happened when the movement to desegregate urban schools moved north. In 1973 in *Morgan v. Hennigan,* Judge W. Arthur Garrity of the United States District Court for Massachusetts found that the de facto pattern of the Boston Schools was unconstitutional.[12] The judge then, with the advice of experts whom he had appointed, drew up a desegregation plan and compelled the city's school board to implement it. In effect, the city schools were, so far as crucial decisions went, and some minor ones as well, was being run by Judge Garrity. The plan, in brief, divided the city into a number of zones radiating out from the city center. In general, the zones had relatively more Black students close to the center and more White students in their peripheral parts. Within the zones, White students were bused toward the center of the city, and Black students toward the periphery. Because the White-Black percentages varied considerably between zones, there was also considerable busing between zones as well. White resistance to the plan was enormous, and the plan was implemented at the price of considerable disorder, violence, and racial animosity. Altogether, it was a very ugly scene.[13] Ultimately, the court prevailed and the schools were integrated.

However, to a considerable extent the intent of the court was undone by "White flight," over which neither the courts nor the school board had any control. In 1972, when *Morgan v. Hennigan* came to Judge Garrity, about 60 percent of the city's 90,000 public school students were White. By 1976, total enrollment had fallen to 71,000 students of whom 44 percent were White.[14] By 1980, the White percentage had dropped further to 40 percent.[15] Though the city had moved far toward integration in the statistical sense of achieving similar proportions of Whites and Blacks in its various schools, the larger goal of integration had largely been defeated by the actions of White parents. Had the mixing of students been carried to the point of mathematical perfection, then every Black student in the system would have been in a majority Black classroom. The letter of the judge's ruling would clearly have been satisfied. But whether the intentions of those who fought for integration and who applauded the *Brown vs. Board of Education* decision two decades earlier would have been satisfied is a very different matter.

Where had all the Whites gone? The 1980 census showed that at both the elementary and the high school levels, 47 percent of all White children in Boston now attended private schools. Of these the great majority attended religious institutions, overwhelmingly Catholic parochial schools. This was not surprising. Boston's White population, with large numbers of Irish and Italian Americans, is heavily Catholic. And the Catholic parochial schools enjoyed a reputation for offering a solid education in a disciplined environment at low tuition.

Some parents escaped busing and integration by moving across the Boston city line into the Boston suburbs or beyond. There they were beyond the reach of the judge's orders for, as had been settled by the Supreme Court of the United States in *Milliken v. Bradley* in 1974, courts could not order busing across municipal lines.

The impartial observer who neither favored not opposed court mandated integration might wonder whether by inadvertently reshaping the demography of the city schools and, to a considerable extent, the demography of the city itself, Judge Garrity's decision (legally correct as it was, for it was easily sustained on appeal) had actually been counterproductive. It could easily be argued that with so many Whites gone from the schools the chance of gradual integration over the years had been destroyed. On this point one can only speculate.

The reader might wonder why in this discussion there is so much mention of the courts and of court cases and no mention of the legislative branch of government. After all, is it not the legislative function to make the laws and the courts' function to interpret them? The fact is that few if any laws were made upon the subject. Both Congress and state legislatures stayed far away from the very contentious subject of school integration. By default, then, policy was made by the courts, primarily the federal district courts and the U.S. Supreme Court, with the former following the lead of the latter. The pattern described in Boston, in which a federal judge (sometimes a panel of judges) found the city at fault, developed a plan or mandated quantitative goals, and then compelled the city to take steps and make expenditures to meet them, was common. Many city school districts have been under judicial control for years as they strived to comply with the mandate of the court. In many cities, it did not quite come to that because the city administration or school board, seeing the trend of judicial decision, took action before it was forced to do so. In any case, the driving force behind busing and other "social engineering" to achieve de facto integration clearly came from the judiciary. It did not well up from the public, nor did it come from legislative bodies.

In some ways the fact that the push for de facto integration came from the judiciary is unfortunate, for judicial decisions necessarily tend to be of the either/or type—guilty or innocent, legal or illegal, obligated or not obligated, appeal sustained or appeal denied, and so on. The legislative process, by contrast, is very different. Politics is "the art of compromise" in a way that the law is not. Thus in the case of Boston, a plan that came out of the legislative process, which had longer timetables and more concessions to local feelings and special situations, would probably have been much better received, with less violence and less hurling of rocks and epithets. But there was no such plan, for there was not enough public support for any legislative body to have enacted such a plan.

Some school districts have attempted to achieve some integration without compulsory busing. This has been done through the use of magnet schools. The school receives extra funding so as to be able to offer special programs or facilities that will attract students from outside its usual catchment area. The usual intention is to attract enough White students to keep the school integrated. Often, the school administrators will strive for a White/non-White ratio that they think will avoid the "tipping point" phenomenon. In general, the concept has not been very successful. In many cases the pull of the "magnet" has not been sufficiently strong to overcome the larger forces behind White flight. Kansas City, Missouri, spent $1.4 billion over a number of years on an extensive magnet school program, largely because of pressure from the courts to end de facto segregation, yet the general consensus is that the effort has failed. The magnet school has also, at times, put school administrators in a very awkward position. If the number of White students in the school is "too low," then administrators may give preference to White students to prevent the school from resegregating. But that means discriminating against Black students who wish to attend. Discriminating against Blacks seems like a strange way to achieve integration, and it has resulted in lawsuits by Black parents whose children were turned away from magnet schools. In Prince Georges County, Maryland, a federal district court prevented the school district from allowing Black students to take unfilled magnet school "slots" reserved for White, Latino, and Asian students in the interest of preserving court-ordered racial balance guidelines.[16] In the city of Arlington, Virginia, Black parents were outraged when the school board refused to appeal a court ruling that would, for reasons of racial balance, reduce the number of Black students in magnet schools.[17]

The Present State of Busing

By and large, busing has not been a success. The biggest factor behind the failure to achieve widespread de facto integration has been White flight. By the mid 1990s, a number of cities had been released by the courts from earlier busing requirements simply because the courts had concluded that further busing was futile. For example in 1995 the courts released the city of Denver from a

1974 busing requirement that had caused the long-distance busing of many children. In 1974 there had been 63,000 White students in the Denver public schools. By 1995, despite Denver's substantial growth in the succeeding two decades, there were only 18,000 Whites left. At that point Whites constituted less than a third of all students, so that meaningful integration was not mathematically possible. Not only had Whites, particularly more prosperous ones, fled in large numbers, but as the city's schools became more troubled, many middle-class Blacks and Hispanics also left. This left the student body not only predominantly minority but also largely poor.[18]

White support for busing has never been strong. In recent years Black opposition to busing has grown considerably. Some Blacks had always opposed busing simply because they, like many White parents, favored neighborhood schools. Some did not want their children bused to distant schools where they might be the objects of prejudice and discrimination. Some Black parents did not favor busing because they, themselves, did not favor integration.[19] By the 1990s, some very prominent Black voices were expressing doubts about or opposition to busing.

> It's not just the mayor is Black; it's that her civil-rights credentials are so in order. All of which makes Mayor [Sharon Sayles] Benton's own crusade seem that much more remarkable: she wants to end court-ordered busing in her city. Better for African Americans, she says, to spend the millions in transportation money improving inner city schools. Better to build affordable housing throughout Minneapolis. Better to rely on children "going to school in their own neighborhoods," she told Newsweek. If that means fewer integrated classrooms, so be it.[20]

The National Association for the Advancement of Colored People (NAACP) has long taken the goal of integration as axiomatic. In fact, NAACP attorneys were prime movers in litigation to achieve integration in education (including *Brown v. Board of Education*), housing, public accommodations, and the workplace. Yet even that organization is beginning to split over the issue of busing. As of 1997 the organization was still officially for busing, but a dissident minority of younger members was making itself heard. According to one of the dissidents:

> You're beating your head up against the wall until it's bloody. At some point you have to ask, "Should I continue to beat up against this wall?" To ask the question is not a terrible thing.[21]

At this writing, America's experiment with busing appears to be coming to a close. Unhappily, the goal of ending de facto segregation in the schools of many cities is not much closer than it was several decades ago. In the writer's view it is simply not possible to achieve very much school integration until there is considerably more integration in housing. As Chapter 10 suggests, for many cities, particularly older cities in the Northeast and North Central regions of the nation, that process is proceeding, at best, very slowly.

The Controversy over Bilingual Education

One of the most serious challenges for many urban schools, particularly in cities such as New York, Chicago, or Los Angeles where there are large immigrant populations, has been how to educate children whose native tongue is not English. One response has been bilingual education.

The initial impetus for bilingual education came from Congress in the form of the Bilingual Education Act of 1968. Since then bilingual education has spread both because of a variety of court decisions and because it has developed a considerable political constituency, particularly among Hispanics.

In the typical bilingual program the student receives instruction in most subjects in his or her native language. Then the student receives instruction in the English language for perhaps an hour a day. The idea is that after some years the child's English becomes good enough so that the child can be switched out of the bilingual program and receive all of his or her instruction in English. In the meantime the child will have been learning mathematics, science, social studies, and other subjects in a familiar language and so will not have fallen behind in subject matter.

To have a bilingual education program the school system must have enough students in any one language group to form classes. It also must be able to find people who are both qualified as teachers and also have the language skills. Thus not every linguistic minority can be served. By far the largest language group served by bilingual education has been Spanish speakers.

The idea seems simple and straightforward, but it has been embroiled in a great deal of controversy, some over whether or not it is good pedagogy and some over ideological issues. Those who support bilingual education argue for it on several grounds. They claim that it allows children to keep up with their grade in subject matter and that it makes school a happier and less threatening experience, thus reducing high school dropout rates. They point, in particular, to high dropout rates among Hispanic students and tout bilingual education as a way to keep Hispanic students in school.[22]

Those who oppose bilingual education do so on several grounds. First, and most important, they claim that bilingual education delays the learning of English. They argue that the most effective way to learn a language is by total immersion, or as close to that as it is possible to come. They argue that bilingual education takes children in exactly the opposite direction. Consider, for example, the child who comes from a Spanish-speaking home situated in a Spanish-speaking neighborhood, perhaps in a part of the country where Spanish-language radio and TV are widely available, and who is in a Spanish bilingual program at school. Is it reasonable to expect that the child will become fluent in English on the strength of, say, an hour of English language instruction for the 180 days of the school year? Opponents argue that even if the child learns more subject matter for a few years than he or she would have in an English-speaking classroom, the delay in acquiring fluency in English more than outweighs any gains in knowledge of subject matter, self-esteem, or sense of comfort in school. Critics may also note that in the late ninteenth and early twentieth centuries there were even higher percentages of non–English-speaking students in the public schools of many cities and that schools did not offer bilingual education. Rather, the child from the non–English-speaking home got total immersion in English for the full length of the school day. And, critics might argue, such students learned English faster than if they had, by mistaken kindness, been instructed in their native Italian, Polish, Hungarian, Yiddish, or other language.

The issue of bilingual education has gotten tangled up in an ideological issue. Those who take a multicultural view often favor it because it will help to preserve the culture of the linguistic minority. If one takes the mosaic or salad bowl view of America, one is likely to favor bilingual education. If one takes the melting pot view, one may see bilingual education as separating one group from another and sowing the seeds of future ethnic conflict.

Among ethnic minorities, attitudes have been mixed. For example, some Hispanic groups have supported it both for pedagogical and preservation-of-culture reasons. But others have not. In New York City some Hispanic parents sued to have their children removed from bilingual education programs. The city's policy had been to require that all children with a Hispanic surname take an English proficiency test. Students who finished in the bottom 40 percent were assigned to a Spanish bilingual program. Parents took the position that the policy retarded the process of learning English and was more designed to fill places in bilingual education classes than to advance the education of school children.[23]

In the latest chapter in the battle over bilingual education, voters in California in 1998 by a substantial majority passed Proposition 227, which, if enforced as written, would effectively end bilingual education in the California schools. How stringently it will be enforced is not clear at this writing. Many educators expressed great unhappiness with the vote and indicated they would do their best to preserve as much bilingual education as possible. Then, too, there is always the possibility of legal challenge, such as the challenge that invalidated Proposition 187 in that state (see Chapter 12).

Competition in Education: Vouchers and Charter Schools

Dissatisfaction with the public schools, whether or not justified, has produced calls to introduce more competition into elementary and high school education. Much, though not all, the pressure has come from conservatives, who embrace the virtues of competition and see its relative absence in public education as a problem. They argue that introducing competition among schools will improve education just as competition among manufacturers leads to better consumer goods.

The public schools are, of course, in competition with private schools, both secular and religious. But the field is steeply tipped to the public schools for they are tax supported. Those who advocate increasing competition would move to level the playing field by providing public funding for competing schools.

One proposal to level the playing field is the school voucher.[24] The central idea is that every parent of a school-age child would receive a voucher for the child. The parent would be free to enroll the child in any school that she chooses. The parent would then use the voucher to pay the tuition. If the tuition is less than or equal to the amount of the voucher, the voucher covers the entire tuition. If the tuition is higher than the voucher, the parent pays the difference. There are variations on the basic theme. In the most extreme form public schools would receive no direct funding from public sources but would be supported entirely by vouchers. They would be in direct competition with private schools that would also be supported by vouchers. Schools would have to compete for students so as to get enough voucher money to survive. Those that were unable to do so would perish, just as the business that cannot take in enough revenues to cover its costs will perish. In a less extreme version public schools would be provided directly with some public funds, but not enough to survive without also taking in money from vouchers. Therefore, they would still have to compete successfully with private schools in order to survive. Vouchers might be set sufficiently high so that they would cover tuition in many or most private schools. Alternatively, they might be set much lower, so that for many private schools parents would have to provide a substantial sum above and beyond the voucher. One legal issue is whether the giving of vouchers to parents who would then use the vouchers at parochial schools violates the establishment of religion clause of the First Amendment ("Congress shall make no law respecting an establishment of religion. . . ."). As of this writing, this issue has not been before the Supreme Court, but such a test seems inevitable.

Is some variation of the voucher plan a good idea? In its favor one can argue that it would put pressure on public schools to improve their "product," just as competition puts pressure on firms to do the same. It would increase parental choice for many parents who might like to send their children to private schools and cannot now afford to do so but who would be able to do so if the voucher paid at least part of the tuition. Giving parents more choice of schools should improve the match between child and school and lead to happier children and better educational outcomes.

There are also serious arguments against the voucher system. The opponents of vouchers make an argument along the following lines. Assume that the voucher amount is set at $3 thousand per year and that the average tuition at secular private schools is $6 thousand per year. What would happen? People who are already sending their children to private schools would simply receive a windfall because their own out-of-pocket tuition expense would fall to $3 thousand.[25] Some people who could afford to pay $3 thousand in tuition but who could not afford $6 thousand would now pull their children out of public schools and place them in private schools. Those people for whom $3 thousand in tuition was still beyond reach would have no choice but to leave their children in the public schools. The net effect would be to pull the children of many middle-income people out of the public schools, leaving the enrollment in the public schools both smaller and, in percentage terms, poorer. That change will diminish the quality of public school education and move us further in the direction of a society segregated by income. Is that what we want to do?

The opponent of vouchers might go further and argue that as middle-class children leave the public schools the political constituency for good public school education will shrink. As that support weakens, the financial support behind the public schools will diminish. State legislators will be less likely to vote for adequate funding levels. At the school district level, parents who have withdrawn their children from the public schools will be more likely to vote no on the next school budget referendum. As the quality of public education falls, the process will feed on itself, with more parents pulling their children out and support for public education being further weakened.

The opponent of vouchers might also argue that public education fills a national need that is not strictly educational. The United States is a large nation with a population that is diverse in cultural, religious, ethnic, and racial backgrounds. To function well it must have some unifying institutions. The public schools are one such institution for they put people of very different backgrounds into the same schools and classrooms.[26] If we allow increasing numbers of people to opt out of the public schools, we are weakening that unifying institution and taking a step toward cultural separatism.

Regardless of their merits or demerits, vouchers have much public support. In New York City a group of Wall Street executives set up a foundation to provide vouchers to parents who wished to send their children to private or parochial schools. The group put together enough money to provide 1,300 vouchers at $1,400 per child. The organizers of the plan were stunned to receive over 17 thousand applications, more than double the number that they had anticipated.[27]

Charter Schools

Charter schools are another way to introduce more competition into primary and secondary education.[28] The basic idea is that a group, perhaps composed of educators and parents, formulates a plan for an independent school and then obtains a charter for this school from the state education department. Admission to the charter school is by lottery. The school is supported by the state and school district at the same rate per pupil as are the public schools. In effect, the child who attends the school brings with himself or herself "one student's worth" of public funding. The charter school thus competes directly with the public schools for funding. The school must meet state education law requirements, but beyond that it has considerable freedom in curriculum and method of instruction. In principle, a charter school can be shut down if it fails to meet its stated goals and the normal educational standards. However, that may not always be politically feasible.

Proponents of charter schools see them as providing flexibility, innovation, and the ability to tailor a school to the needs of special groups of students. Charter schools have received considerable support from Black parents who feel that the public schools are failing their children. The state of Connecticut legislation permitting the creation of charter schools states that

> Charter schools can serve as another vehicle in the creation of innovative and diverse educational settings for our students. Through a charter, a private entity or coalition of private individuals is given the public authority to run an independent public school which is legally autonomous from the local school district. If properly developed, they can create opportunities for improved student learning and academic excellence for all students by allowing for flexibility in the design of each school's educational program without compromising accountability for success.

By 1997 charter school legislation had been passed in over twenty states and more than two hundred charter schools were in operation. Their numbers are growing rapidly.[29]

There are, of course, arguments against charter schools. As with the voucher concept, there is the risk that in some way charter schools will skim off some of the better students from the public schools and thus weaken public education. The risk is presumably not as great as with the voucher system because charter schools, funded at the same per pupil rate as public schools, would not charge tuition. Thus they should not have the economic segregation effect that might occur with a voucher system. The charter school is essentially a private school totally funded with public money. There is always the possibility that the charter school will take the public money and then use it in a way that is in opposition to the will of the majority of citizens in that district or municipality. Groups at very different points on the political spectrum may all support charter schools because each group thinks that charter schools will sing its song, even though the songs are mutually exclusive.

> Conservatives like charter schools because they think the school's autonomy will allow the teaching once again of conservative virtues—old fashioned education, discipline, religious instruction. The race-and-gender left likes charter schools because autonomy will allow the teaching of its values: Afrocentric schools for Blacks and feminist schools for girls and so on. . . . A pluralistic society cannot sustain a scheme in which the citizenry pays for a school but has no influence over how the school is run. Public money is shared money, and it is to be used for the furtherance of shared values, in the interest of *e pluribus unum*

(from many, one). Charter schools and their like are definitionally antithetical to this American promise. They take from the pluribus to destroy the unum.[30]

At this writing charter schools are too new for us to form a judgment on them. However, given their present numbers and the evident popularity of the idea, we should soon have a much clearer picture of their faults and virtues.

The problem of achieving quality education in many urban areas is not a simple one, for most of the problems of American society sooner or later come to the schools. Conversely, there are few if any issues more central to the fate of cities than the results that their school systems achieve. There are few things that affect people's life chances more than how they feel about themselves, what they know, and what they can do when they emerge from school.

SUMMARY

Local governments devote about 40 percent of their total budgets to education (grades K through 12) and employ more people in public education than in all other activities combined. About 47 percent of the cost of public education is borne by local governments, primarily through the property tax. A similar amount comes to local governments and school districts as aid from the states. The remaining 6 percent or so comes from the federal government. We note that we have very high expectations for the public schools and that the task of the schools is complicated by many problems in the larger society. These include problems of family structure, de facto racial segregation, and the problems of large numbers of non–English-speaking students, among others.

In the second part of the chapter we discuss several public education issues over which there has been much controversy. We note the controversy over school financing and the efforts of many to compel the equalization of per pupil expenditures across school districts. We discuss the history of school busing to achieve de facto integration in the wake of the *Brown v. Board of Education* decision. To a substantial extent this effort has failed primarily because of "White flight." There is now a substantial retreat from busing as a solution to the problem of de facto segregation.

We note the controversy over bilingual education and that there are both pedagogical and ideological issues involved. Dissatisfaction with the public schools has prompted much support for both school vouchers and charter schools. These innovations have in common the idea of introducing more choice and more competition into the provision of public education. Proponents claim that this competition will improve the "product" just as competition among firms promotes product improvement. Opponents argue that these plans will draw off many of the more able pupils and also weaken political support for the public schools. They also argue that the public schools are an important unifying institution in a pluralistic society. They claim that enabling more families to opt out of the public school system will lead to greater cultural fragmentation.

NOTES

1. Edward A. Krug, *Salient Dates in American Education, 1635–1964* (New York: Harper & Row, 1966), p. 77.
2. *Pierce, Governor of Oregon, et al., v. Society of the Holy Names of Jesus and Mary.*
3. Educating children with physical, mental, or emotional handicaps along with nonhandicapped students to the maximum extent possible.
4. For an ardent defense of the schools in this regard, see David C. Berliner and Bruce J. Biddle, *The Manufactured Crisis* (Reading, Mass.: Addison Wesley, 1995).
5. James Coleman et al., *Equality of Educational Opportunity* (Washington, D.C.: U.S. Dept. of Health, Education, and Welfare (HEW), Office of Education, 1966). Note: The Dept. of Health, Education, and Welfare no longer exists. During the Carter administration, 1977–81, HEW was split into two departments, the Department of Education (DOE) and the Department of Health and Human Services (HHS).
6. Coleman, op. cit. p. 22.
7. For details see Kern Alexander and Richard G. Salmon, *Public School Finance* (Boston: Allyn and Bacon, 1995), especially Chapter 9.
8. Abby Goodnough, "New Jersey's School Financing Is Again Held Unconstitutional," *New York Times* (May 15, 1997), p. A1.
9. The reader should not conclude that all differences in per pupil expenditure result from differences in tax base. The writer's examination of school finance statistics in Virginia shows that in many instances the most affluent districts also make more tax effort (as measured by property tax rates) than do poorer districts. There are also wide variations in tax effort between places of comparable affluence. Thus, the extent to which the citizens value education also affects the level of expenditures.
10. The *New York Times* of May 18, 1954, provides extensive coverage of the decision and background conditions, as well as a wide range of comment on the decision.
11. *New York Times,* op. cit.
12. Though de jure school segregation had long been illegal in Massachusetts, the court found that school officials had, in effect, conspired to maintain a pattern of segregation by the manner of drawing school district lines and other devices.
13. For a detailed account, see J. Anthony Lukas, *Common Ground* (New York: Alfred A. Knopf, 1986).
14. Lukas, op. cit. p. 649.
15. Computed by the author from data in *General Social and Economic Characteristics of the Population*, Massachusetts volumes for 1970 and 1980, Tables 119 and 126, (Washington, D.C., Bureau of the Census).
16. Lisa Frazier, "Prince Georges School Rules Will Stand," *Washington Post* (August 21, 1997), p. A1.
17. Mike Allen, "School Board Won't Appeal Ruling on Minority Spaces," *Washington Post* (June 20, 1997), p. B1.
18. "Stopping the Bus: Desegregation," *The Economist* (September 30, 1995), p. 28.
19. Black America has never been of one mind on the subject of integration. For example, Martin Luther King was clearly an integrationist, but his contemporary Malcolm X was not. A couple of generations earlier, W. E. B DuBois and Booker T. Washington were similarly split on the issue.
20. "Redrawing the Color Lines," *Newsweek* (April 29, 1996), pp. 34–35.
21. Ted Shaw, Associate Director Counsel of the NAACP Legal Defense and Educational Fund, quoted in James M. Kunen, "Integration Forever? A New Generation of African Americans Questions the Bedrock Beliefs of an Aging NAACP," *Time* (July 21, 1997), p. 39.
22. For articles favorable to bilingual education, see the *Journal of Bilingual Education.*

23. Diane Ravitch, "Children in Prison," *Forbes* (June 3, 1996), p. 94.
24. For arguments pro and con, see Jerome J. Hanus, "They Are Fair and They Are Practical," *Education Week* (July 10, 1996), p. 60; and Peter W. Cookson, Jr., "There's No Escape Clause in the Social Contract," *Education Week,* same edition.
25. In the example given, the $3,000 voucher might not actually push the parents' out-of-pocket costs for a year of private school all the way down to $3,000, for as vouchers increase the demand for private school education, the total cost of private school tuition might rise above $6,000 just by the workings of the law of supply and demand.
26. Before the draft was ended in 1973, it was argued that it too was a major unifying institution because men from all backgrounds were drafted and together put through the same military experience. With the end of the draft and the coming of the all-volunteer army, that unifying effect has undoubtedly been weakened.
27. Jacques Steinberg, "School Choice Program Gets 17,000 Applications," *New York Times* (April 24, 1997), p. B4.
28. Ray Budde, "The Evolution of the Charter Concept," *Phi Delta Kappan* (September, 1996), p. 72. Budde is generally considered to be the inventor of the charter school concept.
29. Robin D. Barnes, "Black America and School Choice; Charting a New Course," *Yale Law Journal* 106, no. 8 (June 1997) p. 2403.
30. Michael Kelly, "Dangerous Minds," *New Republic* (December 30, 1996), p. 6. The particular charter school that evoked Kelly's anger was an Afrocentric charter school in Washington, D.C. that he felt purveyed a virulent hostility to Whites.

REFERENCES

Berliner, David C., and Bruce J. Biddle. *The Manufactured Crisis*. Reading, Mass: Addison-Wesley, 1995.

Finn, Jr., Chester E., and Theodor Reberber. *Education Reform in the 90's*. New York: Macmillan, 1992.

Photo Credits

Chapter 2:   p. 12, Beacon Press, from "Boston Observed" by Carl Seaburg. Copyright © 1970 by Carl Seaburg. Reprinted by permission of Beacon Press, Boston; p. 14, Museum of the City of New York, 'Hester Street, Vendors," 1898. Bryon Collection. 93.1.1.18122. © Museum of the City of New York; p. 19, Museum of the City of New York, "Greeley Square." Bryon Collection. 93.1.1.17917. © Museum of the City of New York.

Chapter 3:   p. 24, Beacon Press, from "Boston Observed" by Carl Seaburg. Copyright © 1970 by Carl Seaburg. Reprinted by permission of Beacon Press, Boston; p. 33, Corbis; p. 34, Corbis; p. 42, Fairfax County Economic Development Agency.

Chapter 9:   p. 171, New York Daily News, © New York Daily News, L.P. Reprinted with permission.

Index